PROFESSIONAL IMAGINATIVE WRITING IN ENGLAND, 1670–1740

Professional Imaginative Writing in England, 1670–1740

'HACKNEY FOR BREAD'

BREAN S. HAMMOND

CLARENDON PRESS · OXFORD
1997

Oxford University Press, Great Clarendon Street, Oxford OX2 6DP

Oxford New York
Athens Auckland Bangkok Bogota Bombay
Buenos Aires Calcutta Cape Town Dar es Salaam
Delhi Florence Hong Kong Istanbul Karachi
Kuala Lumpur Madras Madrid Melbourne
Mexico City Nairobi Paris Singapore
Taipei Tokyo Toronto
and associated companies in
Berlin Ibadan

Oxford is a trade mark of Oxford University Press

Published in the United States
by Oxford University Press Inc., New York

British Library Cataloguing in Publication Data
Data available

Library of Congress Cataloging in Publication Data
Data available
ISBN 0–19–811299–8

1 3 5 7 9 10 8 6 4 2

Typeset by Vera A. Keep, Cheltenham
Printed in Great Britain
on acid-free paper by
Bookcraft Ltd,
Midsomer Norton, Somerset

For the uncles and aunts whose turn has come:
Dave and Debbie, Tony and Shirine.
And especially for the most recent Hammond arrival,
Robert Darius

Acknowledgements

This book began life as a conversation over lunch with Kim Scott Walwyn in Melbourne, Australia. It was she, and later Andrew Lockett from the Oxford University Press, who encouraged me to think that I could write a more ambitious book than the one I originally proposed. I must thank the three anonymous readers who (I am embarrassed to recall when I think of its crude condition) read that original proposal and supported the idea of a broadly based study of the period's writing.

Alexander Pope's punning advice to would-be authors in the *Epistle to Dr. Arbuthnot* is to 'keep your piece nine years'. For modern scholars working under current employment conditions in the U.K., that advice is all too easy to heed. Under current employment conditions, a book that has been nine years in the writing is likely to have had around nine months actually devoted to it. I have been working on a study of the professionalization of imaginative writing in England since 1991, but the truth is that I have been *not* working on it since that date; and its completion is due to the generosity of the R. D. Roberts bequest of the University of Wales, Aberystwyth, which funded a sabbatical year in 1994–5. That I was able to take the period of leave was due to the willing and unstinting co-operation of my colleague Professor Lyn Pykett, who assumed the duties of head of department and has discharged them so well that it is unlikely my colleagues will ever want me back. To Lyn Pykett and to my other colleagues who also took a share of extra tasks, and have provided me with opportunities at research seminars to air my ideas, I am more grateful than I can say.

Once the writing got under way, several colleagues and friends were instrumental in reading drafts, which they did with unfailing generosity and unflagging vigilance: to Ian Bell, Tanya Caldwell, Steve Copley, Simon Dentith, Edmund Fryde, Paul Hunter, Michael McKeon, Gill Manning, Valerie Pedlar, David Shuttleton, Harold Weber, and Peter Wright, I am especially grateful. Very many other individuals have contributed to the making of

viii ACKNOWLEDGEMENTS

this book by means of discussion and conversation, and I forbear from naming them only because in doing so I would risk the sin of omission. To those editors who have published earlier versions of material that appears in the book, I owe my thanks for their labours and permission to reprint. A recognizable version of Chapter 3 appeared as '*An Allusion to Horace*, Jonson's Ghost, and the Second Poets' War', in Edward Burns (ed.), *Reading Rochester*, Liverpool Texts and Studies (Liverpool University Press, 1995). Chapter 7 contains material culled from several earlier articles, though I like to think that it is thoroughly revised and integrated into the new book: material on John Gay in '"A Poet, and a Patron, and Ten Pound": John Gay and Patronage', in Nigel Wood and Peter Lewis (eds.), *John Gay and the Scriblerians* (London: Vision Press, 1989); material on Henry Fielding in 'Politics and Cultural Politics: The Early Career of Henry Fielding', *Eighteenth-Century Life*, 16/1 (1992), 76–93; and material on Alexander Pope in '"Guard the sure barrier": Pope and the Partitioning of Culture', in David Fairer (ed.), *Pope: New Contexts* (Hemel Hempstead: Harvester Press, 1990). To Shaun Regan I am indebted for his scrupulous compilation of the index.

My greatest debt is, as it always is, to my wife, Ann. She will not want me to inscribe this, but for some time during the writing of the book, she was seriously ill. Her astonishing courage during that awful period gave me the will and confidence to go on with the relatively minor challenge of completing it.

B.S.H.

Aberystwyth, 1996

Contents

Introduction

I

Permit me to begin by giving an account, necessarily autobiographical, of this book's genesis. If any single book can be credited with kindling my enthusiasm for the study of early eighteenth-century English writing, it is Pat Rogers's *Grub Street: Studies in a Subculture*, which I read when I was an undergraduate.[1] In that book, Rogers set out to show that the London topography of the realm of duncehood in Alexander Pope's *The Dunciad*, however it may be elaborated into metaphor and urban myth, nevertheless has a literal and realistic foundation. There really *was* a loose union of hack writers whose way of life had enough in common to constitute a subculture; and they *did* live in the manner and in the locations depicted by Pope in the poem. I read Rogers and reading him made me want to read more Pope. The work that I went on to do on my own account was more concerned, however, with politics and the history of ideas than with literary sociology. Elaborating upon earlier work by Maynard Mack, Isaac Kramnick, Bertrand Goldgar, H. T. Dickinson, and others, my first book examined the interplay of personality, ideas, and experience between Alexander Pope and Henry St John, Lord Bolingbroke.[2] I argued that Pope's poems written in the 1730s were conceived as a form of political action. His satire and Bolingbroke's political and philosophical writings were two wings of a campaign to arrest a decline in the nation's moral fibre.[3] Between finishing the writing of this book

[1] Pat Rogers, *Grub Street: Studies in a Subculture* (London: Methuen, 1972).
[2] Brean S. Hammond, *Pope and Bolingbroke: A Study of Friendship and Influence* (Columbia: University of Missouri Press, 1984).
[3] 'Because Bolingbroke's philosophy claimed moral reform as its objective and because it applied to public life a model of virtuous conduct that was based on friendship and cultivation of the domestic virtues and that was partly lived out at Dawley and at Twickenham, its appeal for Pope was very great. This emphasis on friendship and the domestic virtues gives an identifiable consistency to Pope's poetic voice in the series of *Imitations of Horace* that Bolingbroke urged him to write in the

and its printing in 1984 (I had a recurrent nightmare that the title, *Pope and Bolingbroke*, would be misprinted *Poop and Boring-bloke*—but all was well), the effects of the revolution in literary theory first began to impact upon eighteenth-century studies, though they had already been felt in other fields, and doubtless by individuals more avant-garde than myself, for some years. The result, for me, of a growing interest in literary theory and of developing methodological awareness was a dissatisfaction with my reading of Pope at the very moment of its publication. I felt that I had taken Pope too much at face value, that I had fallen victim to his publicity and bought too far into the myth. His poetic voice was not actually as consistent as I had made it out to be and his 'alienation from the direction being taken by progress' that I had referred to was only one part of the story. In some respects, Pope *embodied* the direction being taken by progress. Growing familiarity with structural Marxist theories of ideology taught me to distrust the overt formulations of attitude and belief expressed in Pope's poems.

It took me many years to begin to feel that I was in any position to argue with Pat Rogers (and perhaps I am not yet). Revisiting *Grub Street* some years later, however, I found myself even more attracted to the materialist assumptions behind its project, but I came to feel that it had certain deficiencies. It seemed to take on trust Pope's own adjudications of literary value: writers like Colley Cibber, John Dennis, Susanna Centlivre, Eliza Haywood, Aaron Hill, James Ralph, and a multitude of others, really *were*, Rogers confirmed, the hacks and dunces that Pope branded them. Rogers accepted the poem's tendency to guard, police, exclude, demote, and seal off; he accepted the series of cultural *coupures* by means of which Pope endeavoured to construct a canon of British worthies from which writers with a professional orientation would be excluded. Pope was properly to be distinguished, on this view, from those writers he condemned by the formal dexterity of his couplets and the higher seriousness of his moral mission. It seemed to me, however, that if Pope's own version of the literary topography was not simply to dictate reality to succeeding cultural

1730s. They held in common ideals, concepts, a specialized vocabulary containing key words like *liberty*, *corruption*, and *constitution*, and a myth for the times that derives from their mutual alienation from the direction being taken by progress' (Hammond, *Pope and Bolingbroke*, 9).

historians, then his condemnation of career-professional writers and valorization of the independent amateur of letters needed to be called into question. Pope's placing of himself at the centre of a coterie of aristocratic persons of taste required to be exposed as a partial (in both senses) account of his own significance to the development of literary institutions and practices. Secondly, the relationship Rogers posited between material reality and literary text seemed too reductive. To argue that there really was a Grub Street and that there really were toilers in the salt-mines of the publishing industry was perhaps to redress the balance too far against the constructedness of Pope's *Dunciad*. The poem's representations seemed to me to be *generating*, rather than merely mediating, particular forms of aesthetic consciousness.

Given an opportunity to write for the Harvester New Readings series an account of Pope's *œuvre* that would be self-consciously new and provocative, I wrote a book that treated Pope suspiciously, in some measure. I tried to render the facts of Pope's life in such a way as to throw doubt on his claim to be the phallus, the yardstick of contemporary poetic virility ('if he pleas'd, he pleas'd by manly ways', as the *Epistle to Dr. Arbuthnot* has it). I argued that Pope's rhetoric of moderation, 'the middle way', 'steering betwixt the extremes of doctrine seemingly opposite' (*An Essay on Man*), was itself an ideological justification for a series of political and partisan commitments. I paid particular attention to the *Epistle to Dr. Arbuthnot* as a poem in which Pope dealt with the anxiety emanating from his own relentless careerism by covering his tracks, denying all evidence of the process by which he secured financial independence. In respect of *The Dunciad*, I argued that the confidence to write such a poem as the 1728–9 *Dunciad* actually derived from the successful commercial exploitation of classical and 'native classical' writing (Homer and Shakespeare) that turned Pope (his Catholicism aside) into a member of the financially independent gentry amongst whom he recruited so many friends. The 1743 four-book revision of *The Dunciad* I saw as in some ways an old man's poem, referring back to the (by then) archaic disputes between the ancients and the moderns that had riven the intellectual community at the turn of the century and that had been the crucible of Pope's early creativity. Again, my purpose was to expose some of the ideological determinants behind *The Dunciad*'s vision of cultural decline to uncover the intellectual matrix from which it arose, in order to make the point that this vision is not an objective, value-free description of social reality. In the new fourth book, Pope concerned himself not with the particularities of duncehood, but with its deep structure. A trivialized educational system is held responsible for the wholesale devaluation of culture and the separation of the material forms of words from the spiritual realm of meaning.

My book on Pope was published in 1986, a year after Laura Brown's iconoclastic study of Pope in Blackwell's Rereading Literature series appeared, the intention behind which she presented thus:

> This book contends that we must begin on the offensive. As a consistent advocate of the beliefs and ambitions of the capitalist landlords and of an imperialist consensus, Pope must be scrutinized, doubted and demystified. That is, the explicit values—the conscious political, social and even aesthetic positions of his poetry—must be critically and remorselessly questioned. This process of demystification, with its systematic refusal to see things as Pope would have us see them, to accept the world as Pope constructs it or to accede to Pope's assertions of meaning, coherence and morality, can be described as a critique of ideology: a critique of the conscious or unconscious values of the poet and his poems.[4]

Although I shared with Brown an interest in the way in which economic realities are embedded in imaginative writing, my concern was not primarily with Pope as 'a consistent advocate of the beliefs and ambitions of the capitalist landlords and of an imperial consensus', because I do not believe him to have *consistently* advocated any set of beliefs, much less those of capitalist landlords and imperialists. My interest was in Pope as a cultural broker, and it was his *inconsistency* that most intrigued me. I was promoting a perspective on Pope that is now far more available, thanks to James McLaverty's nursing into print of David Foxon's *Pope and the Early Eighteenth-Century Book Trade*: that Pope was, despite his overt ideology, the first writer who owed his success entirely to the adroit manipulation of the publishing industry.[5] Whereas Pope's writing has helped to shape a lasting distaste for profit as a motive in the production of literature that the writer hopes will be considered of enduring value, he was himself profit's creature.

[4] Laura Brown, *Alexander Pope* (Oxford: Basil Blackwell, 1985), 3.
[5] David Foxon, *Pope and the Early Eighteenth-Century Book Trade*, rev. and ed. James McLaverty (Oxford: Clarendon Press, 1991).

The reading of Pope that I undertook in my earlier book convinced me that there were wider issues at stake than those affecting the career of an individual writer. The present book is motivated by my conviction that our current understanding of what is termed 'Augustan' writing, and of what is valuable in it, has been constructed against the grain of the very professionalization of imaginative writing that is its greater significance. Those authors who contrived to have themselves perceived as least professional, who evolved a *raison d'être* for the writer's career that most artfully concealed the profit motive, and who created an art that could plausibly be seen to transcend its material conditions of production are today the most studied. The 'self-crowned laureates' of the period have had their ideological victories taken at face value, accepted as objective verdicts of an unerring literary taste. This study seeks to revalidate the enterprise and the results of writing that can be orientated towards the 'palpable design' (in Keatsian phrase) that we pay for it.

The unifying theme in the book is a concentration on the respects in which the discourse that later came to be known as 'literature' was shaped by the imperatives of making a living in the period after the Civil War. It is in the century following the Civil War that imaginative writing becomes a widely consumed commodity, that literacy improves demonstrably, that women enter the literary workplace as consumers and producers, that theatre becomes big business, that newspapers and periodicals emerge as distinct forms, that the novel is born out of a typographical 'primal soup', and that arguments begin to be made about the unique status of 'wit' as intellectual property. In this period, conflicts between an older, patronage-based model of authorship as the result of prolonged study and immersion in the classics, and a newer model of professionalism gradually being constituted, are at their most dramatic. Here is the view, for example, of John Dennis: 'nothing [is] more a Man's own than his Thoughts and Inventions . . . a Man ha[s] absolute Property in his Thoughts and Inventions alone' (*The Characters . . . of Sir John Edgar*, 1723). Later, Lord Chesterfield, opposing the 1737 Licensing Act in the Lords, movingly contended that 'Wit, my Lords, is a sort of property: it is the property of those who have it, and too often the only property they have to depend on.' It is at this time that individual careers and texts, and literary genres, are most obviously striated by profound changes in the underlying geology of authorship. In this book, I seek to demonstrate respects in which literary forms and the writing careers of 'major' and 'minor' authors are affected by collaboration with or resistance to these tectonic movements. Conservative reaction against and anxiety over proliferating print, and its apparent corollary declining literary standards, is an important determinant of satiric 'voice': yet study of the writing careers of writers like Dryden, Pope, and Gay should reveal that the attempt to preserve writing as the enclave of anti-professional purity could only proceed by capitalizing on the energies that this stance affects to despise.

II

The study is divided into three parts. In Part I, entitled 'Hackney for Bread' (the phrase comes from a song sung in Fielding's *The Author's Farce*), I devote two chapters to the conceptual, ideological, and material conditions within which writers in my chosen period worked. There is, I suggest, a symbiotic relationship between an economy that offers greatly enhanced opportunities for literate and imaginative individuals to exploit their talents and the legitimization of authorship as a means of making a living. Successful authorship is seen to depend on the possession of 'wit', a form of capital situated somewhere between the stock of goods or investment funding required to launch oneself in any trading concern and the sump of knowledge improved by mental training required to prepare oneself for a profession. As the eighteenth century progressed and it became necessary within a legal framework to clarify the nature of literary property, 'wit' was developed into a conception of 'original genius' that captured for the products of the literary imagination a quasi-mystical status. That, in turn, led to post-Kantian conceptions of aesthetics that valorized both the production and consumption of art as autonomous domains of 'disinterestedness' in which commercial motives ought to play no part. Chapter 2 works in an empirical environment of facts and figures, determining the earnings potentials of imaginative writers working in different genres, and arguing that the theatre, the most directly market-orientated of the verbal arts, was the main dynamo of literary production in other genres.

Writers for the stage were at least semi-autonomous with respect to the publishing industry, having a straightforward means at their disposal of reaping the fruits of their labours: remuneration for poets, translators, and fiction-writers was relatively indirect and open to appropriation by middle-men. The opening chapters provide a material context of economic formations and institutions in which to study the relationship between literary text, author, and the modes of production current in society.

Part II is entitled 'Cultural Broking' and consists of three chapters devoted to the analysis of textual sites within which the status of professional *vis-à-vis* amateur writing can be observed in the process of emergence and contestation. Chapter 3 initiates my account of authorial formation in textual embodiment by considering the quarrels of the 1670s in the light of an amateur versus professional dialectic. Despite our modern reading of Dryden as in the 'laureate' succession of canonical great writers, a seventeenth-century evaluation of him is very different. Just as much as was his great rival Shadwell, Dryden was a 'modern' rather than an 'ancient', a professional rather than an aristocratic amateur. The chapter examines Dryden's quarrels with Shadwell and Rochester as landmarks in the self-definition of professional authorship. Its departure-point is Rochester's representation of Dryden and Shadwell and other writers of the later seventeenth century in the poem *An Allusion to Horace*. Plagiarism is an accusation foregrounded in these quarrels that speaks to the remodelling of older, courtly notions of literary property. I examine the tension created by Dryden's desire to represent himself in a respectable Jonsonian tradition of dramatic writing, at the same time as he wishes to secure value for his plays by stressing their novelty and originality, their preciousness as commodities to a highly competitive theatrical environment eager for audience-pleasing forms of entertainment. This chapter initiates a reappraisal of Dryden's career that is developed in Chapter 4. Dryden is sometimes misrepresented in literary history as a canonical great writer who inherits the literary mantle from illustrious predecessors and takes his place in an unbroken line of succession. His own poem *Mac-Fleckno* has had a success comparable to *The Dunciad*, if on a smaller scale, in determining the taste by which he would later be evaluated. In the chapter on epic in the 1690s, to which Dryden is again central, I suggest that the failure of epic in that decade, and its mutation into the demonized Other of mock-epic, can be treated as a case-study for the effect on traditional literary forms of incipient professionalization. Chapter 4 examines his ambitions to succeed as an epic poet in the 1690s that would have secured for him an exalted niche in the annals of English literature. Dryden was struggling for status in a political climate of uncertainty, caught between gentleman-amateurs like Sedley and Rochester and those like Shadwell, Otway, and Lee who were to be dismissed as mere artisans. A reluctant professional whose plays were money-spinners intended to finance the Stuart epic that would establish his enduring literary fame, Dryden furnishes a particularly poignant example of the writer's dependence on a changing political and economic system. My argument is that he did not, and could not, succeed in realizing his aspirations as an epicist because the conditions that created the literary market-place and the professionalization of authorship (essentially the same conditions that transformed England into a major commercial and trading nation during this historical period) brought about a wholesale shift in taste that rendered the epic anachronistic. The 1690s provides a particularly clear observation-point upon the tendency of epics to metamorphose into mock-epics as the cultural imperative is felt to make stories relevant, realistic, narrative, and domestic. In this chapter, the term 'novelization' is borrowed from Mikhail Bakhtin to put a name to just this underlying process of aesthetic change, as a shorthand way of referring to the cultural forces that render epic anachronistic at the turn of the eighteenth century.

Chapter 5 amplifies my account of the 'novelization' of literary culture. Many of the socio-economic factors that bring professional writing into being are active also in the constitution of polite discourse: and the chapter attempts to map the professionalization of writing on to aspects of the textual formation of politeness that I perceive to have particular significance for my argument. Expanding opportunities for professional writers, such as those afforded by the newly emergent literary periodicals, are the result of a newly domesticated ideological agenda carried by polite and first-wave sentimental writing. Professionalization, novelization, the polite: these were all broad cultural tendencies that provoked a backlash in those pockets of early eighteenth-century cultural practice that valorized the amateur, gentlemanly, classically trained, allusive model of authorship. Between, roughly, 1690 and 1720 wholly new forms of literary production and thoroughly hybridized literary kinds emerged or were in their gestation period (newspapers, literary periodicals, the novel) that provided new opportunities for workers in the writing industry. Various means of controlling this production were sought, but one pan-institutional discursive framework emerged that recent commentators have considered to be particularly important: the 'polite'. Polite discourse was a means of facilitating social intermingling between disparate status-groups in a society rendered increasingly mobile and fluid by the requirements of trade and commerce. Under its terms, protocols were established governing behaviour and conversation in newly emergent public spaces, including the textualized public spaces of established literary genres like pastoral, in the theatre, and in the new literary periodicals. My discussion dwells mainly, though not exclusively, on the role played by professional writers in the development of vital organs of the polite movement such as John Dunton's *Athenian Mercury* and Addison and Steele's *Spectator*, stressing the importance of the profit motive in bringing about discourses that functioned, in part, to occlude the very commercial interests that brought them into being. Aesthetics itself was, I hold, one of the most important innovations of polite discourse, seeking as it did to sponsor and regulate the consumption of culture amongst the newly leisured middle classes. My argument will stress the importance in constituting the polite realm of figures from opposing social and ideological provenances, Shaftesbury and Dennis—the one superior to the middling-status nature of politeness and the other both temperamentally suspicious of it and cast outside its boundaries by his literary opponents. Dennis is the true type of the Popean Dunce, caught between his miserable poverty and his boundless ambition to be the most influential critic of the age. He was a vital transitional figure in his desire to retain the mould of neoclassicism yet simultaneously discovering its limits. His criterion of passionate expressivity was embodied in his sponsorship of the 'sublime', in his promulgation of ideals of genius and spontaneity at a time when such notions were thought to be deranged, in his own writing, and in his personal demeanour. Dennis's analysis of Addison's *Cato* paves the way for a discussion of the respects in which the literary periodicals created by Addison and

Steele adapted his aesthetics to the emerging taste of the new urban bourgeois readership. The celebrated 'Pleasures of the Imagination' papers published in the *Spectator* develop further Dennis's advocacy of the Miltonic sublime, but they do so in a way that creates a conception of aesthetic property, widening the scope of the aesthetically enfranchised but carefully drawing new boundaries. I will suggest that mediation of perspectives contributed by such writers as Shaftesbury and Dennis was the crowning achievement of Addison and Steele.

Part III is entitled 'The Scriblerians and their Enemies' and it derives directly from interests that, in the first section of this introduction, I described as emerging. Chapter 6 considers the forms of resistance that developed towards, in particular, female professional writers who wished to have their work taken seriously while earning a decent living. Pope's quarrels with Susanna Centlivre and Eliza Haywood conducted through *The Dunciad* and elsewhere are taken as symptomatic of this tendency. The terms in which Pope opposed female writers are gender-specific, but women writers were to him indications of a wider cultural malaise. His desire to distinguish between writers of value and mere hacks has some resonance with that discussion as it was conducted through the copyright debates, but for Pope the basis for this distinction could not reside in any pure, untrammelled notion of 'originality' such as Young and the proponents of perpetual copyright sought unsuccessfully to advance. Although in his early career Pope needed to swim with the tide of 'polite' writing characterized in Chapter 5, and his early works can be read as co-operating with this spirit, the post-1726 Pope established himself as a conduit of opposition to some of the major cultural tendencies that he saw as prevalent in his period: professionalization of writing, increasing literary production, literary production undertaken by socially inappropriate individuals—even by women—patronization of worthless writers, hybridization, and debasement of literary forms. The material in this final part takes as a starting-point Pope's attempts in *The Dunciad* and elsewhere to banish women writers, particularly Centlivre and Haywood, from the purlieus of literary respectability. In the case of the former, patronage at the hands of the Addisonian circle of powerful Whigs—protection within the pale of politeness—was one reason for Pope's particular animus. Haywood is more straightforwardly viewed by him as a personal enemy and as a writer in the worthless genre of romantic prose fiction. Chapter 6 moves outside the period mainly under examination in the book to consider some enduring issues of canonicity, asking why it is that some writers are accepted as fit for study whereas others are not. A comparison between the kinds of fiction produced by Haywood and Defoe, both attempting to succeed in a volatile and incompletely understood market-place, sheds some light on these problems.

As Chapter 7 argues, the group of 'Scriblerian' writers who were most opposed to the democratization of culture and to aspects of its mediation by politeness—Pope's fellow writers Gay, Fielding, and Swift—were also 'infected' by pronounced elements of it. Indeed, the energy appropriated by their satire is energy primordially generated by professional writers intent upon developing forms that could succeed in the literary market-place. Despite various attempts in debates over copyright legislation and in aesthetic theory to mystify the fact, writing for money provides the ongoing dynamic for literary production of all kinds, both at the 'quality' and the 'popular' ends of the market. Chapter 7 discerns the consistency behind the oppositional programme that Pope orchestrated or inspired amongst Gay, Swift, and Fielding. Fielding's early career as a dramatist and periodical writer is examined, to show how Fielding created a cultural politics out of his vexed class position as a well-educated, classically trained, aristocratic writer who was compelled to adjust to the growth of the literary market-place. Gay's writing career, I try to show, was shaped by Pope and Swift against the grain of its own significance. In his life and art, Gay wrestled with the Scylla and Charybdis of being a hack on the one hand and a client on the other; his Scriblerian partners created for him a choice of roles—the neglected poet who is the living proof that existing forms of patronage are tainted, or the poor but virtuous independent writer born to blush unseen. Together the Scriblerians articulated a cultural critique in the late 1720s and into the 1730s which called attention to the transgressiveness created by the promiscuous mingling of high and low literary and dramatic forms in poetry, fiction, and popular stage entertainment. Yet they were all able to draw energy from the cultural forms that they simultaneously despised. Just as in *The Dunciad* Pope subjected the culture of the populace and the market-place to the comic control of a dominating and

prestigious cultural form—classical epic—so Fielding's major in-
novation was the dramatic burlesque, a form that could trade on
all of the energy of lowbrow pantomime and comic or ballad opera
while using the rehearsal framework to accuse it of meaninglessness and to put an ironic distance between it and the standards of
true drama. What can be said of *The Beggar's Opera* and *The
Dunciad*, that the authority of the controlling pretexts is itself
destabilized by the valency of the new form, can be posited of
Fielding's burlesques and of Swift's *Gulliver's Travels*.

The power and charisma of the Scriblerian cultural analysis,
and the innovative vivacity of the burlesque forms they evolved to
articulate it, has won for them a leading position in the literary
history of their era. And yet it is in some respects a false position.
There is an eighteenth-century line of succession alternative to
that of Dryden, Pope, Swift, and the conservative satirists thread-
ing its way through this book, which comprises writers like Dennis,
Blackmore, Addison and Steele, Aaron Hill, Mallet, and Thomson. Aaron Hill manifested throughout his variegated career a
consistent preoccupation with improvement of public taste and
with a range of interests traceable to Dennis: advocacy of the
sublime, of Hebrew poetry, of passion and expression in writing
and performing. A figure first stigmatized by Pope in *The Dunciad*
but later reprieved, Hill's career can seem to interrogate the
cultural canon and its fodder established in *The Dunciad*. The
representative writer of the first half of the century, Chapter 7
hints, might not be Pope or Swift or Fielding, but Aaron Hill, an
entrepreneur whose desire to gain honorary status as an intimate
of Pope's and a sharer of his sense of cultural value was contradicted by the circle of professional writers and actors whose
endeavours he tried to nourish.

The book's final chapter is cast in the form of a brief epilogue,
or coda, that comments further on the various contradictions and
perplexes embodied in the person and career of Alexander Pope,
which, as my Introduction confesses, have been the genesis of the
entire book. It revisits the paradoxes and complexities of Pope's
ideology, concentrating on the elusive nature of the 'country'
ideology embodied in some of his most significant poetry. It is
appropriate that I should end the book where it began in an
attempt to understand the cultural significance of Alexander
Pope's poetic achievements.

Writers of every sort commonly experience the phenomenon that what they have written is not altogether what they expected to write. I am glad that this has also been my experience in writing this book, because it is what guarantees that one has participated at some level in a creative process. To conclude the book, I have tried to stand back a little from what I have written and to deal with the most obvious difficulty or weakness that the argument presents. This is (in my opinion) that I have used a comprehensive category (professionalization) to define what I take to be the most significant shift in the conditions under which imaginative writing was produced in the period, affecting everyone who aspired to publish, and yet as the book progresses, pro- and anti-professional stances seem to emerge. In the conclusion therefore, I emphasize a dialectical approach to the phenomenon of literary professionalization, requiring that we understand it both as integral and coherent *and* as comprising separate cells that have their own distinctive cultural politics.

III

Any aspirations I might have had towards writing a comprehensive literary sociology of my chosen period did not survive the first few weeks of working on the project. Such totalizing ambitions perished on the rock of a desire to say something significant about the writers and texts selected, rather than merely deluging the reader with names, facts, and details. The dates I cite to delimit the field of enquiry are to some extent arbitrary. They correspond roughly to the lifetime of Alexander Pope and they define very approximately a period during which men and women who produce imaginative writing for a living first emerge in England and establish themselves as in the ascendant, visible to the extent that for conservative writers like Pope they appear to constitute a serious threat to cultural value. My approach is not defined primarily by chronology, though there is a chronological progression operating in that each chapter focuses on a specific decade and on writers, texts, and forms of literary production that seem to me to be of paramount importance within it. My material is approached, rather, through particular 'problematics' that interest me and that I want to investigate. But these are identified and investigated in the first instance because they illuminate and are illuminated by the overarching theme of literary professionalization with which I am fundamentally concerned. Authors and texts are chosen to some extent symptomatically, as case-studies for a broad range of developments that could be documented across a much wider range of examples. This produces a book that is looser in structure than some that I have read and admired; but it does possess a consecutive argument that, if it does not reach into every single nook and cranny of the textual case-studies adumbrated, nevertheless prevents the book from dwindling (I hope) into mere self-indulgence.

This book's theoretical provenance is less apparent than my first attempts to conceive it would have had it be. Nevertheless there is one, apparent in my overall ambition to lay the foundations for a new biography of writing in the period. This was a period of profound transformation in the structure—economic, social, and political—of English society and in the imaginative literature that it produced. Its enterprising, innovative, projecting spirit can be harnessed to liberate us, on the threshold of the twenty-first century, from some of the ways of reading that still restrict our approaches to literary study. We are heirs to a powerful prejudice, still operative, against the configuration of writing perceived to be valuable within the material field of its production. Financial gain is not, even now, an altogether respectable reason for *producing* good writing—witness the débâcle over the size of the advance for Martin Amis's novel *The Information*. And as regards consumption, or appreciation, of 'great' literature or 'high' art, there is still a tendency to see it as existing in a realm that transcends the quotidian reality in which individuals make a living. It is contaminated by any reminder that perhaps the two provinces are not entirely distinct. In a film I once saw, a movie studio boss invited a much-sought-after director to his office to discuss a project. While the mogul spouted figures and profits, the director wandered over to a Shakespeare first folio displayed in a cabinet on the wall, which he proceeded to admire rhapsodically. 'You like the book?' drawled the tycoon. 'Here, take it.' He lifted the cabinet off its plinth and handed it over to the director. The director, appalled at the ugliness of the gesture, tries weakly to explain that he doesn't *want* the artefact. Yes, he likes it. Yes, he admires it. But no, he doesn't want to *own* it. Ownership, business, commerce, trade—a movie boss talking money—is an intrusion on the space that the soulful individual creates for the awe-stricken contemplation of immortal genius. It might almost be said that until recently, the literary texts that have been most highly valued have been those that can most plausibly be examined in isolation from the broader culture of which they are an aspect—as the free-standing creations of an original genius.

Feminist, cultural materialist, and other recent schools of thought have altered our way of looking at such matters. Evaluation, the central activity of the scholar-critic that Alan Sinfield would deem the 'essentialist-humanist', is not any longer regarded as the desired end-product of literary discussion.[6] Feminists have taught us to suspect the entire value system that makes such determinations as inherently skewed by gender-bias. The emphasis has shifted towards processes of cultural production, to the idea that the significance possessed by a text depends on the cultural field, the broad institutional context, within which it is situated. This way of thinking was initiated for the English scholarly community by Raymond Williams. As part of a fundamentally Marxist commitment, Williams insisted that works of art make a clear application to the world, that they are the products not of the free-floating creative imagination, but of the economic system through which they are produced. More than that, works of art are *in themselves* forms of production. The business of literary analysis, Williams advocated, should not involve looking at isolated texts and analysing their components; it should involve discerning the conditions within which the practices that bring literature into being operate. We should be looking at art as *practice* rather than as a museum of discrete *objects*.[7] Further, we are now in the moment of 'cultural studies'. Popular cultural forms like film and pop music are now academically respectable and highly theorized. Study of popular forms has made us much more aware than we were of the trade-offs between 'high' and 'popular' culture; and the terms themselves, with the evaluations implied by them, have come under close interrogation. This study is motivated by

[6] Alan Sinfield, *Faultlines: Cultural Materialism and the Politics of Dissident Reading* (Oxford University Press, 1992).

[7] Perhaps the most influential single item in Raymond Williams's long bibliography is 'Base and Superstructure in Marxist Cultural Theory', *New Left Review* (1973); repr. in id., *Problems in Materialism and Culture: Selected Essays* (London: New Left Books, 1980).

convictions that derive something from all of these various theoretical provenances. Its major concentration is, however, upon imaginative writing, albeit unconfined to any particular genre. Literary texts are what I was trained to read and they are what I remain most interested in reading.

PART I

'Hackney for Bread'

1
Literary Property

Aphra Behn's play *The Rover* was entered to its publisher John Amery in the Stationer's Company Register on 7 July 1677.[1] In its first printed edition, the play includes an intriguing postscript, composed in a different type-face from the text itself and crammed into a small space between the last few lines of the epilogue and the 'finis', suggesting that it was hastily added to the page just before publication:

This play had been sooner in print, but for a report about the town . . . that 'twas *Thomaso* altered; which made the booksellers fear some trouble from the proprietor of that admirable play, which indeed has wit enough to stock a poet, and is not to be pieced or mended by any but the excellent author himself. That I have stolen some hints from it may be a proof, that I valued it more than to pretend to alter it, had I had the dexterity of some poets, who are not more expert in stealing than in the art of concealing . . . I might have appropriated all to myself, but I, vainly proud of my judgment, hang out the sign of Angellica (the only stolen object) to give notice where a great part of the wit dwelt, though if the play of the novella were as well worth remembering as *Thomaso*, they might (bating the name) have as well said, I took it from thence. I will only say the plot and business (not to boast on't) is my own . . . though had this succeeded ill, I should have had no need of imploring that justice from the critics, who . . . would doubtless have given me the whole honour on't. Therefore I will only say in English what the famous Virgil does in Latin; I make verses, and others have the fame.[2]

What exactly is going on here? How could Henry Herringman, the formidable proprietor of Killigrew's *Thomaso*, act to prevent the

---

[1] *A Transcript of the Registers of the Worshipful Company of Stationers from 1640 to 1708 A.D.*, ed. G. E. Briscoe Eyre and C. R. Rivington, 3 vols. (London, 1913; repr. New York: Peter Smith, 1950), iii. 39.

[2] Aphra Behn, *The Rover* (1677), ed. Janet Todd (Harmondsworth: Penguin, 1992), 248. Todd's editing is faulty here. She does not indicate, by the use of italics, that, 'the play of the novella' is a reference to Richard Brome's play *The Novella* (1632); so that the passage is confusing for the modern reader and some of its force is lost.

publication of Behn's play? Assuredly, Herringman had a considerable investment to protect. He had registered with the Stationers' Company a volume of plays by Killigrew, including the two-part *Thomaso*, in 1663 and was still advertising it in 1679.[3] He might well have perceived a play that was very close to *Thomaso* as a threat to the assignable value of his property, given the copies still unsold of that edition. Nevertheless, it is very difficult to see, given the state of the contemporary law governing literary property, how Herringman could prevent the publication of *The Rover*. According to the wording of this postscript, what is at issue is not *piracy*, the unlicensed verbatim reprinting of a work owned by someone else, but rather plagiarism, 'the wrongful act of taking the product of another person's mind, and presenting it as one's own'.[4] Behn's edgy postscript appears to draw attention to the legal dimension of copyright infringement: though what a comparison of the two plays reveals is that she has entirely redacted the original, using some of its characters, situations, and plot-elements (and even some of its dialogue), but condensing and rearranging the whole as well as introducing some original elements.[5] To prosecute her on these grounds, Herringman would have required a conception of copyright that would take more than two centuries to evolve—a conception to which the notion of an author's originality was central. Perhaps Herringman himself concluded that he could do nothing under the law and, we might conjecture, a compromise was reached that Behn would smooth his ruffled feathers, and maybe Killigrew's, by dubbing an apology into the printed copy.

It is a brilliantly worded piece, the apology of a consummate professional. Behn charms Killigrew by praising his wit and states the contemporary quasi-legal understanding that only an author had the right to 'piece or mend' his own work. Self-glorification and self-advertisement come next. The sign of Angellica in the

---

[3] *Stationers' Register*, ii. 331. The advertisement is carried in copies of Villedieu's *The Unfortunate Heroes* (1679).

[4] The definition is that given by Alexander Lindey, *Plagiarism and Originality* (New York: Harper & Brothers, 1952), 2. Maureen Duffy's discussion of this postscript in *The Passionate Shepherdess: Aphra Behn, 1640–89* (London: Jonathan Cape, 1977), pp. 144, 152–4, is conducted in terms of plagiarism (conflict between authors) rather than piracy (conflict between booksellers) and therefore muddles the issue.

[5] See the discussion in Aphra Behn, *The Rover*, ed. Frederick M. Link (London: Edward Arnold, 1967), pp. xi–xii.

play is a picture of the whore Angellica Bianca displayed like an inn sign on the balcony of her house. She is a woman for hire; and in associating herself with this other A.B., Aphra Behn seems to glory in her own literary form of prostitution. She too is a professional for hire. Including this sign in her play, the most identifiable of her borrowings from Killigrew, is an open invitation to readers and spectators to recognize its provenance. Introducing Brome's *The Novella* is a masterstroke. By suggesting that *Thomaso* itself might have a precursor, might not itself be an entirely original work, Behn opens up the possibility that literature is ineluctably textual, always made out of other literature. Brome's play has also furnished her with a few ideas, but in general, she claims, the plot and incidents are her own. And if the play had been judged a bad one, she wryly comments, critics would have been quite happy then to consider it entirely original! The final sentence is a professional's credo. 'I make verse, and others have the fame.' Behn is a toiler in the field, an artisan. She writes to live now, she implies, not to live on in posterity.

The accusation of plagiarism (the word is derived from the Latin *plagiarius*, which means literally the 'kidnapper' of someone's child or slave) is mud that is being thrown by many writers at their rivals in the 1670s and 1680s. In Chapter 3 of this book, I will explore the operation of plagiarism rhetoric in textual embodiments by Rochester, Dryden, and Shadwell. At present, I want to suggest that around this time there was some movement in the conceptual understanding of authorship such that the priority between imitation of sources and original composition was being realigned. To accuse a fellow writer of plagiarism, given the overtones of theft and invasion of territory, entails some thickening of the conception of literary property. Devices, characters, and motifs existing in the common stock are being hived off by individual writers into a domain of private property that they wish to see protected. In this period therefore, earlier than is sometimes supposed, when the stage was hungry for repertoire, and adaptation of French, Spanish, and earlier English plays was the quickest way for professional writers to furnish it, there was the beginning of an attempt to define 'originality' in writing and the ur-conception of proprietary authorship. That the accusations of plagiarism should be so frequently made in respect of writing for the theatre is unsurprising. It was in the theatre that literary artefacts presented themselves most tangibly as forms of property. Given the cutthroat competition between the two patent theatres for audiences, it was easy to perceive how valuable a commodity was a successful play. Theatre presented with stark immediacy the relationship between the paying patron and the dramatic product that was less apparent in writing intended for an individual patron or for a nebulous wider readership the constitution of which the writer hardly understood. In the theatre, writers could actually watch their brainchildren in the very process of being consumed by an audience who would quickly tell them whether or not they liked the taste. There is a materiality, a tangibility, about this that one thinks must have affected prevailing notions of authorship and literary property. The creation of a literary market and the evolution of literary professionalism—writing undertaken by those whose primary means of earning a living it was—occurred in symbiotic relationship with changing conceptions of literary property and the nature of authorship. In this chapter, I will investigate some of the factors that produce a conceptual alteration in what Michel Foucault terms the 'author-function' during the early period of literary professionalization.

I

In the earliest days of book publishing, in the period shortly after the invention of a mechanical means of reproducing handwriting, we find that the writer's place in the incipient printing and publishing industry was fraught with uncertainty, governed by a complex set of protocols that arrested the development of a straightforward market. In the early modern period, ambitious writers did not necessarily consider their literary works as valuable *per se*. Literary endeavours were a means of flagging up their abilities and of putting in a claim for advancement; and for that purpose, what was required was that their performances should circulate in manuscript in suitable coteries. John Donne exemplifies the kind of writer whose aristocratic conception of authorship implied a fierce contempt for the publicity attached to the print medium. Writing to Sir Henry Goodyer in December 1614, he speaks of the ignominy and difficulty involved in gathering up poems circulating in manuscript for the purpose of preparing a printed edition (which he did not, in fact, go on to print):

I am brought to a necessity of printing my Poems, and addressing them to my L. Chamberlain. This I mean to do forthwith; not for much publique view, but at mine own cost, a few Copies. I apprehend some incongruities in the resolution; and I know what I shall suffer from many interpretations: but I am at an end, of much considering that; and, if I were as startling in that kinde, as ever I was, yet in this particular, I am under an inescapable necessity . . . By this occasion I am made a Rhapsoder of mine own rags, and that cost me more diligence, to seek them, then it did to make them.[6]

Ted-Larry Pebworth is correct to stress that 'the poetry written by the coterie with which Donne was associated was determinedly non-professional . . . while the writing of poetry might be necessary for initial advancement, it was regarded as something one grew out of, an activity inappropriate for sober, mature men'.[7] During this period, as Foucault points out in the landmark essay published in 1969 'What is an Author?' (a seminal document in the contemporary phase of thinking about such matters), authorship functioned primarily in legal discourse. Authors' names were first prominently annexed to books in the Renaissance period, when it became important to the state to prosecute them under the laws of blasphemy or libel. Foucault speaks not of authors, therefore, but of the 'author-function', which was a regulatory one at this juncture. Authored discourse is *owned* discourse, which usually brought some form of opprobrium upon its owner.[8]

Authorship could only develop as a profession when it became respectable for individuals to live off their wits. Opposition to this was deeply entrenched, and it required an ideological shift of seismic proportions to effect it. Some idea of the ferocity of the

---

[6] John Donne, *Letters to Severall Persons of Honour: Written by John Donne, Sometime Deane of St. Paul's London*, 2 vols. (London, 1654), i. 196–7.

[7] Ted-Larry Pebworth, 'John Donne, Coterie Poetry, and the Text as Performance', *Studies in English Literature*, 29 (1989), 61–75: 63. Pebworth quotes Richard Helgerson's remark that Donne and his fellow place-seekers 'shared the short literary careers and the gentlemanly disdain for literature that had characterized the Elizabethan amateurs'. See Helgerson's *Self-Crowned Laureates: Spenser, Jonson, Milton, and the Literary System* (Berkeley: University of California Press, 1983), 108–9 and *passim*.

[8] Michel Foucault, 'What is an Author?' (1969), in *Language, Counter-Memory, Practice*, ed. and introd. Donald F. Bouchard, trans. Donald F. Bouchard and Sherry Simon (Oxford, 1977), 113–38.

prejudice against professional writing is gained from a speech made by Lord Camden in the House of Lords as late as 1774, on the occasion of the *Donaldson* v. *Becket* copyright hearing:

> Glory is the Reward of Science, and those who deserve it, scorn all meaner Views: I speak not of the Scribblers for bread, who teize the Press with their wretched Productions; fourteen Years [the duration of copyright under the 1710 Act] is too long a Privilege for their perishable Trash. It was not for Gain, that *Bacon, Newton, Milton, Locke,* instructed and delighted the World; it would be unworthy such Men to traffic with a dirty Bookseller for so much as a Sheet of Letter-press. When the Bookseller offered *Milton* Five Pounds for his Paradise Lost, he did not reject it, and commit his Poem to the Flames, nor did he accept the miserable Pittance as the Reward of his Labor; he knew that the real price of his Work was Immortality, and that Posterity would pay it.[9]

Samuel Simmons was the bookseller who bought *Paradise Lost* for a fiver. What Lord Camden fails to observe is that when Posterity paid the price, the recipient was the publisher Jacob Tonson, without whose active midwifery Milton's great work might not have survived. Tonson bought a half-share in the copyright from Brabazon Aylmer in 1683, spent several years preparing a good text, and issued it in 1688 as a subscription edition in conjunction with the publisher Richard Bentley.[10] Subsequently, the copyright on Milton's works became an immensely valuable commodity to the Tonson dynasty. This suggests that the development of modern authorship needs to be understood in the conceptual terms of ideas of literary property. For true professionalization of writing could only emerge when authors saw themselves as having something valuable to sell.

Even when the prevailing ideology of authorship was the regulatory one, there were individuals who dissented from it and wanted very much to be of account. Mark Rose suggests in his *Authors and Owners*, an elegant and important study of the invention of copyright to which I will be referring more extensively below, that the first author who appears to have what Rose terms a

---

[9] *The Cases of the Appellants and Respondents in the Cause of Literary Property Before the House of Lords* (London, 1774), 54. Quoted by Mark Rose, 'The Author as Proprietor: *Donaldson* v. *Becket* and the Genealogy of Modern Authorship', *Representations*, 23 (Summer 1988), 51–85: 54. This article has subsequently been elaborated into an important book, referred to in my text.

[10] Kathleen M. Lynch, *Jacob Tonson: Kit-Kat Publisher* (Knoxville: University of Tennessee Press, 1971), 103.

'proprietary' view of himself as a creative agent of some individual worth was indeed John Milton. The very fact that Milton signed a contract with Simmons is, irrespective of the fact that he sold himself too cheap, evidence of a great change in the nature of authorship.[11] An earlier candidate, I would suggest, is George Wither, whose career dramatizes the clash between the regulatory and the proprietary models of authorship during this era and who therefore becomes a fulcral figure in the prehistory of professional writing. Wither spent three years adapting biblical passages into metrical forms, his *Hymns and Songs for the Church*, with which he approached the king directly, gaining on 17 February 1623 letters patent conferring a copyright for fifty-one years. By compulsory order, Wither's *Hymns* were directed to be bound up with every copy of the Psalms printed and distributed by the Stationers' Company. This provoked a furious backlash from the Stationers, who saw their monopoly being broken by an independent author who appeared to be performing an economic act of levitation, cutting himself free from all existing publishing institutions and arguing the respectability of writing for subsistence. Wither intended to publish his pastoral eclogue *Fidelia* (1615) by subscription, and wrote a preface in which he showed his gratitude for the disinterestedness of public subscribers as against the otiose and servile relationships that usually subtended with patrons:

By this means I shall be sure to be beholding to none but those that love virtue or me, and preserve the unequalled happiness of a free spirit. Whereas else, being forced to accept of some particular bounties, it may be, blinded by seeming courtesies, I might fall into the common baseness incident to flatterers, and so at length become like those great clergymen of our times, who dare not upbraid all sins for fear they should seem so saucy as to reprehend their patrons.[12]

In *The Schollers Purgatory, Discovered in the Stationers Common-wealth* (*c.*1625), Wither cut himself off from the other mechanism for publishing, the Stationers' Company, by asserting the author's right to a reasonable reward for his labours and

[11] Mark Rose, *Authors and Owners: The Invention of Copyright* (Cambridge, Mass.: Harvard University Press, 1993), 27–30.
[12] Quoted by Sarah L. C. Clapp, 'The Beginnings of Subscription Publication in the Seventeenth Century', *Modern Philology*, 29 (1931–2), 199–224: 208. For a fuller account of 17th-century subscription ventures, see her article 'Subscription Publishers Prior to Jacob Tonson', *Library*, 4th ser., 13 (1932–3), 158–83.

disclosing the various means at the Stationers' disposal to prevent him from exercising it. His sympathy for the practical trades involved in the printing industry, as against the redundant middlemen, is of a piece with the popularizing and populist intentions behind the *Hymns*, which gained the contempt of the élite:

conceive me not, I pray you, that I goe about to lay a generall imputation upon all Stationers. For, to disparage the whole profession, were an act neither becoming an honest man to doe, nor a prudent Auditory to suffer. Their mystery . . . consists of divers Trades incorporated together: as Printers, Booke-binders, Claspmakers, Booksellers &c. And of all these be some honest men, who to my knowledge are so greeved being overborn by the notorious oppressions and proceedings of the rest, that they have wished themselves of some other calling. The Printers mystery, is ingenious, paynefull, and profitable: the Booke-binders necessary; the Claspemakers usefull. And in deed, the retailer of bookes, commonly called a Booke-seller, is a Trade, which being wel governed, and lymited in certaine bounds, might become somewhat serviceable to the rest. But as it is now (for the most part abused) the Bookeseller hath not onely made the Printer, the Binder, and the Claspemaker a slave to him: but hath brought Authors, yea the whole Commonwealth, and all the liberall Sciences into bondage. For he makes all professors of Art, labour for his profit, at his owne price, and utters it to the Common-wealth in such fashion, and at those rates, which please himselfe.

In so-much, that I wonder so insupportable, and so impertinent a thing, as a meere Booke-seller . . . was ever permitted to grow up in the Commonwealth. For, many of our moderne booke-sellers, are but needlesse excrements, or rather vermine, who being ingendred by the sweat of schollers, Printers, and book-binders, doe (as wormes in timber, or like the generation of vipers) devour those that bred them. While they did like fleas, but sucke now and then a dropp of the writers blood from him, and skipp off when he found himselfe diseased, it was somewhat tollerable: but since they began to feed on him, like the third plague of Ægipt without remooving, and to lay clayme to each Authors labours, as if they had been purposely brought up to studye for their mayntenance.[13]

Wither looks back here to what he perceives as a golden age of printing, when, as described below by the modern historian of print Elizabeth Eisenstein, the early printing-house was a cultural centre and vital dynamo of literary production:

---

[13] George Wither, *The Schollers Purgatory, Discovered in the Stationers Commonwealth* ([*c*.1625]), in *Miscellaneous Works of George Wither: First Collection* (London: printed for the Spenser Society, 1872), 17–18.

The romantic figure of the aristocratic or patrician patron has tended to obscure the more plebeian and prosaic early capitalist entrepreneur who hired scholars, translators, editors and compilers when not serving in these capacities himself. Partly because copyists had, after all, never paid those whose works they copied, partly because new books were a small portion of the early book trade, and partly because divisions of literary labor remained blurred, the author retained a quasi-amateur status until the eighteenth century. During this interval, printers served as patrons for authors, acted as their own authors, and sought patronage, privileges, and favors from official quarters as well. This was the era when men of letters and learning were likely to be familiar with print technology and commercial trade routes in a manner that later observers overlook.[14]

Yet despite Eisenstein's admiration for the Crusoesque early printer, and the high opinion held by Puritans like Wither and Milton of independent authorship, a division of labour between authors and printers, printers and publishers, and subsequently between publishers and booksellers was a prerequisite for the emergence of authorship as a profession. By the mid-seventeenth century, as Wither observed, the bookseller-publisher had separated from the printer and was in undisputed control over the entire publishing industry; and while printers and binders could fight for an equitable cutting of the cake, as Marjorie Plant puts it, 'the person who was of no account whatsoever . . . was the author'.[15] Authorship could only develop as a profession when educated, literate individuals who possessed imaginative fecundity could earn sufficient money to purchase for themselves a standard of living commensurate with this stock-in-trade. That, in turn, could only come about when there were no longer enough aristocratic patrons around to subsidize authors in the provision of manuscripts that bookseller-publishers needed to turn into printed books, and when there were enough readers around to create a demand that could not be satisfied by interested amateur authors of independent means.

[14] Elizabeth L. Eisenstein, *The Printing Revolution in Early Modern Europe* (Cambridge University Press, 1983; repr. 1990), 100.
[15] Marjorie Plant, *The English Book Trade: An Economic History of the Making and Sale of Books* (London: George Allen & Unwin, 1939; repr. 1974), 68.

II

John Milton's *Areopagitica* (1643), written at a thrilling moment when censorship was temporarily in abeyance, embodies a heady vision of readers and writers whose 'pens and heads' are as effective as 'anvils and hammers' in the defence of justice and truth, their lamplit studies providing the intellectual spearhead for the 'shop of war':

> Behold now this vast City; a City of refuge, the mansion house of liberty, encompass'd and surrounded with His protection; the shop of warre hath not there more anvils and hammers waking, to fashion out the plates and instruments of armed Justice in defence of beleaguer'd Truth, then there be pens and heads there, sitting by their studious lamps, musing, search-ing, revolving new notions and idea's wherewith to present, as with their homage and their fealty the approaching Reformation: others as fast reading, trying all things, assenting to the force of reason and convince-ment.[16]

Less than a century later, in 1730, Henry Fielding staged *The Author's Farce*, in which a literary hack called Blotpage sings the following pathetic ditty (and, incidentally, furnishes me with the catch-title for this book):

> How unhappy's the fate
> To live by one's pate
> And be forced to write hackney for bread!
> An author's a joke
> To all manner of folk
> Wherever he pops up his head, his head,
> Wherever he pops up his head.
>
> Though he mount on that hack,
> Old Pegasus' back,
> And of Helicon drink till he burst,
> Yet a curse of those streams,
> Poetical dreams,
> They never can quench one's thirst, etc.

[16] *The Complete Prose Works of John Milton*, 8 vols. (New Haven: Yale University Press, and London: Oxford University Press, 1953–82), ii (1953), 553–4. Milton's attitude towards his writing was never that of a professional, exactly, but he had enormous respect for print as the disseminating medium. See J. W. Saunders, *The Profession of English Letters* (London: Routledge & Kegan Paul, and Toronto: University of Toronto Press, 1964), 85–92.

Ah, how should he fly
On fancy so high
When his limbs are in durance and hold?
Or how should he charm
With genius so warm,
When his poor naked body's acold, etc.[17]

These thin, sad lyrics capture perfectly the gap between aspiration and actuality experienced by the hungry labourer in the growing literary market-place. They recapitulate the visual cues, made familiar by Pope's 1728 *Dunciad,* of the creative soul imprisoned by its tenement of clay. Bodily appetites clamour to be satisfied, but the products of genius command an insufficient price to see to their satisfaction. The classical attributes of literary inspiration— Helicon, the muses, 'fancy'—are metaphors played out by the brute actuality of making a living. Shortly afterwards, there occurs the following scene in Bookweight's house, a bookseller-publisher who supervises the mechanical compositions of three writers, Dash, Quibble, and Blotpage:

BOOKWEIGHT. Fie upon it, gentlemen! What, not at your pens? Do you consider, Mr. Quibble, that it is above a fortnight since your Letter from a Friend in the Country was published? Is it not high time for an Answer to come out? At this rate, before your Answer is printed your Letter will be forgot. I love to keep a controversy up warm. I have had authors who have writ a pamphlet in the morning, answered it in the afternoon, and compromised the matter at night.

QUIBBLE. Sir, I will be as expeditious as possible.

BOOKWEIGHT. Well, Mr. Dash, have you done that murder yet?

DASH. Yes, sir, the murder is done. I am only about a few moral reflections to place before it.

BOOKWEIGHT. Very well. Then let me have the ghost finished by this day sevennight.

DASH. What sort of a ghost would you have, sir? The last was a pale one.

BOOKWEIGHT. Then let this be a bloody one. Mr. Blotpage, what have your lucubrations produced? [*Reads.*] 'Poetical advice to a certain —— from a certain —— on a certain —— from a certain ——.' Very good! I will say, Mr. Blotpage writes as good a dash as any man in Europe.

To them Index.

[17] Henry Fielding, *The Author's Farce* (1730), ed. C. B. Woods (Lincoln: University of Nebraska Press, 1966), II. iii.

BOOKWEIGHT. So, Mr. Index, what news with you?

INDEX. I have brought my bill, sir.

BOOKWEIGHT. What's here?—'For adapting the motto of *Risum teneatis amici* to a dozen pamphlets at sixpence per each, six shillings. For *Omnia vincit amor et nos cedamus amori*, sixpence. For *Difficile est satyram non scribere*, sixpence.' Hum, hum, hum. Ah. 'A sum total, for thirty-six Latin mottos, eighteen shillings; ditto English, seven, one shilling and ninepence; ditto Greek, four, one shilling'—Why, friend, are your Latin mottos dearer than your Greek?

INDEX. Yes marry are they, sir. For as nobody now understands Greek, so I may use any sentence in that language to whatsoever purpose I please.

BOOKWEIGHT. You shall have your money immediately. And pray remember that I must have two Latin sedition mottos and one Greek moral motto for pamphlets by tomorrow morning.   (II. iv–v)

Milton's independent truth-seekers have become, in Fielding's farce, the alienated labourers in a cynical and exploitative book factory, the nature of their output entirely specified by the requirements of the middle-man. The publisher and marketeer Bookweight creates an artificial demand for controversial pamphlets, potboiling crime and horror stories, and the most mind-numbing subgenres of poetry. Judging from the nature of their literary endeavours, Dash, Quibble, and Blotpage could all be manifestations of a writer such as the not-yet-deceased Daniel Defoe, who was frequently accused in his own lifetime of writing on both sides of a question and who had recently written extensively on ghosts and apparitions.[18] The job of rifling through pages of the reputable periodicals to filch mottoes calculated to raise the tone of Bookweight's gutter productions is subcontracted to a character whose name, Index, specifies his status as a literary appendage. A noble tradition of classical learning is commodified, traduced by being turned directly into money. Greek mottoes are worth less than Latin because, in the case of the latter, there is still some vestigial ability on the part of readers to translate them, so that more labour goes into their selection. In II. vi Bookweight is offered a new translation of the *Aeneid* by a hack who subsequently admits that he is monoglot and has 'translated' it out of Dryden. To this, Bookweight has no objection. His scruple is purely financial: he

---

[18] P. N. Furbank and W. R. Owens, *The Canonisation of Daniel Defoe* (New Haven: Yale University Press, 1988), 10–11, 151–60.

will not buy the translation, but will hire the writer's pen and will put him (Scarecrow by name) in his stable with the others.

What accounts for this wide gap in the perception of writing between the eras of Milton and Fielding? One important answer is the growth of writing as a profession: as a calling or occupation by means of which large numbers of individuals were by 1730 attempting to earn their living. In Milton's vision, writers and readers mutually reinforce each other as seekers after a just appraisal of divine and human truth. They operate without brokers and have no wish to make a living by their writing. Although Milton is discussing scriptural exposition rather than imaginative writing, the two categories merge in his own later literary work. His radical championing of freedom of speech, perpetuated in the Civil War, was certainly a constituting condition of the literary market-place to which Fielding's farce reacts. Some thirty years after Milton's broadside against pre-publication censorship, when Andrew Marvell sought to parody the position of those like Samuel Parker who sponsored religious persecution, he has his Parker-persona revisit this passage in *Areopagitica* and twist it as follows:

The Press (that *villanous* Engine) invented much about the same time with the Reformation, that hath done more mischief to the Discipline of our Church, than all the Doctrine can make amends for. 'Twas an happy time when all Learning was in Manuscript, and some little Officer, like our Author, did keep the Keys of the Library . . . But now, since Printing came into the World, such is the mischief, that a Man cannot write a Book but presently he is answered . . . Two or three brawny Fellows in a Corner, with meer Ink and Elbow-grease, do more harm than an *hundred Systematical Divines* with their *sweaty Preaching* . . . *O Printing*! How hast thou disturb'd the Peace of Mankind! that Lead, when moulded into Bullets, is not so mortal as when founded into Letters![19]

Proliferation of print is given in Marvell's parody a pedigree that traces it back through Dissent to radical sectarianism, an association of ideas that was often subliminally present in the writings of those later writers, like Henry Fielding, who made it an important theme. Fielding is all too conscious of the materiality of the means of production, distribution, and exchange employed by the crescent printing industry in Walpolean England and, in sympathy

[19] Andrew Marvell, *The Rehearsal Transpros'd* (1672), ed. D. I. B. Smith (Oxford: Oxford University Press, 1971), 32–3.

with the reaction to it formulated by Pope and his circle, is deeply distrustful of its effect on cultural standards. In recent historical and sociological analysis, the growth of the English book market is understood to be an aspect of the 'commercial capitalism' that transformed pre-industrial Britain into a mass consumer society in the period between the English Civil War and the mid-eighteenth century.[20] Demand for printed materials is recognized to have been stimulated by the Civil War itself, and literacy rates, steadily rising throughout the early modern period, are thought to have grown especially fast, and particularly amongst women, in the decades following the Restoration. In a society becoming capable of delivering a standard of living considerably above that of mere subsistence to an increasing number of its members, books were amongst the possessions that these improving citizens wanted to consume. Indeed, they were high on the list of such consumables, because, as people grew richer, they required the trappings of what David Hume would call 'refinement' to distance themselves from those who could not afford to acquire it and to narrow the gap between themselves and those who had possessed such refinement effortlessly for several generations. By the 1690s, when newspapers and periodicals, as well as review publications that performed the service of sifting through new material and advising busy people of what was particularly worth their notice in the world of learning, had become a permanent part of the publishing scene, we can speak of the beginnings of a mass market for literature. Publishers were trying to locate it with ever-greater precision and directness, writers were responding to their sense of what comprised it and trying to stimulate it, and readers were eager to participate in it. Writing could not remain what it had been—manuscript material circulated narrowly amongst coteries or inaccessible printed books, the production of which was supported by noble patrons.

One important measure of the changing nature and status of the

[20] The term is used by G. J. Barker-Benfield in his valuable and comprehensive synthesis of this process given in *The Culture of Sensibility: Sex and Society in Eighteenth-Century Britain* (Chicago: University of Chicago Press, 1992). Commercial capitalism itself comprises a network of interconnecting developments and practices ranging from naval strength, ensuring trade routes and colonial success; improving internal communications infrastructure; agricultural breakthroughs, enabling more plentiful supplies of cheaper food; to the emergence of a stable political regime, the new empirical science, the 'financial revolution', and the Act of Union.

authorial profession was the growing demand in the late seventeenth century for a copyright statute. As Elizabeth Eisenstein suggestively indicates, the impetus that culminated in the Copyright Act of 1710 was part of a broad cultural movement towards the constitution of private property: 'Competition over the right to publish a given text also introduced controversy over the issues involving monopoly and piracy. Printing forced a definition of what belonged in the public domain. A literary "common" became subject to "enclosure movements", and possessive individualism began to characterize the attitude of writers to their work.'[21] 'Possessive individualism' designates the political theory propounded by John Locke as part of his legitimization of the Revolution Settlement in the *Two Treatises of Government* (1690). Powerful confirmation of the relationship between copyright legislation and the promotion of liberty and property is found in the terms of Locke's opposition to renewal of the Licensing Act when this fell due in 1695. The desire to protect literary productions by preventing acquirers of them from making copies at will stemmed from two different impulses: the need for those in the printing and publishing business to protect their investment in machinery, labour, paper, and other materials; and the state's need to inhibit the circulation of seditious writing.[22] Monopoly over copyright was invested in the Stationers' Company (incorporated 1556), and copyright involved the licensing of books by the Wardens of the Company, followed by their registration in a ledger after payment of a fee.[23] Copyright was the stationer's right to print and reprint copy that he had been the first to license and register. It was precisely this link between ownership of literary property and a state system of surveillance that Locke wished to see broken. Raymond Astbury's detailed study of the background to the lapse of the 1662 Licensing Act in 1695 makes clear how Locke attempted to influence the Commons towards its non-renewal, on

[21] Eisenstein, *The Printing Revolution in Early Modern Europe*, 83–4.

[22] There is by now an extensive literature on aspects of state censorship: one might single out Annabel Patterson, *Censorship and Interpretation: The Conditions of Writing and Reading in Early Modern England* (Madison: University of Wisconsin Press, 1984); and Joseph Loewenstein, 'For a History of Literary Property', *English Literary Renaissance*, 18/3 (Autumn 1988), 389–412.

[23] On the precise mechanics of this, see W. W. Greg, *Some Aspects and Problems of London Publishing between 1550 and 1650* (Oxford: Clarendon Press, 1956), chs. 3, 4.

the grounds that it granted a monopoly that was a clog on the book trade and that pre-publication censorship of books was unnecessary provided they were identified by author. The suggestions he made for a redrafted law included the idea of limited copyright (limited to fifty or seventy years after the author's death or the first printing of the book in question) and the proposition that authors themselves should have the sole rights to reprint their own books for a certain term.[24] Thus Locke anticipated the terms of the 1710 Act. His interventions provide evidence of a growing demand for the recognition of authors as property-owners entitled to protection under the law, also apparent in the objections of such as Daniel Defoe to the unfair practices that proliferated in the printing industry in the vacuum created by the lapsing of the old act. In *An Essay on the Regulation of the Press* (1704), Defoe described the hack butchery that passed for abridgement and the undercutting of authors by cheap pirated editions: and he links the two aspects of existing copyright practice (press regulation and protection of investment) in the argument that 'if an Author has not the right of a Book, after he has made it, and the benefit be not his own, and the Law will not protect him in that Benefit, 'twould be very hard the Law should pretend to punish him for it'.[25]

For much of the time in the intervening period between 1695 and the passage of the 1710 'Act for the Encouragement of Learning, by vesting the Copies of printed Books in the Authors or Purchasers of such Copies, during the Times therein mentioned' authors continued to be puppets in this legal debate. Upon the lapse of the 1695 Licensing Act, when pre-publication censorship was discontinued, bookseller-publishers found that they had lost the old quid pro quo of ownership rights in return for operating the censorship mechanism. There was now no means of curtailing piracy, and they found in the assertion of *authors'* rights to reap the fruits of their labours a convenient cloak for their own interests. In the wordings of the successive petitions that they presented to Parliament, the trade purported to be representing the economic interests of their workers and of the authors who supplied them with copy. On 12–13 December 1709, for example, a

[24] Raymond Astbury, 'The Renewal of the Licensing Act in 1693 and its Lapse in 1695', *Library*, 33 (1978), 296–322, esp. 305–13.

[25] Daniel Defoe, *An Essay on the Regulation of the Press* (1704), ed. J. R. Moore (Oxford: Basil Blackwell for the Luttrell Society, 1948), 28.

petition brought in by sixteen bookseller-publishers was read in the House, setting forth:

> that it had been the constant Usage, for the Writers of Books, to sell their Copies to Booksellers or Printers, to the end they might hold those Copies as their Property, and enjoy the Profit of making, and vending, Impressions of them; yet divers Persons have of late invaded the Properties of others, by reprinting several Books, without the Consent, and to the great Injury, of the Proprietors, even to their utter Ruin, and the Discouragement of all Writers in any useful Part of Learning.[26]

In the following February the printers and bookbinders were encouraged to present a petition that spoke in apocalyptic terms of the 'Poverty and Want' to which the 5,000 members of the trades were being reduced by the absence of legal protection for copy.[27] The justificatory wording of the 1709 Bill gives to authors a proprietary significance that was in practice denied to them because few authors considered it a possibility to retain their own copyrights: 'Whereas Printers, Booksellers and other Persons have of late frequently taken the Liberty of printing, reprinting and publishing, or causing to be printed, reprinted and published, Books and other Writings without the Consent of the Authors or Proprietors of such Books and Writings, to their very great Detriment, and too often to the Ruin of them and their Families . . .'.[28] The wording of an earlier version of the Act to be found in the Bodleian Library states books to be the 'undoubted Property' of authors and leaves open the possibility that they would retain copyrights in part or in full. This constitutes evidence that, prior to the passing of the Act, the booksellers were prepared to represent authors' interests in the original productions of their imagination even more strongly, but that, in the final version, they reneged to some extent and protected the rights, not of authors directly, but of those to whom authors had assigned their rights.[29] Whatever the motives of the printing trade, however, the vital point is that in the wording of the 1710 Act, authors were for the first time given

---

[26] *Journals of the House of Commons*, 16 (1803), 16 Nov. 1708–9 Oct. 1711, 240.

[27] 2 Feb. 1710: *Journals of the House of Commons*, 16: 291.

[28] Anno 8° Annae, c. 19. AD 1709.

[29] See A. J. K. Robinson, 'The Evolution of Copyright, 1476–1776', *Cambrian Law Review*, 21–2 (1990–1), 55–77: 67; and John Feather, 'The Book Trade in Politics: The Making of the Copyright Act of 1710', *Publishing History*, 8 (1980), 19–44: 36. I am indebted to P. J. Wright for the information that another early version of the Bill exists in Lincoln's Inn Library.

legal recognition. It may be, therefore, that we should correct Foucault. The important date for the 'invention' of authors is not some time in the Renaissance, but 1710, when they were first given legal personalities. Furthermore, this degree of recognition was the result of the new power exerted by professionals of the print industry, a grouping that included, prominently, professional writers.

The Act provides that from 10 April 1710 books already printed would be protected for a period of twenty-one years, while new books published after that date would be protected for fourteen years, renewable for a further term of fourteen if the author or owner was still alive. The drafters of the legislation appear to have modelled the Act's provisions on earlier statutes governing patents, in particular on the Statute of Monopolies of 1624 (21 Jac. 1 c. 3) that prevented individuals from having a monopoly on branches of manufacture and commerce, with the exception of existing patents that would be protected for twenty-one years and future patents for fourteen. Letters patent were sought in the early seventeenth century to safeguard inventions, as also for land, mineral extraction, collecting rags for paper, and a very wide range of activities for which a monopoly was sought. The Stationers' Company seemed to regard literary property as exactly on a par with other commodities that could be monopolized and transferred by their owners in perpetuity. This is implied by, for instance, the Company's petition to the Long Parliament for new press regulation in 1643: 'there is no reason apparent why the production of the brain should not be as assignable . . . as the right of any goods or chattels whatsoever'.[30] Was the 1710 Act, therefore, declaring books to be like inventions, that is to say, artefacts in the public domain that could and should be multiplied for the public good, subject only to the proviso that the original inventor should be rewarded for the labour and creativity put into them? The clause limiting the duration of copyright was added at a very late stage in the Bill's progress through Parliament. It appears first in a list of the House of Lords' amendments reported on 5 April 1710;[31] and it left a crucial area of ambiguity. What happened after the twenty-eight years were over? Who owned copyright in the

[30] Quoted in Arnold Plant, 'The Economic Aspects of Copyright in Books', *Economica*, NS 1–4 (May 1934), 167–95: 178.
[31] *Journals of the House of Commons*, 16: 394.

final analysis? This central ambiguity in the Act foregrounded the legal question whether this statute is a law that *supplements* an existing common law right, or whether it is actually a new law that becomes the sole foundation of literary property, limiting any natural right that can be supposed to have existed. And what exactly *is* literary property? Its nature was not determined by the 1710 Act.

III

In the aftermath of the Act, pressure mounted to have the nature of literary property clarified and its worth fully recognized. Very considerable financial interests were at stake, as the struggle for ownership of Shakespeare's works might exemplify. The Tonson dynasty's claim to 'ownership' of Shakespeare was based on the purchase, in 1707 and 1709, of two copyright assignments; and it was their practice to buy out competing editions, as they did in 1747, when they paid Warburton (himself a considerable literary property magnate, whose rights to Pope earned him over £2,600) £500 for his. As Don Nichol remarks, the Tonsons contracted new editors of Shakespeare every so often to assert their rights by improving their property.[32] There was a growing sense of disquiet, however, about a situation persisting in which powerful publishing cartels could engross the dissemination of valuable cultural productions that should belong by rights to their originators if alive and to the people at large if dead. In 1720 one of John Dennis's many feuds erupted, this time with Sir Richard Steele over the failure of his version of *Coriolanus* entitled *The Invader of his Country*. In revenge, Dennis published *The Characters and Conduct of Sir John Edgar* (1720), which makes direct and specific charges of plagiarism against Steele (a little ironic, in view of Dennis's own debt to Shakespeare) and, in so doing, develops a comparison between intellectual property and both movable and

[32] Don Nichol, 'Warburton (Not!) on Copyright: Clearing up the Misattribution of *An Enquiry into the Nature and Origin of Literary Property* (1762)', *British Journal for Eighteenth-Century Studies* (forthcoming). For information on Warburton's profits from publishing editions of Pope, see Don Nichol, *Pope's Literary Legacy: The Book-Trade Correspondence of William Warburton and John Knapton with Other Letters and Related Documents (1744–1780)* (Oxford: Oxford Bibliographical Society, 1990), 191–2.

immovable forms of tangible property well before the copyright debate does so:

> I was formerly so weak as to think, that nothing was more a Man's own than his Thoughts and Inventions. Nay, I have been often inclin'd to think, that a Man had absolute Property in his Thoughts and Inventions alone. I have been apt to think, with a great Poet, that every Thing else which the World calls Property, is very improperly nam'd so [there, Dennis quotes Horace's *Epistles*, II. 2] The Money that is mine, was somebody's else before, and will be hereafter another's.
>
> Houses and Lands too are certain to change their Landlords; sometimes by Gift, sometimes by Purchase, and sometimes by Might; but always, to be sure, by Death. But my Thoughts are unalterably and unalienably mine, and never can be another's . . . I have therefore formerly been inclin'd to think, That nothing ought to be so sacred as a Man's Thoughts and Inventions: And I have more than once observ'd, That the impudent Plagiary, who makes it the Business of his Life to seize on them, and usurp them, has stuck at no other Property, but has dar'd to violate all that is Sacred among Men.[33]

Speaking as a professional writer, Dennis emphasizes that 'Thoughts and Inventions' are the most inviolable guarantees of personal identity; and it is the very immateriality of them, their very intangibility, that makes them most real. Plagiarism is virtually a form of rape. Later, the intellectual property argument surfaced in the parliamentary debate concerning the theatrical Licensing Bill of 1737, following closely on the heels of the various attempts made by the booksellers in 1735 and 1736 to lengthen copyright terms for a further twenty-one years. Lord Chesterfield's dextrous speech on that occasion conjures with the Whig watchwords of liberty and property and puns skilfully on the excise, still a very hot potato in the aftermath of the 1734 Excise crisis that nearly brought Walpole down. It specifically introduces the proprietary model of authorship in the theatrical context, implicitly contrasting mental property with the more tangible assets of landed wealth incident to their lordships, and then goes on to show the absurdity of dealing with intellectual property, with wit, as if it were goods to be subjected to excise duty inspectors.

[33] John Dennis, *The Characters and Conduct of Sir John Edgar, Call'd by Himself Sole Monarch of the Stage in Drury-Lane; and his Three Deputy-Governors. In Two Letters to Sir John Edgar* (1720), in *The Critical Works of John Dennis*, ed. E. N. Hooker, 2 vols. (Baltimore: Johns Hopkins University Press, 1943), ii. 191–2.

Chesterfield's argument would make writing for money an acceptable way to market one's natural assets:

[The Licensing Bill] is not only an encroachment upon liberty, but it is an encroachment upon property. Wit, my Lords, is a sort of property: it is the property of those who have it, and too often the only property they have to depend on. It is indeed but a precarious dependence. Thank God! we, my Lords have a dependence of another kind; we have a much less precarious support, and therefore cannot feel the inconveniences of the bill now before us. But it is our duty to encourage and protect wit, whosoever's property it may be. Those gentlemen who have any such property, are all, I hope, our friends. Do not let us subject them to any unnecessary or arbitrary restraint. I must own, I cannot easily agree to the laying of any tax upon wit. But by this bill it is to be heavily taxed, it is to be excised. For, if this bill passes, it cannot be retailed in a proper way without a permit, and the Lord Chamberlain is to have the honour of being chief-gauger, supervisor, commissioner, judge and jury. But what is still more hard, though the poor author, *the proprietor I should say* [italics mine], cannot perhaps dine till he has found out and agreed with a purchaser, yet, before he can propose to seek for a purchaser, he must patiently submit to have his goods rummaged at this new excise office, where they may be detained for fourteen days, and even then he may find them returned as prohibited goods, by which his chief and best market will be forever shut against him.[34]

One very clear indication that by the 1730s there was a strong desire to legitimize the professional author-function and even to address the degree of economic exploitation by the publishing trade is to be found in the wording of the proposal drawn up on 1 August 1735 to form a Society for the Encouragement of Learning: 'Proposal to Supply the want of a regular & publick Encouragement of Learning: to assist Authors in the publication: & to secure to them the entire profits of their own Works: to institute a Republick of Letters for the promoting of Arts & Sciences by the necessary means of Profit, as well as by the nobler motives of Praise & Emulation.'[35] Each of the thirty-one signatories to the proposal are to subscribe to a fund. Authors send in proposals and the society's managers choose which to support, paying all printing and publication costs. Once those costs are met out of sales, all

[34] Quoted in David Thomas and Arnold Hare (eds.), *Theatre in Europe: A Documentary History. Restoration and Georgian England, 1660–1788* (Cambridge University Press, 1989), 213 (my italics).
[35] BL Add. MS 47131, fo. 96.

profits go to the authors, and all rights to future editions go to them. Under this scheme, the forerunner in its administration of many later charitable associations, authors would for the first time in printing history reap all of the financial benefits of their own work.[36] Once having had their existence legally recognized, authors had a soil in which to plant claims for a better deal. As late as 1758 it was possible for James Ralph, in his characteristically exuberant and exaggerated manner, to present the travails of professional writing in terms not much different from those of George Wither:

There is no Difference between the Writer in his Garret, and the Slave in the Mines; but that the former has his Situation in the Air, and the latter in the Bowels of the Earth: Both have their Tasks assigned them alike; Both must drudge *and* Starve; and neither can hope for Deliverance. The Compiler must compile; the Composer must compose on; sick or well; in Spirit or out; whether furnish'd with Matter or not; till, by the joint Pressure of Labour, Penury, and Sorrow, he has worn out his Parts, his Constitution, and all the little Stock of Reputation he had acquir'd among *the Trade*; Who were All, perhaps, that ever heard of his Name.[37]

By the time Ralph was making his graphic case for the hack writer, test-cases in the wake of the 1710 Act, and legal attempts to clarify its nature, had taken the copyright debate into areas of metaphysical complexity. These are studied by Mark Rose in his *Authors and Owners*, to which the following paragraphs are much indebted. As he argues, it was Alexander Pope's use of the courts in prosecuting Curll over illicit publications of his letters (*Pope* v. *Curll*, 1741) that prompted Lord Chancellor Hardwicke into making a decision to the effect that literary property was not equivalent to any physical object with which it might be identified. Hardwicke decided that letters written *by* Pope were his property, but those written *to* him were not. So Pope was the owner of property that he no longer possessed and was not the owner of property that he did possess. As Rose puts it: 'in Hardwicke's decision, the authors' words have in effect flown free from the page on which they are written. Not ink and paper but pure signs, separated from any material support, have become the protected

[36] On the charity movement later in the century and its form of organization, see Paul Langford, *A Polite and Commercial People: England, 1727–1783* (Oxford University Press, 1992), 481–7.

[37] James Ralph, *The Case of Authors by Profession or Trade, Stated with Regard to Booksellers, the Stage and the Public* (London, 1758), 22.

property' (p. 65). Over the next thirty years, the fundamental issue affecting copyright would be that of whether the author had perpetual rights to his copy under common law, or whether the 1710 statute was a new law that determined literary copy to be on a level with patented inventions, to be protected for a fixed period of time only. Underlying that question was the prior question of the nature of literary property. William Warburton was a key player in the legal debate, who, in his *Letter from an Author . . . Concerning Literary Property* (1747), took the view that a book differed from a 'mechanick Engine' in that it represented the 'Work of the Mind' (p. 9), to which authors were entitled to perpetual rights, unlike any material object. A later response to Warburton, the unidentified *Enquiry Into the Nature and Origin of Literary Property* (1762), however, takes the opposite view, denying that ideas can be protected by copyright and outlining the frightening practical consequences of trying to define originality.[38] By this time, it was clear that the judicial interpretation of the 1710 Act was not necessarily in the interests of a reading public avid for cheap reprints of literary works becoming canonical. Alexander Donaldson, the Scottish publisher who had already commenced the cheap reprinting of the most prestigious literary titles, pointed to the London monopoly, protected by 'the specious pretence of their having purchased from the authors immediately, or by progress, the sole and exclusive property of said books'.[39] Learning could not be served by restricting rights to reprint books and giving to booksellers' cartels the privilege of inflating prices. Judges continued to uphold this right and to deny that it had been limited by the statute of 1710 until 1774 when, as is well known, the House of Lords upheld Donaldson's right to reprint Thomson's *Seasons* in despite of the London bookseller Becket's claim that he owned perpetual copyright.

Rose's work demonstrates the interpenetration of legal-economic and aesthetic ideologies in creating a climate hospitable to changes in thinking about the nature of authorship and the products of the literary imagination. He shows how, in the various

[38] This later work is very frequently identified as being by Warburton, which is strange considering that it is written in direct opposition to Warburton's 1747 *Letter.* Don Nichol, in 'Warburton (Not!) on Copyright', corrects the misattribution and puts forward the suggestion that the true author is Arthur Murphy.

[39] Alexander Donaldson, *Some Thoughts on the State of Literary Property humbly submitted to the Consideration of the Public* (London, 1764), 3.

court cases leading up to *Donaldson* v. *Becket*, counsel for the proponents of perpetual authorial rights claimed that literary property resided neither in the physical book nor in the ideas communicated by it, but in 'an entity consisting of style and sentiment combined'—in the literary 'work' (p. 91). Our present-day literary universe, claims Rose, is constellated around the central idea of the proprietary author, who is the creative originator of an unique and original literary work. This culturally powerful representation of authorship emerged as a function of the legal debates surrounding the settlement of the copyright issue, even though it did not actually succeed in carrying the day. Authorial property is confirmed by the conception of the author as an original genius with an individual personality to express. At the same time as perpetual copyright was being contested by different sections of the book trade and the counsel they employed, the rhetoric of originality and genius was being propounded by Edward Young in the landmark essay *Conjectures on Original Composition* (1759). The *Conjectures* is a belated contribution to the ancients–moderns dispute, which, despite its paradoxical unoriginality in so being, drew a distinction between an original art informed by genius and a derivative art informed by mere learning that would become very potent when planted in the proper soil. Young may be indebted to Warburton's *Letter from an Author* for the distinction drawn between organic works of genius and mechanic works of imitation:

An original may be said to be of a vegetable nature, it rises spontaneously from the vital root of genius; it grows, it is not made: imitations are often a sort of manufacture wrought up by those mechanics, art and labour, out of pre-existent materials not their own.[40]

Young establishes a link between works of genius and literary property:

His works will stand distinguished; his the sole property of them; which property alone can confer the noble title of an author: that is, of one who, to speak accurately, thinks and composes; while other invaders of the press, how voluminous and learned soever, (with due respect be it spoken,) only read and write.[41]

---

[40] Edward Young, *Conjectures on Original Composition in a Letter to the Author of Sir Charles Grandison* (1759), in *The Complete Works, Poetry and Prose, of the Rev. Edward Young, LL.D.*, 2 vols. (London: William Tegg, 1854), ii. 552.

[41] Ibid. 565.

Influence from past works of literature should be by 'a sort of noble contagion' for 'hope we from plagiarism any dominion in literature, as that of Rome arose from a nest of thieves?' (ii. 556). For Young then, ownership of the literary work of genius indisputably belongs to the author who stamps his proprietorship on it with the unmistakable brand of his own voice. The judges in the *Donaldson* v. *Becket* case were to decide in 1774 that Young's enabling distinction between originality and imitation (genius and learning) was one that simply could not be drawn in law; and the strain experienced by Young in trying to make it good is obvious. When he comes across a really original work, Swift's *Gulliver's Travels*, he has to rule it entirely out of court because it does not accord with his Christian view of the limits to be placed on original thought, nor does his view of Pope as derivative, based on the Homer translation, permit him to consider those aspects of Pope's *œuvre* that have the strongest claim on originality.

Mark Rose does not consider Young to have been an influential voice in the English context, where the burden of arguing for an idealized conception of the literary work was carried by the legal commentator William Blackstone and the justice Joseph Yates, who took Blackstone's line in defence of the London booksellers. It was in the European context of proto-Romanticism, argues Martha Woodmansee, studying the situation in Germany, that the export of the English culture of originality, inspiration, and literary genius was most effective, giving rise to demands for a' proper copyright law.[42] Woodmansee's argument is that there were two models of authorship developed in the Renaissance: the writer as mere craftsman and the writer as inspired by the Muses. When the inspirational model became the dominant, as it did in the Germany of Herder and Goethe, writers became reluctant to alienate their property. As I suggested at the beginning of this chapter, however, there is a prehistory to the conception of originality, at least in English culture, that suggests a longer gestation period than either Woodmansee or Rose allow. My exploration, in a subsequent chapter, of the cultural contests between Rochester, Dryden, and Shadwell over theatrical originality and indebtedness suggests that in England the concept of literary property pre-dates

---

[42] Martha Woodmansee, 'The Genius and the Copyright: Economic and Legal Conditions of the Emergence of the "Author"', *Eighteenth-Century Studies*, 17 (1983–4), 425–48.

the ideology of originality as inspirational genius, though works like Edward Young's *Conjectures on Original Composition* (1759) undoubtedly helped to shape it in the public domain. Part of the cultural difference here is certainly the existence of the theatre in Britain, which provided a third model of authorship distinct from the two advanced by Woodmansee—to wit, the writer as entertainer of a paying public. As our initial discussion of Aphra Behn suggests, there had long been in Britain a material context in which issues surrounding plagiarism were prominent and visible in the public domain: and theatrical practice was an important and too often neglected crucible for the conception of the proprietary author.

IV

A standard modern legal manual defines 'copyright' as follows:

> The purpose of the copyright laws is to encourage and reward authors . . . and other creative people as well as the entrepreneurs—publishers, for example—who risk their capital in putting their works before the public. This is done by giving the author . . . certain exclusive rights to enjoy the benefit of the created subject matter for a limited time, usually the life of the author and 50 entire calendar years. This right is called the copyright, because initially it consisted of the right to prevent others from copying the work without permission, for instance by printing copies of a book or play . . . A copyright, then, is not a right to do anything, but to stop others from doing something . . . Copyright is therefore a negative right.[43]

One might take issue with Laddie, Prescott, and Vitoria on their assumption that copyright is a 'negative right'. One might think that the statutory exclusive right bestowed upon an author to publish and authorize others to publish a work is a positive right that entails a further negative right to take legal action against those who infringe it. They go on to examine the many problematic terms that occur in any attempt to define copyright. Only 'original' works can be protected by copyright, where 'original' means that the work concerned must be 'the result of the expenditure of at least a substantial amount of independent skill, knowledge or creative labour' (p. 3). Skill and hard work

[43] Hugh Laddie, Peter Prescott, and Mary Vitoria, *The Modern Law of Copyright* (London: Butterworth, 1980), 1.

are categories that modern legislation prefers to 'aesthetic merit' as a prerequisite for originality, taking cognizance of the fearful difficulty experienced in the eighteenth century in trying to define it in terms of literary value. Even 'skill' is not entirely unproblematic. And what is a 'work'? Is it the ideas in the originator's mind, or the material expression of these on paper or other medium? If the former, can a distinction be made between the ideas themselves and the specific expression of them in a particular linguistic style, so that, even if the ideas in a literary work are part of a common stock, *this particular* embodiment of them is original and is protected by copyright? Our modern jurists argue that no distinction of this kind between form and content can be drawn in law. Anyone who takes a novel and turns it into another medium can be in breach of copyright even if not a single word from the original survives into the copy. To breach copyright, they argue, it is necessary to employ more than a general idea or broad concept—they speak in terms of 'a detailed collection of ideas, or pattern of incidents, or compilation of information' (p. 33)—but cases have to be treated on their individual merits, since no general rule can be established. Most important, however, is their summary of what copyright legislation has sought to do ever since 1774: 'There has to be an accommodation between two principles: the first, that authors should reap the fruits of their work and skill; the second, that composition does not occur in a vacuum, but that each author is inspired, whether he knows it or not, by the efforts of his fellows' (p. 38).

Our discussion has made clear that in the eighteenth century resolving the dispute over perpetual versus limited copyright would not benefit authors directly since the majority of them would alienate their rights to a bookseller-publisher on a 'once and for all' basis and would not therefore have any further financial interest in the progress of the work. Arguably, authorship did not become fully professionalized, or take on anything like its contemporary signification, until new methods of calculating fair compensation for writers became current. According to James Hepburn, the royalty system was developed in the United States by the Hurd and Houghton company and was in operation in the 1860s. According to this system, the publisher estimates his total expenses and desired profit on an edition-size of a particular title and then determines the percentage rate he can afford to offer the author on sales.[44] Thus, authors would know what they stood to gain and could profit proportionably to their sales. The Copyright Act of 1911 wrote the royalty system into its terms by allowing, as a major exception to its copyright period of lifetime plus fifty years, the right to reproduce a work twenty-five years after an author's death on payment of a 10 per cent royalty to the copyright owner. However, the gradual legitimization of professional writing in the eighteenth century gained for authors the respect of many decent and important publishers; and the success of any title established for them a reputation upon which they could drive a harder bargain next time. This was clearly important.

Having given some account of the legal-conceptual conditions affecting an altering authorial *mentalité*, it will be important to discuss, on an empirical level, the material conditions of writers at this time. That is the project of the next chapter.

[44] James Hepburn, *The Author's Empty Purse and the Rise of the Literary Agent* (London: Oxford University Press, 1968), 12–14.

2
Marketing the Literary Imagination

The cloak-and-dagger story of the way in which the manuscript of *Gulliver's Travels* was conveyed to the publisher Benjamin Motte is well known. The package was 'dropp'd at his house in the dark, from a Hackney-coach' and contained a covering letter written by one 'Richard Sympson', the supposed cousin of Lemuel Gulliver.[1] Even the handwriting was disguised: it has been attributed to John Gay. Sympson wrote:

As the printing these Travels will probably be of great value to you, so as a Manager for my Friend and Cousin I expect you will give a due consideration for it, because I know the Author intends the Profit for the use of Poor Sea-men, and I am advised to say that two Hundred pounds is the least Summ I will receive on his account, but if it shall happen that the Sale will not answer as I expect and believe, then whatever shall be thought too much even upon your own word shall be duly repaid.[2]

Not the least audacious element in that story is the fact that Swift had the confidence in the value of his own literary product to ask no less than £200 for the copyright, even if he had to hedge the price around with badinage about poor seamen. For a work of prose fiction, that was a demand without precedent. In the wake of the Drapier campaign, Swift was, of course, an extremely famous writer; but the sum of money involved still suggests that he perceived *Gulliver's Travels* to be in a category altogether apart from the standard prose romance or travel book routinely offered to the trade. An important source of information on writers' earnings in the period is the collection made by William Upcott in 1825 of 'Original Assignments of MS between Authors and Publishers principally for Dramatic Works, from the year 1703 to

[1] *The Correspondence of Jonathan Swift*, ed. Harold Williams, 5 vols. (Oxford University Press, 1965), iii. 181.
[2] Ibid. 153.

1810' housed in the British Library.[3] What little the Upcott Collection has on prose offers a stark comparison: in the same year as *Gulliver's Travels* was sold (1726), John Clarke was given by Edmund Curll 1 guinea for each of two titles, *The Virgin Seducer* and *The Bachelor's Keeper*. Another justly famous anecdote might be cited to mark a point in the eighteenth century at which prose fiction first displayed a potential to rival playwriting as a means to earn a living. Fielding negotiates with the publisher Andrew Millar over the copyright for *Joseph Andrews*:

'I am a man,' said Millar, 'of few words, and fond of coming to the point; but really, after giving every consideration I am able to your novel, I do not think I can afford to give you more than 200*l.* for it.' 'What!' exclaimed Fielding, 'two hundred pounds!' 'Indeed, Mr. Fielding,' returned Millar, 'indeed I am sensible of your talents; but my mind is made up.' 'Two hundred pounds!' continued Fielding in a tone of perfect astonishment; '*two hundred pounds* did you say?' 'Upon my word, Sir, I mean no disparagement to the writer or his great merit; but my mind is made up, and I cannot give one farthing more.' 'Allow me to ask you,' continued Fielding with undiminished surprise, 'allow me, Mr. Millar, to ask you, whether you are *serious*?' 'Never more so,' replied Millar, 'in all my life; and I hope you will candidly acquit me of every intention to injure your feelings or depreciate your abilities, when I repeat that I positively cannot afford you more than two hundred pounds for your novel.' 'Then, my good Sir,' said Fielding, recovering himself from this unexpected stroke of fortune, 'give me your hand; the book is yours.'[4]

As the Upcott Collection informs us, the highest prices routinely paid for copyrights at this time were for plays: Cibber received £105 for his *Caesar in Egypt* and the same for *The Provoked Husband*, while Addison gained £107. 10*s.* from Tonson for the rights to *Cato*—all plays that will receive further attention in subsequent chapters of this book. Writers for the theatre had more avenues to profit than had poets and novelists. In addition to selling copyrights, dramatists stood to gain the box-office profits from the third night's performance of the play, if it lasted that long. The theatre was temporally prior to the publishing industry in affording a living to imaginative writers. More than a century before poets and novelists had any experience of interaction with

---

[3] BL Add. MS 38728.

[4] Quoted (as possibly apocryphal) by Martin and Ruthe Battestin, *Henry Fielding: A Life* (London: Routledge, 1989), 325.

paying consumers, the theatre offered those who furnished its material a direct and often brutally frank form of access. Seventeenth- and eighteenth-century accounts of this process stress its moment-by-moment precariousness, the interventions and disturbances in varying degrees relevant to the product itself that could turn an audience in favour of or against a play. Such accounts make clear that the drama of consumption was as significant as the aesthetic object being consumed. Logically, therefore, it is to the theatre that we turn first in the following necessarily brief account of living on creative wits.

I

In his various writings on the London theatre, John Dennis manifested a characteristically shrewd awareness of the fact that *theatre* was the economic powerhouse of the imaginative and creative arts in the period. William Law, author of *A Serious Call*, had recapitulated older Puritan objections to theatre in writing *The Absolute Unlawfulness of the Stage-Entertainment Fully Demonstrated* (1726), a work reminiscent of Prynne in its fanatical excessiveness. Dennis replied to Law in *The Stage Defended*, arguing powerfully that the commercial theatre had played a much more valuable role in the development of the arts than any royal or political patron:

By taking the *British* Theatre into your Protection and Patronage, you would protect and patronize every other Branch of the *British* Poetry. For as the *British* Theatre, as long as it was justly and judiciously managed among us, was the only publick Rewarder of Dramatick Poetry, so it has been the chief Support and Encouragement of every other Species of that noble Art. It has cherish'd and inflamed the Spirit of Poetry, and raised a noble Emulation among us, more than all our Kings and all our Ministers together. From the very building of *London*, to the erecting the first Theatre in it, which Time contains about thirty Centuries, we had but two *British* Poets who deserve to be read: But from the Establishment of our Theatres to the present Time, which contains scarce a Century and a half, we may boldly affirm, that more than ten times that Number of Poets have appear'd and flourish'd in *England* . . . some [poets] who were by Nature qualified to succeed better in other Kinds of Poetry than the Dramatick, had, by Reason of the Lowness of their Fortunes, been uncapable of exerting their Genius's in those other Kinds, if they had not been first encouraged, and raised, and supported by the Stage. And 'tis very natural to conceive, that several others, who at the same time that they had large revenues, were qualified both by Nature and Art to excel in the other Kinds, were rouzed and excited to try their Fortunes in them, by the animating Applauses which they saw that our Dramatick Poets received from their ravish'd Audiences.[5]

Doubtless, Dennis's view of the theatrical public as a constantly benevolent patron is over-sanguine, but he is nevertheless correct that the existence of the theatre made other forms of literary, musical, and visual art economically viable until his own time and beyond. In his ground-breaking study *The Profession of English Letters* (1964), J. W. Saunders establishes the growing importance to imaginative writing of the printed-book market in the early seventeenth century, while giving due weight to the many factors that inhibited its development: the powerful manuscript culture of court and coterie writers that downgraded the value of printed dissemination, Puritan opposition to secular literary forms, the unpredictabilities of the censorship mechanism, and the difficulty in locating an audience. Theatre, by contrast, was triumphantly successful precisely because, while it enjoyed staunch support at court, it also had the means to appeal to a wider public:

Theatre managed to avoid that dichotomy between the literary interests of the Court and the literary interests of the man in the street, which . . . proved an insuperable obstacle to the establishment of a literary profession in the printed book-market. In the theatre there was a happy union of interests which gave writers, on the one hand, assured status and security, and on the other hand, broadly-based public support.[6]

The economic returns from the writing of poetry never rivalled those for a successful play, with the spectacular exception of one or two long poems and translations, and it was well into the eighteenth century before the writing of prose could do so.

Theatre audiences were not always, in Dennis's term, 'ravish'd', and they did not always express themselves in 'animating Applauses', but he is right to stress the unique directness, the immediacy, of the relationship between the theatre patron and the writer. Since the erection of James Burbage's uninspiringly named

[5] John Dennis, *The Stage Defended, from Scripture, Reason, Experience, and the Common Sense of Mankind for Two Thousand Years. Occasion'd by Mr. Law's Late Pamphlet Against Stage-Entertainments* (1726), in *Critical Works*, ii. 302–3.
[6] Saunders, *The Profession of English Letters*, 69.

The Theatre in 1576, the first custom-built theatre venue in London, it had been possible for writers to test their product directly against audience reaction, obtaining a very potent, if not wholly reliable, measure of its worth. Throughout his career, Ben Jonson wrestled with the complexities of public patronage. Whereas a poem written for a private patron could be judged to hit exactly the vanities and predilections of the individual—and if it did not, the poet was not likely to learn this too painfully—the attempt to meld together a disparate mob of theatre-goers into an audience fit to appreciate Jonson's complex manipulations of dramatic form was one that struck despair into his fainting soul. It must indeed have been an unfathomably alienating experience for a poet who aspired to be the instructor of monarchs and courts to find his work exposed to vociferous, but in his opinion unqualified, criticism from paying customers whose opinions he did not value at a rope's end. Much effort was expended, during the course of his career, on the attempt to educate his audience's taste. In the famous Induction to *Bartholomew Fair*, this effort takes on quasi-contractual form, the writer virtually treating his audience as apprentices who need to be bound by agreement to the master-freeman of a notional guild of professional writers.[7] The audience is to be bound over for good behaviour; and the dramatist tries to create the taste by which he wishes to be judged. At the close of his writing life, Jonson appears the perplexed victim of the early literary market-place, which developed in advance of the formation of an ideology capable of mediating its conditions to literary practitioners.[8] His disillusionment culminated in the famous 'Ode to Himself' begotten by '*the just indignation the author took at the vulgar censure of his play* [*The New Inn*] *by some malicious spectators*'. Jonson's attitude to his paying audience expressed in the second stanza calls to mind Bertolt Brecht's comic dictum that 'the government should dissolve the people and elect a new one':

> Say that thou pour'st them wheat,
> And they will acorns eat:
> 'Twere simple fury still thyself to waste
> On such as have no taste:

[7] For an engrossing account of this contract and of Jonson's place in the development of literary property, see Joseph Loewenstein, 'The Script in the Marketplace', *Representations*, 12 (Fall 1985), 101–14.

[8] See the discussion in Helgerson, *Self-Crowned Laureates*.

To offer them a surfeit of pure bread
Whose appetites are dead.
No, give them grains their fill,
Husks, draff to drink, and swill;
If they love lees, and leave the lusty wine,
Envy them not, their palate's with the swine.[9]

II

As a rough comparator for the sums of money that will inevitably
be bandied about in this chapter, we can look at the spending-
power of money around the turn of the century, relative to income.
On an annual income of £50, which was at least three times that of
a labourer but was a typical enough wage for a better-paid journey-
man such as a printer, a family could afford to eat well, employ a
servant, and live comfortably, assuming that behind this annual
income was an accumulation of a few hundred pounds in capital,
enough for a family to own the long lease of a house, furnish it,
and plough left-over capital into a business. A personal fortune of
£1,000–£2,000 enabled its owner to live very well indeed, while
£10,000 was enormous wealth. Arguably, the established profes-
sions (the Church, the law, teaching) provide the best grounds of
comparison for the earnings of writers. Emoluments from professional practice vary tremendously: top-flight barristers could earn
£3,000–£4,000 per annum, whereas a London curate would earn
around £60, and a schoolteacher would be well paid at £50. The
annual rent for a good London leasehold address was £50–£60.
To cut any kind of sartorial dash, a man would have to lay out
around £6–£7 for a complete outfit.[10]

By the time the most famous actor-director of his era, David
Garrick, had assumed the patent of the Drury Lane Theatre at the
end of 1746–7 season, professional theatre was discernibly big
business. Box-office takings at Drury Lane could reach £200 on a
good night; and at the rival Covent Garden Theatre, they three

---

[9] Ben Jonson, *The New Inn* (1631), ed. Michael Hattaway (Manchester University Press, 1984), 204–5.

[10] Information is culled from Peter Earle, *The Making of the English Middle Class:
Business, Society and Family Life in London, 1660–1730* (London: Methuen, 1989).

times exceeded £250 in that season.[11] H. W. Pedicord calculates that in 1750 an average of 11,874 people were patronizing the theatre every week, against population figures of 676,250: that is, around 1.7 per cent of the population, though these figures may be on the conservative side.[12] In Lance Bertelsen's words, the theatre was 'the centre of a web of economic influence linking actors, managers, playwrights, publishers, critics, coffee-houses and taverns'.[13] Examining the account books for the patent houses reveals that dozens of small trades and several hundred employees depended on theatre business. Stone and Kahrl, biographers of Garrick, describe Drury Lane's patrons as being from 'nine sources in the community':

Parliamentarians and their relatives; readers and subscribers to published books of plays and the dance; students and lawyers from the Inns of Court; apprentices from some 94 trades that supported the theatres in London and profited from the dealings; the tradesmen and merchants themselves who did a thriving business with the theatres; the renters (investors in theatre shares, each of whom held a free seat each night); visitors to London . . . Garrick's friends, neighbours and correspondents . . . and the friends of all the other actors, as well as the intellectuals who wrote critiques for the *Monthly, Critical,* and other reviews.[14]

So far as it is possible to judge profitability in the ensuing period (and it is impossible to do so with certainty because no absolutely complete set of accounting ledgers exists), the theatre made a decent return. Although the figures show no spectacular increase in profitability over the period, and there is certainly not a constant curve, there is a very steady increase in turnover, from £14,323 in 1741 to £37,917 in 1776. This reflects gradual inflation in prices, ongoing alterations to theatre interiors to increase capacity, and the augmenting of the audience. Perhaps the best economic indicator of the theatre's growing status as a business in the period is the continuing rise in value of the theatrical patent

[11] New information on this has recently come to light and is reported by Judith Milhous and Robert D. Hume in 'Receipts at Drury Lane: Richard Cross's Diary for 1746–7', *Theatre Notebook,* 49/1 (1995), 12–26; 49/2 (1995), 69–90.

[12] H. W. Pedicord, *The Theatrical Public in the Time of Garrick* (New York: King's Crown Press, 1954), 16–17. Pat Rogers gives slightly higher figures in his *Henry Fielding: A Biography* (London: Elek, 1979), 68.

[13] Lance Bertelsen, *The Nonsense Club: Literature and Popular Culture, 1749–1764* (Oxford: Clarendon Press, 1986), 71.

[14] George Winchester Stone, Jr. and George M. Kahrl, *David Garrick: A Critical Biography* (Carbondale: Southern Illinois University Press, 1979), 81–2.

that conferred monopoly performance rights on the two officially sanctioned theatres at Drury Lane and Covent Garden.

Reaching this volume of business and profitability had been a gradual process, dependent on the trickling down of participation in theatre-going to merchants, successful tradesmen and shop-keepers, manufacturers, financial brokers and professionals, and to their wives and servants. By the turn of the eighteenth century, these groups were swelling the ranks of the book-buying public and were achieving the social clout to demand that their leisure time should be filled by representations of the lives of individuals that they could recognize, identify with, and profit from. As the theatrical public widened, and its comfort requirements became more sophisticated, new theatre buildings were required and old ones needed to be revamped. Another vital determinant of the nature of the theatrical institution in the seventeenth and eighteenth centuries was the success that the two large patent companies had in protecting their monopoly and preventing the dilution of their audiences as a result of competition in the estab-lished playing season. In this respect, the steady growth that is observable in the eighteenth century does not quite add up to progress. Opera apart, the story of the London theatre at this time is overwhelmingly the story of the patent companies. Theatrical performances did take place in other venues during this period, but the patentees jealously guarded their monopoly and were ready to invoke the Licensing Act wherever there was a possibility of high-season competition. Suppression in 1737 of an incipient 'alternative' theatre through the Licensing Act meant that the London public was served by the culturally conservative cartels of Drury Lane and Covent Garden, despite the ample evidence that more people wanted to see plays than the grand theatres could provide for. Already in the 1760s and 1770s patent companies were being rapidly established in important regional centres. If these much smaller towns could support one patent company, it is clear that London could support more than two.

The two-company model of London theatrical organization dates to the Restoration. Prior to the Restoration, there were several theatres operating in London, organized on two different models. Public theatres housed companies like Shakespeare's, the enormously successful King's Men, which ran as actors' co-operatives. At the Rose Playhouse in the 1590s, for example, the core of the Admiral's Men comprised six or eight sharers who invested money (a 'share') and were then responsible for running the theatre, mounting productions, paying the landlord (Philip Henslowe) his rent, paying the salaries of hired actors and other staff, and taking their cut of profits or shouldering the burden of losses. Playwrights normally sold their plays to acting companies for a flat fee of between £6 and £10.[15] Private theatre development after 1608 threw up another model, the impresario-cum-business-manager like Christopher Beeston, who installed his own company in the Phoenix in 1617; or Sir William Davenant, who provided historical continuity for the theatre by obtaining a patent to run one of the two monopoly companies created after the Restoration. Along with the other patentee, Thomas Killigrew, he established the two-company competition that became the staple diet for London theatre-goers. After 1714 a third model of theatrical organization emerged—group management. The Drury Lane regime of actor-managers, Wilks, Cibber, and Barton Booth, dominated the London stage for more than twenty years. In 1714 opposition to 'the Triumvirate' emerged. Christopher Rich had suffered the indignity of having Drury Lane closed on him by order of the Lord Chamberlain in 1709. Five years later, his son John established the family dynasty by inheriting his father's patent, reopening the theatre at Lincoln's Inn Fields (refurbished expensively in 1725), and in 1732 causing to be built the Theatre Royal, Covent Garden. Theatrical vitality would come to depend on the competence and commitment of management and on the effect of direct competition at the box-office.

Given the considerable appetite for new playscripts in the immediately post-Restoration theatre, writers stood to make a reasonable living. Efforts were made to recruit successful authors as house writers, on the model of the Elizabethan theatre, when the King's Men enjoyed the richness of Shakespeare, Fletcher, Massinger, and Shirley as contracted professionals. Dryden was given 1¼ shares in the King's Company in the late 1660s and his share of the profits from this, according to his fellow sharers, amounted to £300 or £400 per annum.[16] Shadwell, Lee, and

<hr>

[15] Figures given by E. K. Chambers in *The Elizabethan Stage*, 4 vols. (Oxford: Clarendon Press, 1923), i. 373.

[16] James A. Winn, *John Dryden and his World* (New Haven: Yale University Press, 1987), p. 191.

Crowne were also retained to satisfy the Restoration appetite for new plays and would have received a stipend of £50. Actor-playwrights like Betterton and playwrights like Congreve, who was for a short time a licensee at the Haymarket Theatre, are typical of the breed of professional writer whose commitment to the entire business of performance was intense. Little precise information is available on the relationship between dramatists and theatre companies in this period, but some plays were bought from free-lance writers trying to obtain the best price they could from the companies. It could be worth a playwright's while to approach another, better-known writer to solicit a prologue, which acted as a seal of approval on the new play. Thomas Southerne, it is reported, approached Dryden in this way:

> who, when Southern first wrote for the stage, was so famous for his Prologues, that the players would act nothing without that decoration. His usual price till then has been four guineas. But when Southern came to him for the Prologue he had bespoke, Dryden told him he must have six guineas for it; 'which (said he) young man, is out of no disrespect to you, but the Players have had my goods too cheap'.[17]

Southerne was a dramatist typical enough of the post-Restoration period, a man who turned to the theatre whenever he needed to repair his damaged fortunes, as he did when William of Orange's invasion resulted in the loss of his army commission. Typically, too, he found public taste very fickle and profitability far from guaranteed. Theophilus Cibber speaks of Southerne's hard-selling methods and comes up with an astonishingly high figure—perhaps an incredible one—for his total profits from box-office and additional earnings for a single play:

> Mr Southern was industrious to draw all imaginable profits from his poetical labours. Mr. Dryden once took occasion to ask him how much he got by one of his plays; to which he answered, that he was really ashamed to inform him. But Mr. Dryden being a little importunate to know, he plainly told him, that by his last play he cleared seven hundred pounds; which appeared astonishing to Mr. Dryden, as he himself had never been able to acquire more than one hundred by any of his most successful pieces. The secret is, Mr. Southern was not beneath the drudgery of solicitation, and often sold his tickets at a very high price, by making

---

[17] *The Works of Thomas Southerne*, ed. Robert Jordan and Harold Love, 2 vols. (Oxford: Clarendon Press, 1988), vol. i, p. xiv.

applications to persons of distinction: a degree of servility which perhaps
Mr Dryden thought was much beneath the dignity of a poet; and too
much in the character of an under-player.[18]

While *Sir Anthony Love*, *The Fatal Marriage*, and *Oroonoko* were
all successes, *The Wives Excuse* and *The Maid's Last Prayer*
failed. Of *The Fatal Marriage*, an anonymous letter of 1694
records that 'never was poet better rewarded or incouraged by the
town; for besides an extraordinary full house, which brought him
about 140*l.*, 50 noblemen . . . gave him guineas apiece, and the
printer 36*l.* for his copy'.[19] This is the earnings ceiling for a
professional playwright in the period.

As a market commodity, however, dramatic entertainment was
very vulnerable to many outside influences. Then as now, the
factors affecting house size on any given evening were nebulous
and difficult for a management to pin down. A survey of half a
century's repertory yields a number of plays that met with extreme
success—nine performances or more on an initial run, or frequent
performances over a period of time: Sir Samuel Tuke's *The
Adventures of Five Hours* ran thirteen nights in 1663 and, according to John Evelyn, "twas believed would be worth the Comedians
4 or 500 pounds';[20] Dryden and Davenant's *The Tempest* was that
rare thing, a financially successful opera; Otway's *Don Carlos*,
acted in June 1676, 'got more Money than any preceding Modern
Tragedy' to John Downes's knowledge.[21] Dryden's *Don Sebastian*
was clearly a society event in late 1689, since there exists a record
of Queen Mary and her maids of honour paying £15 for a box.
And the following information from the *Entring Book* of Roger
Morrice, though culpable for its geography (Don Sebastian being
king of Portugal, not Poland), hints at the possibility that playwrights as successful as Dryden might negotiate a fixed sum for a
benefit night and make over the actual return to the theatre:

TRAGOEDIA. This Weeke the Queene and the Prince of Denmarke were
at the Playhouse to see Mr Dreydens new Play called *Sebastion* King of
Poland. It was well liked, but very much Curtled before it was suffered to

---

[18] Ibid., p. xxiii.   [19] Ibid. ii. 5.
[20] *The London Stage, 1660–1800: A Calendar of Plays, Entertainments and
Afterpieces etc.* Pt. 1, ed. William Van Lennep (Carbondale, Ill.: Southern Illinois
University Press, 1960–), pt. 2, vol. i, ed. Emmett L. Avery, 195.
[21] John Downes, *Roscius Anglicanus; or, An Historical Review of the Stage* (1708),
ed. Judith Milhous and Robert D. Hume (London: Society for Theatre Research,
1987), 76.

be Acted. The concourse was great at the Playhouse, as of late it Ordinarily useth to be. It's said that Poet hath sold his day for 120 Guinneas.[22]

Shadwell's *The Squire of Alsatia* set new box-office records in 1687–8; the plays of Otway did well and those of Congreve, whose *The Mourning Bride* was perhaps the most successful tragedy in the period, did excellent business in the main (yet the failure of both *The Double Dealer* and *The Way of the World* shows what an elusive vocation writing for the stage was); Farquhar's *The Constant Couple* 'brought the Play-house some fifty Audiences in five Months';[23] Cibber's plays were, in his own opinion, highly successful. What factors affected the general health of the theatre at any given time? Then as now, 'word of mouth', the spread of good publicity from those who had seen the show commending it to their friends, was an important factor in a play's success. Word of mouth does not become formally absorbed into the institution of the review until later, but by the first decade of the eighteenth century, the *Spectator* is perceived to have considerable influence on the average playgoer. A pamphlet published by Defoe in 1715 entitled *The Fears of the Pretender Turn'd into the Fears of Debauchery with a Hint to Richard Steele, Esq.* stresses this:

Here, what he [Mr Spectator] pleas'd to mention, was ever admir'd; and for the *Spectator* to give a good Word to a Play, was to fill the House. In process of Time, his Name was put to the Prologue and Epilogue, to push a Play into the World; and for a grave Person, in an Antik Dress, with a Comic Gravity, to sit in a Box, and suppos'd, tho' but in Banter, to be the *Spectator*, was sufficient to draw the whole Town to the Theatre.[24]

The theatrical 'unit of currency' throughout the period was the 'acting night', and accounting was based on the number of acting nights successfully squeezed into a season. This number could be affected by unpredictable factors like plague and royal funerals. Plague closed the theatres between 5 June 1665 and the early winter of 1666–7. When King William died on Sunday 8 March 1702, the theatres closed until after the coronation on 23 April. Six weeks was customary, though after Charles II's death, there appears to have been an eleven-week closure. 'None will suffer by

[22] *The London Stage*, pt. 2, vol. i, 15.
[23] Ibid., pt. 1, vol. i, ed. Van Lennep, p. clxi.
[24] Daniel Defoe, *The Fears of the Pretender Turn'd into the Fears of Debauchery with a Hint to Richard Steele, Esq.* (London, 1715), 21.

the King's death but the poor players, who are ready to starve', Sir
John Perceval wrote, regarding William's demise.[25] External political events had an effect on the soundness of audiences. The
1688–9 season was sabotaged by James II's departure. As the
Epilogue to Shadwell's *Bury-Fair* repines:

> But could he Write with never so much *Wit*,
> He must despair of seeing a full Pit:
> Most of our constant Friends have left the Town,
> Bravely to serve their *King* and *Country* gone.[26]

In 1701–2, thoughts of war with France were uppermost in Lon-
doners' minds, rendering the theatre a frivolous irrelevance. Earlier, in the period 1678–81, the theatres were affected by the
anti-Catholic atmosphere. Lee's *Lucius Junius Brutus*, as well as
the attraction in the rival house, Tate's adaptation of *Richard II*
entitled *The Sicilian Usurper*, were banned as politically inflammatory. Desperately low receipts at the King's Company
box-office—£3. 2*s.* for 30 May 1681—made the merger with the
Duke's Company inevitable, and for a period of years there was
only one single United Company operating in the capital. This
was in part a result of political insecurity tainting the appetite for
theatre. This was a period of extraordinary hardship for those who
were trying to eke out a living from the theatre. Aphra Behn's
biographer records her subject's extreme penury and her desperate
attempts to persuade her publisher Jacob Tonson to give her £30
rather than £25 for a prose romance; while the poet Robert Gould
wrote of Thomas Otway: 'Otway can hardly guts from jail preserve
| For though he's very fat, he's like to starve.'[27] On his own behalf,
Otway had published in 1680 a melancholy poem entitled 'The
Poet's Complaint of his Muse; or, A Satyr against Libells', which
narrates the story of a poet being seduced by his Muse with prospects of riches and honours. She deserts him, because "twas never
known a Muse e're staid | When Fortune fled' (lines 185–6), and
thereafter he manages only monstrous births:

> A Line came forth, but such a one,
> No trav'ling Matron in her Child-birth pains,

[25] *The London Stage*, pt. 2, vol. i, p. 15.
[26] Thomas Shadwell, Epilogue to *Bury-Fair*, in *The Complete Works of Thomas Shadwell*, ed. Montague Summers, 5 vols. (London: Benjamin Blom, 1927; repr. New York, 1968), iv. 369 (italics reversed).
[27] Cited by Angeline Goreau, *Reconstructing Aphra: A Social Biography of Aphra Behn* (Oxford University Press, 1980), 253.

> Full of the joyful Hopes to bear a Son,
> Was more astonish't at th' unlookt-for shape
> Of some deform'd Baboon or Ape,
> Then I was at the hideous Issue of my Brains.[28]

Glancing at Thomas Shadwell's career will serve to underline the point that even the most established and popular dramatists of the day experienced considerable vicissitude in their financial affairs. In his first play, *The Sullen Lovers* (1668), the young Shadwell is confident enough to poke fun at the poet Ninny's (John Dryden's) attempts to make his profession pay, while also attacking the gentleman-playwrights (Sir Robert and Edward Howard) who do not actually *need* to write for a living: as Emilia says, 'would it not distract one to see a Gentleman of 5,000*l.* a year write Playes, and as Poets venture their Reputations against a Sum of Money, they venture theirs against Nothing?'[29] As the period wore on, this debate between professional playwrights and gentleman-amateurs became more embattled. Dryden's coolly ironic attack on those who 'not having the Vocation of Poverty to scribble, out of mere wantonness take pains to make themselves ridiculous' in the Preface to *All for Love* (1677), was still causing ripples in the 1690s.[30] Mary Pix, in *The Deceiver Deceived* (1698), dramatizes the foppish aristocrat Lord Insulls's contempt for the jobbing professional playwright:

INS. If your Ladiship did but see in *France* how the poor Poets at a new Play sneak, and wou'd creep into an Augur-hole; when I come in, by the Muses, I have often wish'd my self a Woman, that I might have gone in a Mask, and not frighten the little Dogs (that write for Bread) out of their Wits.

ARIA. Does your Lordship never write Plays?

INS. Yes, often, but I could never get either of the Houses to play one.

ARIA. What's the reason of that? . . .

INS. I believe they think, and that wisely, should they once play a Play of mine no other would ever be receiv'd afterwards, and, you know, a man of Quality can't be their Drudge.[31]

---

[28] Lines 158–64, in *Works of Thomas Otway*, ed. J. C. Ghosh, 2 vols. (Oxford: Clarendon Press, 1932). [29] Shadwell, *Complete Works*, i. 45.
[30] *The Works of John Dryden*, ed. H. T. Swedenberg, Jr., *et al.*, 20 vols. (Berkeley and Los Angeles: University of California Press, 1956–), xiii, ed. Maximillian Novak (1984), 14. (Hereafter the California Dryden.)
[31] *The Plays of Mary Pix and Catharine Trotter*, ed. Edna L. Steeves, 2 vols. (New York: Garland, 1982), i. 16.

Yet the relationship between gentleman-amateur and professional was, at least in their earlier period, a complex symbiosis, as is clear in Shadwell's case. After *The Lancashire Witches* was caught up in the controversy surrounding the Popish plot, Shadwell's work was suppressed and he was kept alive by the Earl of Dorset, himself a playwright, whose invitations to Copt Hall and pension of £10 per quarter were the playwright's lifeline.[32] His return to the stage in 1688 with *The Squire of Alsatia*, however, was a triumph, supporting as it did the Whig cause and Lockean theories of education.

Until 1714, then, the theatre afforded a precarious living for a small number of people and a potentially good living for a few. We have already glanced at the prospects for 'attached' playwrights—those who were on a retainer against the performing rights to a certain number of new plays per year. For them and for other less successful writers, the major source of revenue was the proceeds, once house charges had been deducted, from the third-night performance, and gradually, after 1690, from every third night of an extended run. After the initial run, however, the dramatist made nothing out of revivals: and, in assessing his earnings, we must remember that his work did not end when he persuaded the management to take on the play. The author was usually present at the early read-throughs, and gave advice on scenery, actors' delivery, and other technical matters. In addition, the playwright might be able to sell his play to a bookseller-publisher, and, if he was very lucky, he might be paid anything from 10 to 25 guineas for a dedication to a gentle or noble patron. Prospects for dramatists depended on the demand for new writing and, after a repertoire of revivals, adaptations, and new plays was established post-Restoration, the market for new plays became increasingly difficult to tap.

Extremes of fortune in the theatre can be represented by Sir Richard Steele and Colley Cibber at the prosperous end of the spectrum and unfashionable jobbing playwrights at the other. Robert Hume reviews the profitability of various new plays in the season 1726–7 by such unfashionable writers as Philip Frowde and Leonard Welsted, to find that, even if the writer was lucky enough to persuade his friends to turn out to his benefit night,

[32] Thomas Shadwell, *The Squire of Alsatia: A Critical Edition* (1688), ed. J. C. Ross (New York: Garland, 1987), 9.

there was seldom enough of a 'take' to make the new play worth the theatre's while to present. This explains the legendary reluctance on the part of the managers to mount new plays; and Hume's conclusion is that 'no one was making a living by writing plays in the mid-1720s'.[33] In stark comparison stand those dominant eighteenth-century men of the theatre who were able to participate in every aspect of it: acting, playwriting, and managing in the case of Colley Cibber. In 1693 Cibber was working for Christopher Rich and making 15s. per week, but when Kynaston's illness gave him an opportunity to act Touchwood in Congreve's *The Double Dealer*, his salary was raised to £1. After his *Love's Last Shift* proved that he had the makings of a writer in 1696, Rich and his partner Skipwith were prepared to negotiate individual terms with him because they were so keen to gain the performing rights to his subsequent plays. November 1704 saw him under contract to Rich for £3. 10s. per week, with a separate agreement giving him 10s. per week for casting and reading plays, plus 20s. weekly for management services. By 1709 he was in a position to demand £200 per annum clear benefit for becoming a co-manager of Drury Lane. By 1714 Cibber was earning £1,000 per annum from his share of Drury Lane profits, nor was his career as a successful playwright yet over. Despite the derision heaped upon his anti-Jacobite agitprop play *The Non-Juror*, the king liked it enough to award Cibber £200, the copyright was worth £105 to the printer Lintot, and Cibber was said to have made £1,000 from that play alone. By 1730 he could add the Poet Laureate's salary to the proceeds from twenty years of usually successful management. After he retired as sharer in 1732, he was still commanding a salary of 12 guineas weekly, and, coming out of retirement in the 1735–6 season, he was demanding pop-star rates, 50 guineas an appearance.[34] Sir Richard Steele was invited to join the actor-managers at Drury Lane in 1714 because they needed a powerful figurehead with court influence to protect them from the Lord Chamberlain's interference. Initially, Steele received a handsome stipend of £700, until profits diminished when Rich started up in

[33] Robert D. Hume, *Henry Fielding and the London Theatre, 1728–1737* (Oxford: Clarendon Press, 1988), 145–6.

[34] See the entry on Cibber in *A Biographical Dictionary of Actors etc., 1660–1800*, ed. Philip H. Highfill, Jr., Kalman A. Burnim, and Edward A. Langhans, 16 vols. (Carbondale: Southern Illinois University Press, 1973–93), iii. 213–42; and Helene Koon, *Colley Cibber: A Biography* (Lexington: Kentucky University Press, 1986).

competition, and Steele then became an equal sharer in the triumvirate's profits. Later, he got himself into appalling financial difficulties, but from a lawsuit we discover that he estimated his average annual earnings from profit-sharing in Drury Lane at £600, though Cibber put it as high as £1,000. Precise figures are found for some seasons: £700. 18*s*. 2*d*. for 1721–2; £868. 10*s*. for 1722–3; £617. 4*s*. 11*d*. for 1723–4. His finest hour came when his play *The Conscious Lovers* exactly hit the taste of the town, as *The Beggar's Opera* was to do five years later. According to a deposition of 11 May 1727, the play grossed £2,536. 3*s*. 6*d*. for the company in its eighteen-night run, while Steele estimated that it had earned him £600, £329. 5*s*. from benefits. Printing rights to the play were sold to Jacob Tonson, Jr., for which he made £40 and 'other good Causes and Consideration'.[35] This was more than £21. 10*s*. paid by Lintot for his *The Lying Lover* back in 1704. Dedicating the play to George I in the printed version earned him a handsome gift of 500 guineas, a sum previously rivalled only by Dryden, who was reputed to have received that amount from James Bertie, Earl of Abingdon for his memorial poem *Eleonora*.[36]

By the mid-1720s the major theatrical earner was no longer serious drama but the art of pantomime. In 1723 the actor-managers of Drury Lane scored a spectacular success with the dancing-master James Thurmond's raunchy pantomime *Harlequin Dr. Faustus*, which provoked a rash of imitators. Box-office receipts for Lewis Theobald's *Harlequin, A Sorceror* show the earning potential of the pantomime-afterpiece: at its première in January 1725, it grossed £174. 8*s*. and thereafter seldom less than £130 for its next twenty performances. In the 1726–7 season Theobald's *The Rape of Proserpine* grossed over £200 on each of its first eight nights, close to capacity figures for Lincoln's Inn Fields. Arthur Scouten has commented on the two-hundred-year-old adage that *The Beggar's Opera* made Gay rich and Rich gay: '*The Beggar's Opera* may have made Rich gay, but according to the treasurer's account books it was the pantomime *Perseus and Andromeda* that made him rich.'[37] What the spectacular success of *The Beggar's Opera* did achieve was a new impetus for theatrical

[35] Hume, *Henry Fielding and the London Theatre*, 26.

[36] Winn, *John Dryden and his World*, 454.

[37] Arthur M. Scouten, 'The Increase in Popularity in Shakespeare's Plays in the Eighteenth Century', *Shakespeare Quarterly*, 7 (Spring 1956), 191.

activity in the 1730s, perhaps the most exciting theatrical decade in the entire century. Running for thirty-two continuous nights, achieving an unprecedented sixty-two performances in the season, the gross take of *The Beggar's Opera*'s initial run was £5,535, on average £173 per night, playing to average houses of 1,250. Of that massive income, the lion's share certainly went to the manager John Rich. John Gay himself earned between £500 and £700, depending on which source one believes; and 90 guineas for the sale of publishing rights (including those to his poetic Fables) to Tonson and Watts.[38] Clearly, if around 40,000 spectators saw this initial run, it had attracted numerous repeat attenders and also casual or first-time patrons who might become regulars. Unsurprisingly, this success initiated a period of unprecedented activity on the London stage, some of it experimental. Since 1720 there had existed a small third house in the Haymarket, built by John Potter at the low cost of around £1,000, plus £200 worth of scenery, tackle, and costumes. It may have accommodated some 650 patrons. Throughout the period under discussion, this house appears to have functioned as a touring venue, occupied by various troupes who used it for differing purposes, and in the 1730s several of Fielding's plays were premièred there. Its seat prices were around a shilling less than the patent theatre prices. From 1729 theatre provision also existed in the Goodman's Fields area, the most important housing Henry Giffard's company. So, by the late 1720s and into the 1730s, London theatre-goers had four main venues to choose from: the two patent houses, as ever, and two little theatres. They charged lower prices, and, as Robert Hume has argued, competed in the case of the Little Theatre, Haymarket by means of a radically experimental repertory policy geared to contemporary plays, some of them anti-Establishment; and in the case of Goodman's Fields, by mounting the most attractive of the patent theatres' shows in a different location.[39] It is not merely a case of more theatre, but of the embryonic evolution of theatres with an independent programming policy, defined in opposition to the

[38] See the discussion in David Nokes, *John Gay: A Profession of Friendship* (Oxford University Press, 1995), 423 n.
[39] See Robert Hume's account of the building of these theatres in Hume, *Henry Fielding and the London Theatre*, 42–3, 146–7; and on the programming policy, see his article 'Henry Fielding and the Politics at the Little Haymarket, 1728–1737', in John M. Wallace (ed.), *The Golden and the Brazen World* (Berkeley: University of California Press, 1985), 79–124.

conservative large houses. Audiences in the 1730s were eager both for more conventional provision and for radical experimental plays, given the continuing stifling conservatism of the patent houses in the 1730s.

Conditions were favourable to the playwriting debut of Henry Fielding, the most creative playwright, and latterly manager, of his generation. Fielding's theatrical career, rapidly reviewed, is a story of exuberant inventiveness precariously succeeding over frighteningly unstable conditions. When he utilized forms like the burlesque and mock-opera or mock-pantomime that capitalized on the lowbrow energies to which the public was responding, he usually did well. When his ambition prompted him towards five-act mainpieces, he risked failure. *Tom Thumb* was an enormous success, though its precise financial arrangements are unknown; *The Coffee-House Politician* was a failure. Contemporary sources affirm that he made 'little less than a thousand Pounds' from *The Lottery* and *The Modern Husband*; but his personal finances are complicated in several ways. He regularly arranged for publication of his playtexts to coincide with the first night performance, so that a receipt of 4 April 1732 testifies to his having sold the copyrights for two plays to John Watts for 20 guineas; and later Watts handed over at least £100 for *The Miser*, which was 'the usual price paid to authors for plays which met with uncommon success', according to Thomas Davies. And if his recent biographers' suspicions are correct, he was paid for keeping at least one play, *The Grub-street Opera, out* of print.[40] Yet Fielding's earnings alone cannot determine his overall financial position since he was such a spendthrift that he would have been in want with double his income. Though the 1736–7 season was a boom period for him, to the extent that he is found publishing plans in the *Daily Advertiser* for 2 February 1736 for the building of a new theatre, he had by then weathered the storms of Theophilus Cibber's actors' rebellion and Sir John Barnard's attempt to cut theatre operation back to minimum level, an attempt that succeeded in June 1737 with the passing of the Licensing Act.

By far the biggest problem for playwrights was the uncertainty of their income. Very rarely were they commissioned to write plays. The playwright simply approached the manager with his script

---

[40] See Battestin and Battestin, *Henry Fielding*, 119, 131, 164.

(and that was not made easy: Barton Booth is on record as saying that 'if he were not obliged to [produce new plays], he would seldom give his consent to perform one of them') and if the manager agreed to mount it, the author would receive benefit rights.[41] To illustrate the difficulty here, Fielding, in the Preface to his 1743 *Miscellanies*, discusses the première of his early play *The Wedding-Day*, which was not performed until 1743, at Garrick's request. In reply to Garrick's initial enquiry, Fielding says, 'I conceived it so little the Manager's Interest to produce anything new on his Stage this Season, that I should not think of offering it him, as I apprehended he would find some Excuse to refuse me, and adhere to the Theatrical Politics, of never introducing new Plays on the Stage, but when driven to it by absolute Necessity.'[42] At about the same time as Fielding was despairing of *The Wedding-Day*, his associate James Ralph was raising his voice in protest at the conservative, mercenary ways of the theatre impressarios in his amusing tract *The Touch-Stone* (1728):

the Managers . . . don't consider a PLAY as to its Merit; the Reputation it would bring to their Art, or the pleasure, or Instruction it would give the Town; but what Expences must we be at, to fit it for the Stage? What Time must we lose, to study the Parts? and what Money will it bring in, to answer our pains and Expences?

We may proceed with those *Stock-Plays* we are perfect in, or revive those which have lain dormant half an Age: They'll be new to the Town, and save us the Trouble of getting by Rote, more Parts than we can remember, and anticipate the Charge of Cloaths, Scenes, and the *Poet's* third Night.[43]

Apart from the receipts of the '*Poet's* third Night', playwrights would not normally be paid any flat-rate fee by the theatre, but they had the opportunity of submitting the text to a publisher. This, however, was not as lucrative as might be expected, partly owing to the marketing risks and trade ploys of booksellers, and to a lesser extent because copyright was too uncertain to motivate them to pay well. Especially with plays, there was no safeguard

[41] Cited by Robert D. Hume in 'The London Theatre from *The Beggar's Opera* to the Licensing Act', in id., *The Rakish Stage: Studies in English Drama, 1600–1800* (Carbondale: Southern University Press, 1983), 275.

[42] Henry Fielding, *Miscellanies*, i, ed. Henry Knight Miller (Oxford: Clarendon Press, 1972), 5.

[43] James Ralph, *The Touch-Stone* (1728), ed. Arthur Freeman (New York: Garland, 1973), 66–7.

against pirates seeing the play and publishing it.[44] Unperformed plays could sometimes be worth more than performed ones. Subscription printing of Henry Brooke's proscribed 'patriot' play *Gustavus Vasa* was said to have made him £1,000 in 1738. The notoriety attached to the suppression of Gay's *Polly* made him 'a publick person a little Sacheverel' and saw to it that the edition, printed by subscription, made more than £1,200 for the author in 1729.[45] Some typical figures are provided by Lintot's purchases: £3. 4s. 6d. for a third share in Cibber's *Love's Last Shift*; £21. 10s. for Dennis's *Appius and Virginia* (1705); £25 for Gay's *Wife of Bath*; £43. 2s. 6d. for his *Three Hours after Marriage* in 1717.[46] Back in 1691 Dryden had received 30 guineas from Tonson, Sen. for *Cleomenes, the Spartan Hero*.[47] According to John Nichols, Mrs Centlivre received £10 for *The Busie Body*, and Farquhar £16. 2s. 6d. for *The Recruiting Officer* and £30 for *The Beaux Stratagem*.[48] It is unsurprising that publishers seldom paid more than £30–£40 for printing-rights, since the playbook might sell for 1s. 6d., so that 400 copies needed to be sold to recoup the £30 payment, and many more to make a profit.[49] Playwrights could do very well out of writing, therefore, but they could never be *certain* of any income at all. As time went on and publishers were able to hold limited but more secure copyrights, agreements with authors did improve. For obvious reasons, the publisher who owned copyright tried to get the book of the play on sale as soon as possible. Pepys's diary attests to the fact that plays had been printed as soon

[44] There is not a great deal of evidence of piratical activity for run-of-the-mill plays in this period, unlike the Elizabethan–Jacobean epoch. Samuel Richardson's problems with Dublin piracies were to become considerable a little later.

[45] *John Gay: Dramatic Works*, ed. John Fuller, 2 vols. (Oxford: Clarendon Press, 1983), i. 54.

[46] Figures are given in F. A. Mumby and Ian Norrie, *Publishing and Bookselling*, pt. I: *From the Earliest Times to 1870* (London: Jonathan Cape, 1930; rev. edn. 1974), 137.

[47] Winn, *John Dryden and his World*, 451.

[48] John Nichols, *Literary Anecdotes of the Eighteenth Century*, 9 vols. (London, 1812–15), viii. 293–303.

[49] Hume, *Henry Fielding and the London Theatre*, 26. Prices seldom appear on booksellers' catalogues or advertisements (probably because retail prices of books depended on whether they were bound or unbound, and on the quality of the binding), and, actually, the calculation made by Hume is not entirely meaningful, since trade practices like selling to the wholesale trade or exchanging with other booksellers introduced all sorts of variables and no bookseller of the period could have made a calculation on the basis given. The edition size is another parameter required.

as acted since the early Restoration, but the trend seemed to accelerate after 1690.[50] It was most desirable to have the playbook available in the theatre during the run, which, as we have seen, was Fielding's usual practice. The advertisement published in the *Daily Post* for 23 March 1731 announcing his revision of *Tom Thumb* as *The Tragedy of Tragedies* and the new farcical afterpiece *The Letter Writers* informs the public that 'Books of the Tragedy, with Notes by way of Key etc. will be sold at the Theatre; as also Books of the Farce.'[51] It must have been a curious experience to follow the text of the annotated *Thumb* (which alerts the reader to the various parallels in standard-repertoire tragedies to the situations presented) while watching the play on stage. One index of the improving situation for play publishing is furnished by the fact that in 1764 Lowndes was willing to pay £32. 10s. for an eighth share in Bickerstaffe's entertainment based on *Pamela, The Maid of the Mill*, before its première, astutely guessing that it would succeed. During his tenure at Drury Lane, Garrick did pay fees to dramatists whose work he accepted, but not more often than he had to.

From this discussion of the theatre as a livelihood, it appears that the business was not set up primarily to benefit the writers who furnished it with its vital raw material, but that nevertheless it afforded writers an opportunity to participate very directly in a market once the author had overcome the difficulties of gaining entry into it. Summarizing the above account, we find that dramatists would gain money by selling performance rights of a manuscript to a theatre company, but they would retain copyright in the printed version of the play, which they could make over to a publisher. Performance was the most important channel of publication for plays, and by the end of the seventeenth century, the benefit night system had emerged, according to which the author took the profits of every third night's performance of his play. After 1712 benefits were confined to late-season productions. By then, three distinct species of benefit existed, each type occurring at a designated time in the season: the actors' and house servants' benefit; the author's benefit; and, beginning to become more

[50] See the comment in Kerry Downes, *Sir John Vanbrugh: A Biography* (London: Sidgwick & Jackson, 1987), 93.

[51] Wilbur L. Cross, *The History of Henry Fielding*, 3 vols. (New Haven: Yale University Press, 1918), i. 99.

common from the 1730s on, the charitable benefit. Authors and actors hoped to make large profits from their benefits and, to that end, would put much energy into selling tickets, ensuring that the play was a popular one and that the best possible cast could be assembled. Arthur Murphy's benefit earnings show the range of possible variation for an author. In round figures, his *Alzuma* netted £270, *Zenobia* (halted in its run by Mrs Barry's supposed indisposition) £476, *The Grecian Daughter* £600, and *The Apprentice* £800.[52] Earnings would depend on whether they had 'clear' benefits, from which house charges were not deducted.

III

With respect to the publication of other literary genres, matters were less straightforward and it was far more difficult for authors to reap direct rewards from their labours. A mechanism evolved during the seventeenth century, growing in popularity in the early eighteenth, for testing the market while avoiding some of the opprobrium that relying exclusively on a market could bring. This was the institution of subscription publishing. Publishing by public subscription was a device through which authors and booksellers were able to gain access to a market at the same time as they protected themselves from its hostile indifference and from what was perceived as the demeaning stigma of writing for bread. An author or bookseller agrees to publish a book with a specified content and price and in an established format, in exchange for the guarantee given by a number of named subscribers to buy it. The principle behind this, that of the subscription, was similar to the joint-stock method of financing that operated widely in the printing trade, whereby printers' consortia would combine to spread the risk of publishing expensive and possibly uneconomical titles. After 1680 the so-called cartel of printers frequently operated thus. Joint stock also enabled much seventeenth-century theatre building. The first post-Restoration theatre to be built, the Theatre Royal, Bridges Street, was built by means of a floated building fund. Indeed this financial system was central to a wide range of economic activity in the era of early capitalism

---

[52] Figures cited in Kalman A. Burnim, *David Garrick: Director* (Pittsburgh: University of Pennsylvania Press, 1961), 18–19.

encompassing the great trading companies and the banking and insurance industry, and later formed the basis for many charitable endeavours. Subscription publishing differed from joint-stock financing in that it was the *consumers* rather than the *producers* who financed copies of titles otherwise unavailable to them. This transitional phase in the financing of book publishing, poised between aristocratic patronage (because the author tried to persuade his important and influential friends to subscribe and to gain new subscribers) and an impersonal market (because the publisher will know how much income he can expect from the edition and will have agreed terms with the author), was one of the enabling conditions of modern authorship. The majority of subscription editions were organized by the bookseller and depended for their success more on the middling sort than on the *haut monde*; but to head a subscription list with aristocratic or, better still, royal names was a recipe for success. On this foundation were built the earliest literary fortunes, those of John Dryden and Alexander Pope.

Subscription publishing operated both at the prestigious end of the market and, interestingly, at the charitable end of it. Hannah More collected enough money in subscriptions from over 1,000 subscribers to enable the poet Anne Yearsley to gain her independence as the proprietrix of a circulating library. At the other end of the spectrum, Fanny Burney's subscription edition of *Camilla* cleared between £2,000 and £3,000 profit for her in 1796.[53] In the cases of John Dryden and Alexander Pope, however, publishing by subscription did more to develop the profession of authorship than merely enriching them personally. The point is properly emphasized with respect to Dryden's great Virgil edition, by the editors of the California Dryden.

The true significance of the Dryden–Tonson enterprise in 1697 was as a watershed in the economic liberation of authorship from the exclusive reliance on the stage, on patronage, or on politics, which had theretofore prevailed . . . Dryden's Virgil was . . . the first work of imaginative literature, requiring years of a distinguished author's effort, to be directly funded by a reading public rather than by theatre audiences, noble patrons or any political faction.[54]

[53] For the effect of subscription publishing on women writers, see Cheryl Turner, *Living by the Pen: Women Writers of the Eighteenth Century* (London: Routledge, 1992; repr. in paperback 1994), 108–13.
[54] The California Dryden, vi. 848.

Dryden's agreement with the publisher Jacob Tonson signed on 15 June 1694 for his translation of Virgil illustrates the subscription mechanism's function in the professionalizing of authorship, By its terms, Dryden was not permitted to work on any other project apart from stated exceptions (thus eliminating delay—the greatest disincentive to potential subscribers); he was to receive £200 from Tonson in four carefully timed instalments; Tonson was to procure 100 subscribers who would each pay 5 guineas and would have a plate inscribed to them with their coat of arms; Dryden would be paid extra by any subscriber who, out of esteem for him, should subscribe more than 5 guineas; Dryden had the right to purchase extra copies for his own disposal at preferential rates; and after the first edition had sold out, Dryden could advertise a second subscription edition for 2 guineas only inferior in that the coats of arms would not be engraved for the subscribers. The accounting procedures that enabled Dryden to keep tabs on Tonson's income from subscriptions are as impressive as are the terms themselves.[55] For both Dryden's translation of Virgil and Pope's later translation of Homer, business considerations interacted with aesthetic desiderata to produce beautiful books and considerable profits.

How typical were Dryden and Pope of the authorial profession at large? Those who derive their conceptions of eighteenth-century authorship from Pope's *Dunciad* are likely to overstate the degree of poverty and servitude in which writers existed.[56] Nevertheless, as Stephen Parks makes clear in his account of the bookseller John Dunton's career, the majority of authors working in the burgeoning literary profession at the end of the seventeenth century were entirely at the mercy of powerful bookseller-publisher associations known as 'congers':

Although it was possible for an author to circumvent the bookseller and to contract directly with a printer to produce his work, few authors could muster the necessary capital or credit. More important, the writer lacked also the means of publishing his work; were he sufficiently self-confident

---

[55] See ibid., 1179–87; Lynch, *Jacob Tonson*, 30; Winn, *John Dryden and his World*, 475–7.

[56] The point is made by John Feather, 'The Commerce of Letters: The Study of the Eighteenth-Century Book Trade', *Eighteenth-Century Studies*, 17 (1983–4), 405–24: 418.

to attempt to reach the public directly, he found normal retail channels of distribution closed to him.[57]

Very many writers never achieved any measure of individual recognition, though some were talented enough to discharge booksellers' commissions and earn a substantial living without any prospect of literary fame. To subsist, the average writer had to be prepared to diversify very considerably the kinds of commission he was prepared to accept. Dunton himself counselled against trying to earn a living by means of writing poetry:

When I see an ingenious man set up for a mere Poet, and steer his course through life towards that Point of the Compass, I give him up, as one pricked down by Fate for misery and misfortune . . . one would incline to think there is some indispensable Law, whereby Poverty and Disappointment are entailed upon Poets . . . I would not . . . dissuade any noble Genius to pursue this Art as a little pretty Divertisement; but where it is made the very Trade of life, I am pretty positive the man is in the wrong box.[58]

Amongst aspiring poets, the entrée into the literary world made by William Diaper is perhaps more typical than the extraordinarily precocious Alexander Pope's, who was recognized by the printers as a hot property from the outset. As he reports in the *Journal to Stella*, Swift introduced Diaper's marine eclogues *Nereides* to the influential members of the Brothers Club in 1712, and they raised a gift of 1 guinea each for him. Later, Swift reports Diaper's success with a follow-up collection *Dryades*:

This morning I presented one Diaper a poet to Ld Bolingbroke, with a new Poem, which is a very good one; and I am to give him a Sum of money from my Ld; and I have contrivd to make a Parson of him; for he is half a one already, being in Deacons Orders, and serves a small Cure in the Country, but has a sword at his A—— here in Town. Tis a poor little short Wretch, but will do best in a Gown, & we will make Ld Keepr give him a Living.[59]

[57] Stephen Parks, *John Dunton and the English Book Trade: A Study of his Career with a Checklist of his Publications* (New York: Garland, 1976), 184.
[58] John Dunton, *The Life and Errors of John Dunton, late Citizen of London: written by Himself in Solitude* (London, 1705), 183–4.
[59] Jonathan Swift, *Journal to Stella*, ed. Harold Williams, 2 vols. (Oxford: Clarendon Press, 1948; 2nd edn. 1974), ii. 519, 586. I am indebted for this reference to Shane Flynn, 'The Scriblerus Club and the Interaction of Politics and Literature, 1710–1714', Ph.D. thesis (Aberystwyth, 1994).

This blend of career advancement and cash payment is typical enough of what a minor poet of good family could expect at the twilight of the age of patronage. By this time, the going rate for separately printed poems of substantial length was around 10 guineas—the sum paid by Robert Dodsley to Samuel Johnson for *London*, who refused to take less than he knew Paul Whitehead had been offered a little earlier. Apart from one or two celebrated cases like those of Dryden and Pope mentioned earlier, to which we might add the 4,000 guineas earned by Matthew Prior for the Tonson subscription edition of *Poems on Several Occasions*; there was comparatively little to be earned from poetry.[60] James Thomson's recent biographer James Sambrook notes that the poet's profit from performances of his play *Sophonisba* (around £300) amounted to more than the total of all his copyright sales for such labour-intensive works as *The Seasons*, though the subscription edition of *The Seasons* published in 1730 made him 1,000 guineas.[61]

Although the price commanded by poetry did not improve much as the period wore on, opportunities to publish it certainly increased as a result of the proliferation of literary periodicals. Prose essays published in periodicals became one of the most significant aspects of authorial income in the eighteenth century, the price paid ranging from 1 to 6 guineas. Walter Graham, the historian of the English literary periodical, considers that 'the stipends paid by the rapidly increasing numbers of newspapers, essay-serials, magazines and reviews' marks a watershed in the history of patronage.[62] When such lucrative publishing opportunities existed, the pensioning of writers like Addison and Prior was no longer necessary and, after the accession of George I, no longer a real possibility. Angus Ross's valuable summary of the evidence pertaining to the *Tatler*'s business footing deserves to be cited:

A press printed on one day about 2,000–2,500 folio half-sheets, so that up to *Tatler* 117 the sale of papers was probably less than 2,500. It has been shown that from *Tatler* 118 to the end of the series, two settings of each number on two separate presses were called for. This implies a sale

[60] For an informative summary of approximate earnings figures for poetry, see Harry Ransom, 'The Rewards of Authorship in the Eighteenth Century', *University of Texas Studies in English*, 18 (1938), 47–66: 51–5.

[61] James Sambrook, *James Thomson, 1700–1748: A Life* (Oxford: Clarendon Press, 1991), 91, 104.

[62] Walter Graham, *English Literary Periodicals* (New York: Nelson, 1930), 20.

of 3,000–4,000 . . . It should be remembered that each paper was read by several people, especially the papers in coffee-houses and taverns, so that a readership of 10,000 or more would not be out of the way . . . [At a cost of 15s. per 1,000 copies] 9,000 *Tatlers* . . . [3,000 thrice weekly] would cost £7 4 shillings, with unknown other costs. Sold at 1 penny each, they would bring in £37 10 shillings. In addition, there was a considerable advertising revenue . . . There are more than 2,000 advertisement entries in *The Tatler*, which at a reasonable guess of 2s 6d each would have brought in £250.[63]

Daniel Defoe's career is the prime example in the period of how far an industrious individual devoted to a life of writing could hope to prosper by the early eighteenth century. Although his most recent biographer doubts whether he ever made more than £100 for any of the great novels for which he is now remembered, he experienced the various different payment systems current at the time and set himself up in a comfortably bourgeois style of living in his latter days. As a pamphleteer in Queen Anne's reign and afterwards, Defoe would be paid 2 guineas on every 500 sixpenny pamphlets printed by his publisher John Baker, whereas another publisher, Janeway, gave him 4 guineas plus a number of free copies for every 1,000 sold. During the period of his notorious double agency, when he was writing for Nathaniel Mist's Tory *Mist's Weekly Journal* but was actually spying on its activities for the government, he was receiving 20s. per week, increased to 40s. in 1718. It was the periodicals that he owned himself, however, that made him his fortune. As Paula Backscheider writes:

Some of Defoe's own eight periodicals made substantial profits, altogether perhaps as much as £1,200 a year, and by the beginning of 1721 he lived the prosperous, serene life of the prominent citizen of Stoke Newington. Now and then he vacationed at Tunbridge Wells, and he seems to have spent his weekends away from the city . . . The papers show us a happy man going from coffeehouse to coffeehouse, mingling easily with the financiers at Jonathan's and Garraway's, with the churchmen at Child's, dropping in at the Temple coffeehouses, and talking politics and economics or exchanging jokes and good-natured jibes.[64]

What about the careers of women writers in the period? Did they face any special difficulties? Judging by the number of women

[63] Richard Steele and Joseph Addison, *Selections from the* Tatler *and the* Spectator, ed. Angus Ross (Harmondsworth: Penguin, 1982; repr. 1988), 52–3.
[64] Paula R. Backscheider, *Daniel Defoe: His Life* (Baltimore: Johns Hopkins University Press, 1989), 465. See also pp. 371, 432.

playwrights who gained at least a partial living from the theatre in the period *c.*1695–1720 following in Aphra Behn's footsteps— women like Catherine Trotter, Mary Pix, Mary Delarivier Manley, Eliza Haywood, and Susanna Centlivre—the answer appears to be negative. There is no evidence that women earned less money from writing for the theatre than did men. Of Susanna Centlivre's earnings, F. P. Lock informs us that she received £21 each from Edmund Curll for the copyrights to *The Wonder*, *The Cruel Gift*, and *The Artifice* (this information is confirmed in the Upcott Collection, where the assignments are to be found) and his estim- ate is that she may have made from £100 to £150 out of each of her more successful plays. This, we can put beside her husband Joseph's salary of £60 per annum from his position as Yeoman of the Mouth (in the royal kitchen).[65] Nevertheless, there is a falling- off after 1720, and women like Elizabeth Cooper in the 1730s, Frances Brooke in the 1750s, Elizabeth Griffith and Frances Sheridan in the 1760s, and the very successful Elizabeth Inchbald, whose farce *The Mogul Tale; or, The Descent of the Balloon* earned 100 guineas from Colman in 1784, were exceptional.[66] Part of the reason for this lies in the changing ideology of womanhood that made it progressively more difficult for women to compete in the bruising business of negotiating with theatrical managements and acting companies to have plays mounted. Janet Todd ex- presses this paradigm shift in the following terms:

The new writer had to conform to the age's ideal of womanhood, whatever the individual reality seemed to be. She had to be virtuous and domestic, writing either from financial necessity, unsupported by the proper guard- ians of femininity such as husband or father, or from desire to teach virtue to the unformed. The work she wrote was not presented aggres- sively to the public as an artful piece desiring to overwhelm the reader and give fame to the author. Instead it was a response to misfortune which had thrown the woman into the unusual necessity of providing financially for herself and her dependants. She would write and earn money while filling as before every possible domestic duty.[67]

[65] F. P. Lock, *Susanna Centlivre*, Twayne English Authors, 254 (Boston: G. K. Hall, 1979), 18–19.
[66] Some of the information in this paragraph is provided by *A Dictionary of British and American Women Writers, 1660–1800*, ed. Janet Todd (London: Methuen, 1987), *passim*.
[67] Janet Todd, *The Sign of Angellica: Women, Writing and Fiction, 1660–1800* (London: Virago, 1989), 126.

An ideology such as this favoured forms of writing that could be conducted relatively impersonally, even anonymously. Some idea of the stamina required to bring a play from manuscript to performance, as well as valuable information about contemporary performance conditions, is given by John Dennis's extraordinary Dedication of his adaptation of *Coriolanus*, entitled *The Invader of his Country*, to the Lord Chamberlain, the Duke of Newcastle. Dennis complains that the Drury Lane managers first postponed the play for a flimsy reason and then refused to postpone it for another week, despite the fact that its third night, his benefit night, would clash with the king's return to England. Further, it would be a Friday, notoriously a bad night for audiences. He continues:

My Lord, the Play was Acted on *Wednesday* the 11th [November 1719] to an Audience of near a Hundred Pound, for so much they own'd to me. It was favourably received by the Audience. There did some Malice appear twice, but it was immediately drown'd by the utmost Clamours of Applause. On *Thursday*, the Play was Acted again to an Audience of between Fifty and Threescore Pounds. And on *Friday* to an Audience of between Sixty and Seventy Pounds. Considering the disadvantages under which we lay, here were fair hopes for the future. And on *Friday*, after the Play was done, these tender-hearted Managers caus'd another to be given out, to the Astonishment of the Audience, the Disappointment of those who had reserv'd themselves for the Sixth Day, and the Retrenching three parts in four of my Profits.[68]

Dennis is enraged by the Managers' claim that no play is worth retaining that fails to net £100: he claims that, by custom, any play that covers its costs and is liked is duty-bound to be retained. As he points out, a dramatist ventures his financial interest and reputation in a play: it is surely the least the managers can do to support him for a day or two when they lose nothing by it. Another example of the rough-and-tumble involved in trying to stage a play at this period is provided by the case of Susanna Centlivre's *The Man's Bewitch'd; or, The Devil to Do about Her*, premièred at the Queen's Theatre, Haymarket on 12 December 1709. The play's pre-performance history had been discussed in the *Female Tatler*, a periodical probably edited by Delarivier Manley perhaps with help from Mandeville, that had been targeting Cibber for attacks

[68] Dennis, *Critical Works*, ii. 177–8.

throughout that autumn. The issue for 12–14 December 1709 praised Centlivre's play exorbitantly (they 'were rejoyc'd to see the inimitable Mrs. *Behn* so nearly reviv'd in Mrs. *Centlivre*') and accused the actors of actually having tried to excise the ghost scene in Act V, which had been a resounding success with the public. Replying, in the Preface to the printed version of her play, to the charge that she herself had written this shameless piece of self-advertisement, Centlivre denied authorship and professed her co-operation with Cibber's editorial interference, though she drew the line at the actor Estcourt's attempt to excise the scene entirely. She goes on:

At present it seems a certain Author [Cibber] has enter'd a Caveat against all Plays running to a sixth Night, but his own. Tho' an Opera interfer'd with this Comedy, yet it brought above Forty Pounds the second Night, which shew'd it had some Merit; for I have known many a Play kept up, that fail'd of half that Money the second Night . . . This play met with a kind Reception in general, and notwithstanding the Disadvantages it had to struggle with, by raising the Prices the first Day, and the nearness of *Christmas*, it would have made its way to a sixth Night, if it had had fair Play.[69]

The point is, then, that the 'new woman' created by the changing construction of femininity in the period is encouraged to believe that she hasn't the stomach for this kind of negotiation. Furthermore, by the mid-eighteenth century, a successful novel was as much of a paying proposition as a play, though the going rate for the sale of copyright on a popular novel was set within the 5–10 guinea range throughout the period. Maxima are indicted by the spectacular fees of £500 and £800 respectively paid to Ann Radcliffe for *The Mysteries of Udolpho* (1794) and *The Italian* (1797). Novel-writing was a more congenial way for increasingly suburbanized women to create, given the exhausting and public way a playwright gained a living. Cheryl Turner's recent study of women writers in the eighteenth century suggests that well before the accepted halcyon period of women writers in the nineteenth century, 'literate women from the lower social strata wrote for

[69] Susanna Centlivre, *The Man's Bewitch'd; or, The Devil to Do About Her* (London, [1710?]), fos. A4ᵛ–A5. On this controversy, see John Wilson Bowyer, *The Celebrated Mrs. Centlivre* (Durham, NC: Duke University Press, 1952), ch. 5. Valuable additional information is supplied in Pierre Danchin (ed.), *The Prologues and Epilogues of the Eighteenth Century*, 2 parts, 4 vols. (Nancy: Presses Universitaires de Nancy, 1990–3), pt. 1 (1701–20), ii. 443–4.

publication seeking a wide readership for their material'.[70] There
were, she argues, two distinct phases of development in women's
writing: 'a steady, rapid rise in output reaching a peak around
1725, followed by an equally substantial decline to a slump around
1740; then a gradual increase in production from the mid-century
onwards until the mid-1780s, followed by an abrupt upward surge
during the next decade' (p. 38). Turner also emphasizes, as does
Janet Todd, the ideological changes that brought women's domestic experience to the forefront of literary representation; and
the growing insistence on the didactic function of literature permitted women to enter the market as novelists without any compromise of their respectability. By the eighteenth century, literary
women were predominantly middle-class and the need to repair
diminishing fortunes was a salient motive for much of the period's
literary output. Many talented women writers were nurtured by the
social, intellectual, and literary coteries of major writers like Swift,
Johnson, and the publisher-writer Richardson; and Turner correctly stresses the role played by the Bluestockings in boosting the
self-confidence of literary women and in introducing them to
influential contacts. A point valuably insisted upon by Turner is
the formative role played by publishers on early women's writing
and on the literary market as a whole. From the viewpoint of
professionalization there is time even for such legendary villains as
the pirate and pornographer Edmund Curll, who published a few of
Susanna Centlivre's plays and several novels by women; but the
publishing giants of the era themselves—Dodsley, Andrew Millar,
the Dilly brothers, and Thomas Cadell—participated in the professionalization of women writers. The extent to which this process
had developed by the end of the century is indicated by Turner:

Although the eighteenth century was an early phase in the growth of
women's participation in the literature market, the range of their activities
was extensive. To appreciate the scope of their work we have only to think
of the provincial poets whose material was issued through subscription;
of women who submitted their correspondence, biographical portraits,
reviews, social commentaries, and verses to magazines; the writers of
polemical and reflective religious pieces and of controversial items on
social issues; translators; and authors of travelogues, treatises on educa-

[70] Turner, *Living by the Pen*, 23. My account of women writers in the period is
deeply indebted to this important study.

tion, histories, and of books offering mixtures of prose and verse, recipes, and advice on childrearing, housewifery and midwifery.   (pp. 125–6)

In view of activity on this scale, it is surprising to say the least that, as Jane Spencer and others have noted, women writers are virtually excluded from the standard accounts of 'the rise of the novel'.[71]

[71] Jane Spencer, *The Rise of the Woman Novelist: From Aphra Behn to Jane Austen* (Oxford: Basil Blackwell, 1986). And not only from the 'classic' accounts like Ian Watt's: Clive T. Probyn's *English Fiction of the Eighteenth Century, 1700–1789* (London: Longman, 1987), a standard and typical student guide, has practically nothing to say on women writers.

PART II

Cultural Broking

3

An Allusion to Horace, Jonson's Ghost, and the Rhetoric of Plagiarism

In the opening chapter of this book, it was suggested that modern conceptions of originality may derive from the urgent demand of the publishing profession that literary property be given a definition. Influential forms of aesthetic theory emanating from Edward Young's *Conjectures on Original Composition* via German and English Romanticism assisted in the dissemination of 'invention' or originality as the *sine qua non* of valuable literary works. New theories of reading were also developing in parallel with those governing composition. Literature could be *created* by writers who had nothing but their genius to recommend them, and, as the 'polite' literary periodicals of the early eighteenth century taught their readers, it could also be *consumed* by members of the literate middle class who had some leisure time rather than any extensive training or cultural pedigree. This point will be developed in Chapter 5. What is clear is that the nature of literary creation and of those involved in it was in a state of evolution. The austere, Miltonic conception of the poet as fitting himself for his profession by years of immersion in the classics and by the amassing of great knowledge was one that could not survive the development of the literary market-place. Cultural forms that gained prestige by advertising their indebtedness to literary tradition through allusion would come under enormous pressure from a new aesthetic based on originality. In poetry, this is the story of the mid-to-late eighteenth century.

Yet there is, I would contend, an earlier cultural formation, that of dramatic writing in the 1670s and 1680s, wherein the problematic nature of borrowing from earlier works was already under heated negotiation. In this milieu, clear financial interests were wrapped up in the issue of allusion. Competing for the production of potentially lucrative playscripts, professional writers saw the theatrical stock of the pre-Civil War era as a rich ground for looting. It was much less prodigal of valuable professional time to annex plots, characters, and dialogue of already proven worth than to create from scratch. Writers could justify this on an aesthetic that required them to make acts of obeisance to eminent literary predecessors. Opponents would seek to deprive them of any honorific status thus collected by making the charge of plagiarism. Thus, Dryden's anxiety about plagiarism was detected and mercilessly exploited by his enemies, as is evident in this passage in *The Rehearsal* (1672), where Buckingham and his cronies home in on it unerringly:

SMITH. But pray, Mr. *Bayes*, among all your other Rules, have you no one Rule for invention?

BAYES. Yes, Sir; that's my third Rule that I have here in my pocket.

SMITH. What Rule can that be, I wonder?

BAYES. Why, Sir, when I have anything to invent, I never trouble my head about it, as other men do; but presently turn over this Book, and there I have, at one view, all that *Perseus, Montaigne, Seneca's Tragedies, Horace, Juvenal, Claudian, Pliny, Plutarch's lives*, and the rest, have ever thought upon this subject: and so, in a trice, by leaving out a few words, or putting in others of my own, the business is done.[1]

Examining dramatic practice and the rhetoric of plagiarism as it operates in the literary quarrels between Rochester, Dryden, and Shadwell should offer a valuable observation-point on the nature of the first phase of professional writing in England.

I

Modern conceptions of originality make the claim appear paradoxical that *An Allusion to Horace*, the poem in which Rochester is most indebted to a precursor, is also one of his most original contributions to English poetry. If Rochester was not quite the first English poet to press a Roman satire into the service of his own times, he was the first to appreciate that this could be done systematically over the length of an entire poem, to wit Horace's

---

[1] George Villiers, Duke of Buckingham, *et al.*, *The Rehearsal*, ed. D. E. L. Crane (University of Durham Publications, 1976), 6.

Satire I. x.[2] Doubtless, Rochester did not intuit the full potential
of this new medium. That would come, not so much through the
greater poetic genius of Alexander Pope, as through Pope's more
developed understanding of the phenomenology of reading the
'imitation'. As soon as you cease to rely on your reader's hazy
memory of the original Latin, and print it in juxtaposition to your
own English, using typography when necessary to call attention to
your own especially felicitous adaptations, knowing departures,
and virtuoso puns, you enable effects that were not possible for
Rochester.[3] Where, for instance, Rochester could simply omit an
Horatian passage that he did not see as having any relevance to
contemporary circumstances, such as that commencing 'scilicet
oblitus patriaeque', in which Horace condemns the practice of
adulterating the native satiric strain with Greek words, later satirists like Pope and Johnson, fearing that the reader would construe
this as an evasion, would invest far more effort in inventing
parallel circumstances. In Pope's hands, the Horatian imitation
offers the reader a pleasure analogous to that of the musical
'variations on a theme of . . .'—extreme formal constraint, from
which every departure is experienced as a glorious freedom.[4]
Rochester's poem is not such a triumph of the baroque, but its
relative lack of polish offers an opportunity to observe certain
aspects of contemporary cultural debate—in particular, the fight
for possession of Ben Jonson, at this time a struggle even more

[2] William Kupersmith observes that 'although Sprat and Cowley wrote the earliest
Imitations of Horace, John Wilmot, Earl of Rochester, first used the Imitation
as a weapon to attack contemporaries', in *Roman Satirists in Seventeenth-Century
England* (Lincoln: Nebraska University Press, 1985), 97. Etherege, it seems, had
produced a systematic imitation of Boileau in 1673, which Dryden had mentioned to
Rochester in a letter. See Winn, *John Dryden and his World*, 251.

[3] Previous important discussions of the *Allusion to Horace* have not always
observed this point, and have had some tendency to condemn Rochester's poem as a
relatively unsuccessful exploitation of its original. See Howard D. Weinbrot, 'The
"Allusion to Horace": Rochester's Imitative Mode', *Studies in Philology*, 69 (1972),
348–68: 364–8; David Farley-Hills, *Rochester's Poetry* (Totowa, NJ: Rowman &
Littlefield, 1978), 203; Pat Rogers, 'An Allusion to Horace', in *Spirit of Wit:
Reconsiderations of Rochester*, ed. Jeremy Treglown (Oxford: Basil Blackwell, 1982);
P. E. Hewison, 'Rochester, the Imitation and *An Allusion to Horace*', *Seventeenth-
Century*, 2/1 (1987), 73–94.

[4] See Frank Stack, *Pope and Horace* (Cambridge University Press, 1985), for the
most detailed discussion available of Popean technique. On pp. 85–8, Stack provides
an excellent example of the way in which Pope employed typography to focus
particular attention on Horace's obscenity. In *Sober Advice from Horace*, Pope
quotes Horace in block capitals, raising the reader's (somewhat salacious) interest in
how he is going to negotiate the translation of 'mirator CUNNI CUPIENNIUS ALBI'.

active than the perennial contest over Shakespeare—and the gradually assembling rhetoric of plagiarism.

In general terms, the reasons for Rochester's mounting an overt attack on Dryden in 1675 are well enough understood. It is not yet clear by 1673–4, from the dedication to Dryden's *Marriage à la Mode* or from his flattering letter to Rochester of that year, that there was considerable personal dislike between them. In his poem *Timon* (1674), Rochester glanced at Dryden's plays and critical opinions. He seems to have found Dryden something of a disappointment in the flesh as opposed to on paper—a 'singing owl', as he once remarked.[5] And in the subsequent years, infighting at Court between Rochester and Mulgrave had consequences for those who depended on their patronage. By 1675, there was an overtly political difference of allegiance between them. At a time of rapidly polarizing politics, Dryden was known to be in the Duke of York's camp, whereas Rochester was a supporter of Buckingham. Mapped on to incipient Tory–Whig political divisions, however, were more volatile and nebulous conflicts over the status of the writer in society. Dryden's failed play *The Assignation; or, Love in a Nunnery* was published in 1673 with a dedication to the court wit Sedley, in which the writer made a bold bid for acceptance into Sedley's inner circle. Celebrating the close friendship of the Roman poets, Dryden had the temerity to describe, from the insider's viewpoint and for the benefit of those who have exaggerated their licentiousness, the typical behaviour of the aristocratic epicureans:

We have . . . our Genial Nights; where our discourse is neither too serious, nor too light; but alwayes pleasant, and for the most part instructive: the raillery neither too sharp upon the present, nor too censorious on the absent; and the Cups, onely such as will raise the Conversation of the Night, without disturbing the business of the Morrow. And thus far not only the Philosophers, but the Fathers of the Church have gone, without lessening their Reputation of good Manners, or of Piety. For this reason I have often Laugh'd at the ignorant and ridiculous Descriptions, which some Pedants have given of the Wits (as they are pleas'd to call them:) which are a Generation of Men as unknown to them, as the People of *Tartary* or the *Terra Australis* are to us . . . Such wits as they describe, I have never been so unfortunate to meet in your Company: but have often heard much better Reasoning at your Table,

[5] See Winn, *John Dryden and his World*, 250.

THE RHETORIC OF PLAGIARISM 87

than I have encounter'd in their Books. The Wits they describe, are the Fops we banish: for Blasphemy and Atheism, if they were neither Sin nor Ill Manners, are subjects so very common, and worn so Thredbare, that people who have sence avoid them, for fear of being suspected to have none.

Later in the dedication, Dryden rebuts the charge that he has habitually disparaged the achievement of earlier authors—Ben Jonson in particular—by citing as a precedent Horace's tactic in the *Satires*, wherein the Roman poet certainly criticized his eminent predecessor Lucilius, but also gave him credit where credit was due:

I am made a Detractor from my Predecessors, whom I confess to have been my Masters in the Art. But this latter was the accusation of the best Judge, and almost the best Poet in the *Latine* Tongue. You find *Horace* complaining, that for taxing some Verses in *Lucilius*, he himself was blamed by others, though his Design was no other than mine now, to improve Knowledge of Poetry: and it was no defence to him, amongst his Enemies, any more than it is for me, that he Prais'd Lucilius where he deserv'd it: *Pagina laudatur eadem*.[6]

It must have been particularly painful, then, for Dryden to discover that Rochester had probably picked up the germ of the idea of applying Horace's Satire I. x from him, and had used it to accuse *Dryden* of plagiarism! Worse still, in the cruellest lines in the poem, entirely unlicensed by Horace, Rochester mocks Dryden's clodhopping attempts to talk bawdy, ridiculing his claim to be intimate with the aristocratic libertines, whose light touch he entirely lacks:

> Dryden, in vaine, try'd this nice way of Witt,
> For he, to be a tearing Blade thought fit,
> But when he wou'd be sharp, he still was blunt,
> To friske his frollique fancy, hed cry Cunt . . .[7]

[6] The California Dryden, xi. 320–1, 322.
[7] Lines 71–4; all quotations from Rochester are taken from *The Poems of John Wilmot, Earl of Rochester*, ed. Keith Walker (Oxford: Basil Blackwell, 1984). Shadwell recorded one of Dryden's allegedly gauche attempts at in-crowd obscenity in *The Medal of John Bayes* (1682):

> Thy Mirth by foolish Bawdry is exprest;
> And so debauch'd, so fulsome, and so odd,
> As . . .
> *Let's Bugger one another now by G–d*
> (When ask'd how they should spend the Afternoon)
> This was the smart reply of the Heroick Clown.

Ironic that Dryden, whose most famous characterization of his satiric art in the *Discourse concerning Satire* (1692) would stress a razor sharpness that separates the head from the body, and leaves it standing in its place, is in Rochester's lines banished as a mere dull fop. The depth of feeling engendered by Rochester's public repudiation of him can be measured by his Preface to the published edition of *All for Love* (1678) in which, in total contrast to the in-crowd intimacies of the dedication to Sedley, Dryden makes a withering irony out of accepting himself as a mere venal professional: 'We who write, if we want the Talent, yet have the excuse that we do it for a poor subsistence; but what can be urg'd in their defence, who not having the Vocation of Poverty to scribble, out of meer wantonness take pains to make themselves ridiculous?'[8] Rochester's tactic in *An Allusion to Horace* is to contrast crowd-pleasing, ill-considered popular entertainment, hastily composed and thrown together, with writing that is carefully constructed and submitted only to those whose rank and education puts them in the best position to judge (lines 12–17, 93–7, 104–9 versus lines 20–9, 98–103, 110–14, 120–4). Practical criticism of specific writers designed to exemplify these broadly contrasting attitudes to composition occupies most of the remainder. The caste or status-group basis of Rochester's attack on Dryden in *An Allusion to Horace* is explicitly enunciated in the final lines:

> I loath the Rabble, 'tis enough for me,
> If Sidley, Shadwell, Shepherd, Witcherley,
> Godolphin, Butler, Buckhurst, Buckingham,
> And some few more, whom I omit to name
> Approve my Sense, I count their Censure Fame.

> (lines 120–4)

Line 120 underwrites its memorability by alluding to one of Horace's most famous lines from the *Odes*, 'Odi profanum vulgus et arceo'. Even more sharply, though, the posture struck by Rochester with regard to 'the false Judgement of an Audience | Of Clapping-Fooles' recalls Ben Jonson's various attempts to educate, cajole, and browbeat his audience into acceptance of his comic genius. As we have seen, Jonson finally, in the 'Ode to Himself' written after the failure of *The New Inn*, expressed a Timonesque

---

[8] The California Dryden, xiii. 14.

resolution not to waste his sweetness on the desert air that was the contemporary Caroline audience. Dryden must have read *An Allusion to Horace* as a public commitment of Rochester's power to Shadwell's side in the struggle, now some seven or eight years old, for possession of Ben Jonson's comic mantle even though Rochester's praise of Shadwell is qualified in important ways. Yet for the modern reader poring over the precise terms of Rochester's sponsorship, the difference between the two rivals is elusive. These terms are as follows:

Shadwell	*Dryden*
Shadwell's unfinisht workes doe yet impart,	But does not Dryden find ev'n Jonson dull?
Great proofes of force of Nature, none of Art.	Fletcher, and Beaumont, uncorrect, and full
With just bold Stroakes, he dashes here and there,	Of Lewd lines as he calls 'em? Shakespeare's Stile
Shewing great Mastery with little care;	Stiffe, and Affected? To his owne the while
And scornes to varnish his good touches o're,	Allowing all the justnesse that his Pride,
To make the Fooles, and Women, praise 'em more.	Soe Arrogantly, had to these deny'd?
(lines 44–9)	And may not I, have leave Impartially
	To search, and Censure, Drydens workes, and try,
	If those grosse faults, his Choyce Pen does Commit
	Proceed from want of Judgment, or of Wit.
	Or if his lumpish fancy does refuse,
	Spirit, and grace to his loose slatterne Muse?
	(lines 81–92)

On the basis of the key critical terms here—'Nature', 'Art', the painting metaphor applied to Shadwell's work, 'Judgment', 'Wit', 'fancy', 'spirit', and 'grace'—it is difficult for the modern reader to understand exactly what was at issue between the two writers. Even if we look beyond the poem to those statements made by Dryden about his attitudes to earlier writers, to which Rochester's passage alludes, there is some difficulty in extrapolating from them to the theatrical practices involved. Typical of the exchanges between the two writers over Jonson's merit as a comic dramatist was Dryden's Preface to *An Evening's Love* (1671), to which Shadwell responded in his Preface to *The Humorists* in the same year. Dryden writes:

To make men appear pleasantly ridiculous on the Stage was . . . [Jonson's] talent: and in this he needed not the acumen of wit, but that of judgement. For the characters and representations of folly are only the effects of observation; and observation is an effect of judgement. Some ingenious men, for whom I have a particular esteem, have thought I have much injur'd *Ben Johnson* when I have not allow'd his wit to be extraordinary: but they confound the notion of what is witty with what is pleasant. That *Ben Johnson*'s Playes were pleasant he must want reason who denyes: But that pleasantness was not properly wit, or the sharpness of conceit; but the natural imitation of folly: which I confess to be excellent in it's kind, but not to be of that kind which they pretend.[9]

Shadwell construes this as an attack on comedy of 'humours' and thus responds:

I cannot be of their opinion who think he wanted wit . . . Nor can I think, to the writing of his humors (which were not only the follies, but vices and subtilties of men) that wit was not required, but judgment; where, by the way, they speak as if judgment were less a thing than wit. But certainly it was meant otherwise by nature, who subjected wit to the government of judgment, which is the noblest faculty of the mind. Fancy rough-draws, but judgment smooths and finishes, nay judgment does in deed comprehend wit, for no man can have that who has not wit.[10]

Shadwell goes on to deny Dryden's argument that Jonsonian comedy of humours is essentially a mimetic art, requiring no imaginative heightening. Applying the categories of faculty psychology, playing and replaying the counters of 'wit' and 'judgement', the disputants never quite develop a language adequate to analyse dramatic performance, and to exemplify the differing comic effects that they strove to achieve. It may be of some critical service, therefore, to try to elucidate this matter, and demonstrate its importance to the cultural status of Rochester's poem.

---

[9] The California Dryden, 205–6 (italics reversed).
[10] Thomas Shadwell, Preface to *The Humorists*, in *Complete Works*, i. 187–8.

II

Rochester, in *An Allusion to Horace*, wants to cut a wide swathe between those poets like Settle, Otway, and Lee who are working dramatists, professional writers eking out a living by marketing their writing talents, and those like Waller, Buckhurst, and Sedley who, by virtue of their social rank and court connections, can obey gentlemanly aesthetic prescriptions like those expressed in lines 20–9, which are then said to be the characteristic excellencies of Shakespeare and Jonson (lines 30–1):

> But within due proportions, circumscribe
> What e're you write; that with a flowing Tyde,
> The Stile, may rise, yet in its rise forbeare,
> With uselesse Words, t'oppresse the wearyed Eare:
> Here be your Language lofty, there more light,
> Your Rethorick, with your Poetry, unite:
> For Elegance sake, sometimes alay the force
> Of Epethets; 'twill soften the discourse;
> A Jeast in Scorne, poynts out, and hits the thing,
> More home, than the Morosest Satyrs Sting.
> Shakespeare, and Johnson, did herein excell,
> And might in this be Immitated well . . .

Waller is the great panegyrist, Buckhurst the satirist extraordinaire, and Sedley a master of the erotic capable of releasing desire so subliminal that it seeps up through cultural barriers:

> For Songs, and Verses, Mannerly Obscene,
> That can stirr Nature up, by Springs unseene,
> And without forceing blushes, warm the Queene:
> Sidley, has that prevailing gentle Art.

(lines 61–4)

There are four writers whose work defies this easy typology, and whose work it is the poem's major task to evaluate: Etherege, Wycherley, Shadwell, and Dryden. The Etherege problem is solved by making him *sui generis*: 'refin'd Etheridge, Coppys not at all, | But is himself a Sheere Originall'. Wycherley is a thorough, painstaking artist (lines 50–4). Shadwell and Dryden remain as the most fluid reputations, antitypes in that the one is said to be a natural writer whose creative energy overrides his attention to detail and the other to have a 'lumpish fancy'. Permitting ourselves to move beyond the confines of the neoclassical critical vocabulary, let us try to examine what is at stake here.

Essentially, the difference between Dryden's comedy of 'wit' and Shadwell's comedy of 'humours' is that between a theatre dominated by its spoken text (Dryden) and one dominated by dramatic action, situation, and gesture (Shadwell). Shadwell's *The Sullen Lovers* and Dryden's *An Evening's Love* were produced within one month of each other in May and June 1668; and although both plays owe a debt to Jonson, it is Shadwell who really understands Jonsonian stagecraft and wishes it to form the basis of a reinvigorated comedy. In Dryden's play, Bellamy's servant Maskall gives him out to be an astrologer in order to explain how he has come by certain knowledge about his inamorata Theodosia's love life. Thereafter, Bellamy is consulted by various individuals, including Theodosia's father Don Alonzo, who wish to benefit from his mystery, rather in the way that Jonson's alchemist Subtle is approached by the various gulls. Don Alonzo knows a good deal of occult lore, and Bellamy's attempts to improvise the language while also satisfying the demands of various clients for clairvoyance are reminiscent of Jonsonian situation management. Act III scene i comes to a recognizably Jonsonian climax of farcical brabble when Don Lopez attempts to inform Don Alonzo that another young gallant is in love with his daughter, but Alonzo, priding himself on the gift of foreknowledge, insists on speaking over him:

ALON. Why, when do you begin, Sir? How long must a man wait for you? pray make an end of what you have to say quickly, that I may speak in my turn too.

LOP. This Cavalier is in Love—

ALON. You told me that before, Sir; Do you speak Oracles that you require this strict attention? either let me share the talk with you or I am gone.

LOP. Why, Sir, I am almost mad to tell you, and you will not suffer me.

ALON. Will you never have done, Sir? I must tell you, Sir, you have tatled long enough; and 'tis now good Manners to hear me speak. Here's a Torrent of words indeed; a very *impetus dicendi*; Will you never have done?

LOP. I will be heard in spight of you.

This next Speech of Lopez, *and the next of* Alonzo's, *with both their*

*Replies, are to be spoken at one time; both raising their voices by little
and little, till they baul, and come up close to shoulder one another.*

LOP. There's one *Don Melchor de Guzman*, a Friend and Acquaintance
of mine, that is desperately in Love with your eldest Daughter *Donna
Theodosia*.

ALON. [*at the same time*] 'Tis the sentence of a Philosopher, *Loquere ut
te videam*; Speak that I may know thee . . .[11]

It is doubtless merely coincidence, because Dryden's direct source
here is Molière, that Alonzo's (mistranslated) philosophical sentence was profoundly important to Jonson, cited in his *Discoveries*
as a fundamental principle of epistemology: '*language* most shewes
a man: speake that I may see thee'.[12] Lopez, unsuccessful in
capturing Alonzo's attention with legal gibberish, runs off to find a
bell, with which he manages to interrupt Alonzo's next diatribe
against 'perpetual Talkers, Disputants, Controverters, and Duel-
lers of the Tongue'. Yet, for all that this frenetic activity has a
Jonsonian texture, the play as an entirety lacks the Jonsonian
satiric impulse. Bellamy and Maskall are not, as are Subtle and
Face, calculatedly manipulating the gullible and the greedy. Cant,
trade-talk, argot—the various languages of duplicity that take on
such a perverse malevolence in Jonson—are a temporary discom-
fiture for Lopez and a short-lived test for Bellamy's powers of
invention. This point about Dryden's fundamental *difference* from
Jonson might be pursued in respect of another of his plays, the
fabulously successful *The Feign'd Innocence; or, Sir Martin Mar-
all*, premièred in August 1667. The plot is simple and monolithic.
Sir Martin Mar-all foils all the plans laid by his servant Warner to
capture Mrs Millisent for him, by counterplotting ineptly. Despite
the argument made by John Loftis, editor of the California edition
of Dryden's works, for Jonsonian influence, the uncomplicated
structure of this play, its formula of repeated situations, its over-
reliance on a single actor's performance (Nokes was apparently a
huge success in the title role)—in short, its failure to build into
any degree of farcical complexity—make it a singularly inept
imitation of Jonson.[13] It suggests that Dryden had no real talent
for, or understanding of, Jonsonian stagecraft. Far more central to

[11] III. i. 342–60: The California Dryden, x. 259.
[12] Ben Jonson, *Works*, ed. C. H. Herford and Percy and Evelyn Simpson, 11 vols.
(Oxford: Clarendon Press, 1925–52), viii. 625.
[13] The California Dryden, ix. 352–69, *passim*.

Dryden are those scenes in which the witty couples engage in 'repartie', the combats of thrust and parry, innuendo and counter-implication, that define the young protagonists as suited to each other through intelligence, rank, and sexual appetite. Shadwell would complain that such couples as Wildblood and Jacinta in *An Evening's Love*, or Frederick and Lucretia in *The Assignation*, or Palamede and Doralice in *Marriage à la Mode* are entirely interchangeable, mouthpieces for the author's wit, prompted by no internal imperatives of character.

Shadwell's response to a kind of comedy in which speech and action are not integrally related is to develop 'humours' characters, where that connection is as tight and predictable as possible. Stanford and Emilia are the 'sullen lovers' of Shadwell's play. Recalling Jonson's Morose (*The Silent Woman*), who cannot abide noise, and his Lovel (*The New Inn*), who can take no pleasure in the present age, this couple are attracted to each other not by the sexual friction of their discourse but by discovery of their symmetrical aberrations. In the characters of the fustian poet Ninny, the squeaking musician Woodcock, and the self-appointed polymath Sir Positive At-All, Shadwell is able to satirize quite identifiably the contemporary figure of the virtuoso, a theme to which he returns in his play *The Virtuoso*. There are moments in *The Sullen Lovers* superficially similar to the passage of action from *An Evening's Love* examined above, but they are more genuinely Jonsonian moments. In Act IV scene i Woodcock and Ninny have been torturing Emilia with simultaneously rendered examples of their art, when Sir Positive enters and in short succession proclaims himself to be master of languages, ship-building, painting, athletics, mathematics, music, metaphysics, gambling, legerdemain, diplomacy, rope-dancing (perhaps a not altogether innocent juxtaposition, anticipating the rope-dancing in Swift's Lilliput and the connection established between moral philosophy and gymnastics in Stoppard's *Jumpers*) . . . and so on, until Caroline and Lovel, by dint of speaking very quickly one after the other, provoke the following orgy of self-adulation in Sir Positive:

CAR. ——Now *Lovel* to your post.
LOV. Navigation.
SIR POS. Navigation d'ye talk of?
CAR. Geography.

LOV. Physick.
CAR. Divinity.
LOV. Surgery.

SIR PAS. Geography d'ye talk of?

LOV. Astronomy.

SIR POS. Astronomy, d'ye talk of?

CAR. Palmistry.

CAR. Arithmetick.

LOV. Logick.

CAR. Cookery.

LOV. Magick.

SIR POS. Hold, hold, hold, hold! Navigation, Geography, Astronomy, Palmistry, Physick, Divinity, Surgery, Arithmetick, Logick, Cookery and Magick: I'le speak to every one of these in their order; if I don't understand e'm every one in perfection, nay, if I don't Fence, Dance, Ride, Sing, Fight a Duel, speak *French*, Command an Army, play on the Violin, Bag-pipe, Organ, Harp, Hoboy, Sackbut, and double Curtal, speak Spanish, Italian, Greek, Hebrew, Dutch, Welch and Irish, Dance a Jigg, throw the Barr, Swear, Drink, Swagger, Whore, Quarrel, Cuffe, break Windowes, manage Affairs of State, Hunt, Hawke, Shoot, Angle, play at Catte, Stool-ball, Scotch-hope and Trap-ball, Preach, Dispute, make Speeches —— [*Coughs*]

Prethee, get me a glass of small beere, *Roger.*

STANF. Hell and Furies!

EMIL. Oh, oh——

SIR POS. Nay, hold, I have not told you halfe; if I don't do all these, and fifty times more, I am the greatest Owle, Pimp, Monkey, Jack-a-napes, Baboon, Rascal, Oafe, Ignoramus, Logger-head, Cur-dog, Block-head, Buffoone, Jack-pudden, Tony, or what you will; spit upon me, kick me, cuff me, lugg me by the eares, pull me by the Nose, tread upon me, and despise me more than the World now values me.[14]

There is a physicality about Shadwell's comedy, evident here in the turning of Sir Positive into a demented automaton, a crazed pointer revolving madly round a dial, that is absent from Dryden and that Dryden would finally have condemned as 'low'. Shadwell is always looking for the stage-picture that will transform a character into the graphic emblem of his humour.[15] It is Shadwell, rather

[14] Shadwell, *Complete Works*, i. 74.

[15] A few examples might help to elucidate this point. When we are first introduced to Sir Nicholas Gimcrack, the title figure of *The Virtuoso* (1676), the '*scene opens and discovers* Sir Nicholas *learning to swim upon a table*': or the marvellous stage direction that opens *Bury Fair* (1689): 'Trim stands jetting out his bum, and bowing all the while.' Throughout his career Shadwell exploited the possibilities of claustrophobic staging pioneered by Jonson in plays like *The Alchemist* and *The Silent Woman*, enjoying nothing more than to bring together in the same confined space characters who are rivals and antipathetic to one another. Ninny and Woodcock in *The Sullen Lovers* are lured to the same room in an inn, both under the impression that Emilia is to be there. In *The Humorists* (1671), Crazy and Drybob have both been told by the maid Bridget to climb into a window that they understand to be Theodosia's, there to be discovered and beaten by Raymond and Brisk. This device is taken to unprecedented lengths in *The Virtuoso* when Sir Formal Trifle and Sir Samuel Hearty, dressed in drag, find themselves sharing the same pitch-dark vault.

than Dryden, who genuinely enjoys the juxtaposition of bizarre idiolects, the construction of a linguistic tower of Babel so familiar in Jonson. Dryden will certainly entertain an individual linguistic humour like the absurdly Frenchified Amalthea in *Marriage à la Mode*, but as a one-off portrait of vanity and affectation, not as a sign that irresponsible language has turned the world upside-down. Shadwell's coarse, frequently grotesque, physicality—Snarl being beaten by Mrs Figgup in *The Virtuoso*, Crazy groaning in pain from his pox while being arrested by the bailiffs in *The Humorists*, the cudgelling of La Roch the barber disguised as a count in *Bury Fair*—is quite unlike anything in Dryden's comedy, but very common in Jonson. Violence seeps up through every crack in Shadwell, whereas in Dryden it is controlled by codes of aristocratic honour. It is possible to read *The Virtuoso* as a play written in conscious allusion to *Marriage à la Mode*, since it echoes the basic situations in the subplot of the earlier play, and if that exercise is undertaken, it becomes apparent that Dryden's comedy, at best, was a comedy of ideas to which Shadwell's never aspired. Of *Marriage à la Mode*, it makes sense to ask what are Dryden's underlying concerns, a question that is likely to elicit only disappointing answers in the case of Shadwell, whose comic art is one of surfaces.

III

Some of the tension to be detected in Dryden's critical writings of this period, then, derives from the fact that he was developing *non*-Jonsonian forms of comedy while still being obliged to own Jonson as a model. Such was the power of Jonson's reputation that Edward Howard, in his play *The Women's Conquest* (1671), went to the length of bringing Jonson's ghost on-stage to protest about the low Frenchified farces that have displaced the native strain of comedy:

> Did I instruct you (well ne're half an Age)
> To understand the Grandeur of the Stage,
> With the exactest Rules of Comedy,
> Yet now y'are pleased with Wits low frippery,
> Admitting Farce, the trifling mode of France,
> T'infect you with fantastick ignorance,

> Forgetting 'twas your glory to behold,
> Plays wisely form'd such as I made of old . . .[16]

In Rochester's poem *An Allusion to Horace*, Dryden was blamed for failing to follow Jonson's instruction and to respect the eminences of a bygone age:

> But does not Dryden find ev'n Johnson dull?
> Fletcher, and Beaumont, uncorrect and full
> Of Lewd lines as he calls em? Shakespeares Stile
> Stiffe, and Affected?
>
> (lines 81–4)

And yet the opposite charge, that he followed the example of his literary predecessors *far too closely*, is also being preferred. Plagiarism, with its implication that there exists a violable category of literary property, announces itself as an issue at the very outset of *An Allusion*. Where Horace had begun his poem recalling the terms of his earlier critique of Lucilius in Satire I. iv, 'Nempe incomposito dixi pede currere versus | Lucili' ('True, I did say that Lucilius' verses lurched awkwardly along'),[17] Rochester's version registers not just the aesthetic objection to Dryden's 'Rhimes' that they are 'unequal', nor the reception of them as 'dull', but the moral difficulty that they are 'stol'n':

> Well Sir, 'tis granted, I said Dryden's Rhimes,
> Were stol'n, unequal, nay dull many times . . .   (lines 1–2)

The éclat of this opening derives, then, not only from the fact that whereas Lucilius was safely dead, Dryden is very much alive—and this is the most overt attack on him that Rochester had so far made. It also derives from the specific terms in which that attack is constructed. The uneasy suggestion of literary theft continues in lines 5–7:

> But that his Plays, Embroider'd up and downe,
> With Witt, and Learning, justly pleas'd the Towne,
> In the same paper, I as freely owne . . .

The suggestion of 'Embroider'd' is that Dryden embellishes with his wit and learning some base clay that is not his own: and it is

[16] The Hon. Edward Howard, *The Women's Conquest* (London, 1671), Second Prologue, lines 11–18.
[17] The translation is that of Niall Rudd, *The Satires of Horace and Persius* (Harmondsworth: Penguin, 1973; repr. 1976), 67.

right ('justly') that this confection should please those theatrical patrons whose judgement is no better ('the Towne'). Here is a second, more elusive respect in which Jonson's ghost haunts Rochester's poem. In this accusation of lack of originality, and in the development of a binary opposition between the merely popular writer and the writer with long-term ambition, Rochester is recapitulating the terms of previous literary controversy— in particular the so-called *poetomachia* involving Jonson, Dekker, and Marston at the beginning of the century. In reversing some of the polarities of that earlier struggle, however, Rochester's poem sounds a characteristic note of the 1670s. In *Poetaster*, the bricklayer's son Ben Jonson had figured himself as the English Horace, a court dramatist enjoying the protection of his monarch, ennobled by his talent and chosen for his outstanding ability to advise the ruler. Proving his credentials entailed the exposure of smaller fry like Marston and Dekker (the Crispinus and Demetrius Fannius of the play), the former of whom, through a magnificent literalization of the metaphor of satire as an emetic, is forced to vomit up all the outlandish words in his extraordinary thesaurus. Dekker, in his revenge play *Satiromastix*, ridicules Jonson's pretensions to noble patronage, portraying him as a mere literary hack who is first discovered hopelessly attempting to find rhymes for a routine epithalamium to celebrate a gentleman's wedding. What appeared to sting Jonson more than any other palpable hit in *Satiromastix* was the repeated claim that he was extremely slow in composition, and could not, or would not, dash off his productions quickly:

TUC. What wut end? wut hang thy selfe now? has he not writ Finis yet *Iacke*? what will he bee fifteene weekes about this Cockatrices egge too? has he not cackeld yet? not laide yet?

BLUNT. Not yet, hee sweares hee will within this houre.

TUC. His wittes are somewhat hard bound: the Puncke his Muse has sore labour ere the whoore bee deliuered: the poore saffron-cheeke Sunburnt Gipsie wants Phisicke; give the hungrie-face pudding-pye-eater ten Pilles: ten shillings my faire Angelica, they'l make his Muse as yare as a tumbler.[18]

---

[18] Thomas Dekker, *Satiromastix* (1602), ed. Fredson Bowers (Cambridge University Press, 1953), I. ii. 362–70. For an excellent account of the quarrel, see David Riggs, *Ben Jonson: A Life* (Cambridge, Mass.: Harvard University Press, 1989), 72–85.

Should Jonson be inclined to consider himself the kind of writer whose work is the product of much study, prolonged revision, and careful nurture, Dekker here asserts that his is a prostituted muse just like all the others and will yield its offspring with the help of the customary midwife money. So acutely did Jonson feel this accusation—that he was pretentiously trying to raise dramatic writing to an undue dignity—that he specifically rebutted it in the Prologue to *Volpone*:

> And, when his playes come forth, thinke they can flout them,
> With saying, he was a yeere about them.
> To these there needs no lie, but this his creature,
> Which was, two months since, no feature;
> And, though he dares give them five lives to mend it,
> 'Tis knowne, five weekes fully pen'd it:
> From his owne hand, without a co-adiutor,
> Novice, journey-man, or tutor.[19]

As Jonson's career developed, he became less defensive about the degree of creative energy he was prepared to invest in his plays, as their authorized publication in 1616 would suggest.

In Rochester's poem, this gradual shift in the construction of poetic value is apparent. It is seen to lie not in a professional ability to write to order, but in a willingness to ponder carefully every aspect of one's art—implying a rejection of the professional 'time is money' ethos:

> To write what may securely stand the test
> Of being well read over Thrice at least
> Compare each Phrase, examin ev'ry Line,
> Weigh ev'ry word, and ev'ry thought refine;
> Scorne all Applause the Vile Rout can bestow,
> And be content to please those few, who know.

(lines 98–103)

Plagiarism takes its place as another corner-cutting, shoddy technique that the genuinely aspiring author must now outgrow. Interestingly, one charge that is *not* made in *Satiromastix* against Jonson is that of plagiarism, presumably because Dekker saw no particular stigma attaching to dependency on earlier works. Rochester's strictures against it tap a rich vein of guilt that runs just beneath the surface of the culture. For the professional writers

---

[19] Jonson, *Works*, v. 23–4.

of the time, who experienced at first hand, as Rochester did not, the pressures that gave rise to such expedients, his Horatian advice was difficult to take. Shadwell's Preface to *The Sullen Lovers* (1668), for example, acknowledges while minimizing the extent of his debt to Molière, and in nothing-to-lose fashion (since he has as yet no reputation as a dramatist) confesses that it has been hastily put together:

I freely confess my Theft, and am asham'd on't, though I have the example of some that never yet wrote a Play without stealing most of it; And (like Men that lye so long, till they believe themselves) at length, by continual Thieving, reckon their stolne goods their own too: which is so ignoble a thing, that I cannot but believe that he that makes a common practice of stealing other mens Witt, would, if he could, with the same safety steall any thing else . . . Look upon [this play] as it really was, wrote in haste, by a Young Writer, and you will easily pardon it . . . Nor can you expect a very Correct *Play*, under a Years pains at the least, from the Wittiest Man of the Nation; It is so difficult a thing to write well in this kind. Men of quality, that write for their pleasure, will not trouble themselves with exactness in their *Playes*; and those, that write for profit, would find too little incouragement for so much paines as a correct *Play* would require.[20]

Shadwell was able to manage such 'turd i' your teeth' insouciance in his prefaces, and never more so than in the Preface to *Psyche* (1675), where he writes that 'in a thing written in five weeks, as this was, there must needs be many Errors' which must be excused 'since there are so many splendid Objects in the Play'.[21] For Dryden, however, the whole business was far more anguished, and it forced out of him, at times, astonishingly frank and painful confessions, as in the following passage from *A Defence of an Essay of Dramatique Poesie* (1668):

For I confess my chief endeavours are to delight the Age in which I live. If the humour of this, be for low Comedy, small Accidents, and Raillery, I will force my Genius to obey it, though with more reputation I could write in Verse. I know I am not so fitted by Nature to write Comedy: I want that gayety of humour which is required to it. My Conversation is slow and dull, my humour Saturnine and reserv'd: In short, I am none of those who endeavour to break Jests in Company, or make reparties.[22]

[20] Thomas Shadwell, Preface to *The Sullen Lovers*, in *Complete Works*, i. 10, 12.
[21] Shadwell, *Complete Works*, ii. 279.
[22] Dryden, *A Defence of an Essay of Dramatique Poesie* (London, 1668), 7.

Equally direct is Dryden's dismissal of his tragedy capitalizing on the outbreak of war with the Dutch, *Amboyna*, as 'scarcely [worth] a serious perusal, it being contrived and written in a month, the subject barren, the persons low, and the writing not heightened with many labored scenes'.[23] One measure of the extent to which the exigencies of professionalism were bearing upon literary production at this period is furnished by the confession, made by both Dryden and Shadwell (even if not entirely seriously), that they have abandoned rhyme because it represents poor value for money! It takes too long to write, and brings too little in profit. Shadwell writes, in the Prologue to *The Virtuoso* (1676):

> Yet since y'have had Rhime for a relishing Bit,
> To give a better taste to Comick Wit.
> But this requires expence of time and pains,
> Too great, alas, for Poets slender gains.
> For Wit, like *China*, should long buri'd lie,
> Before it ripens to good Comedy;
> A thing we ne'er have seen since *Johnson*'s days,
> And but a few of his were perfect Plays.
> Now Drudges of the Stage must oft appear,
> They must be bound to scribble twice a year.[24]

When, in 1687, Gerard Langbaine published his extraordinary catalogue of all the English plays known to him, he gave his biographical project a polemical edge apparent in its title—*Momus Triumphans; or, The Plagiaries of the English Stage*. Langbaine's Preface was dedicated to exposing the difference between classical and modern ways of using sources. The ancients, as a mark of respect to their forebears, borrowed only what was beautiful in them, and modestly acknowledged their debts. The moderns are thieves, trying to gain credit for invention not their own, and the worst offender is John Dryden, to whom is preached this homily:

I cannot but blame him for taxing others with stealing Characters from him . . . when he himself does the same, almost in all the Plays he writes; and for arraigning his Predecessours for stealing from the *Ancients*, as he does *Johnson*; which tis evident that he himself is guilty of the same. I

---

[23] *Dramatic Works of John Dryden*, ed. George Saintsbury, 8 vols. (Edinburgh: William Paterson, 1882), v. 8.

[24] Thomas Shadwell, Prologue to *The Virtuoso* (1676), lines 5–14; repr. in Richard L. Oden (ed.), *Dryden and Shadwell: The Literary Controversy* (Delmar, NY: Scholars Facsimiles and Reprints, 1977).

would therefore desire our Laureate, that he would follow that good Advice which the modest Professor Mr. *Wheare* gives to the young Academick in his *Antelogium, to shun this, Confidence and Self-love, as the worst of Plagues; and to* consider that *Modesty is it which becomes every Age, and leads all that follow her in the Streight, and right Path to solid Glory.*[25]

Perhaps Langbaine has in mind Dryden's double-edged compliment made to Jonson in *An Essay of Dramatick Poesie* that 'he invades Authours like a Monarch, and what would be theft in other Poets, is onely victory in him'.[26] From these charges of plagiarism and duplicity, Shadwell is explicitly excepted by Langbaine. He borrows very little and never without acknowledgement. For those whose view of these matters is conditioned by *Mac-Fleckno*, this relative positioning of Dryden and Shadwell comes as something of a surprise.

It should be clear that when, in *An Allusion to Horace*, Rochester counterposes Shadwell to Dryden as 'mighty Opposites' and makes this contest the armature of the poem, he is expressing an important insight into the present condition of his culture. *MacFleckno* will accuse Shadwell of plagiarism wittily:

> When did his Muse [Jonson's] from *Fletcher* scenes purloin,
> As thou whole *Eth'ridg* dost transfuse to thine?
> But so transfus'd as Oyl on Waters flow,
> His always floats above, thine sinks below.[27]

And Shadwell's *The Medal of John Bayes* (1682) will make the countercharge bluntly:

> Were from thy Works cull'd out what thou'st purloin'd,
> Even D—fey would excel what's left behind.
> Should all thy borrow'd plumes we from thee tear,
> How truly *Poet Squab* would'st thou appear! . . .
> Thou plunder'st all, t' advance thy mighty Name,
> Look'st big, and triumph'st with thy borrow'd fame.
> But art (while swelling thus thou think'st th'art Chief)
> *A servile Imitator and a Thief.*

---

[25] Gerard Langbaine, *Momus Triumphans; or, The Plagiaries of the English Stage* (1687), ed. David Stuart Rodes, Augustan Reprint 150 (Los Angeles: William Andrews Clark Library, 1971), sig. A3ᵛ (italics reversed).
[26] The California Dryden, xvii. 57.
[27] Lines 183–6; quoted from *The Poems and Fables of John Dryden*, ed. James Kinsley (Oxford University Press, 1958; repr. 1962), 242.

Plagiarism will eventually come to be apprehended as a legal matter in increasingly individualistic and professionalized institutions of literature. Already in the 1670s the aesthetic foundation is being laid for this, as writers argue over the question whether 'invention' is to be given a higher priority than learning in literary production. As Edward Howard puts it in his Preface to *The Women's Conquest*:

It is very observable, since Translating hath been so much practis'd, and taking from Romances and Foreign Plays, the compositions arising from them appear not less disproportion'd and uneven, then if a Painter undertaking to describe a History, should from the drawings of Masters, and Figures in Print . . . take a posture from one, a head from another, a body from a third, and having put them on such legs as he shall make for them, confidently averre he hath performed the noble invention and design that belongs to a Story Painter. (Sig. a2ᵛ)

At this historical juncture there is some unresolved contradiction in the demonstrable degree of mounting anxiety over plagiarism and literary theft, coexisting with the desire to be most clearly indebted to an eminent predecessor. What Langbaine upbraids as intellectual dishonesty is not usually what would now be considered plagiarism: the adaptation of plots from plays and novels written by authors no longer living, and/or in languages other than English. In the absence of a law of copyright, which would define any precise sense in which, to use Chesterfield's expression, wit could be considered 'a kind of Property', this cultural tension could not be diffused. If, then, the reader detects in Rochester's *An Allusion to Horace* some degree of inconsistency—Dryden accused of literary theft in the opening lines but later censured for his upstart refusal to serve the literary gods of Elizabethan and Jacobean England in his critical opinions—it may be that s/he has stumbled across a genuine enough *aporia*. The contradiction here could not admit of resolution from within the institutional boundaries of literature, but required the Copyright Act of 1709 and subsequent clarificatory legislation that established the pre-eminence of originality as a criterion of literary value, to make sense out of it.

In the next chapter, Dryden's fortunes as a writer of epic in the last decade of his lifetime will be the subject of enquiry. In the 1690s Dryden was, less ambiguously than at any previous point in his career, a professional writer. Stripped of political and royal patronage, having lost his pension and his place, he had to write to live in a straightforward manner. Paradoxically, however, it was at this time that he yearned most wistfully to rival the achievement of his eminent Greek, Roman, and European predecessors in composing an epic. I will contend that the time for that was over. The same forces that expanded the literary market-place and professionalized the production of imaginative writing brought about an alteration in taste that rendered epic an unachievable form in English poetry. There were attempts, but they failed. Writers who understood the developing tastes of their times would not write epic, but would translate it, or deploy it in new mock and hybrid forms to comic effect.

4

The Mock-Heroic Moment
in the 1690s

In January 1692 the poet and dramatist John Crowne published
his Anglicized version of Boileau's *Le Lutrin*, under the title
Daeneids. His Dedication of the poem to that ubiquitous patron
and gentleman of letters the Earl of Mulgrave captures a sense of
the split between amateur and professional writers that in the last
chapter we saw distancing Dryden from Rochester. Crowne regrets
that Mulgrave has not been his patron previously because not to
have *his* seal of approval is to be wanting in the world's eyes: 'Your
Fortune, and, most Men believe, Your Inclinations, fixes You on
the top of Ease and Pleasure, therefore you wou'd never have
written one Line, if it had cost you any pains, yet have you
perform'd Masteries, which we who make Poetry the whole Business of our Lives, cou'd never equal.'[1] Within a very short time,
Crowne had published as an offshoot to *Daeneids* a love-episode
between one of the choristers of Notre-Dame and a society lady.
Basing itself on the Dido and Aeneas episode in Virgil's *Aeneid*, it
has a claim to importance as the first proper mock-heroic poem in
English: *The History of the Famous and Passionate Love, between
a Fair Noble Parisian Lady and a Beautiful Young Singing-Man*
(1692).

This chapter explores the epic and mock-epic writing of the
1690s from the perspective of the emergent professionalization of
writing. Throughout the later seventeenth century, and into the
eighteenth, there is a growing imperative to mediate classical texts
to English readers through translation and imitation. This phenomenon represents an awareness on the part of market-conscious

[1] John Crowne, *Daeneids; or, The Noble Labours of the Great Dean of Notre-
Dame in Paris, for the Erecting in his Quire a Throne for his Glory, and the Eclipsing
the Pride of an Imperious, Usurping Chanter. An Heroique POEM in Four Canto's,
Containing a True History, and shews the Folly, Foppery, Luxury, Laziness, Pride,
Ambition and Contention of the Romish Clergy* (London, 1692), fo. 1ʳ⁻ᵛ.

writers that new readerships are being constituted of individuals
who do not understand the classical languages in the original
or who do not have the time to spend in making them out. Such
readers want to enjoy the narrative pleasures afforded by wonder-
ful stories. Yet in the process of making epic stories available,
writers like Dryden and Pope also made perceptible the distance
between the value systems governing these earlier, martial cultures
and the *politesse* demanded by current taste. Epic and mytho-
logical tales were opened up to humour as a means of bridging the
credibility gap created by changing criteria of plausibility. Epic in
translation was always already (as they say) infected with an
instability that threatened to turn it into self-parody. The achievement of major mock-epics such as Garth's *The Dispensary* and
Pope's *The Rape of the Lock* was to harness that inherent instability and to turn it into a distinctive, precariously balanced form.

I

It has been an article of faith in definitions of the mock-heroic
that, whatever the genre is doing, it is *not* mocking the heroic.
Ulrich Broich's study *The Eighteenth-Century Mock-Heroic
Poem* gives this *aperçu* a standard formulation: 'Another feature
that our examples have in common is the fact that the model—
whether Horace or the classical epic—is never mocked. Even if
the style and intention of the imitation depart from the panegyric
or the heroic, in order to use irony or comedy to fulfil the parodic
intention, the poetic quality of the model is not impugned.'[2] This
is a line that Broich discovers he cannot hold. A few pages later, he
gives a much more adequate and flexible account of the position at
the latter end of the seventeenth century. There is an ambivalence
towards antiquity and towards the contemporary world that results
in a veneration for the epic at the same time as there is a growing
conviction that the values epic represents have disappeared
beyond recall. Therefore the mock-heroic 'not only deliberately
made fun of the contemporary classical-style epic as well as the
"rules" laid down by pedantic neo-classical commentators, but it
also—often quite unconsciously—set the classical epic itself in a

---

[2] Ulrich Broich, *The Eighteenth-Century Mock-Heroic Poem*, trans. David Henry
Wilson (Cambridge University Press, 1990; original German version 1968), 58–9.

comic light . . . At one and the same time the mock-heroic poem took the epic up and put it down' (pp. 66–7). In what follows, I want to elaborate on this very promising starting-point, offering an account of the complicated mechanism through which the English mock-heroic emerged and became the single most characteristic and individual literary form of the neoclassical era. I will argue that the mock-heroic form is an important stage of development in, and manifestation of, a broad tendency in post-Restoration writing towards the 'novelization' of all forms of imaginative writing, one product of which is the modern novel itself. To the extent that this has been overlooked, it is the result of a common-sense tendency to confine the investigation of the 'rise of the novel' to prose forms.

In an essay entitled 'Epic and Novel: Towards a Methodology for the Study of the Novel', the first of the four essays published in English as *The Dialogic Imagination*, Mikhail Bakhtin offers an account of the nature and development of the novel in terms of a comparison with epic.[3] Epic and the novel are for Bakhtin at opposite ends of the mimetic spectrum. Where epic is monologic and monoglossic, dominated by a single authoritative voice, the novel is dialogic and polyglossic, representing an orchestra of diverse discourses and giving to no one of these any position of authority over any other. Epic represents an absolute closure and impersonality: its world is untouchable, located in an unchangeable past that is called to memory but that we have no genuine capacity to inhabit. Whereas epic is 'structured in the zone of the distanced image, a zone outside any possible contact with the present in all its openendedness . . . the novel . . . is associated with the eternally living elements of unofficial language and unofficial thought (holiday forms, familiar speech, profanation)' (pp. 18–20). The roots of the novel are folkloric and all genres that permit laughter have a contribution to make to its development. Epic, therefore, has none because epic takes itself so seriously that 'it is precisely laughter that destroys the epic, and in general destroys any distance' (p. 23). The 'plane of laughter' allows us to walk disrespectfully around objects, perceiving them in undignified postures and from unorthodox vantage-points.

[3] Mikhail Bakhtin, *The Dialogic Imagination: Four Essays*, ed. Michael Holquist, trans. Caryl Emerson and Michael Holquist (Austin: University of Texas Press, 1981).

It is the novelist's privilege to be in a contemporaneous, non-hierarchical relationship to the material reality s/he represents. On characterization, Bakhtin argues that the epic hero is 'complete' but is 'hopelessly ready-made . . . he is, furthermore, completely externalized. There is not the slightest gap between his authentic essence and its external manifestation. All his potential, all his possibilities are realized utterly in his external social position' (p. 34).

Commentators on Bakhtin have made the point that his thinking is too wedded to binarisms: monologic–dialogic, epic–novel, poetry–prose, official–carnivalesque, and so on.[4] Some have been concerned about the effect on the study of poetry of all the attractions of dialogism being attributed to the novel, and would wish to argue that at least relative degrees of it are present in poetic forms.[5] For the student of later seventeenth-century imaginative writing, however, Bakhtin's insights are particularly rich because this was the crucible period in the emergence of the modern novel. At this time the transferral of the protagonist from the distanced realm of epic to the zone of contact with the inconclusive, open-ended dimension of the present was occurring in several literary forms. Bakhtin's theory of the gradual 'novelization' of literary genres suggests that discoverable in the writing of the later seventeenth century should be a movement towards the domestic, the contemporaneous, towards a greater degree of what one is thrown back upon terming 'realism'. Drama, for example, should be, and manifestly is, in a transitional phase of its development. Tragedy and comedy appear to exist at an immense distance from one another at this time, and yet there are pressures operating upon both genres to reduce the gap. There was the contemporary habit of reading tragedy as referring allegorically to affairs of state, which offered one point of entry into the geographical and historical remoteness of the milieu. This tendency to discern present-day relevance in tragedy was greatly assisted by the abandonment of rhyming couplet as its principal medium. This was a crucial move in the 'novelization' of tragedy because rhyme was the semiotic device through which the 'epic' tragedy sealed itself

[4] David Lodge, 'After Bakhtin', in id., *After Bakhtin: Essays on Fiction and Criticism* (London: Routledge, 1990), 87–99, esp. 89–90.
[5] See George Myerson, *The Argumentative Imagination: Wordsworth, Dryden, Religious Dialogues* (Manchester University Press, 1992).

in. There is in late-century tragedy an emotional expressiveness in characters like Dorax in Dryden's *Don Sebastian* and Osmyn in Congreve's *The Mourning Bride*, characters whose excessive feeling discloses more to an audience than is in their own self-knowledge. This, for Bakhtin, is one of the constitutive distinctions between epic and novelistic characterization. Characters are not entirely expressed by the plots that contain them. They can, as Dorax does in *Don Sebastian*, enter confessional, vulnerable modes that give intimations of a deeper psychology and are on the way to the forms of self-display that are recognizably novelistic. From the direction of comic theory and practice, there is a reciprocal move towards a less differentiated dramatic form that results from a readjustment of the relationship between punitive and sympathetic elements in the construction of comic characterization. This is under negotiation, for example, in the correspondence between John Dennis and William Congreve in the mid-1690s:

Is any thing more common, than to have a pretended Comedy, stuff'd with such Grotesques, Figures, and Farce Fools? Things, that either are not in Nature, or if they are, are Monsters, and Births of Mischance; and consequently as such, should be stifled, and huddled out of the way, like *Sooterkins*; that Mankind may not be shock'd with an appearing Possibility of the Degeneration of a God-like *Species*. For my part, I am as willing to Laugh, as any body, and as easily diverted with an Object truly ridiculous: but at the same time, I can never care for seeing things, that force me to entertain low thoughts of my Nature.[6]

Although implacably hostile to Jeremy Collier and his former-day moral majority who wanted to soften and sentimentalize comic representation from a standpoint fundamentally hostile to theatre, Dennis and Congreve were arriving at a similar destination from the inside.[7] In practice, comedy in the 1690s moves towards the integration of Fletcherian and Jonsonian elements and, certainly in plays like Southerne's *The Wives' Excuse* and Congreve's *The Way of the World*, arrives at resolutions that generations of readers and spectators have perceived to be more adequate to the

[6] William Congreve to John Dennis, 10 July 1695, in *William Congreve: Letters and Documents*, ed. John C. Hodges (London: Macmillan, 1964), 178.

[7] This point emerges from Brian Corman's study *Genre and Generic Change in English Comedy, 1660–1710* (University of Toronto Press, 1993), ch. 4 and pp. 137–8. Dennis's rejection of Collier is made abundantly clear in the excoriating satirical attack made upon him in *The Usefulness of the Stage, etc.* (1698).

complexity of life as it is actually lived, by breaking the strict boundaries of established convention.

Congreve is again a significant figure in the theorizing, if not so much in the practice, of narrative prose that also manifests a move towards contemporaneity at this time. In the Preface to *Incognita* (1692), he couches a distinction between romance and the novel in terms of familiarity and plausibility that is again evidence of a Bakhtinian 'novelization' process at work:

Romances are generally composed of the Constant Loves and invincible Courages of Hero's, Heroins, Kings and Queens, Mortals of the first Rank, and so forth; where lofty Language, miraculous Contingencies and impossible Performances, elevate and surprize the Reader into a giddy Delight, which leaves him flat upon the Ground whenever he gives of, and vexes him to think how he has suffer'd himself to be pleased and transported, concern'd and afflicted at the several Passages which he has Read, *viz.* these Knights Success to their Damosels Misfortunes, and such like, when he is forced to be very well convinced that 'tis all a lye. Novels are of a more familiar nature; Come near us, and represent to us Intrigues in practice, delight us with Accidents and odd Events, but not such as are wholly unusual or unpresidented, such which not being so distant from our Belief bring also the pleasure nearer us. Romances give more of Wonder, Novels more Delight.[8]

In terms of this distinction, the story that Congreve goes on to narrate is a spoof romance, a carnivalized form that would provide one of the novel's generic roots. A gentle irony controls the narrative throughout, a mannered distortion of romance motifs that makes everywhere for anti-romantic bathos. The Preface is actually more relevant to the bold prose experiments being undertaken at the time by Aphra Behn than it is to Congreve himself. Not only do Behn's prose narratives like *Oroonoko* (1688) and *The Fair Jilt* (1688) claim to be based on factual sources and build in metafictional references that reach beyond the boundaries of the framing fictions: in Behn's writing, romance motifs and assumptions are struggling against elements that appear to belong to another order of authenticity altogether. *The Fair Jilt*, for example, puts its protagonist, Prince Henrick, into a typically absolute love-versus-honour dilemma when his elder brother marries his inamorata through deception: but since the princess's

[8] William Congreve, Preface to the Reader of *Incognita*, in *Letters and Documents*, 158–9.

'honour could never permit her to ease any part of his flame; nor was he so vicious, to entertain a thought that should stain her virtue', Henrick has had to flee and become a friar.[9] He attracts the amatory attention of Miranda, the Fair Jilt, whose erotic fantasies about the Confessional are detailed with surprising frankness. Her advances rejected by Henrick, she uses the Confessional to compromise him and falsely charge him with rape, in a scene that, at the same time as it addresses a surprisingly realistic predicament—what we would now term sexual harassment—employs a highly stylized dialogue. At various points both in *Oroonoko* and *The Fair Jilt*, the reader senses that the standard didactic purpose of fiction is being overwhelmed altogether by a loving attention to grisly realistic detail. *The Fair Jilt* is trying to tell the story of Prince Tarquin, whose infatuation with Miranda is so total that he is prepared to go to any lengths of criminality to appease her. As the story ends, its attempt to articulate this moral is entirely drowned out by a description of a botched execution so mordantly exact that it becomes a source of interest entirely in and of itself. *Oroonoko* is similarly crammed with such moments, many of them also revolving around sado-masochistic episodes of bodily dismemberment.

II

From the epic side of the equation just as surely as from the novelistic, there is evidence of a growing ambivalence of response to the classical world and the belief systems that supported it. In one way of thinking about the subject, as Claude Rawson has observed, there never has been a true English epic. Milton retreated from the principal subject-matter of the epic: 'Warrs, hitherto the onely Argument | Heroic deem'd' (*Paradise Lost* IX. 28–9). In Rawson's words:

Such language, within the poem, puts Milton into an adversary relation with the epic tradition which is in some ways ambiguous as the relation of mock-heroic to the epic was ambiguous. It retains Milton's reverence for the classical models, whose form and structure and whose elevation of

---

[9] Aphra Behn, *Oroonoko, The Rover and Other Works*, ed. Janet Todd (Harmondsworth: Penguin, 1992), 39.

style and perspective he 'imitated', while conveying that neither he nor his age was in tune with their ethos.[10]

In the drama and the prose of post-Restoration England, as I have suggested above, there is a tendency for forms to emerge that break down boundaries between monologic discourses deriving from epic and dialogic, polyglossic, carnivalesque-comic discourses. Typically, the forms of the 1690s are mixed: tragicomic, sentimentalized drama and fiction that admits realistic elements into romance paradigms. That this is the leading tendency of the period is signalled in the reluctance of tragic protagonists ever to *die*. Sebastian in Dryden's *Don Sebastian* is persuaded not to commit suicide, while at the end of *The Mourning Bride*, Almeria is weeping beside the decapitated trunk of what she believes is her lover Alphonso, who then enters in time to prevent her poisoning herself. Standards of plausibility and authenticity demanded by readers are changing: and this 'plausibility crisis', as I shall term it, also affects the way the classical world is represented in original writing and in the translation of epic. The developing tastes and reading habits that the new forms had to satisfy made for 'carnivalized' representations of the classical world in burlesque and even pornographic mutations. One or two examples might serve as an *hors d'œuvre* to the discussion below. In Dryden's translation of Virgil's *Aeneid*, there is a terrifying description of the Cyclops given by Achaemonides in book 3, lines 808–56. Polyphemus is a bloodthirsty man-eater, whose image traumatizes the Greek narrator:

> Bellowing his Voice, and horrid in his Hue:
> Ye Gods, remove this Plague from Mortal View!
> The Joints of slaughter'd Wretches are his Food:
> And for his Wine he quaffs the streaming Blood.
> These Eyes beheld, when with his spacious Hand
> He seiz'd two Captives of our *Grecian* Band;
> Stretch'd on his Back, he dash'd against the Stones
> Their broken Bodies, and their crackling Bones:
> With spouting Blood the Purple Pavement swims,
> While the dire Glutton grinds the trembling Limbs.[11]

[10] Claude Rawson, 'Pope's *Waste Land*: Reflections on Mock-Heroic', in id., *Order from Confusion Sprung: Studies in Eighteenth-Century Literature from Swift to Cowper* (London: Allen & Unwin, 1985), 204.
[11] 3. 814–23; quoted from the California Dryden, v. 444.

Just a few months earlier, in November 1696, the audience for Motteux's masque *The Loves of Mars and Venus* could see Virgil's fearsome cyclops galumphing around the stage in a dance that has them making thunderbolts for Jove which they aim 'At a *Ninny* who finds a Gallant with his Wife, | Then begs both their Pardons for making a Strife'. The 'ninny' is Vulcan, rendered a complaisant cuckold by Venus' deceptive infidelity with Mars. Already in 1694, Motteux had presented the Ovidian story of the *Rape of Europa* in the form of a masque that interrupts its principal story-line of Jupiter transforming into a bull to ravish Europa with a bawdy rustic interlude in which Coridon, represented by the comic actor Doggett, sets upon his mistress:

> From thence as I went
> To see th'Moniment,
> I met with a Girl in *Cheapside* 'a,
> That for half a Crown
> Pluck'd up her silk Gown,
> And show'd me how far she cou'd stride 'a.

Motteux's version of *Acis and Galatea* (1701) similarly punctuates its pathetic story of the murder of Acis by the cyclops Polyphemus with a country wedding in which the husband exults: 'I have her, I have her. Heigh, I'm a made man: I'll marry her now; and we'll jigg it anon.'[12] By the beginning of the new century, then, one form of consumption of the classics was in the semi-operatic masque, a transitional form between English and Italian opera that licensed a bawdy visual confection. Some years later, the loves of Mars and Venus were to become the basis for the 'story-board' of the first English pantomime, John Weaver's *The Loves of Mars and Venus* (1717); and in the following year, the representation of Polyphemus in Handel and Gay's entertainment *Acis & Galatea* (1718) has the Cyclops singing the intimidating *recitativo accompagnato* 'I rage, I melt, I burn' followed by the aria 'O ruddier than the cherry', a leaping, irregular melody that suggests considerable uncertainty in the characterization.[13] One final example of the

---

[12] Peter Motteux and John Eccles, *Rape of Europa by Jupiter* and *Acis and Galatea*, ed. Lucyle Hook, Augustan Reprint Society, 208 (Los Angeles, 1981).
[13] See Robert King's note to the 1989 Hyperion recording (CDA6636/2): 'Of the four characters, it is the monster Polyphemus who is the most complex, for we are left unsure whether to take him seriously or not' (p. 5).

strange disjunction between the epic world and that of contemporary reality that seemed to be occurring in the public consciousness by the beginning of the eighteenth century is furnished by the epilogue to Ambrose Philips's immensely popular play *The Distrest Mother*, premièred at Drury Lane on 17 March 1712. Having played the dignified tragic role of Hector's widow Andromache, a perfectly maternal being prepared to make any sacrifice to protect the life of her son Astyanax, including marrying a man she does not love, the actress Anne Oldfield delivers an epilogue that comically deflates the entire idea of any woman acting in so absolute a fashion. The Homeric epic is exposed to the cynical sensibilities of a contemporary woman about town:

> But why you'll say was all this Grief exprest
> For a first Husband, laid long since at Rest?
> Why so much Coldness to my kind Protector?
> —Ah Ladies! Had you known the good Man *Hector*!
> *Homer* will tell you (or I'm misinform'd)
> That when enrag'd the *Grecian* Camp he Storm'd,
> To break the ten-fold Barriers of the Gate
> He threw a Stone of such prodigious Weight
> As no two Men could lift: not even of those
> Who in that Age of thund'ring Mortals rose:
> —It would have sprain'd a Dozen modern Beaux.[14]

In theory, the distance between the epic and the risible was still infinite. Dryden's view of the necessary separation of epic from the more realistic genre of comedy is remarkably close to Bakhtin's account of the relationship between epic and the novel. In 1695 Dryden was taking a short break from the main business of his Virgil translation. He was diverted into translating Du Fresnoy's *De Arte Graphica*, for which he wrote a *Preface of the Translator, with a Parallel of Poetry and Painting*. In this purist work of theory, Dryden argued for a strict separation between those genres in poetry and painting whose business is to perfect nature—epic and history painting—and those that must incorporate deficiencies—comedy–tragedy and portraits. Consequently, epic and farce are as far apart on the literary spectrum as it is possible to be because while epic imitates nature at its grandest, farce renders

---

[14] Text taken from Danchin (ed.), *The Prologues and Epilogues of the Eighteenth Century*, pt. 1, vol. ii, pp. 504–5. Danchin records the controversy to which this irreverent epilogue gave rise, and its popularity; see vol. i, p. xxviii.

nature grotesque. They are entirely sealed off from one another, epic enshrining the noblest, most perfectly rational forms of human pleasure where farce offers a bestial, debased form of merely popular entertainment. Dryden's animus against trivial laughter is frighteningly intense:

Farce-scribblers make use of the same noble invention to entertain citizens, country-gentlemen, and Covent Garden fops. If they are merry, all goes well on the poet's side. The better sort go thither too, but in despair of sense and the just images of nature, which are the adequate pleasures of the mind. But the author can give the stage no better than what was given him by nature; and the actors must represent such things as they are capable to perform, and by which both they and the scribbler may get their living. After all, 'tis a good thing to laugh at any rate, and if a straw can tickle a man, 'tis an instrument of happiness.[15]

Yet in the practice of translating Virgil's *Aeneid* into English, Dryden would discover, perhaps not that the epic world was laughable or wholly implausible, but that it incorporated more farcical potential than the theoretical blueprints would sanction. Writing to John Dennis in 1694, Dryden expresses his awareness that the composer of a modern epic faces a formidable barrage of difficulties, none greater than the problem of creating plausible 'machines' in a Christian context. As the publication of Blackmore's *Prince Arthur* comes ever closer, Dryden anticipates that this is likely to be a flop; and as the librettist of a heroic Arthurian opera himself, he is at some pains to distance himself from it:

If I undertake the translation of Virgil, the little which I can perform will shew at least that no man is fit to write after him in a barbarous modern tongue. Neither will his machines be of any service to a Christian poet. We see how ineffectually they have been tried by Tasso and by Ariosto. 'Tis using them too dully if we only make devils of his gods: as if, for example, I would raise a storm and make use of Aeolus, with this only difference of calling him Prince of the Air. What invention of mine would there be in this; or who would not see Virgil through me; only the same trick played over again by a bungling juggler? Boileau has well observed that it is an easy matter in a Christian poem for God to bring the Devil to reason. I think I have given a better hint for new machines in my preface to Juvenal, where I have particularly recommended two subjects, one of

[15] John Dryden, *A Parallel of Poetry and Painting* (1695), in *Of Dramatic Poesy and Other Critical Essays*, ed. George Watson, 2 vols. (London: Dent, 1962; repr. 1968), ii. 190.

King Arthur's conquest of the Saxons, and the other of the Black Prince in his conquest of Spain. But the guardian angels of Monarchies and Kingdoms are not to be touched by every hand. A man must be deeply conversant in the Platonic philosophy to deal with them: and therefore I may reasonably expect that no poet of our age will presume to handle those machines for fear of discovering his own ignorance; or if he should, he might perhaps be ingrateful enough not to own me for his benefactor.[16]

That representations of the classical world of gods, demi-gods, and heroes in English writing, in particular the world of the Homeric and Virgilian epic, were often coloured by scepticism is apparent to anyone who has read *Troilus and Cressida: [cunnus] teterrima belli causa*, as Swift would put it in *A Tale of a Tub*, ribaldly misquoting Horace on Helen of Troy in Satire I. iii. In a similar vein the Dido and Aeneas episode in the *Aeneid*, book 4 has a farcical potential that is capable of compromising the hero's dignity—epic high seriousness curdled by the infusion of an unedifying romantic tiff and the billingsgate curse of a woman scorned. The episode raises the issue of extra-marital sex, as well as the ethics of Aeneas' abandoning Dido. Was that not the cowardly act of a sexually gratified male who does not wish to accept the consequences of his actions? Or is Dido a nymphomaniac whose excessive carnal demands threaten to blunt the purpose of a man of destiny? Despite its tragic outcome, this story has a potential for subversive comedy, even farce, that previous English versions had sometimes registered. Marlowe's play *The Tragedy of Dido, Queen of Carthage*, for example, frequently provides the audience with amusement at Dido's expense, as in the ludicrous punning apostrophe she makes to Aeneas' tackle, oars, and sails, which she has confiscated in order to confine him to Carthage:

> Is this the wood that grew in Carthage plains,
> And would be toiling in the watery billows,
> To rob their mistress of her Trojan guest?
> O cursed tree, hadst thou but wit or sense,
> To measure how I prize Aeneas' love,
> Thou wouldst have leapt from out the sailors' hands,
> And told me that Aeneas meant to go!
> And yet I blame thee not; thou art but wood.[17]

---

[16] Dryden, *A Parallel Betwixt Painting and Poetry*, ii. 178.
[17] IV. iv. 136–43: Christopher Marlowe, *The Complete Plays*, ed. J. B. Steane (Harmondsworth: Penguin, 1969), 86.

In *The Tempest,* Gonzalo's quaint reference to Dido as 'widow Dido' provides Sebastian and Antonio with an opportunity to exercise their loutish badinage:

ANTONIO. Widow! A pox o' that! How came that widow in? widow Dido!
SEBASTIAN. What if he had said 'widower Aeneas' too?[18]

at the same time as it reminds the audience of Dido's position as the wife of the deceased Sichaeus and underscores the lasciviousness of her sexual encounter with Aeneas in a cave. As Stephen Orgel, editor of the recent Oxford Shakespeare edition of *The Tempest* explains, two traditions of representing Dido come down from antiquity: one a heroic and moral tradition in which she was an exemplary ruler famed for chastity and uxorial devotion; and the other, introduced by Virgil, in which she is a fallen woman who sins with the wanton Aeneas.[19] In 1665 Charles Cotton's English octosyllabic version of Scarron's *Virgile Travestie* made the smutty potential of the episode explicit, transforming all motives into the lowest venereal denominator, making deities speak like fishwives. Aeneas' rival Iarbas' prayer to Jupiter will give a typical flavour:

> A wand'ring Woman that had scarce
> A Rag to hang upon her——
> When she came hither first and wou'd
> Have then been glad to —— for Food.
> Is now forsooth, so proud (what else!)
> And stands so on her Pantables,
> That she has said me nay most slightly,
> And (on the very nonce to spite me)
> Has marry'd a spruce Youth they say,
> (Whom some ill Wind blew that away)
> One Squire *Aeneas*, a great Kelf,
> Some wandring Hangman like her self:
> And now this Swabber, by the Maskins,
> Thunders up *Dido*'s Gally-Gaskins.[20]

---

[18] II. i. 74–7: William Shakespeare, *The Tempest,* ed. Frank Kermode (London: Methuen, 1954; repr. 1980), 46–7.

[19] William Shakespeare, *The Tempest,* ed. Stephen Orgel (Oxford University Press, 1987; repr. 1994), 40–3.

[20] Charles Cotton, *Scarronides; or, Virgile Travestie: A Mock-Poem on the First and Fourth Books of Virgil's Aenaeis in English Burlesque* (1670; 10th edn. 1715), 76.

Dido commits suicide, in Cotton's version, by hanging herself from the noose she has strung to lynch Aeneas in effigy, and the author's experience of public executions is brought to bear on her undignified end, in which she parodies a Newgate felon's speech, calls out for the comforts of Hopkins's hymnody, and loses control of her bowels as she concludes 'the dismal Dance'. Even in the version of the story most recently to hand, Nahum Tate and Henry Purcell's operatic collaboration staged in 1689 (the year before Purcell's collaboration with Dryden over the music for *Amphitryon*), in which Dido is given a lament celebrated for its moving dignity and tragic pathos, dignity is compromised by those scenes of 'freakish glee', as the musicologist Curtis Price calls them, amongst the Sorceress and her enchantresses. Deriving from Tate's play *Brutus of Alba; or, The Enchanted Lovers* (1678), which the author had originally intended to be a direct dramatization of the *Aeneid*, book 4, but had been persuaded to disguise behind the Brutus legend, this libretto explains the indecency of the lovers' sexual encounter in a cave as the result of demonic enchantment. Finally, the purpose of these scenes seems to be to provide a black parody of court sentiment and ritual.[21] Given this pedigree of treatment, it is unsurprising that when pantomime came into vogue on the English stage in the 1720s, writers should want to get their hands on the Dido and Aeneas story; and that the veteran professional Thomas D'Urfey should actually do so. His pantomime *The English Stage Italianiz'd in a New Dramatic Entertainment, called Dido and Aeneas; or, Harlequin, a Butler, a Pimp, a Minister of State, Generalissimo, and Lord High Admiral; dead and alive again, and at last crown'd King of* Carthage *by* Dido (1727) is introduced to the reader by a paean to the health-giving qualities of his shameless brand of commercialism:

How much will it add to the Interest and Glory of *Great Britain*, if we can bring our Tragedy and Comedy to the same Perfection! I know of no better a Method, than at once to abolish our old-fashion'd Stuff, and for ever to banish from the Stage, *Shakespear, Johnson, Dryden, Otway, Wycherly, Congreve, Rowe, Addison*, and all those formal Fellows, who with their ponderous *Sentiments*, thicken the Blood of their Auditors: Whereas these light airy Performances, quicken the Circulation, give new

---

[21] Curtis Price, *Henry Purcell and the London Stage* (Cambridge University Press, 1984), 251. Price accepts Roger Savage's view of the function of the unsettling scenes at the beginning of Act II.

Life, and as it were, quite another manner of Air to the whole human Microcosm . . . Let us judge, therefore, of these *Italian* Comedies and Comedians, not by the Report of illiterate and peevish Criticks, but by their full Houses.[22]

A typical scene (II. xii) does not suggest that anything happened on stage much to the 'interest and glory of *Great Britain*': '*Colombine's* Apartment. *Colombine* asleep. Enter *Harlequin*, followed by *Aeneas* with a dark Lanthorn; they strive which shall most express their Love in dumb Shew: *Aeneas* kisses her Hand, *Harlequin* kisses her Foot, *Aeneas* her Face, *Harlequin* her A–se. After many Struggles, *Aeneas* takes the Chamber-Pot and drinks it all off—*Harlequin* overcome retires, wishing his Master a good Night and good Success.' Aeneas drinking the contents of a piss-pot for love of Dido—what a falling off was there!

Given the nature of the Dido and Aeneas story as an episode in the warrior's private life, and given the long association in literature and iconography between sexual involvement and emasculation, it is bound to sit somewhat awkwardly in a heroic epic.[23] Ambivalent responses to the belief systems of the classical world are, however, more widely disseminated in the culture. Some years earlier, Thomas Duffett had in his burlesque mock-opera *Psyche Debauch'd* (1675) handled the story of Psyche and Cupid, with its attendant machinery of Delphic oracles and supernatural manifestations, with such irreverent hilarity that it is difficult not to perceive here evidence of the weakening of the classical world's hold on the poetic imagination, and of a desire to bring its solemnities up sharp against the demythologizing power of laughter. Directly in Duffett's sights is what he considers to be the multimedia pretentiousness and lavish fustian deceit of Shadwell's opera *Psyche* (1675); but his systematic substitution of folkloric, quotidian, and proletarian equivalents for the world of Psyche, her sisters Cidippe and Aglaura, and their suitors Nicander and Polynices has a depth of cut that saws off more than opera itself.[24]

[22] Thomas D'Urfey, *The English Stage Italianiz'd in a New Dramatic Entertainment, called Dido and Aeneas; or, Harlequin, a Butler, a Pimp, a Minister of State, Generalissimo, and Lord High Admiral; dead and alive again, and at last crown'd King of Carthage by Dido* (London, 1727), pp. iii–iv.

[23] I have in mind representations like Poussin's painting of Mars being disarmed by Venus.

[24] Peter Lewis comes down, finally, on the side of the view that Duffett's burlesques were no more than exercises in crowd-pulling without greater seriousness of purpose (*Fielding's Burlesque Drama: Its Place in the Tradition* (Edinburgh University Press, 1987), 26–31).

Venus, Cupid, and the oracle of Apollo appear in *Psyche De-bauch'd* as Mother Woosat, a pimping witch, her son Bruin, and a wishing-chair that is operated by Woosat as a transparent money-grubbing hoax. Psyche and her wicked sisters become None-so-fair, Woudhamore, and Sweet-lips, whose idiom is a coarsened and insistently carnal Spenserian mock-pastoral. It is clear from the dramatis personae that several roles, including that of the heroine 'Nonsy', were played against gender, thus imparting a pantomimic hilarity to the whole show. As a typical example of Duffett's technique, the magnificence of Cupid's palace and sculpture garden in *Psyche* becomes 'an Arbour dress'd up with gaudy Play-games for Children', and the vision of luxury with which the god charms Psyche's imagination in the original is transformed into a confection that Jonson's Sir Epicure Mammon would have envied:

Thou shalt be both my pretty *Romp* in Luxury and Pomp, thy eyes shall watch; while thy ears are ravished, and all thy other Senses shall dance *Bobbing-Joan* for joy. I'le keep thee in thy Hair, and thy Slippers; thou shalt eat like a Cameleon, and drink like a Flitter-mouse; thy House shall be made of one intire Sugar-Plum, out of which thou shalt every day eat thy passage like a lovely Viper out of his Dam's Belly, thy Closet shall be furnished with Sun-beams, thy Cloaths shall be all Marmalade powdered with Caraways for spangles, thy Bed shall be made of a great Blue-Fig, and thy Curtains of Dyet-bread Paper, where thou shalt lye like the Lady in the Lobster . . .[25]

Duffett implies that Rabelaisian greed and vulgarian failure of imagination are the real presiding deities of Shadwell's vision in *Psyche*. The classical world is so mercilessly stripped of its dignity that it appears as a naked and emaciated illusion.

Against this background, Dryden's magnificent comedy *Amphi-tryon; or, The Two Sosia's* (1690), which is only now beginning to be recognized for the masterpiece that it is, emerges as an import-ant landmark.[26] It is the work of a writer steeped in Virgil, who is responding to the scepticism engendered by epic machinery and

---

[25] Thomas Duffett, *Psyche Debauch'd* (1678), 40.

[26] Earl Miner, editor of the California Dryden edition of the play, comments: 'Only those who know Dryden or Restoration drama thoroughly have hitherto understood that *Amphitryon* is one of the unrecognized masterpieces of English comedy' (California Dryden, xv. 472). Brian Corman also recognizes its quality: 'In producing a farcical comedy with tragic overtones complete with gods and goddesses, Dryden stretched the boundaries of the comedy of his time almost beyond recognition' (*Genre and Generic Change in English Comedy*, 64).

by the conduct of deities who behave in a venal and capricious manner towards the mortals whose destinies they control. Jupiter comes down to earth to seduce Alcmena, wife of Amphitryon, by disguising himself as her husband and anticipating his imminent return from the wars, while Mercury impersonates his servant Sosia and in that guise tries to seduce Alcmena's waiting woman Phaedra while avoiding the conjugal attentions of his own 'wife' Bromia. The real Amphitryon and Sosia are cruelly bested at every turn by the deities, so tormented that they no longer remain in control of their own identities. That the birth of the hero Hercules is to be the result of Jupiter's seduction of Alcmena can only be, for Amphitryon, the gilding of a bitter pill. Nominally employing the three-tier structure of gods, nobles, and servants, the plot actually folds the tiers into each other so that the gods behave in a way that is virtually indistinguishable from the low characters:

MERC. 'Tis our Part to obey our Father; for, to confess the Truth, we two are little better than Sons of Harlots: and if *Jupiter* had not been pleas'd to take a little pains with our Mothers, instead of being Gods, we might have been a couple of Linck-Boys.[27]

A little later in the act, Mercury commands Night to extend her sway for some extra hours, giving Jupiter time to conclude his intrigue with Alcmena. The dialogue that follows sets out the vision of classical heaven that Dryden wishes to prevail, a vision refracted through the lens of late Caroline theatrical orthodoxies about sexual boredom and the complexion of Charles II's court:

NIGHT. *Jupiter* would do well to stick to his Wife *Juno*.
MERC. He has been marry'd to her above these hundred years; and that's long enough in conscience to stick to one Woman.
NIGHT. She's his Sister too, as well as his Wife: that's a double tie of affection to her.
MERC. Nay, if he made bold with his own Flesh and Blood, 'tis likely he will not spare his Neighbours.
NIGHT. If I were his Wife, I would raise a Rebellion against him, for the violation of my Bed.
MERC. Thou art mistaken, *Old Night*: his Wife cou'd raise no faction: all the Deities in Heaven wou'd take the part of the Cuckold-making God; for they are given to the Flesh most damnably. Nay the very Goddesses wou'd stickle in the cause of Love; 'tis the way to be

---

[27] I. i. 15–19; all quotations from *Amphitryon* are from the California Dryden, xv. Link boys were men employed to light the way for those walking home at night.

Popular, to Whore and Love. For what dost thou think old *Saturn* was depos'd, but that he was cold and impotent; and made no Court to the fair Ladies. *Pallas* and *Juno* themselves, as chaste as they are, cry'd shame on him. I say unto thee, *Old Night*, Wo be to the Monarch that has not the Women on his side.

NIGHT. Then by your rule, *Mercury*, A King who wou'd live happily, must debauch his whole Nation of Women.

MERC. As far as his ready Money will go, I mean: for *Jupiter* himself can't please all of 'em.   (I. i. 222–44)

This dialogue exemplifies the play's deft and skilful way of conducting a discussion about the public and private body of the king at the same time as it employs an allegory so tantalizingly flexible that its central equivalences are constantly shifting. There are, it seems, a set of references to the circumstances of 1688 and the Glorious Revolution running through the play. Jupiter is to be identified with William and the unfortunate Amphitryon with James. Alcmena is the kingdom of Britain, who, asked to choose between her two identical 'husbands', opts for the racy exoticism of her conquering seducer in preference to the dull legitimacy of her genuine lord and master. We might commiserate with Amphitryon for the desperately raw deal he is given by the potent god, but the sexual attraction of that power cannot be gainsaid. Jupiter's rake-philosophy has a clear topical application:

JUP. In me (my charming Mistris) you behold
     A Lover that disdains a Lawful Title;
     Such as of Monarchs to successive Thrones:
     The Generous Lover holds by force of Arms;
     And claims his Crown by Conquest.   (II. ii. 83–7)

Yet the issue raised by a king who behaves so promiscuously as to bring the monarchy into disrepute, defending himself by insisting on the separation between the public and the private body, was one that flared up in the reign of Charles. Promiscuity was not a significant factor in the homosexually inclined William's make-up and it would have been difficult for an audience to identify him with Jupiter. Caroline nostalgia, combined with a clear-sighted appraisal of the dangers of Charles's excess, is as significant a factor in the play as is a grudging adjustment to the Williamite status quo. Without ever endangering the decorum of comedy, Dryden is also able to raise the issues of the power of royal prerogative to suspend the common law, and the philosophical question of freewill versus predestination, both of which are debated between Jupiter, Mercury, and Phoebus in the opening scene:

> JUP. I love, because 'twas in the Fates I shou'd.
> PHOEB. With reverence be it spoke, a bad excuse.
> Thus every wicked Act in Heav'n or Earth,
> May make the same defence; but what is Fate?
> Is it a blind contingence of Events?
> Or sure necessity of Causes, linck'd,
> That must produce Effects? or is't a Pow'r
> That orders all things by superior Will,
> Foresees his Work, and works in that foresight?
> JUP. Fate is, what I
> By vertue of Omnipotence have made it:
> And pow'r Omnipotent can do no wrong:
> Not to my self, because I will'd it so:
> Nor yet to Men, for what they are is mine.   (II. i. 93–106)

In its philosophical ambitions, Dryden employs a texture earlier introduced by Duffett's *Psyche Debauch'd*, which has tremendous fun with Shadwell's earnest attempts in *Psyche* to make philosophical sense of questions like the operation of miracles. Do miracles, like oracular pronouncements, confirm heaven's power or bear witness to the essential weakness of gods who must rule by disordering nature? Prince Nick, in *Psyche Debauch'd*, cogitates impenetrably:

The Power is governed by the Order, which commands the Power and the Order, Rules the Beauty which governs the Order, which is found ty'd fast to the end of the Creation, in a long round Chain; and things, and things loose fast upon one another, I don't know howish, like bunches of Paper at a Kite's tail, and so by plain orderly method of Power and Order, and Order without Power, and Power without Order; and no Power, and no Order, and no Order, but a kind of Dis-orderly Powerful Order. (p. 26)

Without descending to the anarchic slapstick of Duffett, Dryden's play treats serious philosophical and constitutional issues with a wonderfully deft touch. For the purposes of my argument, however, the most significant aspect of *Amphitryon* is that it presents a servant's-eye view of Jupiter and the Olympians, conceived by a writer who is certainly not suffering from fascination. In Bakhtin's terms, this classical world is anything but sealed off from that of contemporary actuality: on the contrary, it is governed by the same instinctive drives and equally uncontrolled by ethical norms. This is the John Dryden that we should call to mind when reading his translation of Virgil.

It is against this demythologizing background that we should set the publication of the first proper mock-heroic poem in English: John Crowne's *The History of the Famous and Passionate Love, between a Fair Noble Parisian Lady and a Beautiful Young Singing-Man* (1692), in imitation of the Dido and Aeneas episode. This developed, as we have noted, from Crowne's rendering into English of Boileau's *Le Lutrin* under the title *Daeneids, etc.* (1692), which he turned into anti-Catholic and anti-French propaganda in support of William's wars in Ireland and against France. Crowne's version of Boileau is characterized by a Rabelaisian inversion of values. Fat, food, gargantuan appetite, imperturbable sloth: these are the true articles of Roman Catholic faith and it is in defence of them that the quarrel between the Dean and Choirmaster of Notre-Dame Cathedral is prosecuted. *The History of the Famous and Passionate Love* chronicles an affair between a married society lady and a singer called Minnum who first appeared in *Daeneids* as one of the heroes set the task of rescuing the Dean's pulpit from the cellar of Notre-Dame. Both in this work and in *The History of the Famous and Passionate Love*, Crowne wants to bring a carnivalesque spirit of appetitive, mocking laughter to the Virgilian epic structure: and he is impatient to handle issues of direct relevance to present-day society. His Epistle to the Reader prefacing *The History of the Famous and Passionate Love* first distinguishes mock-heroic from burlesque: 'a kind of Burlesque, directly contrary to that of *Virgil* Travestie, for that makes a *Hero* and *Heroine* talk like *Higlers* or *Costardmongers*, and this represents *Priests, Chanters* and *Vergers*, like *Gods* and *Heroes*' and goes on to deny that there is anything wrong with his having set the incidents against a background of *English* church practices.[28] With unpleasant braggadocio, Crowne boasts that the English built Notre-Dame, 'therefore we have a

---

[28] John Crowne, *The History of the Famous and Passionate Love, between a Fair Noble Parisian Lady and a Beautiful Young Singing-Man; a Chanter in the Quire of Notre Dame in Paris and a Singer in Opera's Being in Imitation of Virgil's Dido and Aeneas* (London, 1692), sig. A2 (italics reversed).

right to *Pews* there, and I hope we shall have the Possession o'
some, by the help of our King's Valour and Conduct' (sig. A2ᵛ).
Underscoring this Anglicization of the mock-heroic form is a
clearly discernible class basis to the satirical attack on Minnum,
most apparent in Crowne's version of Dido's curse:

> Let him be plagu'd with a vexatious Race:
> Foul and lewd Whores lay waste his conqu'ring Face.
> For him bold Fools write and set ev'ry Song,
> Blockheads as daring hiss him right or wrong.
> Give him a plenteous Portion with his Wife,
> Of open Infamy, domestick Strife,
> Of Brats he'll dote upon, and not beget;
> And from their Arms let him be torn by Debt.
> Let horrid Lewdness drive him from the Quire,
> Then let not Players think him worth their hire.
> From them a starving Bargain let him pray,
> When he has gain'd it, forfeit all his Pay.
> Out of all Rule let him both sing and live,
> But Rules of Gaols; and those let him deceive;
> Till he's an universal Nuisance grown,
> For Debts and Riots into Dungeons thrown.
> His Beauty, Voice, Wife's Love, and Skill in Song,
> Oh! may he long survive, yet perish Young.
> Then may his Wife be forc'd to beg a Grave,
> And that be all the Land she'll ever have.
> May all my Friends all Harmony abhor,
> And with it wage an Everlasting War.
> Let fierce Dissenters from my Womb arise,
> Which may pursue all singing Colonies.
> In Churches, Musick-Meetings, on the Stage,
> And with the Edge of Wit and Fire of Rage
> Be th'entire Extirpation of 'em all,
> And 'stead of Musick fill the World with Brawl.

Minnum is to be punished by the destruction of his livelihood and
the entire apparatus of professional musicianship that allows him
to support it. The gentry are urged to suspend their powers of
patronage and ally themselves with traditional enemies to music
like the Dissenters. There is a close and detailed understanding of
the structuration of an incipient music profession in the dunce's
progress that is here wished upon poor Minnum. In rejecting the
lady and marrying the Dean's niece, Minnum has had the audacity

to assert his sexual independence, snubbing his social superior. Her revenge is to be economic. Crowne here anticipates one of the prime functions of the mock-heroic as it is to develop: that of mediating clashes in class and professional interests by articulating an epic structure of episodes and incidents through the deeds of demotic, self-interested agents. In Garth's *Dispensary* (1699), as we shall see, this function is raised to an entirely conscious and intentional level. Mock-heroic's generic function, one is tempted to assert, is to act as missing link between the epic and the novel. It begins the work of mediating between class interests that the novel will perform to a greater degree. Both arise out of the same ideological matrix.

III

That there was a 'plausibility crisis' affecting an entire penumbra of discourses in which epic participated in the late seventeenth century emerges clearly from the outstanding work of Joseph Levine.[29] He cites Charles Perrault's *Parallèle des anciens et des modernes* (1688–92) as a work that establishes Homeric and Virgilian epic as the front line in the battle between the ancients and the moderns. Perrault drew up a series of parallels between ancient and modern achievement in the arts, eloquence, and drama, very much in favour of the moderns. Aristotle and Plato achieved nothing in science compared to the invention of the telescope; Homer was a great poet, but he had the misfortune to live in coarse and brutal times, and his gods were capricious and venal. The Homeric epics are punctuated by tedious irrelevant digressions, the most ridiculous of which was the digression describing the Shield of Achilles in the *Iliad*, book 18. This weapon is described as having so many engraved scenes on it that it would have been too massive and unwieldy actually to construct or to don. Gradually, Perrault built up the view that the very existence of 'Homer' was doubtful, that the great epics were not single works displaying coherent structure but were assembly jobs, that the story was deficient, the characters badly drawn, the manners of gods and heroes gross, and the whole lacking the politeness and

---

[29] Joseph M. Levine, *The Battle of the Books: History and Literature in the Augustan Age* (Ithaca, NY: Cornell University Press, 1991; repr. 1994), esp. ch. 4, 5.

refinement of seventeenth-century France. Later, Homer found able defenders in the husband-and-wife team of André and Anne Dacier, the latter of whom was an outstanding Greek scholar who produced a French prose translation of Homer published in 1711 and, in so doing, defended Homer and his times in scholarly commentaries. Behind the somewhat pointless question of whether the ancients or the moderns were superior was a real and vital issue—the nature of the past and the nature of the kind of historical scholarship best suited to retrieve it. For supporters of the moderns, the main point was that Homer, whoever he was, had written his epics in a world that had long ago vanished. The manners and customs of late seventeenth-century France and England were not those of ancient Greece: but on the other hand, contemporary writers found themselves without heroes that they could put in Homer's place. The supporters of the ancients insisted on the 'presentness' of the past: classical poetry was applicable to modern life, human nature and manners were universal, the epics taught moral lessons that we need to learn. In the late seventeenth century, in England and in France, there was emerging a new breed of scholar, antiquarians and classical philologists who increasingly had the equipment to understand the culture and the language of ancient Greece. The news they were bringing back from the front line was alarming to the ancients, defenders of *politesse*, defenders of a gentlemanly, humane way of studying the classics. Scholars like the German Ludolph Kuster, who produced a synthesis of ancient and recent Homeric scholarship, and the Englishman Joshua Barnes, who produced a new edition of Homer's complete works in 1711, had to go over all the important previous editions of Homer and all the massive storehouse of commentary from Byzantine to recent times: and they had to consider the archaeological evidence that had a bearing on classical customs and beliefs. To edit Homer, or to translate him, it was necessary to be knowledgeable about, for example, methods of mowing and ploughing the land, burial customs, religious beliefs, forms of political organization, measurement of time, distance, and money, military matters, and so on.

Against this material background, the 1690s emerge as a watershed decade in the history of the English epic. In that serio-comic period, Dryden signalled the defeat of his ambition to write an English epic by translating one, while Blackmore proved Dryden's

instinct sound by writing one. If, as Dryden said, 'a heroick Poem
. . . is undoubtedly the greatest Work which the Soul of Man is
capable to perform', why is it that Blackmore's heroic poems have
been objects of ridicule since the day they were first published?[30]
Perhaps the explanation lies in the two words omitted from Dryden's statement cited above: 'truly such'. It is not merely that
Blackmore's *Prince Arthur* (1695) can be so effectively mined for
bathos, as it was by Pope in *Peri Bathous* (1728)—lines like 'With
strutting Teats the Herds come lowing home' from book II, or the
falsetto attempts to astonish in lines like 'The lab'ring Mounts
belch drossy Vomit out, | And throw their melted Bowels round
about' in book III.[31] There is an infelicitous absurdity deeply
ingrained in the poem's structure as when, in book I, Arthur on his
way to Albion is diverted by a storm on to the Armorican coast. He
expounds the wisdom of Providence and immediately provides his
fellow mariners with a meal of meat, fruit, Burgundy, and cham-
pagne. If that's what it's like, we all want to be shipwrecked as
soon as possible; and, clearly, Providence is an excellent vintner.
Minor though it is, this incident is a clue to the broader shortcom-
ings of Blackmore's epic vision, manifest in the Preface. Here,
Blackmore confides that he is not actually a writer by profession
but has taken time out from his day job (of physician to the king)
to write an epic because he is concerned at the state of contemporary letters:

Our Poets seem engag'd in a general *Confederacy* to ruin the End of their
own Art, to expose *Religion* and *Virtue*, and bring *Vice* and *Corruption of
Manners* into esteem and reputation . . . I was willing to make one *Effort*
towards the rescuing the *Muses* out of the hands of these *Ravishers*, to
restore them to their sweet and chast Mansions, and to engage them in an
Employment suitable to their *Dignity*. (Preface, unpaginated; italics
reversed)

In the spirit of Collier and the Society for the Reformation of
Manners, Blackmore absolutely denies that pleasure is a significant end of poetry (perhaps a wise precaution in view of the
particular poem he has the task of introducing), seeing it instead
as an arm of divine instruction. Above everything else, Blackmore
wishes to claim that the epic genre is entirely consistent with

[30] John Dryden, Dedication of the *Aeneis* (1697), in the California Dryden, v. 267.
[31] All quotations from *Prince Arthur* are from the Scolar facsimile edition
(Menston: Scolar Press, 1971). Page numbers are supplied, not line numbers.

Christian morality and even theology: epic is intended 'to give Men right and just Conceptions of *Religion* and *Virtue*, to aid their Reason in restraining their Exorbitant Appetites and Impetuous Passions, and to bring their Lives under the Rules and Guidance of true Wisdom' (Preface, unpaginated). Has Blackmore, one may wonder, ever actually *read* an epic? That *Prince Arthur* is a 'cit's epic' appears in the clearly enunciated class politics of the Preface. Blackmore defends 'the Diligent, Thriving *Citizen*', the Alderman, and the JP from the merciless ridicule of contemporary comedy and thinks it would be a good thing if poets and preachers were kept under a rigid system of state licensing—a timely reminder that the Licensing Laws were coming up for renewal and that the government seemed unaware of their importance. In the teeth of the objection that poets have a duty to entertain, Blackmore brings out seriously the argument that, in *The Dunciad*, Pope kept up his sleeve:

They say, 'tis their *Profession* to Write for the Stage; and that Poets must Starve if they will not in this way humour the *Audience*. The *Theater* will be as *unfrequented*, as the *Churches*, and the Poet and the Parson *equally* neglected. Let the Poet then abandon his Profession, and take up some honest, lawful Calling, where joyning Industry to his great Wit, he may soon get above the Complaints of *Poverty*, so common among these ingenious Men, and lye under no necessity of prostituting his Wit to any such *vile* Purposes as are here censur'd. (Preface, unpaginated, italics reversed)

Here is a clear expression of Blackmore's cultural politics. And the epic that this cultural manifesto produces is testimony to its crippling narrowness—the epic as composed by Shimei or Sir Balaam.

In the early books, we are given a pop-up picture-book account of the Gospel and the Day of Judgement illustrated by predictably opulent and vulgar visions of the Eternal City, all informed by a smug and pettily vengeful sense of the damned getting their just deserts. When the narrative moves out of analepse into present tense, it becomes, in line with Blackmore's opinion that epic should proceed on one very clear level of allegorical significance, a transparent account of William's being called over to Britain to defend Protestant interests against the Catholic monarch James II, who is abetted by the French king Louis. Ariosto and Spenser have gone wrong, Blackmore explains in his Preface, by being 'hurried on with a *boundless, impetuous* Fancy over Hill and Dale, till they are both lost in a Wood of Allegories. Allegories so *wild, unnatural,* and *extravagant,* as greatly displease the Reader' (Preface, unpaginated). One feels for Blackmore reading Spenser, being pained by all that waste of imagination. Through his narrative of Arthur's heroic deeds in leading the early Britons against the Saxon king Octa aided by the Neustrian Odar can be discerned the invitation to William to free Britain from the Catholic yoke, his landing in Devon, down to the storm that delayed this event initially, the failure to engage militarily with James in England, and the subsequent Jacobite wars in Ireland and Scotland. Despite the professed Christianity of its aspiration, the poem is shockingly prejudiced, losing no opportunity to engage in anti-French, anti-Catholic, anti-Scottish, and anti-Irish polemic. Very early on, the Fury Persecution is associated with Rome, which takes on the Gothic character of an unnatural, vampirical dam, the vampirism implicitly an attack on the Catholic literal interpretation of the Eucharist:

> Fierce Tygers, Dragons, Wolves about her stay,
> They grin, and snap, and bite, and snarling play.
> I to her Jaws, throw Infants newly Born;
> She sucks their Blood, and by her Teeth are torn
> Their tender Limbs, while I rejoyce to see
> Such noble proofs of growing Cruelty.
> To her wide Breast, and vast capacious Soul,
> I often Torrents of black Poyson rowl:
> She drinks the livid Flood, and through her Veins
> Mad Fury runs, and wild Distraction reigns.
> I'll lead her from the Rocks, her strength full grown,
> Fix her high Seat in the Imperial Town,
> And give her Scarlet, and a threefold Crown.
>
> (I, p. 20)

In Arthur's time, we learn,

> . . . a rude, cruel People, bred to Spoil,
> To Blood, and Rapine, from th' *Hibernian* Isle,
> Did in this Age, infest th'*Albanian* Coast,
> And landed there at last their barb'rous Host.
>
> (VIII, p. 265)

And the poem comes to its appointedly Williamite conclusion, finding means in the prophetic section in book v to celebrate the house of Nassau, commemorating the still-recent death of Queen Mary, and in book VII providing a long paean in praise of the city of London as a centre of empire and world trade. Here Blackmore advises neighbouring states that, if they are not *actually* quaking with fear of Britain's potency during the current war of the League of Augsburg, they should be:

> Her Power by trembling, Neighbour States is fear'd,
> By distant Empires, and new Worlds rever'd.
> . . . *Britannia*'s Head she reigns in Wealth and Ease,
> Mart of the World, and Emp'ress of the Seas.
>
> (VII, p. 191)

Promoting the good of mankind, therefore, the true poet's vocation as stipulated by Blackmore, turns out to be identical with promoting the Revolution Settlement and Britain's world destiny as conceived by William.

Yet the very local specificity of this cultural politics prevents Blackmore from taking advantage of the genuine imaginative achievements of Virgilian epic at the same time as it ensures that he cannot deliver on his promise to Christianize it. There is no equivalent found for the Dido and Aeneas episode, for obvious moralistic reasons, nor can Blackmore endorse paganism to the extent of sending Arthur into any underworld. Thus the episodes that, above all others, haunted Dryden's imagination are simply excised by Blackmore. Although in much of the text a strict Providential system operates, the sheer bloodthirstiness of the closing accounts of battle make them very difficult to reconcile with a central emphasis in Christianity on pacifism and mercy. Here is a sample of Arthur's running amok:

> Thro' the bright Helmet which his Head encas'd,
> Thro' bones, and Brains the furious Javelin pass'd;
> And his left Eye from out its Circle struck,
> On the sharp Point, a ghastly Prospect stuck.
> Then *Ethelrick* a stout west Saxon Lord,
> And *Ida* fell, by his victorious Sword.
> The first his Head down to his Shoulders cleft,
> Fell to the Ground, of Breath and sense bereft.
> The heavy Blade falling with oblique Sway,
> Half thro' the other's Neck, did make its way.

The Head half sever'd on his Shoulders hung,
And from the Wound a bloody Torrent sprung.

(x, p. 283)

Representations of war on the one hand, and, on the other, of what were called in the period 'machines', that is to say the supernatural agencies of the epic, provoke in *Prince Arthur* the probability crisis that I have been arguing makes for an inherent instability in the condition of English epic. Contemporary dissatisfaction with the epic ethos can be studied in the treatise in which the critic John Dennis made his early reputation, the *Remarks on* Prince Arthur (1696). So often dismissed as an unthinking apologist for prescriptive Aristotelian 'rules', Dennis shows in this essay that impressive combination of common sense and analytical power that is to become the distinctive feature of his critical voice. There is, he points out, a pervasive incoherence in Arthurian epic given that we actually take our descent from the Saxons and Normans so that Arthur's victory over the Saxons is, in terms of the epic's genealogical function, a sideshow. Of 'machines', Dennis comments that he has often wondered: 'why I could never be pleas'd with the Machines in a Christian Poem. At length, I believe I have found out the reason. Poetry pleases by an imitation of Nature. Now the Christian Machines are quite out of Nature, and consequently cannot delight. The Heathen Machines are enough out of Nature to be admirable, and enough in Nature to delight.'[32] Gods and goddesses in classical epic, that is to say, behave in a manner that is identifiably human, whereas the Christian God and Devil simply cannot be rendered plausibly. Throughout the treatise, Dennis is in search of a degree of plausibility—of 'realism', as we might put it—that Blackmore's epic (and, arguably, the genre in English) cannot provide. Even if he employs the Aristotelian term 'unity' to express his desideratum with respect to character, Dennis really wants characters to act in a psychologically consistent and plausible manner. He wants depth, interaction—rather than the boring predictabilities of long, rhetorical speeches. Hence, commenting on Blackmore's characterization of the Armorican king Hoel, Dennis's voice take on a coruscating irony, recalling at the outset the jokes against inscrutable politicians in Buckingham's *Rehearsal*:

---

[32] John Dennis, *Remarks on* Prince Arthur (1696), in *Critical Works*, i. 105.

Now I defie any Man in the World to give me this *Hoel*'s Character. *Hoel* is as obscure, and as much conceal'd, as if he were a Politician: Tho' it is manifest that he is none. For notwithstanding he is every-where mention'd throughout a Third Part of the Narrative, yet he has very little hand in the Plot . . . He seems to have neither Life nor Soul of his own, but is actuated by invisible Springs at first from below, and by and by from above. The first news we hear of him, is, when that Devil Persecution, appears to him in the reverend Shape of *Alman*. She gives him an account of *Arthur*'s being thrown upon his Coast; and tells him, that the most obliging way of receiving him, will be to cut his Throat . . . This, she assures him, in a long Speech of above forty Lines. It seems, Mr. *Blackmore* judiciously saw, that this Fury ought to make a long Speech, or else she would go out of her Character, and that her very words ought to appear to persecute the passive Ears of *Hoel*. He hears all this with a great deal of Patience, and without the least Interruption, and what is still more wonderfull, without the least Reply. So that hitherto we have found in *Hoel* neither Thought, nor Voice, nor Motion.[33]

Obscurely formulated in Dennis, then, is a critique of epic that anticipates the desiderata of psychological consistency and realistic dialogue to be developed by Defoe in his novels published in the 1720s. If, as Rawson remarks, Dryden and Pope could only write epic 'by proxy, or through a filter of irony' (p. 203), it was because conditions of narrative plausibility had changed. Blackmore's domestication seems to get the worst of all possible worlds.

John Dryden makes a cameo appearance in book VI of *Prince Arthur as* the seditious, godless, and importunate poet Laurus who wearies Sakil of Stourus (Sackville, Earl of Dorset) with his petitions for patronage:

> *Laurus* amidst the meagre Crowd appear'd,
> An old, revolted, unbelieving Bard,
> Who throng'd, and shov'd, and prest, and would be heard.
> Distinguish'd by his louder craving Tone,
> So well to all the Muses Patrons known,
> He did the voice of modest Poets drown.
> *Sakil*'s high Roof, the Muses Palace rung
> With endless Cries, and endless Songs he sung.
> To bless good *Sakil Laurus* would be first.
> But *Sakil*'s Prince, and *Sakil*'s God he curst.
>
> (VI. clxvii)

[33] Ibid. 88.

Dryden is represented as engrossing more than his fair share of patrons' money without giving the expected service in exchange: promotion of the patrons' ideology. Blackmore gets his retaliation in first for what he presumes will be the pro-Catholic, anti-Williamite translation of the *Aeneid* that Dryden was known to be preparing. Given the contours, however, of the *Aeneid*'s story, in which a foreign conqueror (Aeneas) is destined to inherit the lands and the queen already promised to a native heir (Turnus), it is difficult to see how a faithful version could be *other* than Williamite. Dryden's task, therefore, is not the familiar one of exculpating himself from the charge of sedition, but the more embarrassing one of justifying his seeming acceptance of the status quo. For Dryden himself, heroism was an ideal over which contemporary events had cast an ironic pallor. In 1688 a British king had been presented with an opportunity to act heroically, and had not only failed to live up to it in retreating before William's army, but had plumbed depths of comic farce when, after sneaking off to a vessel in Sheerness, he was apprehended by some Kentish fishermen and brought back to London. All of Dryden's writing in the last decade of the century was, in one way or another, a coming to terms with the mock-heroic complexion of the times he lived in. In a lengthy Dedication of the translation to the Earl of Mulgrave, Dryden identifies several important pressure-points, the major one being the political implications of his task. These he expounds by means of a masterly lesson in Roman history that implies an inexact parallel between his own position and Virgil's. Virgil is represented as a closet republican who had reconciled himself to the Augustan imperial order partly because it was a political fact and partly because the last days of the republic had been so obviously corrupt. The nature of Virgil's political compromise is described at considerable length, and his poem is seen to be instrumental in promoting acceptance of that compromise by the Roman people. Yet the poet's freedom to express scepticism, reminding the Emperor that his title was not divinely sanctioned or hereditary and that there may be certain flaws in the conception of Roman history as inaugurated by the fugitive hero of Troy, is emphasized.[34] This role as public apologist

---

[34] I cannot agree with David Bywaters where he argues that, in the Dedication, Dryden wishes to belittle all political systems, intentionally failing to adapt the details of Roman history to contemporary events in order to prepare the way for an eagle's-nest view of the latter (*Dryden in Revolutionary England* (Berkeley and Los Angeles:

and private conscience of the king is one to which Dryden now aspires.

Dido and Aeneas present another kind of problem. Dryden finds a political reason for the episode, justifying Augustus' recent divorce and discomfiting the Carthaginians, chief enemies to the Romans. In the translation itself, Dido's cursing fury may be undignified, but it is certainly not comic. Nevertheless, this is a clear point at which the *Aeneid*'s heroic agenda comes into conflict with the domestic-romantic story of an intense human passion. It is one of several points in Dryden's translation at which, I would wish to argue, there is registered an inherent instability in the epic universe as perceived by late seventeenth-century English sensibilities. In the act of translating the entire *Aeneid*, Dryden is always alive to the split between a heroic ideal and an unheroic reality, conscious exploitation of which would create the conditions of the mock-heroic. Epic in the 1690s, that is to say, contains the seeds of its own obverse, the mock-epic. The scepticism that tinges treatments of the Dido and Aeneas episode in English writing discussed above is one seam of a rich vein running right through the English reception of the Trojan war as one not worth fighting. It is a vein mined by Dryden at various points in his translation. Ironic glimpses of the campaign as one whose outcome is determined by a ham actor and an oversized stage prop appear in Aeneas' account of Sinon's thespian performance in persuading the Trojans to admit the wooden horse:

> With such Deceits he gain'd their easie Hearts,
> Too prone to credit his perfidious Arts.
> What *Diomede*, nor *Thetis* greater Son,
> A thousand Ships, nor ten years Siege had done:
> False Tears and fawning Words the City won.

> (2. 259–63)

Later in book 2, the episode of Priam's death parodies the heroic ideal, admittedly in the interests of pathos; but the image of the aged king loading his wasted limbs with armour that his body can barely support is one that inevitably compromises the warrior ideal itself:

> In Arms, disus'd, invests his Limbs, decay'd
> Like them, with Age; a late and useless aid.

University of California Press, 1991), 110). It seems to me that there is a very evident parallel in the roles of the two poets.

His feeble shoulders scarce the weight sustain:
Loaded, not arm'd, he creeps along, with pain;
Despairing of Success; ambitious to be slain!

(2. 695–9)

Priam arrives at an altar shaded by a laurel tree that, 'Dodder'd with Age', is a mocking emblem of himself. There he meets Hecuba with her women 'Driv'n like a Flock of Doves along the skie', who upbraids Priam for his juvenile attempt at resistance, soon to be put into perspective by Pyrrhus' sportive slaughter of their son Polites before their very eyes. Priam rails at his barbarity, the impotence of his words underscored by the risible ineffectuality of his weapons:

This said, his feeble hand a Javelin threw,
Which flutt'ring, seem'd to loiter as it flew:
Just, and but barely, to the Mark it held,
And faintly tinckl'd on the Brazen Shield.

(2. 742–5)

It would be difficult to conceive a less dignified death than Priam's at the hands of Pyrrhus:

With that he dragg'd the trembling Sire,
Slidd'ring through clotter'd Blood, and holy Mire,
(The mingl'd Paste his murder'd Son had made,)
Hauled from beneath the violated Shade;
And on the Sacred Pile, the Royal Victim laid . . .
Thus *Priam* fell: and shar'd one common Fate
With *Troy* in Ashes, and his ruin'd State:
He, who the Scepter of all *Asia* sway'd,
Whom Monarchs like domestick Slaves obey'd.
On the bleak Shoar now lies th' abandoned King,
A headless Carcass, and a nameless thing.

(2. 748–52, 758–63)

The atypically vernacular words 'slidd'ring' and 'clotter'd', the 'paste' composed of blood and mud, the sheer physical ugliness of this regicide, are used to introduce a *sic transit gloria mundi* theme that undermines the values of epic.

In the intensely political book 11, a pacifist strain that throws into doubt the martial ethos upon which epic depends is consistently sounded. There is by now dissension in the Rutulian camp and the ordinary citizens who have suffered heavy war casualties are beginning to perceive that they, as opposed to their leaders, have nothing to gain from sustained hostilities. Matters are worsened when envoys sent to Diomede to persuade the Greek hero to send troops return empty-handed. Diomede's response as reported to King Latinus is an elegy for a lost and pointless cause. None of the victorious Greeks gained anything whatsoever out of the Trojan War:

> Not one but suffer'd, and too dearly bought
> The Prize of Honour which in Arms he sought:
> Some doom'd to Death, and some in Exile driv'n,
> Out-casts, abandon'd by the Care of Heav'n . . .
> No Hate remains with me to ruin'd *Troy*.
> I war not with its Dust.

(11. 396–9, 430–1)

Diomede advises the Latians to make peace: and in his 'cold Excuse' is something of the cynicism surrounding the Trojan war as a campaign fought over an undeserving whore most memorably expressed in Shakespeare's *Troilus and Cressida*. Diomede's dignified *Weltschmerz* is followed by a very different tonality—the voice of Drances, who, introduced as 'a close Caballer and Tongue-valiant Lord', clearly does not have authorial endorsement. Accusing Turnus wrongfully of flight as he does, Drances might call to mind the fair-weather friends of James II who were so very quick to round upon him in late 1688. Further, he presumes to speak for the people and tries to drive a wedge between their interests and those of the leaders—populist rabble-rousing politics of which Dryden elsewhere disapproves:

> Your Interest is the War should never cease;
> But we have felt enough, to wish the Peace:
> A Land exhausted to the last remains,
> Depopulated Towns, and driven Plains . . .
> Mankind, it seems, is made for you alone;
> We, but the Slaves who mount you to the Throne:
> A base ignoble Crowd, without a Name,
> Unwept, unworthy of the Fun'ral Flame:
> By Duty bound to forfeit each his Life,
> That *Turnus* may possess a Royal Wife.

(11. 562–5, 570–5)

Turnus is fully aware of the threat this poses to the tissue of understandings composing an aristocratic code of martial honour, and his response is similar to that of Coriolanus when he is accused of cowardice by Tullus Aufidius. He blusters about his heroic prowess, insisting that 'heaps of *Trojans* by this Hand were slain, | And how the bloody *Tyber* swell'd the Main' (606–7), emphasizes that his achievements are *solitary* ones—uses the heroic code, in short, as a stick with which to beat Drances rather than engaging with his point of view. But that point of view has been registered—the dissenting voice has been heard—and it is not satisfactorily silenced. In her comparative study of Dryden's *Aeneis* and the Latin original, Tanya Caldwell observes the systematic way in which Dryden's modifications impose a pattern of gradual disillusionment on the translation. Particularly in books 9–12, Caldwell demonstrates 'a bitterness that seems to grow in proportion to the destruction depicted':

Dryden heightens Vergil's pathos, stresses the cruelty and pointlessness of war and, finally, denies that anything may be accomplished through the struggles ... As Dryden's Aeneas penetrates further into Italy, he becomes less a Stuart figure to be praised or a William figure to be condemned than a fore-runner to Gulliver or Tom Jones: a wanderer adrift in a world which one minute promotes time-honoured, sacrosanct values, the next undercuts them.[35]

Her sense of the epic's trajectory is one with which I profoundly concur.

IV

At the dead centre of Sir Samuel Garth's mock-heroic poem *The Dispensary* (1699), we find ... Sir Richard Blackmore. In Canto III, Dr Horoscope has unsuccessfully attempted to raise the fury Disease by making a sacrificial pyre out of his various herbal remedies and medicaments, using his prescriptions as the touch-paper. It remains to Blackmore in Canto IV to propitiate her successfully with a reading of a typical passage of warlike, met-onymical fustian from *King Arthur*. Disease is roused from her lair

[35] Tanya Caldwell, 'Towards a Carmen Perpetuum: Dryden's *Georgics* and *Aeneis*', Ph.D. thesis (Toronto, 1996), ch. 4, pp. 3, 39.

in the '*Essex* Marshy Hundreds' and spends many lines giving the bard critical advice:

> Then dare not, for the future, once rehearse
> The Dissonance of such untuneful Verse.
> But in your Lines let Energy be found,
> And learn to rise in Sense, and sink in Sound.
> Harsh Words, tho' pertinent, uncouth appear;
> None please the Fancy, who offend the Ear.
> In Sense and Numbers, if you would excel,
> Read W[ycherley], consider D[ryde]n well.
> In one, what vig'rous Turns of Fancy shine,
> In th'other, *Syrens* warble in each Line.[36]

This is all a mite surprising, given that one would not expect Blackmore's lays to have such potency, nor Disease to be an expert on literary matters, which seem anyway to be entirely irrelevant to the quarrel over the dispensing of free medicine that is the poem's ostensible subject. For Garth, however, Blackmore is a fitting symbol of the nexus of bad poetry and self-seeking professional greed that he wishes to satirize and condemn. *Prince Arthur* had brought him to the attention of the court and his pen had been hired to give a partisan account of the failed assassination plot on William in 1696. Blackmore was knighted in February 1697 and appointed to the post of fourth physician to the king at a salary of £219 per annum. Professional patronage was the direct result of his muse's labours; and he was the kind of individual whose advancement it was in the interests of the old guard of the Royal College of Physicians to oppose.

His promotion was an aspect of a much more complex debate surrounding the professionalization of medicine in the period, a little of which it is necessary to understand. Gregory C. Colomb's perceptive and valuable analysis concludes that '*The Dispensary* is . . . a gallery of portraits that are representations by class. It is a class portrait.'[37] The direct occasion for Garth's poem is the construction of a dispensary for medicines in the Warwick Lane premises of the College of Physicians, to be used for the purpose

---

[36] Sir Samuel Garth, *The Dispensary* (1699; 9th edn. London, 1725), ed. Jo Allen Bradham (Delmar, NY: Scholars' Facsimiles and Reprints, 1975), 37.

[37] Gregory C. Colomb, *Designs on Truth: The Poetics of the Mock-Epic* (University Park, Pa.: Penn State University Press, 1992), 162.

of making up cheap remedies for the certified poor of London. For some years, the College had been trying to persuade the London Society of Apothecaries to participate in a scheme that the College would oversee, for remedies to be given to the poor at or near cost price by nominated local dispensers. It is astonishing, at first glance, to encounter such a charitable enterprise anticipating the principles of a public health service in this early period; and the Society of Apothecaries' opposition is difficult to fathom. Garth refers the reader in his Preface to a treatise entitled *A Short Account of the Proceedings of the College of Physicians, London, in Relation to the Sick Poor of the said City and Suburbs thereof* (1697), perusal of which makes it more apparent that the motive behind the College of Physicians' charity is not simply to improve the lot of the poor: 'As to the Offer [the Apothecaries] make in *prescribing Medicines to the Poor in the absence of a Physician gratis* . . . We are sorry to meet with so clear a proof of their great Ambition to meddle with what belongs not to them, to set themselves up for Physicians, and to run themselves into practice upon pretence of Charity to the Poor' (p. 13). At issue is the question of whether physicians are to control prescription or whether, contrariwise, men that they regarded as untrained and unqualified, mere mechanics whose skill lay only in mixing herbs and simples, were to gain the right of prescribing. As Harold J. Cook makes clear, two distinct approaches to medicine were developing in the period, one concerned with the treatment of an individual human subject—a holistic, but expensive approach—and the other concerned with developing treatments for symptoms that could cure large numbers of patients without individual consultation. Cook shows that the latter approach, essentially that of the Apothecaries, was gaining ground as a result of William's need to provide cheap and effective treatments for his combat troops, while the College of Physicians had reason to feel that, under William, it was losing the strengthened powers that James II had conferred upon it as part of his overall project of centralization.[38] Recent improvements in the status of apothecaries had put the Physicians upon their guard; especially since there were parvenus among their own

[38] Harold J. Cook, 'Living in Revolutionary Times: Medical Change under William and Mary', in Bruce T. Moran (ed.), *Patronage and Institutions: Science, Technology and Medicine at the European Court, 1500–1750* (Rochester, NY: Boydell Press, 1991), 111–36.

ranks, like Blackmore and Francis Bernard (Garth's 'Horoscope'), who were in receipt of Whig support and who had sympathy for the apothecarial approach to healing. The dispensary project was really, then, a pre-emptive strike by the Physicians to control both the Apothecaries and the more entrepreneurial section of their own membership, in the absence of any sign that king, Parliament, or city council would regulate them. From all of this, the poor might even benefit incidentally.

Black comedy is created in the poem out of the pervasive presence of financial self-interest linked to death, a texture woven out of life in the shadow of the Grim Reaper that John Gay would harness even more successfully in *The Beggar's Opera*. In terms of the Bakhtinian typology employed at various points in this chapter, I would suggest that the most obvious distinction between the true epic and *The Dispensary* resides precisely in the latter's greater degree of dialogism.[39] The author is in hostile dialogue with the language of the apothecaries and physicians that he represents. Doubtless it is true that language in the poem is not dialogic in the fullest possible realization of Bakhtin's meaning: the dialogic ideal is for languages to be represented without ultimate authority being accorded to any one of them. What Garth offers us is, as it were, a fly-on-the-wall recording of the language actually spoken by the apothecaries and physicians when they think no one is listening. Through irony, he intends to retain authority over that object-language. Language is *displayed*, held up to ridicule, billposted, so to speak, for characters like Horoscope and Mirmillo to condemn themselves out of their own mouths. Yet the implied lack of authorial consent is exactly what imparts energy to the irony. In Canto II, for example, the fury Envy has assumed the persona of Colon (the apothecary Lee, Warden of Apothecaries Hall in Blackfriars Lane) for the purpose of nerving Horoscope up to the combat ahead. One is reminded throughout of Jonson's *The Alchemist*, in particular the scenes in which Rabbi Busy is ritually humiliated by Subtle, being forced to confess his sect's true motives if he is to gain from the alchemist the means to perpetuate them. Colon's exhortation is a comically

---

[39] I would maintain this even though it is clear from what I have said above that I do not regard Dryden's translation of the epic as entirely monologic. One might look, for example, at the representation of Mezentius in Dryden's *Aeneid*, who stands for a form of absolute, tyrannical rule that quite clearly does not gain authorial endorsement.

barefaced acknowledgement of their true motives, there being no necessity to conceal these behind the veil of hypocrisy reserved for patients. The language is subverting itself in the very process of utterance, in a way typical of novelistic discourse:

Forbear, forbear, thy vain Amusements cease,
Thy *Woodcocks* from their *Gines* a while release;
And to that dire Misfortune listen well,
Which thou shou'dst fear to know, or I to tell.
'Tis true, thou ever wast esteem'd by me
The great *Alcides* of our *Company*.
When we with Noble Scorn resolv'd to ease
Our selves from all Parochial Offices;
And to our Wealthier Patients left the Care,
And draggl'd Dignity of Scavenger:
Such Zeal in that Affair thou didst express,
Nought could be equal, but the great Success.
Now call to Mind thy Gen'rous Prowess past,
Be what thou shou'dst, by thinking what thou wast:
The Faculty of *Warwick-Lane* Design,
If not to Storm, at least to Undermine.
Their Gates each Day Ten thousand Night-caps crowd,
And Mortars utter their Attempts aloud.
If they should once unmask our Mystery,
Each Nurse, ere long, wou'd be as learn'd as We;
Our Art expos'd to ev'ry Vulgar Eye,
And none, in Complaisance to us, wou'd dye.
What if We claim their Right t'Assassinate,
Must they needs turn *Apothecaries* strait?
Prevent it, Gods! all Stratagems we try,
To crowd with new Inhabitants your Sky.
'Tis we who wait the Destinies Command,
To purge the troubled Air, and weed the Land.
And dare the *College* insolently aim
To equal our Fraternity in Fame?

(pp. 15–16)

Patients are really woodcocks caught in traps, apothecaries are performing the work of the gods in ridding the land of surplus inhabitants, and what is most important is to preserve the Apothecaries' mystery from the Physicians, whose dispensing experience will soon unmask it. Here, epic references combine with contemporary actuality in a way that Pope will later perfect:

Horoscope's reputation as 'the great *Alcides* of our *Company*' has been gained in the heroic part he played in the Apothecaries' successful petition to Parliament in 1694 for a bill exempting them from performing city offices like those of rubbish-collecting. Their success implied that the Apothecaries were a necessary reserved occupation. They could not be spared for menial tasks— another step on the road to professional acceptability.

As the many detailed descriptions of actual locations and the clearly recognizable portraits of actual individuals confirm, the whole point of *The Dispensary* is to bring the eternal present of the epic into collision with the temporal present of a real occasion. Garth exploits epic to gain a raised vantage-point from which to expose the mercenary deadliness of aspiring semi-professional quacks. But if my argument carries any conviction, he is able to do this only because there is an instability inherent in perceptions of epic and because the classical world is itself already tarnished. Epic can no longer speak to contemporary economic conditions. As John Barrell and Harriet Guest have observed,

> The heroes of epic were now unimaginable, for the essential condition of epic heroism was that the hero should somehow represent, within himself, all the members of his society. But the proliferation of interests and occupational identities within a commercial society meant that no individual could now fulfill that representative task.[40]

This instability is woven into the very fabric of Dryden's Virgil translation undertaken for Tonson in the 1690s. It was the first really profitable example of subscription publishing, itself a conspicuous case of new interests and occupational identities emerging in a commercial society. As I noted in Chapter 2, Dryden and Tonson's Virgil project was financed directly by members of the book-buying public, and the contract issued by Tonson to Dryden is a model for subsequent legal instruments governing relations between the professional writer and his publisher. Act of deep *pietas* as it undoubtedly was, Dryden's translation was also a landmark in the mediation of classical learning to a new reading public who were too impatient or not well enough educated to read classical masterpieces in the original. Different though it

[40] John Barrell and Harriet Guest, 'On the Use of Contradiction: Economics and Morality in the Eighteenth-Century Long Poem', in Felicity Nussbaum and Laura Brown (eds.), *The New Eighteenth Century: Theory, Politics, English Literature* (New York: Routledge, 1987; repr. 1991), 132.

seems, Dryden's Virgil is a product of social forces similar to those that brought about the novel's emergence as a distinct literary form, which are by now well established in the standard histories of the novel and need little recapitulation. The new bourgeois commercial sectors, the merchants, successful tradesmen and shopkeepers, manufacturers, financial brokers, and professionals—and their increasingly ornamental wives—were swelling the ranks of the theatre-going and book-buying public. They were achieving enough cultural power to demand that their leisure time be filled by representations of their own class fraction's way of life. If they were to become acquainted with the great works of classical literature at all, they would do so in translation. Increasingly, however, they would not do so. Mock-heroic's emergence as a separate, if short-lived, poetic form is evidence that they would not do so. Blackmore's epics were an ill-judged attempt to nick the taste of exactly this readership. Although he does not seem to have captured the hearts and minds even of the solid burghers whom his Preface interpellates, much less the wits at Will's, he certainly did succeed in gaining a quality of patronage that would prevent him from having to write such stuff for a living. Soon, the new readership would demand that mock-heroic fictionalized its real occasions and its historical protagonists while preserving the realism of its characterization and the dialogism of its language. That would be the next step in the novelization of English literary culture.

5

Conversing with Pictures:
The Periodical and the Polite

Steele's *Tatler*, no. 217 for 29 August 1710, provides an excellent example of the use to which the Miltonic epic might find itself being put in the fashionable literary periodical of the early eighteenth century. The essay, on the subject of the Bully and the Scold, has the same objective as very many others in the *Tatler* series, to subject male and (mainly) female behaviour to its standard of acceptable sociability. Women who are chaste, argues the essay, think that they have achieved perfection and cannot be reproached with any other misconduct. But modesty is more than merely keeping men out of your bed. Rage, publicly expressed anger, is conduct just as unseemly in a woman, and decibels are the enemies of true modesty: 'Modesty never rages, never murmurs, never pouts; when it is ill-treated, it pines, it beseeches, it languishes.' To illustrate the unpleasantness of the domestic quarrel, Isaac Bickerstaff translates the first postlapsarian contretemps of Adam and Eve in *Paradise Lost*, book IX 'out of heroics, and [put] into domestic style':

'Madam, if my advices had been of any authority with you, when that strange desire of gadding possessed you this morning, we had still been happy; but your cursed vanity and opinion of your own conduct, which is certainly very wavering when it seeks occasions of being proved, has ruined both yourself and me, who trusted you.'

Eve had no fan in her hand to ruffle, or tucker to pull down; but with a reproachful air she answered:

'Sir, do you impute that to my desire of gadding, which might have happened to yourself, with all your wisdom and gravity? The serpent spoke so excellently, and with so good a grace, that—Besides, what harm had I ever done him, that he should design me any? Was I to have been always at your side, I might as well have continued there, and been but your rib still: but if I was so weak a creature as you thought me, why did you not interpose your sage authority more absolutely? You denied me going as faintly, as you say I resisted the serpent. Had you not been too easy, neither you nor I had transgressed.'[1]

Bickerstaff comments on the relatively restrained nature of the quarrel to a modern sensibility, but this he imputes to our first parents' not yet having the terms to express anger; and, reading between the lines, Eve's telling Adam 'how fine a gentleman the devil was' is 'as if she had called him cuckold'. Thus Miltonic epic is domesticated and reduced to a comic blueprint for female fickleness down the ages. Miltonic blank verse has all its awkwardness and ardour schooled into Steele's imitation of a carping couple from a comedy by Dryden or Congreve. One rubric to which we might specify such a transformation is that of 'the polite'.

In the foregoing chapters, I have been arguing that, as the opportunities for professional writers increased, so the legal-conceptual conditions for the legitimization of literary careerism evolved. The idea that it was a moral crime for authors to present unoriginal material as if it were their own presupposed an embryonic notion of literary property and a perception of literary inspiration as a stock-in-trade that had to be protected by those intent upon living on their wits. This was one of the enabling conditions of a demand for copyright legislation that, for the first time, placed the interests of authors, rather than those of trade publishers, under the protection of the law. Another such condition was the loosening grasp on aspiring authors of the courtly amateur *sprezzatura* that, in Thomas Woodman's words, 'included the idea of an apparently effortless ease in the turning of verses and an aristocratic disdain for what has been called "the stigma of print" associated with selling one's work in the marketplace'.[2] In the previous chapter, I investigated the fortunes of a central expression of that aristocratic ambition, the desire to write an original English epic that would be a purer imitation of classical form than the Miltonic and Cowleian religious epic that in so many ways embarrassed rather than executed the design of the courtly poet.

There, I used the Bakhtinian conception of a 'novelization of culture' to refer to changes in taste that left Dryden a beached whale in the 1690s. The point is couched, there, in terms of

[1] Quoted from Steele and Addison, *The Tatler and the Guardian* (Edinburgh: William P. Nimmo, 1880), 395.
[2] Thomas Woodman, *Poetry and Politeness in the Age of Pope* (London: Associated University Presses, 1989), 31.

altering standards of plausibility. New generations of readers, from different social provenances, wanted to read different stories— stories not concerned with remote, ramrod-stiff heroes but rather, stories coloured by humour and concerned with individuals whose destinies might conceivably resemble their own. This call was first answered in the 'polite' writing of the early century. Polite discourse, arguably the most significant crucible of aesthetic and social change in the eighteenth century, was to an extent constituted by the efforts of professional writers. The polite sphere could not have taken the shape that it did without the business acumen of writers like John Dunton, whose indefatigable quest for new and lucrative forms caused him to stumble across the literary periodical. In turn, the discursive spaces shaped by the polite aspiration provided new opportunities for professional writers. One thinks of Pope being called in as a troubleshooter in the Petre v. Fermor quarrel, writing the 1712 *Rape of the Lock* as a means of restoring the quarrelling parties to the fold of politeness: and of the poem immediately being picked up by Bernard Lintot for his collection of *Miscellaneous Poems and Translations*, to Pope's total profit of £26. 19*s.* In what follows, I will begin by defining 'the polite' and considering the ideological work that its various manifestations were required to perform. I follow this up by exploring some developments in the early literary periodical, pre-Addison and Steele, suggestive of the place of literary professionals in the story. Professional writers like Peter Motteux, John Oldmixon, and John Dunton played a part in the shaping of polite discourse, even if their motives were those of commerce and profit and even if they themselves would hardly make membership of the middle class. Others contributed to its formation from a position relatively external to it, like Pope and Swift, or entirely external to it: in the case of John Dennis, implacably hostile to it. And perhaps the single most important negotiator of the polite was Anthony Ashley Cooper, third Earl of Shaftesbury, whose class vantage-point was many miles above it. Addison and Steele were central to its formation, as would be generally agreed. They were so, I will argue, because together they had the range of experience and breadth of attitude necessary to meld widely disparate cultural elements into a witty, tolerant, moderate, and highly marketable literary product.

I

Writing from Paris to Catherine Macaulay in 1763, Tobias Smollett offers a definition of the term 'politeness' and a demonstration of its utility as a weapon in the by then well-advanced Anglo-French cultural battle: 'If I was obliged to define politeness, I should call it, the art of making one's self agreeable. I think it an art that necessarily implies a sense of decorum, and a delicacy of sentiment. These are qualities, of which . . . a Frenchman has no idea; therefore he never can be deemed polite, except by those persons among whom they are as little understood.'[3] Smollett goes on to call attention to the vanity, superficiality, obsession with gallantry, effeminacy, egotism, indiscretion, insincerity, and general ridiculousness of the French *petit maître*, all deriving from his imperfect socialization: his inability to respond sympathetically to the wishes of others that is in Smollett's view the fundamental desideratum of the individual in society, encapsulated in the key notion of 'politeness'.

In 1962 Jürgen Habermas published his influential discussion of the 'public sphere', *Strukturwandel der Öffentlichkeit* (*The Structural Transformation of the Public Sphere*). Habermas argued in this book that the traffic in commodities and in news occasioned by the nature of early capitalist economic relations made for a new kind of 'representative publicness', which he designated 'the bourgeois public sphere'. This new social formation was in symbiotic relationship with the growth of literacy and the development of the press. It was a coming together of private people out of the intimate domains of their conjugal families and into new and constituting forms of public space—coffee-houses, redesigned domestic interiors, clubs and societies, salons in France, and *Tischgesellschaften* in Germany. Its effect was to create a new kind of subjectivity: people who perceived themselves simultaneously as owners of goods and persons, and as part of a common humanity—one human being amongst others. In Habermas's terms: 'The fully developed bourgeois public sphere was based on the fictitious identity of the two roles assumed by the privatized individuals who came together to form a public: the role

---

[3] Tobias Smollett, *Travels through France and Italy* (1766), ed. Frank Felsenstein (Oxford University Press, 1979; repr. 1992), Letter VII, p. 57.

of the property owners and the role of human beings pure and simple' (italics reversed).[4] The most important aspect of the bourgeois public sphere for our purposes is the new discursive formations to which it gave rise: new forms of debate that exalted rationality, new cultural artefacts like the epistolary novel, which publicized the intimate sphere of the family, new forms of law based on common consent. Habermas's view is, indeed, that 'culture' as we know it, the consumption of cultural artefacts and performances for their own sake, was a product of this discursive formation. Its gradual effect was to subject the power of the state to the monitoring of an increasingly influential realm of 'public opinion': 'The bourgeois public sphere may be conceived above all as the sphere of private people come together as a public; they soon claimed the public sphere regulated from above against the public authorities themselves, to engage them in a debate over the general rules governing relations in the basically privatized but publicly relevant sphere of commodity exchange and social labor' (p. 27).

Habermas's ideas were applied to English cultural history in the early 1980s through the further mediation of Foucauldian theories of discourse and of Bakhtinian theories of the dialogic. In such adaptations, they have been exceptionally fertile in the analysis of social and cultural development in post-Restoration society. A particularly limpid formulation of the conception of the public sphere is given by Peter Stallybrass and Allon White in their influential book *The Politics and Poetics of Transgression*:

Patterns of discourse are regulated through the forms of corporate assembly in which they are produced. Alehouse, coffee-house, church, law court, library, drawing-room of a country mansion: each place of assembly is a different site of intercourse requiring different manners and morals. Discursive space is never completely independent of social place and the formation of new kinds of speech can be traced through the emergence of new public sites of discourse and the transformation of old ones. Each 'site of assembly' constitutes a nucleus of material and cultural conditions which regulate what may and may not be said, who may speak, how people may communicate and what importance must be given to what is said. An utterance is legitimated or disregarded according to its

[4] Jürgen Habermas, *The Structural Transformation of the Public Sphere: An Inquiry into a Category of Bourgeois Society* (Darmstadt: Hermann Luchterhand, 1962), trans. Thomas Burger with Frederick Lawrence (Cambridge, Mass.: MIT Press, 1989; repr. 1993), 56.

place of production and so, in large part, the history of political struggle has been the history of the attempts made to control significant sites of assembly and spaces of discourse.[5]

The argument would run that in the period crucial to the development of the middle class in English life, the period of urbanization, commercialization, consumerism, and leisure, there was an unprecedented need to create public spaces that permitted the mingling of individuals from the aristocracy and the upper echelons of the 'middling sort'. Three-dimensional spaces that have been extensively studied in addition to those listed in the quotation above, of which the coffee-house is perhaps the most important, would include meeting-places of learned societies, museum and gallery space, circulating libraries, and the masquerade: and there were many short-lived and temporary attempts to create such milieux, like the so-called Censorium established by Richard Steele in York Buildings in 1712.[6] Discursive spaces can also be two-dimensional, however, and it is in this sense that the literary periodicals of the early century—in particular Steele's *Tatler* and Addison and Steele's *Spectator* and *Guardian*—have been perceived to negotiate a new cultural discourse, that of 'refinement' or 'politeness'. To define the signification of the term 'politeness' at this time, we might refer to Mary Wollstonecraft's later deployment of it in the open letter to Edmund Burke in which she expressed her *Vindication of the Rights of Men*: 'I have not yet learned to twist my periods, nor, in the equivocal idiom of politeness, to disguise my sentiments, and imply what I should be afraid to utter: if, therefore, in the course of this epistle, I chance to express contempt, and even indignation . . .'.[7] To Wollstonecraft in 1790, 'politeness' was a buttoned-up, discredited, hypocritical system of hints and hesitancies, which she counterposes to a radical openness and plain speaking. And, from her political standpoint, she is right to identify politeness as her enemy, because it was indeed a semiotic designed to effect what Gramsci

[5] Peter Stallybrass and Allon White, *The Politics and Poetics of Transgression* (London: Methuen, 1985), 80.

[6] See the discussion in Brean S. Hammond, '"Guard the sure barrier": Pope and the Partitioning of Culture', in David Fairer (ed.), *Pope: New Contexts* (New York: Harvester Wheatsheaf, 1990), 225–40.

[7] Mary Wollstonecraft, *A Vindication of the Rights of Men in a Letter to the Right Honourable Edmund Burke* (1790), ed. Janet Todd (London: William Pickering, 1993), 5.

would term 'incorporation'. 'Politeness' is defined by Lawrence Klein as 'the set of attitudes, strategies, skills and devices that an individual could command to gratify others and thus render the social realm truly sociable'.[8] Those are primarily attitudes and strategies of self-containment: internal sanctions, protocols of speech and behaviour calculated to eliminate conflict and oil the wheels of social intercourse. The making over of the social realm to politeness performed a wide variety of ideological functions that, taken collectively, go a long way towards identifying the nature of dominant culture in the early century. Kathryn Shevelow traces to the mission of the literary periodicals the *gendering* of the split between private and public spheres, where the private is 'the feminine, reproductive, apolitical area of home and family, in opposition to the masculine, productive, political realm of work and society'. She notes, however, the vital paradox through which women were represented as in the private realm by being represented in print, to some extent as writing subjects.[9] A related ideological project effected by polite discourse was a reordering of conceptions of gentility. Paul Langford speaks of 'the debasement of gentility' as 'one of the clearest signs of social change in the eighteenth century, the mark of a fundamental transformation'.[10] Command of a polite discourse could enable an individual who was not from the upper echelons of society to pass himself off as such: gentility became not so much a matter of birth and status as of self-presentation. Further, genuine aristocrats could be encouraged to covet possession of the polite code as a more virtuous and ethical alternative to those, like duelling and hunting, into which they were born.

Recent discussions of the polite phenomenon in the early eighteenth century have stressed the art of conversation as the central domain of inculcation and dissemination.[11] Polite conversation, it can be shown, was governed by rules about the

[8] Lawrence Klein, 'The Third Earl of Shaftesbury and the Progress of Politeness', *Eighteenth-Century Studies*, 18 (1984–5), 186–214: 190.

[9] Kathryn Shevelow, *Women and Print Culture: The Construction of Femininity in the Early Periodical* (London: Routledge, 1989), 15.

[10] Langford, *A Polite and Commercial People*, 66. The title of Langford's book in the Oxford History of England series, and the substantial chapter he devotes to the analysis of politeness, will suggest its salience as a theme in the period.

[11] See Barker-Benfield, *The Culture of Sensibility*, chs. 2–4; and Stephen Copley, 'Commerce, Conversation and Politeness in the Early Eighteenth-Century Periodical', *British Journal for Eighteenth-Century Studies*, 18 (1995), 63–77.

appropriateness of topics, the amount of specialist knowledge that can be deployed, the degree and tone of disagreement that can be tolerated: rules dispositionally apparent in the periodical essays. That the discursive code of polite conversation became part of the fibre of social intercourse is evident from parodies of it such as Swift's *Compleat Collection of Genteel and Ingenious Conversation* (1738), the irony of which depends on the ability to abstract its protocols. In his Introduction, Swift uses the reductive arithmetic so effectively deployed in the fourth of the *Drapier's Letters* to ridicule Walpole's threat that he would make the Irish swallow Wood's coin:

> The Flowers of Wit, Fancy, Wisdom, Humour, and Politeness, scattered in this Volume, amount to one thousand, seventy and four. Allowing then to every Gentleman and Lady thirty visiting Families (not insisting upon Fractions) there will want but a little of an hundred polite Questions, Answers, Replies, Rejoinders, Repartees, and Remarks, to be daily delivered, fresh, in every Company, for twelve solar Months.[12]

Politeness has been of particular interest to students of literature because charismatic accounts of the nature and function of literary conversation, ancestor of institutionalized literary criticism, have been written in its terms. Terry Eagleton's *The Function of Criticism* is such an account, contending as it does that the desire and ability to talk about literature developed as a function of the early eighteenth-century ideal of polite conversation. Polite conversation itself transfuses manifest forms of political power as wielded by an absolutist state into the bloodstream of rational discussion between apparent equals: 'Criticism is a reformative apparatus, scourging deviation and repressing the transgressive; yet this juridical technology is deployed in the name of a certain historical emancipation. The classical public sphere involves a discursive reorganization of social power, redrawing the boundaries between social classes as those who engage in rational argument, and those who do not.'[13] Consonant with the objectives of a

---

[12] Jonathan Swift, *A Compleat Collection of Genteel and Ingenious Conversation, according to the most polite Mode and Method, now used at Court, and in the best Companies of* England. *In several Dialogues. By* Simon Wagstaff, *Esq.* (1738), in *The Prose Works of Jonathan Swift*, ed. Herbert Davis *et al.*, 16 vols. (Oxford: Basil Blackwell, 1939–74), iv. 111.

[13] Terry Eagleton, *The Function of Criticism: From the* Spectator *to Post-Structuralism* (London: Verso, 1984), 12–13.

parliamentary democracy increasingly dedicated to commerce and wealth-creation, literary criticism takes its place as an aspect of a broader cultural politics: 'The examination of literary texts is one relatively marginal moment of a broader enterprise which explores attitudes to servants and the rules of gallantry, the status of women and familial affections, the purity of the English language, the character of conjugal love, the psychology of the sentiments and the laws of the toilet' (p. 18). Addison and Steele are crucial to the development of a literary discourse that, while involving the handing down of verdicts and the arbitration of taste, is capable of concealing its judgemental aspects and of presenting itself as consensual—couched in a style that the writers themselves would have termed 'easy writing'. Eagleton's sense of polite conversation as primarily a masking, concealing discourse that occludes the real nature of material and political circumstances in a society is one that is shared by other commentators. To Stephen Copley, for example, the ideological function of polite conversation was to provide 'a justificatory rationale for consumption by mystifying its relation to economic exchange, and concealing the status of the polite as leisured consumers'.[14] In his view the major project of politeness is to render acceptable the transition between a residual model of citizenship deriving from a tradition of civic republicanism and an emergent model defined by the imperatives of trade and commerce. Polite discourse legitimizes consumption where the more traditional vocabulary would have condemned it as luxury.

In the main this account of the development and function of the bourgeois public sphere is one I find convincing, though in Eagleton's characteristically 'clean' account, uncomplicated by any close engagement with the primary material, there is a tendency to regard Addison and Steele as arising *ex nihilo* and as engrossing the polite entirely in and of themselves. The 'bourgeois public sphere' is discussed as though it were a free-standing creation of the bourgeois for the bourgeois, to the neglect both of aristocratic and of demotic strands within it. In Tom Woodman's formulation of politeness, for example, the phenomenon is an aristocratic

---

[14] Copley, 'Commerce, Conversation and Politeness in the Early Eighteenth-Century Periodical', 67.

concession handed down to social inferiors rather than a genuinely democratic development:

> Politeness . . . represents the modification of traditional aristocratic attitudes and the co-opting of a wider polite élite through subtle instructions in such values. It proposes consensus, but it is in fact a narrow consensus in which the constraints are merely concealed. Politeness is ultimately a way of reconciling an aristocratic ethos with a limited acceptance of the aspirations of other classes in a laissez-faire economic system.[15]

Such a perspective might arise from a consideration of Shaftesbury as the prime mover of politeness rather than Addison or Steele. My own discussion begins with a consideration of John Dunton's *Athenian Mercury*, the progenitor of the literary periodical, as a business venture undertaken by a writer-publisher whose main imperative was to make a living. Thereafter, the prevailing (though not the exclusive) focus will be on the early formulation, in Shaftesbury, Dennis, and Addison and Steele, of a discourse of aesthetics as a function of the need to legitimize the consumption of valuable literature by a new, broad-based readership. Clearly, this was an enterprise in which professional writers' interests were deeply engaged. If, as was suggested in Chapter 1, the discourse of 'originality' served to widen the social constituency of those who could *produce* literature while still imposing severe controls upon it through the inconvenience of having to possess genius, aesthetics was the reciprocal discourse in the domain of consumption. The humanist ideal of a union between writing on the one hand, and wisdom and eloquence on the other, that Milton embodies so powerfully and that Pope still stands on tiptoe to reach, might have given way, after all, to an unashamed aesthetic of writing for the marketplace that Samuel Johnson encapsulates in the famous comment recorded by Boswell: 'No man but a blockhead ever wrote, except for money.' But the aesthetics that developed in the early eighteenth century, promulgated in Shaftesbury, in Hutcheson, and in the *Spectator*, was a 'polite' aesthetics, that assigned appreciation to a domain of the senses, because in that form it could become the property of the new middle class. This is an aesthetic that facilitates the trickling down of élite culture to a broader consuming public at the same time as it occludes the new

---

[15] Woodman, *Poetry and Politeness in the Age of Pope*, 22.

commercial basis on which such a dissemination will be achieved. Through Shaftesbury and Dennis, into the *Spectator*, and on to Aaron Hill's periodical essays shaping taste in the 1720s, contributing in turn to the nature poetry of James Thomson, and finding in Edmund Burke a spokesman as powerful as Young on originality, the natural world was constituted as a proper object of aesthetic attention. Its advantage was that it could be contemplated by most respectable citizens for free.

II

In his *Life and Errors*, the bookseller-publisher John Dunton, citizen of London, gives a description of how his *Athenian Gazette* project came to him in 1691, in terms that almost call spiritual autobiography to mind—for all the world like John Bunyan testifying to his conversion in *Grace Abounding*:

The human Mind, though it has lost its innocence, and made shipwreck of the image of God; yet the desire of Knowledge is undestroyed. Mankind are sunk, as it were, into shadows and darkness, and now and then they see some glimmering apparition of Truth; but yet, though it be as glorious, it is fleeting as a vision. The Soul is also much jilted and juggled with a walking kind of happiness, which is promising enough, but always unperforming. Thus the Human Understanding and the Will being under penal banishment from Truth and Goodness, and yet tantalized with the appearance of both, the Soul must suffer under a world of uneasiness and pain; for, what misery more exquisite than when the Faculties and their Objects are divorced? . . . I had received a very flaming injury, which was so loaded with aggravations that I could scarce get over it. My thoughts were constantly working upon it, and made me strangely uneasy; sometimes I thought to make application to some Divine, but how to conceal myself and the ungrateful wretch, was the difficulty. Whilst this perplexity remained upon me, I was one day walking over St. George's Fields, and Mr. Larkin and Mr. Harris were along with me; and on a sudden I made a stop and said, 'Well, Sirs, I have a thought I will not exchange for fifty Guineas.' They smiled, and were very urgent with me to *discover* it; but they could not get it from me. The first rude *hint* of it was no more than a confused idea, of concealing the Querist, and answering his Question. However, so soon as I came home, I managed it to some better purpose, brought it into form, and hammered out a *Title* for it, which happened to be extremely lucky . . . The inhabitants of Athens were mightily fond of being called *Athenians*, in regard they fancied the title did distinguish them from the rest of mankind, whom they stiled *Barbarians*.[16]

What emerged was an interactive periodical, quickly retitled the *Athenian Mercury*, purporting to be the organ of a group of men called the Athenian Society, dedicated to responding to its readers' queries. It has a seminal place in the history of English literary periodicals, as also in the history of the agony column.[17] Dunton's manner of telling the story—the bathetic transition from souls in torment to what sounds like a venereal misadventure—characterizes exactly the combination of high-cultural pretention and business acumen that was his Athenian scheme. Ancient Athenian society represented, for such as Shaftesbury, the most salient proof of his theory that philosophical and artistic culture flourished best in conditions of political liberty: Athens afforded a gracious, spacious environment for its inhabitants to cultivate polished and agreeable manners while engaging in deep and valuable thought.[18] Capitalizing on such connotations, Dunton's title indeed 'happened to be extremely lucky'. On the other hand, as the contract that Dunton proceeded to draw up with his collaborators Richard Sault and Samuel Wesley attests, the enterprising publisher saw at once that serial publication could be safer and more profitable than book publishing. Sault and Wesley would furnish Dunton with two numbers, each occupying a half-sheet folio, every Friday evening, in exchange for payment of 10*s.* per number. Should Dunton abandon the project, his collaborators would receive 20*s.* compensation each. There would be an editorial meeting every Friday to sort out each number's contents.[19] Although at first the queries handled by Dunton and his band of ersatz Athenians are of a speculative, metaphysical kidney—'Whether the Torments of the damn'd are visible to the Saints in Heaven?'—it soon becomes apparent to them that the human-interest enquiries are a much deeper and more marketable vein—'*How shall a* man *know when*

---

[16] John Dunton, *The Life and Errors of John Dunton, Citizen of London*, 2 vols. (London: J. Nichols & Bentley, 1818), i. 187–9.

[17] On its place in the literary periodical, see Graham, *English Literary Periodicals*, 36 ff.; and on the agony column, Robin Kent, *Agony: Problem Pages throughout the Ages* (1979; repr. London: W. H. Allen, 1987), ch. 1.

[18] See the account given by Lawrence E. Klein, 'Liberty, Manners, and Politeness in Early Eighteenth-Century England', *Historical Journal*, 32/3 (1989), 583–605.

[19] The agreement is Bodl. MS Rawlinson 72, fo. 65. It is reproduced in Parks, *John Dunton and the English Book Trade*, 81–2.

a Lady loves *him*?'[20] Gradually, the questions come to assume the shape of mini-narrative, setting out detailed cases of conscience, from which the form taken by some later *Tatler* and *Spectator* essays is relatively easy to infer. From the outset it is clear that the *Athenian Mercury* operates as an instrument of social control, dispensing sensible if socially conservative advice. One querist, for example, who writes in to complain about the behaviour of unruly apprentices who keep company with a disreputable serving maid, is advised to show them this issue of the *Mercury* and threaten them with publicity and exposure. Some of the queries handled are literary, and in this province the *Mercury*'s cultural policing is especially patent:

Q. Whether 'tis lawful to read Romances? A. Every one grants that 'tis lawful to read *Quintus Curtius*, or *Xenophon*'s Life of *Cyrus*, in both of which the Loves as well as Wars of two great Monarchs are describ'd:— And if so, we think 'tis not easie to assign a reason why the same *Stories* mayn't be read, when the *Heroes* are made greater, and their *Actions* more *compleat* and *lively* than before, as in good Romance they generally are, and particularly in the *Grand Cyrus*, and *Cassandra*; Tho' we think then that the *Reading* these Books may be *lawful*, and have some *Convenience* too, as to forming the *Minds* of *Persons* of *Quality*; yet we think 'em not at all *convenient* for the *vulgar*, because they give 'em extravagant Idea's of *practice*, and before they have *Judgment* to byass their *Fancies*, generally make 'em think themselves some King or Queen, or other:— . . . Add to this, the soft'ning of the *Mind* by *Love*, which are the greatest Subject of these sort of Books, and the *fooling* away so many *hours*, and *days*, and *years*, which might be better employ'd, and which must be repented of: And upon the whole, we think *Young People* wou'd do better, either not to read 'em at all, or to use 'em more sparingly than they generally do, when once they set about 'em. (i. 191–2)

The respect in which Dunton and his team of literary professionals are defining the polite sphere and shaping its inhabitants' reading habits is apparent from the above quotation. Writers who moved in Dunton's circle felt very strongly, however, that although his project might fool such as the inexperienced Jonathan Swift into eulogizing the Athenians in his Ode ('Yet shall these traces of your wit remain | Like a just map to tell the vast extent | Of conquest

[20] This and subsequent quotations are from the compendium of Athenian queries and replies published as *The Athenian Oracle: Being an Entire Collection of all the Valuable Questions and Answers in the Old Athenian Mercuries*, 3 vols. (London: A. Bell, 1703–4), i. 33.

in your short and happy reign'; lines 301–3), this thinly spread
and motley crew of self-appointed pundits certainly did not deserve to be arbitrators of polite taste. Just this element of cultural
pretension, the contrast between the courtly language employed
by the Athenians and the hole-in-corner outfit they actually were,
is exposed in Elkanah Settle's play *The New Athenian Comedy,
containing the Politicks, Oeconomicks, Tacticks, Crypticks, Apo-
calypticks, Stypticks, Scepticks, Pneumaticks, Theologicks, Poeticks, Mathematicks, Sophisticks, Prognosticks, Dogmaticks, etc.
Of that most Learned Society* (1693). The play is set in the loft of
a coffee-house. Two gentlemen, Freeman and Hardy, have been
asked to vacate the cramped premises to make way for a meeting of
the Athenian Society, which the gentlemen are astonished to
learn comprises only four members: Obadiah Grub, Terry Squirt,
Joachim Dash, and Jack Stuff. Act I climaxes with the Athenians in
conclave, brought a query by Dorothy Fetlock from 'the right
famous Colledge in *Blow-bladder* Precinct' on '*Which is the more
Noble Animal, a Louse or a Flea?*' This question, later to be used
by Samuel Johnson as the proverbial expression of distinction
where there is no difference, is earnestly debated by the Athenians, invested with their brand of self-important moralizing and
social engineering:

You forget sure that the main Great End of our Debates and Results is the
Encouragement of true Religion, Virtue and Piety; and the suppression of
Vanity, Vice and Profaneness. And perhaps never was a fairer Topick of
that kind come before us than in these two small animals now in Con-
troversie. For instance, what is the Flea but a perfect image or portraict of
Prodigality, nay the Prodigal himself, that very improvidently, like the
Grasshopper, only hops and dances in Summer, and famishes and starves
in Winter. Nay, what's yet a greater blot in his Scutcheon for . . . he herds
and sociates with Dogs, when on the contrary, the braver-spirited Louse
consorts with Men, and not only so, but is the perfect Emblem of the
provident good Husband.[21]

It is not surprising that writers intimate with Dunton's doings
should object to his setting himself up as a broker of the polite.
In the same year in which Dunton commenced the *Athenian
Mercury*, he published his astonishing work of semi-autobiograph-
ical fiction *A New Voyage Round the World; or, A Pocket Library*,
which is a virtual antidote to polite letters. It professes to be the

[21] E[lkanah] S[ettle], *The New Athenian Comedy, etc.* (London, 1693), 7.

life history of Don Kainophilus, a.k.a. Evander. In its chronic use of digression, rugged indifference towards the reader, constant self-referentiality, interruption, use of different accents and registers of language—in summary its transforming and protean character—this discourse is truly dialogic in a Bakhtinian sense: a sense quite opposite, that is, to the one used by Shaftesbury when, in *Soliloquy; or, Advice to an Author* (1710), he recommends that polite authors should use the Platonic dialogue to retain objectivity over their writing. A suggestive passage from the introduction to *A New Voyage* might call to mind the famous 'spider and bee' passage from Swift's *The Battle of the Books* (1704), permitting us to voice the suspicion that the Dunton of *A New Voyage* was exactly the kind of impolite hack author standing behind the attack on 'modern' authorship in that work and in the persona adopted for *A Tale of a Tub* (1704):

I had forgot one Word, stay a little longer, and then some may *snotter* and *snuffle* at the *many Collections* they'll find in these my Labours, they'll call me *Owl, Jay, Cuckoo, Magpy,* and a hundred *Beasts of Birds* besides, for borrowing so many *Feathers* and gawdy plumes; —but they might, I'll tell them, learn more Civility from an ingenious Person, who has prefixed an ingenious *Poem* to these my Works; and styleth me rather a *Bee,* nay, a mellifluous Bee, or *Brother* to one who gathers *Sweets and Dainties* wherever he comes . . . and how ungrateful were that *rustick Boor,* and foolish withal, who would refuse the delicate present that his *little industrious Tenant* would make him forsooth, because he had stoln it from *other folks Gardens,* and not gathered it only out of his *own,* or as the *Spider* spins his thred drawn from his *own Bowels.*[22]

Later in the text, the connection with Swift's *Tale* is further cemented by a passage, the acme of the impolite, in which Evander meets Dryden in Will's coffee-house, exults over 'Mr. *Laureat*'s' fallen condition—'what in the same Religion for a whole three or four years together! indeed Mr. *Bays* 'tis unconscionable'—and leads him to a Catholic church service, which he likens to puppet show. The passage ends with a commentary on the Catholic belief in transubstantiation during the Eucharist, the height of impoliteness, to put it no worse, expressed in terms that Swift would echo in section IV of *A Tale of a Tub*:

D'ye see this small little tiny scrap of Bread Gentlemen—no bigger than a *Christning Maccaroon*—look upon't all of you—*isn't Bread*

[22] John Dunton, *A Voyage Round the World: or, A Pocket Library* (London, 1691), 7.

Gentlemen—ay Bread, what shou'd it be—well—mark the end on't—
keep your Eyes fix'd—by virtue of *Hocus Pocus*—*Hiccius Doctius, Hey
Presto!* but what is't now—why *Bread* still—nay—then I'll be Burnt for a
Heretick, as you deserve to be for saying so—why 'tis a *Man*, an Errant
Man (ay and more too) with *Eyes* and *Nose, Teeth, Blood, Bones* and
Fingers, as you and I have—Mr. *Bays*—*did you ever see the like in all
your Changes*—here's a turn without an alteration, a very pretty Miracle
where nothing at all's effected . . . get you gone and leave me alone to my
Devotion—agreed—for you are not worth the *Lampooning*, having been
flogg'd and yerkt so long between *Catholick and Heretick*, that there's not
one sound Inch left in Body, Soul or Reputation. (pp. 155–6)[23]

Dunton was therefore an ambivalent figure in the early shaping
of polite discourse, capable, in a ventriloquial way, of representing
both the cynosure of urbane counsel and the height of ill-bred
churlishness at one and the same time. More straightforward was
the part played by another professional writer in the construction
of polite taste, Peter Anthony Motteux, the naturalized Huguenot
refugee who began the *Gentleman's Journal* in 1692. At virtually
the same time as Dunton was lampooning the ex-Laureate so
mercilessly, Motteux was praising Dryden's translations and, in
some of the earliest theatre reviews ever published, defending his
play *Cleomenes* from having offended against the canons of poetic
justice for not punishing Cassandra:

And, as for her coming off with Impunity, which some have reckon'd as a
Scandal to Poetical Justice, let those Judges remember, that 'tis something
severe to Vote for lashing that Vice in Publick, which they constantly hug
in a Corner. On the other side, it is nothing strange, that they should
damn an Hero's Continency (a hard Case, by the way, that a Man should
be damn'd for his Virtue) who come to a Play, on purpose to *ogle* the
orange Wench.[24]

Motteux knew perfectly well how valuable a commodity Dryden
could be if he chose to contribute to his new venture in gentlemanly reading materials. The contents of the issue for February
1692 give an impression of the reader whose interests Motteux
was endeavouring both to create and to reflect:

[23] On the relation between Dunton and Swift, see further J. M. Stedmond, 'Another
Possible Analogue for Swift's *Tale of a Tub*', *Modern Language Notes*, 72 (1957), 13–
18.
[24] Peter Motteux, *The Gentleman's Journal; or, The Monthly Miscellany. By Way
of Letter to a Gentleman in the Country*, 2 vols. (London, 1692), May 1692, i. 21.

Introduction; Stanza's by Mr. *Prior*; An Account of that great Imposter William Morrel; His Epitaph; *Apollo*'s Proclamation; The 9th Ode of *Horace* Imitated; The Friendly Cheat, a Novel; Verses from a Lover to his Mistress, who feared she was too kind; An Account of the Disputes between the Ancients and the Moderns; *Acteon*, or the original of *Horn-Fair*, a Fable in Verse; An account of the last Month's *Enigmatick* Verses; An *Enigma* in Verse; Of the *Marriage-hater Match'd*; of *Cleomenes*, a new Tragedy, by Mr. *Dryden*; of *Juvenal* and *Persius*; News and Remarks; a Latin *Epigram* on my *Lord Dorset*'s being made Knight of the Garter; The same in English; a new *Scotch* song set by Mr. King, the words made to the Tune by the Author of this *Journal*.   (italics reversed)

There were three other songs, the whole coming to thirty-six pages. It is as brilliantly shrewd a miscellany as any modern magazine, ranging as it does from the narrative satisfactions of the short novella in which two errant husbands are dehumoured by a bed-trick that dupes them into enjoying their own wives, to the airing of the latest, most up-to-date controversy in the learned world, the ancients–moderns dispute. Motteux's gift for ribald classical travesty (which we saw in action in the previous chapter) is often exercised in the *Gentleman's Journal*, but this is juxtaposed with serious and meritorious translation. Snippets of news and theatre reviews make the magazine an early *Time Out* for the metro-politan person of fashion. One can imagine that readers would look forward very much to receiving the sheet music for popular songs by some of the greatest composers like Purcell and John Blow, which they could have their wives play and sing. And the *Journal* was a testing-ground for new poets like John Dennis and Matthew Prior who were eager to establish themselves, as well as for well-known writers like Congreve and Nahum Tate. At the end of the year 1692 it seems that Motteux's ambition had soared high enough to solicit translations from the greatest writer of the age, John Dryden. Dryden's publisher, Jacob Tonson, immediately perceived the commercial threat that a publication like the *Gentle-man's Journal* might represent and, in a letter that speaks volumes about the ultra-professional relationship he had with Dryden, he wrote to the poet in early 1693 complaining that Dryden was charging *him* more for translations of Ovid than he was prepared to charge Motteux:

After your arrivall you shew'd Mr. Motteaux what you had done, (wch he told me was to ye end of ye Story of Daphnis) and demanded . . . twenty

guyneas, wch that bookseller refus'd. Now, Sr. I the rather believe there was just soe much done, by reason ye number of lines, you mention in yor letter agrees wth ye quantity of lines that soe much of ye first book makes; wch upon counting ye Ovid I find to be in ye Lattin 566, in ye English 759 . . . then pray, Sr, consider how much dearer I pay then you offered it to ye other bookseller;. for he might have had to ye end of ye story of Daphnis for 20 guyneas, wch is in yor translation.................759 lines
And then suppose 20 guyneas more for the same
number...............................759 lines
that makes 40 guyneas   1518 lines;[25]

Tonson's injured reaction draws attention to the fact that ventures like Motteux's, although they did a tremendous amount to shape the habits and expectations of the class of polite readers whose busy lives prevented them from engaging in sustained acts of reading, were propelled by commercial interests that were the expression of the incipient literary professionalism we have been studying. They led, via imitative publications like the *British Apollo* (1708–11) and John Oldmixon's the *Muses Mercury*, to the triumphs of Steele and Addison.

III

Although the professional writers who were responsible for these early serial publications and who used them to dispense advice and instant literary opinions were very influential upon the shaping of the polite domain, the writer who, more than any other, was to provide an explicit ideological rationale for politeness was Shaftesbury. The treatise *Soliloquy; or, Advice to an Author* (1710), reprinted as Treatise III of the *Characteristics of Men, Manners, Opinions, Times, etc.* (1711) is a landmark in the evolution of a conception of polite writing that was to be successfully mediated for a somewhat different class fraction in the Addisonian periodical. In sharp opposition to such as Dunton, however, Shaftesbury considers professional writing and trade publishing, with its eagerness to satisfy debased reader expecta-

---

[25] Quoted from Sir Walter Scott's edition of Dryden by Robert Newton Cunningham, *Peter Anthony Motteux, 1663–1718: A Biographical and Critical Study* (Oxford: Basil Blackwell, 1933), 21–2. Tonson was under the erroneous impression that Motteux was a bookseller.

tions, to be directly responsible for the malaise that affects contemporary letters:

> In our days the audience makes the poet, and the bookseller the author, with what profit to the public, or what prospect of lasting fame and honour to the writer, let anyone who has judgement imagine . . . Read we must; let writers be ever so indifferent. And this perhaps may be some occasion of the laziness and negligence of our authors, who observing of this need which our curiosity brings on us, and making an exact calculation in the way of trade, to know justly the quality and quantity of the public demand, feed us thus from hand to mouth; resolving not to overstock the market, or be at the pains of more correctness or wit than is absolutely necessary to carry on the traffic.[26]

That Shaftesbury does not consider *himself* to be any part of a bourgeois public sphere is manifest in his answer to the question why he chooses to publish his writings:

> In answer to this I shall only say that for appearing in public or before the world, I do not readily conceive what our worthy objector may understand by it. I can call to mind, indeed, among my acquaintance, certain merchant-adventurers in the letter-trade, who in correspondence with their factor-bookseller are entered into a notable commerce with the world. They have directly, and in due form of preface and epistle dedicatory, solicited the public, and made interest with friends for favour and protection on this account. They have ventured, perhaps, to join some great man's reputation with their own; having obtained his permission to address a work to him on presumption of its passing for something considerable in the eyes of mankind. One may easily imagine that such patronised and avowed authors as these would be shrewdly disappointed if the public took no notice of their labours. But for my own part, 'tis of no concern to me what regard the public bestows on my amusements, or after what manner it comes acquainted with what I write for my private entertainment, or by way of advice to such of my acquaintance as are thus desperately embarked. (p. 197)

This is the purest expression imaginable of the Renaissance *sprezzatura* that affects to despise the print culture. Shaftesbury goes on disingenuously to claim that print is merely a reprographic medium, merely a way of making his deplorable handwriting legible to the few friends that he wishes to reach, though 'I have

[26] *Characteristics of Men, Manners, Opinions, Times, etc.*, ed. John M. Robertson, 2 vols. (London: Grant Richards, 1900), i. 172–3. Subsequent references to Shaftesbury are also taken from this edition.

not indeed forbid my amanuensis the making as many as he pleases for his own benefit . . . 'Tis a traffic I have no share in, though I accidentally furnish the subject-matter. And thus am I nowise more an author for being in print' (p. 198). This wilful posing as the denizen of a pure scribal culture supplements the treatise's emphasis on the need to develop a prose style that expresses good breeding, good argument, good sense, and good grammar. To Shaftesbury, the ideal form of narrative is the dialogue. This allows the author to split the persona into two and hold an inner conversation with the self. Cool rationality and impeccable logic then replaces the frantic, hortatory excitement that is the currency of hack writers. Shaftesbury is implacably opposed to first-person narrative in a piece of writing; memoir, autobiography, love-letters, forms in which authors personalize themselves and speak directly to readers, are condemned because they confer upon writers the power of self-manipulation. (Dunton's *New Voyage Round the World* would have been anathema to him.) Paradoxically, dialogue provides the best vehicle for authorial integrity and self-presence. Dialogue is the formal means of avoiding fanaticism, enthusiasm, 'crudities, indigestions, choler, bile, and particularly . . . a certain tumour or flatulency' (p. 111). One is reminded here of the 'learned Aeolists' in Swift's *A Tale of a Tub*; and, at times, Shaftesbury almost seems to have Swift's hack persona from the *Tale* in mind as the exemplar of debased writing. It is not clear that Shaftesbury would have been capable of penetrating the irony involved in the hack's characterization of modern bookmaking. Parody, the impersonation of a voice not one's own, would not have recommended itself to him as an admissible tactic in the pursuit of a gentlemanly rhetorical ideal. Although Swift and Shaftesbury actually had similar targets in view, the latter may well have read the following passage from section VII as an example of, rather than a satire on, modern 'tumour or flatulency' of style:

In a few Weeks there starts up many a Writer capable of managing the profoundest, and most universal Subjects. For, what though his *Head* be empty provided his *Common-place-Book* be full; And if you will bate him but the Circumstances of *Method*, and *Style*, and *Grammar*, and *Invention*; allow him but the common Priviledges of transcribing from others, and digressing from himself, as often as he shall see Occasion; He will desire no more Ingredients towards fitting up a Treatise, that shall make a very comely Figure on a Bookseller's Shelf.[27]

Apart from his attention to stylistic matters, however, Shaftesbury is a seminal influence upon the polite in two respects, one programmatic and one philosophical. His call, in *Advice to an Author*, to the 'sovereigns', 'prime ministers', and 'grandees' of society to become patrons of arts and letters in order to 'ensure the fortunes of a distressed and ruinous tribe, whose forlorn condition has helped to draw disgrace upon arts and sciences, and kept them far off from that politeness and beauty in which they would soon appear if the aspiring genius of our nation were forwarded by the least care or culture' (i. 140) appears to have been heard very directly by Lord Burlington. This occurred, perhaps, through the mediation of his adviser Lord Somers (to whom Shaftesbury dedicated his *Letter concerning the Art or Science of Design*) and it influenced Burlington's own behaviour as a patron and as a practical, though not a professional, architect. Shaftesbury spoke in defence of the 'virtuoso', though he understood the term to refer to the gentleman-amateur rather than the professional scholar: 'I am persuaded that to be a *virtuoso* (so far as befits a gentleman) is a higher step towards the becoming a man of virtue and good sense than the being what in this age we call a scholar . . . The mere amusements of gentlemen are found more improving than the profound researches of pedants' (i. 214–15). More speculatively, we might consider elements of the neo-Palladian revival to be an instantiation of politeness in its more aristocratic forms. Burlington said almost nothing about the guiding idea behind his remodelling of Chiswick House, but the creation of a small-scale, intimate building that recapitulated Palladian exteriors and Roman decorative interiors, and that functioned as a temple of classical and neoclassical taste, could be viewed as the architectural capstone of Shaftesburian ideals.[28] More significant still, however, was the dialectical movement in which Shaftesbury connected nature, artistic mimesis of nature, ethics, and inherent critical taste. This, I would contend, enabled a conception of aesthetics that made the appreciation of natural

[27] Jonathan Swift, *A Tale of a Tub*, in *Prose Works*, i. 93.
[28] See John Harris, *The Palladian Revival: Lord Burlington, his Villa and Garden at Chiswick*, Exhibition catalogue (New Haven University Press, 1995), esp. 36–7.

and man-made beauty available to a broader section of the consuming public—even if nothing in Shaftesbury's own attitudes to such matters would have suggested that this outcome was desirable.

In *Advice to an Author*, Shaftesbury contends that 'in the very nature of things there must of necessity be the foundation of a right and wrong taste' (i. 216). Here, and in the earlier *An Inquiry Concerning Virtue and Merit* (1699), Shaftesbury argued that we are endowed with a moral sense that enables us to distinguish right from wrong quite naturally, which extends also to the aesthetic distinction between beauty and deformity. Genuine artists are those who possess inherently this sense of the inward beauty of things, and genuine artworks will express it: those alone, therefore, can operate as models and inspirations for developing artists. Living one's life ethically becomes for Shaftesbury very much an *aesthetic* business, very much a matter of taste:

What mortal being, once convinced of a difference in inward character, and of a preference due to one kind above another, would not be concerned to make his own the best? If civility and humanity be a taste; if brutality, insolence, riot, be in the same manner a taste, who, if he could reflect, would not choose to form himself on the amiable and agreeable rather than the odious and perverse model? Who would not endeavour to force Nature as well in this respect as in what relates to a taste or judgement in other arts and sciences? . . . If a natural good taste be not already formed in us, why should not we endeavour to form it, and cultivate it till it became natural? (i. 218)

Premising thus, Shaftesbury is able to lay down strict rules for the kind of reading necessary to cultivate natural good taste: it should not be too omnivorous, it should not be too serious ('task-reading'), it should not be in worthless genres such as travel-writing, or fantastic tales—especially those that suck us in with a great play of circumstantial and realistic detail. But the true aesthetic sense, like the moral sense, does not derive from any reading programme, even such an armigeral one as this. It derives from the contemplation of nature.

Prior to the publication of *Advice*, Shaftesbury had published his influential dialogue *The Moralists: A Philosophical Rhapsody* (1709), reprinted as Treatise V in *Characteristics*, in which his *raisonneur* figure Theocles persuades Philocles that 'there is no real good beside the enjoyment of beauty' (ii. 141). Philocles has been kept in extreme suspense by his friend, who has promised to reveal to him some ultimate insights in a specially appointed location 'with the silvan nymphs'. Theocles first astonishes his companion with an invocation to 'Ye fields and woods, my refuge from the toilsome world of business' to:

receive me in your quiet sanctuaries, and favour my retreat and thoughtful solitude. Ye verdant plains, how gladly I salute ye! Hail all ye blissful mansions! known seats! delightful prospects! majestic beauties of this earth, and all ye rural powers and graces! . . . O glorious nature! supremely fair and sovereignly good! all-loving and all-lovely, all-divine! whose looks are so becoming and of such infinite grace; whose study brings such wisdom, and whose contemplation such delight; whose every single work affords an ampler scene, and is a nobler spectacle than all which ever art presented! (ii. 97–8)

The passage, and the subsequent paean to the cosmos with its appreciation of the wild, barren places upon earth, has been read as an early intimation of Romanticism.[29] My own emphasis is slightly different. It is important to Shaftesbury to create nature as a category of the aesthetic, properly engaging our sense of beauty, because he wishes to liberate a taste for beauty that does not reside in beautiful objects themselves, products of artifice, but in the evidence that beautiful objects give of a shaping intelligence. Shaftesbury constructs a hierarchical ordering of beauty according to which art-objects give place to analogous designing powers in human nature. Benevolent human mental and emotional activity becomes the greatest aesthetic beauty, consonant with Shaftesbury's view that beauty and good are identical. On the way to this position, however, he implicates a form of aesthetic attention that is distinguished sharply from possession-ownership. To appreciate beauty, you don't need to own it: indeed, to experience any urge to possession would be vulgar, impolite, almost on a par with rapine:

Imagine then, good Philocles, if being taken with the beauty of the ocean, which you see yonder at a distance, it should come into your head to seek how to command it, and, like some mighty admiral, ride master of the sea, would not the fancy be a little absurd?

Absurd enough, in conscience. The next thing I should do, 'tis likely,

[29] See the valuable general discussion of Shaftesbury's philosophy and aesthetics given in James Sambrook, *The Eighteenth-Century: The Intellectual and Cultural Context of English Literature, 1700–1789* (London: Longman, 1986), 53–5.

upon this frenzy, would be to hire some bark and go in nuptial ceremony, Venetian-like, to wed the gulf, which I might perhaps as properly call my own.

Let who will call it theirs, replied Theocles, you will own the enjoyment of this kind to be very different from that which should naturally follow from the contemplation of the ocean's beauty. The bridegroom-Doge, who in his stately Bucentaur floats on the bosom of his Thetis, has less possession than the poor shepherd, who from a hanging rock or point of some high promontory, stretched at his ease, forgets his feeding flocks, while he admires her beauty. But to come nearer home, and make the question still more familiar. Suppose (my Philocles) that, viewing such a tract of country as this delicious vale we see beneath us, you should, for the enjoyment of the prospect, require the property or possession of the land.

The covetous fancy, replied I, would be as absurd altogether as that other ambitious one.   (ii. 126–7)

This, as we shall see, is an emphasis considerably developed by Addison in the celebrated 'Pleasures of the Imagination' papers in the *Spectator*. In Addison's hands, appreciation of natural beauty becomes a virtual *substitute* for ownership. We are not all in a position to appreciate works of art, paintings, sculptures—but most of us have nature's gallery at hand; and if we can be persuaded that disinterested contemplation of natural beauty is actually superior to the sordid pleasures of estate-ownership, so much the better for social cohesion.

IV

In *Advice to an Author*, one of Shaftesbury's purposes is to raise respect for informed discussion of the arts as in itself a valuable mode of discourse:

I take upon me absolutely to condemn the fashionable and prevailing custom of inveighing against critics as the common enemies, the pests and incendiaries of the commonwealth of Wit and Letters. I assert, on the contrary, that they are the props and pillars of this building; and that without the encouragement and propagation of such a race, we should remain as Gothic architects as ever.   (i. 153)

It is difficult to imagine that, in so saying, Shaftesbury had such as John Dennis in mind. Undoubtedly, Dennis was an important figure in the development of literary criticism, but a profoundly ambivalent one in the process of incorporating literary talk in the polite domain. As we have seen, Peter Motteux was an early sponsor of Dennis's work, publishing, for example, his patriotic poem 'Upon Our Victory at Sea' in the *Gentleman's Journal* and praising highly his first major critical essay *The Impartial Critick*. By 1713, however, when Pope published his *The Narrative of Dr. Robert Norris, concerning the strange and deplorable frenzy of Mr. John Dennis, an Officer of the Custom-house*, Dennis was well on his way to being permanently exiled from the precincts of *politesse*. Indeed, he was constructed as a composite image of the mad critic—hack, paranoic, choleric, slattern, a raving enthusiast maddened by the anal retentiveness of his adherence to Aristotle's 'rules':

His Aspect was furious, his Eyes were rather fiery than lively, which he roll'd about in an uncommon manner. He often open'd his Mouth, as if he would have utter'd some Matter of Importance, but the Sound seem'd lost inwardly. His Beard was grown, which they told me he would not suffer to be shav'd, believing the modern Dramatick Poets had corrupted all the Barbers in the Town to take the first Opportunity of cutting his Throat . . . I observ'd his Room was hung with *old Tapestry*, which had several Holes in it, caus'd . . . by his having cut out of it the Heads of divers *Tyrants*, the Fierceness of whose Visages had much provoked him. On all sides of his Room were pinned a great many Sheets of a Tragedy called *Cato*, with Notes on the Margin with his own Hand. The Words *Absurd, Monstrous, Execrable*, were everywhere written in such large Characters, that I could read them without my Spectacles.[30]

Dennis jokes became an established genre in the following years. The story circulated that Dennis had told the Duke of Marlborough that he feared the French would call for his (Dennis's) extradition as one of the terms of the Treaty of Utrecht. The duke replied that he himself was not nervous, though perhaps an equally formidable foe to France! In the *Dunciad Variorum*, Pope immortalized the story of Dennis's having claimed to invent a new way of making thunder sound-effects for his play *Appius and Virginia*; on hearing a similar effect at a performance of *Macbeth*, he roared out, 'That is my thunder, by God! the villains will play

[30] Alexander Pope, *The Narrative of Dr. Robert Norris etc.* (1713), in *The Prose Works of Alexander Pope: The Earlier Works, 1711–1720*, ed. Norman Ault (Oxford: Basil Blackwell, 1936; repr. 1968), 157–8.

my thunder but not my plays.' In the Scriblerian farce *Three Hours after Marriage* (1717), Dennis appears as Sir Tremendous in burlesque of his expressive critical vocabulary and his well-aired enthusiasm for Longinus and the sublime. As late as 1731 Fielding was guying Dennis's supposed enslavement to neoclassical canons of decorum in his Scriblerian Preface to *The Tragedy of Tragedies*.

What had Dennis done to deserve such sustained ridicule and opprobrium? An investigation of this question sheds some light on the early construction of politeness by concentrating on a figure who, by failing to observe its protocols, was banished to its margins: and yet whose critical opinions were influential on polite aesthetics. Pope's *Essay on Criticism* first caused Dennis to break the bounds of decorum in a pamphlet accusing Pope of Jacobite sympathies and expressing himself on Pope's person in a manner that would surely have drawn a challenge from an abler-bodied opponent: 'it being impossible that his outward Form, tho' it should be that of a downright Monkey, should differ so much from human Shape, as his immaterial unthinking part does from human Understanding'.[31] It is not difficult to see what, in Pope's *Essay*, would have roused Dennis to fury. The most explosive suggestion made by Pope was that an original genius was capable of breaking established rules and, by his success, forcing the rules themselves to adjust to innovative practice:

> Great Wits sometimes may *gloriously offend*,
> And *rise* to *Faults* true *Criticks dare not mend*;
> From *vulgar Bounds* with *brave Disorder* part,
> And *snatch* a *Grace* beyond the Reach of Art[32]

Dennis's name occurs in a later passage (lines 267–84) in which an anecdote from *Don Quixote* is cited as an example of the folly into which slavish adherence to Aristotle's rules would drag the injudicious critic. Dennis, then, is coupled with the foolish Knight of La Mancha in a poem that, on the whole, is not disposed to take the same charitable view of critics as is Shaftesbury and that is

---

[31] John Dennis, *Reflections on* An Essay Upon Criticism (1711), in *Critical Works*, i. 417.

[32] Lines 152–5, quoted from *The Twickenham Edition of the Poems of Alexander Pope*, ed. John Butt *et al.*, 11 vols. (London: Methuen and New Haven: Yale University Press, 1939–69), i. 257–8. (All quotations from Pope are from this edition, hereafter *The Twickenham Pope*.)

much more approbatory of the ancients than a critic like Dennis can be, who has already been sponsoring Milton in treatise after treatise. Although even at this early stage in his career Pope cannot be unproblematically recruited to the ranks of the polite, the *Essay on Criticism* is certainly his most polite performance:

> True ease in writing comes from art, not chance,
> As those move easiest who have learned to dance
>
> (lines 362–3)

which is why its potential was spotted by Addison and the poem taken up in the *Spectator*, no. 253 (20 Dec. 1711). The poem virtually exiled Dennis from the ranks of polite society and criticism, relegating him to a twilight existence as a companion for the deluded Knight of the Woeful Countenance.[33] Politeness, I would contend, is also behind Dennis's dispute with Addison expressed two years later in his *Remarks upon* Cato, *A Tragedy* (1713), and this is worth considering in some detail.

As Dennis himself admitted in his Introduction, it looked extremely odd for a Williamite Whig, a staunch defender of the Revolution settlement and spokesman for 'liberty', to be attacking a play that was widely perceived to be a defence of exactly these political values in the wake of the Sacheverell conviction. As Alan Downie puts it, 'the eponymous defender of the Roman republic is contrasted for ideological effect with the imperial usurper, Caesar'.[34] Yet the play is much more significant for the expression it gives to some of the binary oppositions that structure polite discourse than for any contribution its impotent hero makes to political thought. Cato dies by his own hand, having first satisfied himself in a Hamletesque soliloquy that his soul is immortal. Given that suicide is what is mainly at issue for Cato, it is difficult to know how he can achieve much in the way of a defence of his people's freedom. Pope's Prologue announces to the audience that, unlike other tragedies whose pathos derives from love, 'Here

---

[33] Dennis tried to earn his living in ways other than writing, but he was continually in financial difficulty and did look to his writing to supplement a meagre income. He considered that Pope's attack on him in the *Essay* took advantage of him at a particularly vulnerable moment when he was seriously in debt. His poverty is hinted at in Pope's *Narrative*. On this, see Dennis, *Critical Works*, i. 524–7, and *The Prose Works of Alexander Pope*, ed. Ault, pp. xcviii–cxxviii.

[34] J. A. Downie, *To Settle the Succession of the State: Literature and Politics, 1678–1750* (Basingstoke: Macmillan, 1994), 84.

tears shall flow from a more generous cause, | Such tears as Patriots shed for dying laws' (lines 13–14).[35] *Cato* presents itself as running against the current of contemporary taste in certain important respects. We have already referred, in the previous chapter, to a 'plausibility crisis', a domestication and bourgeoisification of taste that compromised traditional literary aspirations. An aspect of this is the emergence of a female readership, most obvious in and for the early periodicals, that had a powerful effect on the nature of writing in the early eighteenth century. Kathryn Shevelow puts the point thus:

Periodical editors certainly perceived women as an economic interest group that it was advantageous to attract, and this they did by characterizing them as a social group necessitous of the periodical's oversight. In addition, by orienting their publications to what was generally perceived to be women's typical reading levels, the editors established a common denominator of all reading levels, male and female. Ignorance of classical languages and literature, signifying lack of access to higher forms of education, became a frequently employed sign of the common denominator . . . Eschewing the classics, a pronounced class marker, was an ideological gesture: not only did it define a readership, but it established and celebrated an alternate, popular literary tradition in explicit contrast to an elite one.[36]

Feminization of culture is, as Shevelow's book argues, an important aspect of the new polite discourse. This is apparent in the tragic drama of the early century, especially in the 'she-tragedies' of Nicholas Rowe, the Prologue to whose *The Fair Penitent* (1703) theorizes the point:

> Long has the fate of kings and empires been
> The common business of the tragic scene,
> As if misfortune made the throne her seat,
> And none could be unhappy but the great . . .
> Stories like these with wonder we may hear,
> But far remote, and in a higher sphere,
> We ne're can pity what we ne'er can share . . .
> Therefore an humbler theme our author chose,
> A melancholy tale of private woes;

---

[35] All quotations from *Cato* are from *The Miscellaneous Works of Joseph Addison*, ed. A. C. Guthkelch, 2 vols. (London: G. Bell, 1914), i. Subsequent references to Addison's works other than to the *Spectator* are to this edition.

[36] Shevelow, *Women and Print Culture*, 34–5.

> No princes here lost royalty bemoan,
> But you shall meet with sorrows like your own.[37]

The point is even more obvious in the later *The Tragedy of Jane
Shore* (1714), in which the heroine is ritually humiliated by
Richard of Gloucester and cast out as a beggar for her principled
refusal to seduce her lover into joining Richard's political faction.
Here the domestication and feminization of tragic form is apparent, as *hunger* becomes Shore's durance, not, as in neoclassical
tragedy, some more ethereal sickness at heart. The play renegoti-
ates the valency of the stage cuckold: no longer the Restoration
figure of fun, Shore's husband in an orgy of forgiveness receives
his wife's penitence and gives her to eat. Although Jane dies,
the emotional effect of Shore's absolution is quite transporting,
making for a deliriously happy death.

Cato's Prologue presents itself as very *British* in its manly
refusal of domestic subject-matter, its rigorous attempt to put
political events at the centre of tragic representation. This is,
however, a selective and inaccurate account of the play. Its principal issue is the value of self-control as against the untrammelled
expression of emotion. Cato's sons Portius and Marcus are in love
with Lucia: and from the outset they are contrasted, the former
capable of a philosophical evenness of temper, while the latter has
'a weak distemper'd soul that swells | With sudden gusts, and
sinks as soon in calms, | The sport of passions' (I. i. 110–12).
Which cast of mind is the more effectively Roman? In Act I scene
iv, Juba, the Numidian prince, and his general, Syphax, debate the
question of what makes Rome great. Syphax confesses that he
can't conceal his discontent—he is not yet Roman enough—and
that he does not see why the Romans should be regarded as a
greater race than the Numidians. The answer is given by Juba in
terms of polish, restraint, sociability—all key terms in polite
discourse:

> A *Roman* soul is bent on higher views:
> To civilize the rude unpolish'd world,
> And lay it under the restraint of laws;
> To make Man mild, and sociable to Man;
> To cultivate the wild licentious Savage

[37] Nicholas Rowe, *The Fair Penitent* (1703), ed. Malcolm Goldstein (London:
Edward Arnold, 1969), Prologue, lines 1–4, 9–11, 15–18.

With wisdom, discipline and liberal arts;
Th'embellishments of life: Virtues like these,
Make human nature shine, reform the soul,
And break our fierce barbarians into men.

(I. iv. 30–8)

Juba has clearly been reading his *Spectator* carefully. To Syphax's objection that this sounds all very effeminate to him—merely a reining in of the passions and a breeding-ground for hypocrisy—Juba suggests that he should look at Cato as an example. Cato not only despises sensual pleasure, but he bears affliction with exemplary fortitude. This distinguishes the hero from the brute. The play disposes very conveniently of the emotionally incontinent Marcus and Syphax, who do not possess the Roman virtues, by having the former killed putting down a traitorous rebellion led by the latter, also killed. This leads to the play's climactic moment as the body of his son is brought before Cato by means of a collectable stage direction:

CATO [*meeting the corps*]. Welcome my son! here lay him down, my
   friends,
  Full in my sight, that I may view at leisure
  The bloody coarse, and count those glorious wounds.
  —How beautiful is death, when earn'd by virtue!
  Who would not be that youth? what pity is it
  That we can die but once to serve our country!
  —Why sits this sadness on your brows, my friends?
  I should have blush'd if *Cato*'s house had stood
  Secure, and flourish'd in a civil war.
  —*Portius*, behold thy brother, and remember
  Thy life is not thy own, when *Rome* demands it.
JUBA. Was ever man like this!   [*Aside.*
CATO. Alas my friends!
  Why mourn you thus? let not a private loss
  Afflict your hearts. 'Tis *Rome* requires our tears.
  The mistress of the world, the seat of empire,
  The nurse of heroes, the delight of gods,
  That humbled the proud tyrants of the earth,
  And set the nations free, *Rome* is no more.
  O liberty! O virtue! O my country!
JUBA. Behold that upright man! *Rome* fills his eyes
  With tears, that flow'd not o'er his dead son.   [*Aside.*

(IV. iv. 77–97)

Intended as it is to represent Stoic republican virtue, as exemplified by Cato's ability to put an abstraction like patriotism above the personal love for his son, the passage is, on another level, an expression of polite good manners, an exalted form of 'family hold back'. Cato is admired because, like his true son Portius, he can manage himself and is not given to creating embarrassing emotional scenes. Self-restraint of this superior kind is a central lesson of the literary periodical. Hence, Steele's relentless *Guardian* campaign to puff *Cato* as a play that is in itself an entire 'liberal Education'. Of the Juba–Syphax encounter referred to above, the *Guardian*, no. 33 for 18 April 1713 makes the following somewhat racist observation:

There is not an Idea in all the Part of *Syphax*, which does not apparently arise from the Habits which grow in the Mind of an *African*; and the Scene between *Juba* and his General, where they talk for and against a liberal Education, is full of Instruction: *Syphax* urges all that can be said against Philosophy, as it is made subservient to ill Ends by Men who abuse their Talents; and *Juba* sets the less Excellencies of Activity, Labour, Patience of Hunger, and Strength of Body, which are the admired Qualifications of a *Numidian*, in their proper Subordination to the Accomplishments of the Mind.[38]

Juba, in his role as honorary Roman, underlines the superiority of European cultural achievement over the rude physicality of the African people.

In the *Remarks upon* Cato, Dennis appears to conform to Pope's view of him in the *Essay on Criticism* as a slavish follower of the 'rules' when he offers the most succinct summary in his criticism to date of the tragedian's obligation to enforce poetic justice, an obligation that he believes Addison flouts. Yet it appears that consistency in presentation of character and setting is more important than are the rules in themselves. Dennis outlines his strategy in the *Remarks upon* Cato as follows:

1. I shall shew what perfections are wanting to it, thro' the not observing several of the Rules of *Aristotle.*
2. I shall shew with what Absurdities it abounds, thro' the observing several of the Rules without any manner of Judgment or Discretion.
3. I shall shew some Faults and Absurdities, which are such in Themselves, without any relation to the Rules.   (ii. 44)

---

[38] Richard Steele *et al.*, *The Guardian*, ed. John Calhoun Stephens (Lexington: University of Kentucky Press, 1982), 139. All subsequent quotations from the *Guardian* are from this edition.

It is plain from the above that Dennis's quarrel with Addison is not exactly that the latter fails to adhere to the Aristotelian prescription for tragedy: rather that he does so only partially and in such a random manner that he destroys the plausibility of his play altogether. Throughout, Otway's play *The Orphan* is employed by Dennis as a yardstick against which to measure the improbability and unnaturalness of *Cato*. These weaknesses are illustrated at once with respect to Cato's role. Dennis's way of putting it is that the play inculcates no general moral (is not 'allegorical' in the contemporary acceptation of that term) because, by killing himself at a point when his life was necessary, Cato does not act in a way that allows us to deduce any generalizable code of conduct. Cato's suicide induces, not the classical tragic emotions of pity and terror, but rather burning indignation in the observer. Dennis is utterly outraged by this craven self-murder. The Stoic temperament, emphasizing as it does mastery over the passions, was deeply abhorrent to a critic who had for some years been advocating the expression of passion as the central platform of his critical agenda; and Dennis doubts whether a Stoic can actually *be* a tragic hero, given that drama involves conflict, whereas the Stoic's overriding imperative is to avoid it. The climactic scene in Act IV scene iv quoted above, in which Cato exalts love of his country over love of his son, is closely analysed. Surely they are not mutually exclusive? Surely the truth is that love of one's country is actually the resultant of the close familial ties that, for the individual, actually *constitute* a country? And yet, says Dennis, if we are to have 'a Nest of *Stoicks*', let them at least *be* Stoics. Addison's inconsistency in having Cato advise his son Portius to go into safe rural retirement just at the point where his public service will be most necessary goads Dennis into a mocking irony that becomes, as the treatise goes on, his characteristic tone. Where Dennis exceeds the boundaries of the polite is not only in the mordant tone, but in a critical methodology that prompts him to pick the text to pieces, reducing situations and sentiments to absurdity. With respect to Act IV, Dennis's purpose is to show that Addison's adherence to Aristotle's supposed unity of place has resulted in wholesale implausibility. At that point, the wicked traitor Sempronius has dressed in Juba's clothes to gain access to Marcia:

JUBA. *What do I see? Who's this that dares usurp*
The Guards and Habits of Numidia*'s Prince?*

We see here that *Juba* does but ask him a pertinent Question, when he very rudely makes him an impertinent Answer.

SEMP. *One that was born to scourge thy Arrogance,*
Presumptuous Youth.

Now what is this Arrogance, and what this mighty Presumption? Where lies the Arrogance and the Presumption of a Man's laying claim to his own Cloaths, when he sees them upon another Man's Back?   (ii. 77)

This will serve as one example out of many, both of the ironic tone reminiscent of Thomas Rymer—capable often of making the reader laugh aloud—and of the methodology of close reading that exposes implausibility in the characters and dramatic situations. Pope's advice to would-be critics in the *Essay on Criticism* is to eschew exactly the kind of hostile and detailed analysis undertaken by Dennis. Polite criticism entails getting on to the same wavelength as one's author and seeing the work entire:

> A perfect judge will read each work of wit
> With the same spirit that its author writ:
> Survey the WHOLE, nor seek slight faults to find
> Where nature moves, and rapture warms the mind;
> Nor lose, for that malignant dull delight,
> The generous pleasure to be charmed with wit.

> (lines 233–8)

To Pope, there was nothing generous and much that was malignant in Dennis's way of proceeding and characteristic forms of expression.

Increasingly personal, comic, and closely analytical as his criticism became, Dennis was constructed by his enemies as the antithesis of the polite drawing-room critic. *Cato* infuriated him, despite its political correctness, because it sponsored a buttoned-in self-reliance, a containment that was at the centre of the polite campaign to regulate conduct, to police the boundaries of the self by, *inter alia*, preventing emotions from leaking through them. Dennis favoured passion, the sublime, religious forms of poetry like that of the Old Testament Psalmist that could not altogether be contained by classical canons of decorum. Yet in the important province of aesthetics, one of the polite movement's most significant cultural edifices, there is a direct line of descent leading from Dennis to Addison, Aaron Hill, James Thomson, and the Whig poets of the 1730s.[39] In *The Advancement and Reformation of Modern Poetry* (1701) and *The Grounds of Criticism in Poetry* (1704), Dennis had taken up the modern stance in the ancients versus moderns debate, by arguing that the expression of *passion* was poetry's most important function, that passion can be 'enthusiastic' when it is the result of wonder, terror, and astonishment, that religious poetry is most likely to express this most valuable form of passion and that Christian poetry above all is capable of doing so. Hence, his admiration for the original genius of Milton. Sponsorship of primitive Old Testament poetry, of sublime passions that were more likely to derive from nature than from art objects, and, famously, of Milton's originality was assumed by Addison in the *Spectator*, although he would not acknowledge this as a legacy from Dennis, with whom he would shortly be in furious contention.

V

One way of characterizing the mission of Addison and Steele is to say that they had to fuse the strands of polite ideology to be found in writers as apparently distinct as Shaftesbury and Dennis and to find a mode of expression that would unite as large a section of the potential readership as possible behind this powerful ideological product. The combination of talent and experience that they brought to the task was an extraordinarily fruitful one. Neither is wholly definable as a professional writer, but Steele was less successful at avoiding that fate than Addison, failing in two alternative careers as a soldier and a politician and never achieving the level of financial patronage necessary to service his considerable needs. Steele's literary publications—the extraordinary tract *The Christian Hero; or, An Argument Proving that no Principles but those of Religion are Sufficient to make a Great Man* (1701) and the sentimental comedies *The Lying Lover* (1703) and *The Tender Husband; or, The Accomplished Fool* (1705)—placed him at the dead centre of the early campaign to regulate manners and

[39] See Robert Inglesfield, 'James Thomson, Aaron Hill and the Poetic "Sublime"', *British Journal for Eighteenth-Century Studies*, 13/2 (Autumn 1990), 215–21.

conduct. In the wake of the founding of the London Society for the
Reformation of Manners in 1691 and the Collier controversy,
Steele's early reputation as a moralist was gained on the strength
of his bid, in *The Christian Hero*, to make Christianity occupy
more imaginative space than paganism in our conception of what
is heroic behaviour. Rejecting both Caesar and Cato as types of
heroism, Steele seeks to replace them by Christ and St Paul. A key
paragraph outlines an early manifesto of the sentimental in its
insistence on the innate sociability of mankind and in its isolation
of sympathy as a mechanism by means of which feeling can be
communicated between individuals:

The Eternal God, in whom we Live, and Move, and have our Being, has
Impress'd upon us all one Nature, which as an Emanation from him, who
is Universal Life, presses us by Natural Society to a close Union with each
other; which is, methinks, a sort of Enlargement of our very selves when
we run into the Ideas, Sensations and Concerns of our Brethren: By this
Force of their Make, Men are insensibly hurried into each other, and by a
secret Charm we lament with the Unfortunate, and rejoice with the Glad;
for it is not possible for an human Heart to be averse to any thing that is
Human: But by the very Mein and Gesture of the Joyful and Distress'd we
rise and fall into their Condition; and since Joy is Communicative, 'tis
reasonable that Grief should be Contagious, both which are seen and felt
at a look, for one Man's Eyes are Spectacles to another to Read his Heart:
Those useful and honest Instruments do not only discover Objects to us,
but make our selves also Transparent; for they, in spite of Dissimulation,
when the Heart is full, will brighten into Gladness, and gush into Tears:
From this Foundation in nature is kindled passion, which opens our
Bosoms, and extends our Arms to Embrace all Mankind, and by this it is
that the Amorous Man is not more suddenly melted with Beauty, than the
Compassionate with Misery.[40]

The subsequent emphasis on the heroism of forgiveness leads to a
renegotiation of the aristocratic code of honour, a revision of
gentility that exposed one of its central practices, duelling, as 'an
Imposture, made up of Cowardice, Falshood, and Want of Understanding' (*Tatler*, no. 25 for 4–7 June 1709) which was a vital
contribution to the cultural mediation that created polite society.[41]

[40] *Tracts and Pamphlets by Richard Steele*, ed. Rae Blanchard (Baltimore: Johns
Hopkins University Press, 1944), 54–5.
[41] On duelling as a vital part of the aristocratic ideology, see J. C. D. Clark, *English
Society, 1660–1832: Ideology, Social Structure and Political Practice during the
Ancien Régime* (Cambridge University Press, 1985), 106–18.

Yet, despite his reputation as an arbiter of public morality, on the back of which he obtained the Drury Lane patent in 1715, Steele remained vulnerable to the attack that he himself was no gentleman. The whiff of hypocrisy and fakery continued to emanate from him. Swift exploited the ambiguity in social status of (another) upstart Irishman brilliantly in his campaign against the Whig refusal to insist on the dismantling of French fortifications at Dunkirk as one of the peace terms in ending the war of the Spanish succession. He opens his reply to Steele in *The Importance of the Guardian Considered, in a Second Letter to the Bailiff of Stockbridge* (1713) with a characterization of him as a low-level scribbler and subliterate drinking crony, charges to which Steele, unlike Addison, remained vulnerable:

Mr. *Steele* is author of two tolerable Plays, (or at least of the greatest part of them) which, added to the Company he kept, and, to the continual Conversation and Friendship of Mr. *Addison*, hath given him the Character of a Wit. To take the height of his Learning, you are to suppose a Lad just fit for the University, and sent early from thence into the wide World, where he followed every way of Life that might least improve or preserve the Rudiments he had got. He hath no Invention, nor is Master of a tolerable Style; his chief Talent is Humour, which he sometimes discovers both in Writing and Discourse; for after the first Bottle he is no disagreeable Companion.[42]

Addison already enjoyed a high reputation as a gentleman-author whose *Remarks on Several Parts of Italy* (1705) became essential reading for noblemen on the Grand Tour. Such is the classical orientation of this guidebook that the Italian landscape appears to exist only to vindicate the ancient authors whose writing memorializes it: 'The greatest pleasure I took in my journey from *Rome* to *Naples* was in seeing the fields, towns and rivers that have been described by so many *Classic* Authors, and have been the scenes of so many great actions; for this whole road is extremely barren of curiosities'.[43] In the posthumously published *Dialogues upon the Usefulness of Ancient Medals especially in Relation to the Latin and Greek Poets* (1721—though probably written before 1715), Addison developed the interest in coins, inscriptions, statuary, and classical poetry that is the salient feature of the *Remarks*. The *Dialogues* are cast in the polite Shaftes-

---

[42] Swift, *Prose Works*, viii. 5–6.
[43] Addison, *Miscellaneous Works*, ii. 94.

burian form of a conversation between Philander, very much in favour of ancient numismatology, Cynthio, who can't see the sense in it, and Eugenius, who has an open mind. The discussion takes place in a milieu of gentlemanly retirement, in beautiful surroundings; and, against that background, Cynthio's ridicule of 'the Medallists' strikes a note of aristocratic empty-headedness: 'These gentlemen, says he, value themselves upon being critics in Rust, and will undertake to tell you the different ages of it, by its colour' (ii. 282). Philander gradually persuades his friends that there is nothing ridiculous about this kind of study, provided it does not become an end in itself. Coins must be studied to throw light on ancient history and, above all, on ancient poetry and art, so that numismatics becomes a supplement to the humane pursuits of a gentleman. Philander is positioned between the vulgar pursuits of those antiquarians like the notorious Dr Woodward who mistake means for ends and as a result are embarked on some life-denying mission of stockpiling ancient objects for their own sakes, and the pleasure-seeking philistinism of well-bred aristocrats who are allergic to knowing about anything at all. Eugenius is the reader's representative in the text and it is his heart and mind that the argument sets out to win.

Between them, then, Steele and Addison had experience relevant to the entire social spectrum that in their periodicals they hoped to telescope. First and foremost, the Addisonian periodical was a business venture. We must insist on this just as we did earlier with Dunton's *Athenian Mercury*. In the *Spectator*, no. 10 (12 March 1711), Addison's trumpet-blowing has him estimating a readership of 60,000 and announcing a mission for the periodical that sheds light on its polite aspiration, by means of mass circulation, to take down the partitions between élite and popular forms of discourse:

It is with much Satisfaction that I hear this great City inquiring Day by Day after these my Papers, and receiving my Morning Lectures with a becoming Seriousness and Attention. My Publisher tells me, that there are already Three thousand of them distributed every Day: So that if I allow Twenty Readers to every Paper, which I look upon as a modest Computation, I may reckon about Threescore thousand Disciples in *London* and *Westminster* . . . and I shall be ambitious to have it said of me, that I have brought Philosophy out of Closets and Libraries, Schools and Colleges, to dwell in Clubs and Assemblies, at Tea-Tables and in Coffee-Houses.[44]

Contemporary readers testify to the widespread appeal, and therefore the commercial success, of the *Tatler's* combination of social reformism and good humour: John Gay, in *The Present State of Wit*:

[The *Tatler's*] disappearing seem'd to be bewailed as some general Calamity, every one wanted so agreeable an Amusement, and the Coffee-houses began to be sensible that the Esquires Lucubrations alone, had brought them more Customers than all their other News Papers put together. It must indeed be confess'd, that never Man threw up his Pen under Stronger Temptations to have imployed it longer: His Reputation was at a greater height than, I believe, ever any living Author's was before him. 'Tis reasonable to suppose that his Gains were proportionably considerable . . . He has indeed rescued [Learning] out of the hands of Pedants and Fools, and discover'd the true method of making it amiable and lovely to all mankind: In the dress he gives it, 'tis a most welcome guest at Tea-tables and Assemblies, and is relish'd and caressed by the Merchants on the Change; accordingly, there is not a Lady at Court, nor a Banker in *Lombard-Street*, who is not verily perswaded, that *Captain Steele* is the greatest Scholar, and best Casuist, of any Man in *England*.[45]

Perhaps the ultimate tribute to the *Tatler* was not so much Gay's eagerness to praise it as the publisher Henry Hills's eagerness to pirate it. He rushed into print an edition of the *Tatler's* first 100 numbers, a mere four days after no. 100 appeared, in December 1709.[46] Reasons for the popularity and suggestibility of the periodicals are apparent on first reading. The format of a 2,000-word essay proved to be a median measure of the leisure-gap that readers required this kind of reading material to fill. Within that set format, there seemed to be no end to the inventiveness with which skilled journalists could vary the forms and sonorities of each individual number. Building on the work of their predecessors, the periodicalists stressed the accessibility of their columns, creating an image of their readers as *producers* rather than mere

[44] *The Spectator*, ed. Donald F. Bond, 5 vols. (Oxford: Clarendon Press, 1965), i. 44. All quotations are from this edition.

[45] John Gay, *The Present State of Wit, in a Letter to a Friend in the Country* (1711), in *John Gay: Poetry and Prose*, ed. Vinton A. Dearing with Charles E. Beckwith, 2 vols. (Oxford: Clarendon Press, 1974), ii. 451–2.

[46] See Richmond P. Bond, 'The Pirate and the *Tatler*', *Library*, 5th ser., 28/4 (1963), 257–74.

consumers of the paper, interacting reciprocally with the editors. When Steele published a particularly controversial number of the *Spectator* on the topic of whoring (no. 266 for 4 Jan. 1712), he took advantage of the reaction by publishing a range of readers' responses, some supportive and some critical. Reader-friendly devices like the characterized personae of Isaac Bickerstaff and Mr Spectator and their social circles provide obvious nodes of interest. Generations of commentators have located the *Spectator*'s distinctive achievement in the 'literariness' of its style, commencing with Samuel Johnson, who in the *Life of Addison* spoke of it as a 'model of the middle style' being 'pure without scrupulosity, and exact without apparent elaboration; always equable, and always easy, without glowing words or pointed sentences'.[47] Recently, Michael Ketcham has provided an interesting analysis of the way in which the *Spectator* creates a self-contained and self-referential constellation of key terms, such as the ubiquitous 'good nature', which is duplicated with quasi-synonymous terms like compassion, benevolence, humanity, affability, complaisance, and easiness. By constant repetition and accretion, these become available for use by the reader, who annexes them to his own vocabulary and who, therefore, begins to think in patterns that have been defined for him. Ketcham draws attention both to the referential function of the language and to the 'doubleness' with which it constitutes a sealed-off domain of *Spectator*-speak:

The *Spectator*'s whole program embraces an expanding readership while it creates the illusion of an intimate community. But at the heart of *The Spectator*'s balance of public and private communication is the duality of language: words can modify behaviour because they participate in behaviour, and they control behaviour because they have a structure of their own. *The Spectator*, because it is so deliberately a piece of rhetoric, illuminates the doubleness of whatever we read: it draws from and returns to its society; and it forms a self-enclosed, self-contained, self-reflecting world within itself.[48]

It is worth dwelling upon the middle-way rhetoric that I describe operating in Addison's *Dialogues upon . . . Ancient Medals* because the tactics pursued by the *Tatler*, the *Spectator*, and the

[47] Samuel Johnson, *Life of Addison*, quoted from *The Oxford Authors: Samuel Johnson*, ed. Donald Greene (Oxford University Press, 1984), 676.
[48] Michael G. Ketcham, *Transparent Designs: Reading, Performance and Form in the* Spectator *Papers* (Athens: University of Georgia Press, 1985), 676.

Guardian to *produce* a readership that was simultaneously represented to be the *actual* readership operated in a similar way. The
Spectator, no. 117 (14 July 1711) might serve as a typical example
of the periodical's method of thought-shaping and opinion-form-
ing. It commences:

> There are some Opinions in which a Man should stand Neuter, without
> engaging his Assent to one side or the other. Such a hovering Faith as this,
> which refuses to settle upon any Determination, is absolutely necessary
> in a Mind that is careful to avoid Errors and Prepossessions. When the
> Arguments press equally on both sides in matters that are indifferent to
> us, the safest Method is to give up our selves to neither.   (i. 479)

From the opening generalized philosophical-cum-social observation, encapsulating an attitude of drawing-room scepticism, the
reader cannot predict how the essay will develop. We are eager to
learn what, exactly, will be topic on which we should remain
uncommitted. In the event, the essay is on witchcraft. The next
paragraph balances the evidence for the persistence of stories
about witchcraft against the dubious provenance of such stories
and reaches a conclusion beautifully poised on the rim of irony: 'I
believe in general that there is, and has been such a thing as
Witchcraft; but at the same time can give no Credit to any Particular Instance of it.' Addison's cool formulation is one that the
reader can extract from the essay and take away in capsule form.
One can imagine this being reproduced at a dinner engagement as
the reader's own view, an opinion shaped in exactly the same way
as modern newspaper leaders form detachable opinions for their
readers. The position constructed by Addison is neither zealous
in the persecution of witches nor openly scathing about those
who believe in their existence. In the second sentence, non-
commitment is figured as a hovering Faith, a bird refusing to find
its perch in a personified Mind at large in the dangerous allegorical
landscape of Errors and Prepossessions. 'Matters that are indifferent to us' in the next sentence is an appropriation of a key term in
the new latitudinarian religious vocabulary, where 'indifferent
matters' are those on which the church is not obliged to take a line.
Again, Mr Spectator employs it to reinforce his moderate, anti-
enthusiastic, well-mannered stance. After the two opening paragraphs stating the theme and taking up a position in respect of it,
the essay develops into an anecdote about the lovable Tory squire

Sir Roger de Coverley, who was with Mr Spectator one day when they were accosted by a beggar-woman, Moll White, who has the local reputation of being a witch. Moll White is described through a literary template: a graphic and observant portrait of a country beggar quoted from Otway's *The Orphan*. Thus a reader is invoked who is knowledgeable, well-read, interested in the theatre—cultured to a degree—and who is likely to be arrested by what is in fact a beautifully chosen passage from Otway, almost Words-worthian in its sympathy for the 'wrinkled Hag, with Age grown double', that it describes. Sir Roger and Mr Spectator enter Moll White's hovel, and it becomes apparent that the squire buys into the Moll White story to a considerable extent. He is receptive to many of the rumours circulated about her 'and would frequently have bound her over to the County Sessions, had not his Chaplain with much ado perswaded him to the contrary' (i. 482). Since the reader has already been constructed as superior to this Tory traditionalism (and abuse of justice), the progressive political stance of the essay is communicated. Again, that stance is careful: however much we may smile at the country bumpkins and their community leaders who brand harmless beggars like Moll as witches, it was less than a year after this that the last conviction in England for witchcraft (of Jane Wenham) occurred.[49] Thus, even on a topic not overtly political, the *Spectator* does its work of promoting an *entente cordiale* between the 'social indifference' of the middle class and the 'calcified traditionalism' of the gentry.[50]

It would be possible to document thoroughly and at length the way in which the periodicals function to bring the aristocracy and the literate middle class into contact with each other on the ground of politeness, giving substance to the claim that the periodicals are a cultural arm of the making of the English middle class. It is in the province of aesthetics, however, that we can best demonstrate the *Spectator*'s genius in combining elements from widely scattered ideological provenances and shaping these into a way of thinking about art that would become the philosophical matrix for

[49] She was reprieved and pardoned. The last execution was in 1685 and the Witchcraft Act was repealed in 1736. See Keith Thomas, *Religion and the Decline of Magic* (London: Weidenfeld and Nicolson, 1971), 537–8.

[50] The terms come from Edward A. Bloom and Lillian D. Bloom, *Joseph Addison's Sociable Animal* (Providence, RI: Brown University Press, 1971), 13. They are making the point that the device of using Sir Roger and the Whig merchant Sir Andrew Freeport is vital in achieving the class mediation that is the *Spectator*'s project.

some of the century's major developments. Aesthetic discussion in the *Spectator* also affords a vantage-point from which to observe clearly the cultural politics of the early-century periodicals. Addison's 'Pleasures of the Imagination' papers (*Spectator,* nos. 409 and 411–21) make an initial distinction between 'primary' and 'secondary' pleasures which appropriates John Locke's distinction between primary and secondary qualities of objects. Addison's distinction owes as much, however, to John Dennis's division of 'passion' into 'Vulgar Passion' and 'Enthusiastick Passion' in *The Grounds of Criticism in Poetry,* where enthusiastic passion is the effect produced in us by imagining objects that 'belong not to common Life', objects that strike us with 'Terror, or Admiration, or Horror'—his examples are large-scale phenomena from the natural world.[51] Addison's concern in the opening two papers, however, is for the social licensing of aesthetic pleasure: and this is an emphasis that derives, as I have suggested earlier, from hints in Shaftesbury's *The Moralists.* In the opening paper, no. 409 for 19 June 1712, Addison adduces the metaphor of 'taste' to refer to 'that Faculty of the Mind, which distinguishes all the most concealed Faults and nicest Perfections in Writing' (iii. 527). At this historical juncture, as Andrew Varney puts it, 'the alimentary canal is a major highway of aesthetic discourse', an observation that argues for the interconnection of the rise of aesthetics and the rise of trade.[52] For Addison, literary taste is akin to connoisseurship in tea—though there is an unnoticed glissando from fact to value, since the tea connoisseur's task is only to tell different teas apart whereas the 'Man of a fine Taste in Writing' can not only discern the distinctive characteristics of authors but can discover their 'general Beauties and Imperfections'. To know whether you possess literary taste, you have to read over the celebrated works of antiquity and those modern works 'which have the Sanction of the Politer Part of our Contemporaries' [but who are they, and what gave *them* the right to pass this sanction?] and see whether you feel yourself to be delighted with exactly those passages and aspects of the works that have stood the test of time. If not, *you* and not the classics are in the wrong: the books judge *you,* rather than you judge the *books.* You will take delight, not necessarily in

[51] Dennis, *Critical Works,* i. 338–9.
[52] Andrew Varney, 'Advertising and Vindicating Eighteenth-Century Novels', *Connotations,* 3/2 (1993–4), 133–46: 143–4.

any complexity of thought, but rather in the language in which the thought is '*cloathed*'—language as the dress of thought, another central aesthetic metaphor of the age, again suggesting that reflection about art is being conditioned by an increasingly sumptuous, more luxurious material environment furnished by commercial activity. The question then arises: is taste innate, or is it learned? 'The Faculty must in some degree be born with us' but 'there are several Methods for Cultivating and Improving it' and 'the most natural Method for this Purpose is to be conversant among the Writings of the most Polite Authors'. Addison is clearly having it both ways: taste is *both* innate and learned. It is the property of those who succeed to an aristocratic cultural inheritance, but is not closed to those who wish to acquire it. This is a statement in aesthetic terms of the philosophy of the open élite. 'Conversation with Men of a Polite Genius is another Method for improving our Natural Taste,' Addison goes on to say. In Addison's writing well-educated, well-bred private individuals have become the arbiters of taste rather than the habitués of the royal court who decide these matters in Dryden's critical treatises. Addison has a Shaftesburian sense of the importance of this critical conversation taking place: it shapes a climate in which schools of creative writing can flourish. But his sense of what that conversation should now be *about* is pure Dennis: the rules, inspired by the sublime: 'Altho' in Poetry it be absolutely necessary that the Unities of Time, Place and Action, with other Points of the same Nature should be thoroughly explained and understood; there is still something more essential, to the Art, something that elevates and astonishes the Fancy, and gives a Greatness of Mind to the Reader, which few of the Criticks besides *Longinus* have consider'd' (iii. 530).

In the next number to deal with aesthetics, no. 411 for 21 June 1712, the distinction is introduced between primary and secondary pleasures of the imagination, the former resulting from objects that are actually present to us and the latter resulting from images called to mind by memory or fiction. A further distinction is drawn between pleasures deriving from imagination and those from the understanding (such as a chapter in Aristotle). The former are easier to acquire: indeed those that derive from the natural world are spoken of as instinctive and available to virtually everyone: 'We are struck, we know not how, with the Symmetry of any thing we see, and immediately assent to the Beauty of an Object, without enquiring into the particular Causes and Occasions of it' (iii. 369). However, the next paragraph, perhaps the key paragraph in the entire sequence of papers, pulls back from this degree of democratization at the same time as it constructs aesthetic pleasure as a substitute for commercial ownership:

A man of a Polite Imagination, is let into a great many Pleasures that the Vulgar are not capable of receiving. He can converse with a Picture, and find an agreeable Companion in a Statue. He meets with a secret Refreshment in a Description, and often feels a greater Satisfaction in the Prospect of Fields and Meadows, than another does in the Possession. It gives him, indeed, a kind of Property in every thing he sees, and makes the most rude uncultivated Parts of Nature administer to his Pleasures: So that he looks upon the World, as it were, in another Light, and discovers in it a Multitude of Charms, that conceal themselves from the generality of Mankind.   (iii. 538)

Pleasurable contemplation of art-objects and of the natural world defuses the aspiration to own them. All of nature becomes a landed estate of the imagination, where a man can harmlessly play out his fantasies of cultivation and control: desires that estate-owning aristocrats such as the Cobhams, Burlingtons, and Boyles who were the addressees of Pope's later poems could fully exercise upon their own properties. At the same time, he can take pleasure in the fact that his mental activity is still relatively privileged because 'the vulgar' are not capable of engaging in it. This paragraph gives on to one in which the social programme for aesthetics is spelled out. Art appreciation is constructed as the ultimately desirable activity to fill the new-found leisure time of the middling sort, in a prescription that prefigures the use of it made by such as Matthew Arnold in *Culture and Anarchy*:

There are, indeed, but very few who know how to be idle and innocent, or have a Relish of any Pleasures that are not Criminal . . . A Man should endeavour, therefore, to make the Sphere of his innocent Pleasures as wide as possible, that he may retire into them with Safety, and find in them such a Satisfaction as a wise Man would not blush to take. Of this Nature are those of the Imagination, which do not require such a Bent of Thought as is necessary to our more serious Employments, nor, at the same Time, suffer the Mind to sink into that Negligence and Remissness, which are apt to accompany our more sensual Delights, but, like a gentle Exercise to the Faculties, awaken them from Sloth and Idleness, without putting them upon any Labour or Difficulty.   (iii. 538–9)

Art appreciation as a harmless way of passing the time for those who have the surplus means to consider that man does not live by bread alone is the opportunity that Addison presents here. Shifting the locus of aesthetic attention on to landscape, prospects, the natural world, as the early papers in the 'Pleasures of the Imagination' sequence do, even if it transpires that 'we find the Works of Nature still more pleasant, the more they resemble those of Art' (iii. 549), creates a category of the beautiful that can be appropriated without expenditure. The most explicit and unequivocal expression of this new aesthetic is given in the *Guardian*, no. 49 for 7 May 1713, a paper clearly indebted to the *Spectator*, no. 411 and to Shaftesbury:

The various Objects that compose the World were by Nature formed to delight our Senses; and as it is this alone that makes them desirable to an uncorrupted Taste, a Man may be said naturally to possess them, when he possesseth those Enjoyments which they are fitting by Nature to yield. Hence it is usual with me to consider my self, as having a natural Property in every Object that administers Pleasure to me. When I am in the Country, all the fine Seats near the Place of my Residence, and to which I have Access, I regard as *mine*. The same I think of the Groves and Fields where I walk, and I muse on the Folly of the *civil* Landlord in *London*, who has the fantastical Pleasure of draining dry Rent into his Coffers, but is a Stranger to fresh Air and Rural Enjoyments. By these Principles I am possessed of half a dozen of the finest Seats in *England*, which in the Eye of the Law belong to certain of my Acquaintance, who being Men of Business, chuse to live near the Court.   (pp. 193–4)

The essay goes on to illustrate the maxim that 'he is the true Possessor of a thing who enjoys it' (p. 194) by suggesting that the entire beau monde in its finery is really a spectacle put on for his enjoyment and therefore, in this specialized sense, ownership. Interestingly, the argument is then used to sponsor a domestic, homespun, mass-produced taste in houseware: landscapes and perspectives rather than history paintings or old masters, Irish linen not foreign, coloured glasses but not expensive imported china. Commodities once the exclusive property of the luxurious rich have now become accessible through the techniques of mass production to consumers of the middling sort. In just the same way, cultural appreciation can become a conversation in which all (or at least all consumers) can participate. Overall the effect of the periodicals' aesthetic discussion is to introduce a conception of the beautiful that frees it from the exclusive ownership of a privileged élite and yet makes the enjoyment of it dependent on the cultivation of a particular sensibility that requires leisure time, a level of educational attainment, and a familiarity, even if not at first hand, with the great monuments of classical and modern culture.

In Addison's annexation to the aesthetic domain of 'Prospects of an open Champian Country, a vast uncultivated Desert, of huge Heaps of Mountains, high Rocks and Precipices, or a wide Expanse of Waters, where we are . . . struck . . . with that rude kind of Magnificence which appears in many of these stupendous Works of Nature' (iii. 540) can be discerned a dry run for the Burkean sublime; and the 'Pleasures of the Imagination' papers are also structured by a prototype of that momentous distinction between the sublime and the beautiful spelled out, but certainly not invented, by Burke. Emphasis placed on the *disinterested* nature of aesthetic attention, on a form of contemplation that is opposed to economic ownership, anticipates some of the positions taken in Kant's *Critique of Judgement* (1790). The periodicals' sponsorship of ballad and folk forms (two essays were devoted to the promotion of the Ballad of Chevy-Chase), their softening of the edges of satire in the interests of good breeding, and verdicts against *The Man of Mode* and the muscular Restoration tradition of satirical theatre: all this is evidence of the extent to which they were influential in shaping the climate of mid-century and later literary production and aesthetic discussion.[53] And they achieved such prominence, this chapter has contended, by the suturing of widely disparate influences into an aesthetic credo of polite refinement that had a very widespread appeal. The literary agenda was now firmly in the hands of the middling sort. It was perhaps the first time in literary history that the age-old Horatian prescription —*utile et dulce*—was convincingly realized in a publishing venture that was a huge commercial success. The success of the

[53] *Spectator*, no. 70 (21 May 1711) and no. 74 (25 May 1711) are on the Ballad of Chevy-Chase. Interestingly, however, Walter Graham notes (*English Literary Periodicals*, 61–2) that this poem was first championed by Oldmixon's *Muses Mercury*. The *Tatler*, no. 242 (24–6 Oct. 1710) argues that 'good Nature was an essential Quality in a Satyrist, and . . . all the Sentiments that are beautiful in this Way of Writing must proceed from that Quality in the Author'. *The Man of Mode* is attacked in the *Spectator*, no. 65 (15 May 1711).

literary periodicals masterminded by Addison and Steele ensured that, however bleak the future for aristocratic or government patronage of writers, a living could be secured through the agency of the newspapers, essay-serials, magazines, and reviews.

PART III

The Scriblerians and their Enemies

6

Canon Fodder

Alexander Pope made an appearance in the previous chapter as an avatar of the polite. Author of the *Essay on Criticism* and *The Rape of the Lock,* furnisher of a prologue for Addison's *Cato,* Pope in his early manifestation was hovering on the fringes of the latter's 'little senate'. The story of his break with Addison over Thomas Tickell's rival translation of the *Iliad* is well known.[1] When Pope returned to original composition after several years' toiling in the field of Homer translation and Shakespeare editing, he was anything but polite. He had refashioned himself into an honorary aristocrat and could look down from an Olympian height on the workers in the uncontrolled publishing industry scurrying around his feet. *Peri Bathous,* published in the third (1728) volume of Pope and Swift's *Miscellanies,* and the 1728 *Dunciad* were not the first, but the most overt and powerful indications of a backlash against commercial and popular forms of writing and entertainment that Pope and his allies saw as receiving active encouragement from government circles. There is a politics involved in the anti-polite parodic and satirical forms they adopted to combat writing perceived to be the product of a consumer-driven literary market-place, which will be the subject of the next chapter. At present, we need only note that, whatever else it was, *The Dunciad* was an attempt to influence public taste in a particular, anti-professional direction. It was an act of canon formation.

In the case of at least one writer, the romantic novelist Eliza Haywood, Pope is credited with spectacular success. The lines that he wrote about her in book 2 of the 1729 version, figuring her as the worthy object of competition in a pissing contest between the popular publishers Curll and Chetwood, are still said by critics and literary historians to have been responsible for forcing Haywood to abandon writing. The lines read:

[1] Maynard Mack, *Alexander Pope: A Life* (New Haven: Yale University Press, 1985), 272–82.

See in the circle next, Eliza plac'd;
Two babes of love close clinging to her waste;
Fair as before her works she stands confess'd,
In flow'rs and pearls by bounteous Kirkall dress'd.
The Goddess then: 'Who best can send on high
The salient spout, far-streaming to the sky;
His be yon Juno of majestic size,
With cow-like-udders, and with ox-like eyes.
This China-Jordan, let the chief o'ercome
Replenish, not ingloriously, at home.'

(II. 149–58)

Interest in Haywood has revived recently as a function of a wider concern with the 'mothers of the novel'. Pope's satirical method of collapsing personal into aesthetic judgements is deemed to have caused an enduring neglect both of the writer and of the genre (romantic fiction) in which she wrote. Christine Blouch puts the point thus: '[Pope's] assault on [Haywood's] "morals" was coupled with an attack on the genre in which she had achieved success, a maneuver that effectively positions the poetic Eliza's "babes of love" as interchangeable metaphors for illegitimate children and illegitimate literary offspring.'[2] Employing the mother-whore homology, the satirist can figure the female writer's textual production as a function of her sexual promiscuity. Haywood is represented as one of the 'monstrous mothers' in which, as Susan Gubar has observed, male-authored writing of this period is rich. Since, as she points out, female writers are compared to mothers of misshapen or illegitimate offspring in male-authored satire of the period, it makes sense that in *The Dunciad*, a lady novelist should be first prize in the pissing contest and a chamberpot the second prize! Scriblerus' note heaps coals on the fire. He purports to find a respectable classical precedent in the *Iliad*, book 23 (the funeral games for Patroclus) for heroic games in which 'a Lady and a Kettle' are the prizes, except that his version is claimed to be more humanitarian because at least the china jordan is given only as *second* prize! It is difficult to dissent from Valerie Rumbold's account of woman's place in Pope's world, where she concludes: 'That Dulness herself is female is one of the most important facts about her... her yawn, the formless yet potent opposite of the

[2] Christine Blouch, 'Eliza Haywood and the Romance of Obscurity', *Studies in English Literature*, 31 (1991), 535–53: 540.

divine fiat, like her womb-like cave of pullulating literary monstrosities, draws on Pope's fundamental unease about female creativity; yet her very existence at the centre of his own creation testifies to his need for such a creature.'[3]

As an aspect of the book's concern with the emergence of professional writing, this chapter investigates the part played by two women writers, Susanna Centlivre and Eliza Haywood, in promoting the respectability of writing professionally, and in producing a supply of prose fiction that preserved the novel from premature extinction. These writers were explicitly excluded from the canon by the series of cultural *coupures* made in Scriblerian writing and particularly in *The Dunciad*. As a contrast to the treatment meted out to them by Pope and his colleagues, I discuss attempts made on Congreve's behalf to configure him as a canonical writer before he had actually written anything. To investigate the question of how some forms of writing come to be regarded as culturally valuable where others do not, I draw a comparison between the novels of Eliza Haywood and Daniel Defoe, both writers whose main imperative was to find a market niche, but only the latter of whom is considered to have any enduring literary merit. It seems valuable in this chapter to go beyond the book's allotted time-span to investigate later sites upon which a continuing process of cultural arbitration between the romance and the novel is seen to occur. To this end, I explore an important novel by a mid-century female professional writer, Charlotte Lennox's *The Female Quixote*, in which one can clearly discern a line of separation between valuable and valueless women's fiction that provides an observation-point on the incipient split between the 'art' novel and the merely popular novel, 'classics and trash' in a modern formulation.[4] This chapter might suggest that if we choose not to take Pope at face value, if we refuse to permit his exceptionally charismatic topography of the literary landscape to set our agenda—if, perhaps, we tell the story from below rather than accepting Pope's *ex cathedra* version—-we might find heroes and villains different from those inscribed by the powerful mythology of *The Dunciad*.

[3] Valerie Rumbold, *Woman's Place in Pope's World* (Cambridge University Press, 1991), 166–7.

[4] See Harriet Hawkins, *Classics and Trash: Traditions and Taboos in High Literature and Modern Popular Genres* (London: Harvester Wheatsheaf, 1990), 312 and *passim*.

I

Cultural historians would agree that it was in the period under this book's scrutiny that a recognizably modern conception of 'literature' and 'the literary' began to develop, a conception that narrowed the category of literature by excluding from it long-established non-fictional forms and genres and severing traditional ties with erudition. Explicitly stated in a poem like Milton's *Lycidas* is the conception of poetry as a vocation that cannot be served without unremitting toil:

> Alas! What boots it with uncessant care
> To tend the homely slighted Shepherds trade,
> And strictly meditate the thankless Muse?[5]

Before the poet has a self to express, he must make himself master of as much of the accumulated wisdom contained in books as is humanly possible, and the poetic voice he discovers for himself will be a ventriloquial one because he will be required to demonstrate the fruits of his learning by means of allusion. Professionalization of writing would necessarily transform this conception of the poet's role. Busy professionals striving against deadlines to make a living in the theatre, for example, would have altogether more pragmatic reasons for knowing the plots of plays written by their English, French, and Spanish predecessors: and, as we have seen, within the commercial institution of theatre where literary property took on palpable form the use they made of this knowledge was more likely to be branded 'plagiarism' than honorifically termed 'allusion'. By the time Samuel Johnson wrote *Rasselas*, the Miltonic conception of the poet as a man of extensive learning and encyclopaedic knowledge was one that his Imlac could only maintain at the expense of self-parody:

[The poet's] labour is not yet at an end: he must know many languages and many sciences; and, that his stile may be worthy of his thoughts, must, by incessant practice, familiarize to himself every delicacy of speech and grace of harmony. [Chapter break.] Imlac now felt the enthusiastic fit, and was proceeding to aggrandize his own profession, when the prince

---

[5] Lines 64–6; quoted from *John Milton: The Complete Poems*, intro. Gordon Campbell (London: Dent-Dutton, 1980), 43.

cried out, 'Enough! Thou hast convinced me, that no human being can ever be a poet.'[6]

Poetry was by then a crippling responsibility, quite out of tune with the new climate created by professional writers and by the conception of aesthetics that we saw emerging in the previous chapter. As Douglas Lane Patey suggests in a stimulating discussion, the 'aesthetic' theory of art that is developed by Shaftesbury, Addison, and in Hutcheson's *Inquiry into the Original of our Ideas of Beauty and Virtue* (1725) is one that separates 'the aesthetic from the moral and the intellectual: a fracturing of the humanist ideal of a union of wisdom and eloquence':

> Like paintings in museums, literary works come to be conceived as at once the products of, and objects properly approached with, a special set of mind distinct from any which we bring to bear in other circumstances, a special 'aesthetic attitude', as it has come to be called, characterized precisely by its 'disinterestedness', its disconnection from the rest of human concerns. In the course of the eighteenth century, this special mode of experience becomes the defining property of the aesthetic, relegating the arts to an autonomous realm and, of course, making possible 'aesthetics' as a separate philosophical discipline.[7]

'Literature' operates in the realm of the senses, not in the realm of cognition, according to this new conception of aesthetics: and one root of this is, as we have seen, a desire to bring the beautiful within the grasp of polite consumers who needed emotional rather than economic resources to appreciate it. The new movement had the strangely paradoxical result that those writers like the periodical essayists who sought most earnestly to bring it about were made redundant by it. From the standpoint of post-Romantic writing, Addison and Steele would seem impossibly naïve and designing in the simple clarity of their mission to educate and reform. Their position in the canon would be subject to increasing pressure.[8]

[6] Samuel Johnson, *The History of Rasselas, Prince of Abissinia* (1759), ed. D. J. Enright (Harmondsworth: Penguin, 1976), 62–3.

[7] Douglas Lane Patey, 'The Eighteenth Century Invents the Canon', *Modern Language Studies*, 18/1 (Winter 1988), 17–37: 24. Patey himself makes little of Shaftesbury in the discussion; and his conception of the sociology of this new aesthetics is somewhat attenuated; but his central argument is a powerful one.

[8] See the account given of this by Brian McCrea, 'The Canon and the Eighteenth Century: A Modest Proposal and a Tale of Two Tubs', *Modern Language Studies*, 18/1 (Winter 1988), 58–73.

Not only were the canons for what would be considered 'the literary' under active renegotiation, but the content with which they would be filled out—the actual genres and writers who would meet the new criteria—were in process of contestation. Howard Weinbrot is doubtless correct to argue that the overall trajectory of this process was the replacement of the classical pantheon by a group of British Worthies that, to achieve itself fully, required the rehabilitation of Milton from the taint of republicanism so that Britain could boast an epicist on a par with those of Greece and Rome.[9] His claim, however, that the British canon that finally replaced the classical one was tolerant, open, and inclusive—in that respect a microcosm of the British people themselves and their libertarian principles—appears to be open to challenge on at least two major counts. It ignores such self-conscious acts of canon formation as Pope's *Dunciad*, the tendency of which is to guard, police, exclude, demote, and seal off; and it ignores the fact that so very few women writers (with the exception of Katherine Philips, 'the matchless Orinda', and the occasional exception of Aphra Behn) were ever admitted to it—which, of course, is why feminist critics in our own time have had such rich reclamation opportunities.

For much of its length, *The Dunciad* opposes itself to the forms of social energy that the periodical essayists wished to channel. Whereas Addison and Steele tried to create forms of discourse that permitted the bleeding of one cultural strain into another, the transgressive mingling of social strata in tightly controlled environments, *The Dunciad* is readable as an intervention against what it sees as cultural miscegenation:

> How Tragedy and Comedy embrace;
> How Farce and Epic get a jumbled race;
> How Time himself stands still at her command,
> Realms shift their place, and Ocean turns to land.
> Here gay Description Ægypt glads with showers;
> Or gives to Zembla fruits, to Barca flowers;
> Glitt'ring with ice here hoary hills are seen,
> There painted vallies of eternal green,
> In cold December fragrant chaplets blow,
> And heavy harvests nod beneath the snow.[10]

---

[9] Howard D. Weinbrot, *Britannia's Issue: The Rise of British Literature from Dryden to Ossian* (Cambridge University Press, 1993), 114–41.

[10] I. 69–78; quoted from *The Twickenham Pope*, v. 68. Subsequent references to *The Dunciad* are from this edition.

As the periodicals strove to sanitize and regulate public space—the *Spectator*, no. 132 (1 August 1711), in which the reader is taught how to respect human interaction space when travelling in the close confines of a stagecoach, is a particularly vivacious example—*The Dunciad* anxiously depicts popular and commercial cultural forms subverting this ideal. The 'Smithfield muses' are on the march, polluting the territory of high culture, contaminating the high by the low. Spatializing and concretizing the struggle as a struggle over *Lebensraum*, the poem represents the conflict between the mediators of popular, lowbrow, and irrational culture like Colley Cibber, Eliza Haywood, and Elkanah Settle and those who would prevent their infiltration into respectable artistic vicinities. By implication, *The Dunciad* distinguishes between good and bad writers, between valuable and worthless art forms, rational and irrational printed works, lasting art and commercial, evanescent entertainment: and it tries to hold the line between élite, or 'classic', and merely popular cultural forms: 'Or, if to wit a coxcomb make pretence, | Guard the sure barrier between that and sense' (i. 177–8). In the line of fire is the newly emergent professional writer whose relations with the public are unmediated market relations, and whose art is merely a species of production quite on a level with any other: art as trade. In his autobiographical *Epistle to Dr. Arbuthnot*, Pope had distanced himself from such artisans of print:

> I left no Calling for this idle trade;
> No Duty broke, no Father dis-obey'd . . .
> Yet then did *Gildon* draw his venal quill;
> I wish'd the man a dinner, and sate still:
> Yet then did *Dennis* rave in furious fret;
> I never answer'd, I was not in debt:
> If want provok'd, or madness made them print,
> I waged no war with *Bedlam* or the *Mint*.[11]

Pope's stance on professional writing contributes to the shaping of a lasting prejudice against any kind of commercial motive operating in the production of what is allowed to be 'art'. In ways certainly not acknowledged by Weinbrot, this position has contributed to the formation of the British literary canon, influencing the system of exclusions upon which the nineteenth-century conception of an unbroken literary tradition was based. In its final

---

[11] Lines 129–30, 151–6: ibid. iv. 105, 107.

version, *The Dunciad* is an indictment of an entire educational apparatus that is responsible for the production of *Trivialliteratur*, and that is itself the result of erosion of political liberties. As the footnote to lines 501 ff. of book IV explains:

A Recapitulation of the whole Course of Modern Education describ'd in this book, which confines youth to the study of *Words* only in Schools, subjects them to the authority of *Systems* in the Universities, and deludes them with the names of *Party-distinctions* in the World. All equally concurring to narrow the Understanding, and establish Slavery and Error in Literature, Philosophy and Politics. The whole finished in modern Freethinking; the completion of whatever is vain, wrong, and destructive to the happiness of man-kind, as it establishes *Self-love* for the sole Principle of Action.   (v. 391)

Women who wished to write were, to Pope, examples of debased education and perverse self-love. When Lady Mary Wortley Montagu read the infamous lines 83–4 of Pope's *Imitation of Horace*, Satire II. i—'From furious Sappho scarce a milder fate, | P–xed by her love, or libelled by her hate'—she was, predictably, furious. Through his friend the Earl of Peterborow, Pope transmitted a reply to her to the effect that:

he wonderd how the Town could apply those Lines to any but some noted common woeman, that he should yet be more surprised if you should take them to your Self, He named to me fower remarkable poetesses & scribblers, Mrs Centlivre Mrs Haywood Mrs Manly & Mrs Been, Ladies famous indeed in their generation, and some of them Esteemed to have given very unfortunate favours to their Friends, assuring me that Such only were the objects of his satire.[12]

Four remarkable poetesses and scribblers, Susanna Centlivre, Eliza Haywood, Mary Manley, and Aphra Behn, are more significant to venery than to veneration, in Pope's opinion. When in the Epistle to Augustus (*Imitations of Horace, Epistle* II. i) Pope is offering an overview of Restoration comedy, his characterization of Aphra Behn is in terms of licentiousness:

> The stage how loosely does Astraea tread,
> Who fairly puts all characters to bed.   (lines 290–1)

The note supplied, '*Astraea*. A name taken by Mrs. Behn, authoress of several obscene plays, *etc.*', calls attention to the degenera-

---

[12] Pope, *Correspondence*, ed. George Sherburn, 5 vols. (Oxford, 1956), iii. 352.

tion involved in a lewd playwright's assuming a name once reserved for the great virgin queen Elizabeth.[13] As Jeslyn Medoff has
shown, it was difficult for women writing in the wake of Aphra
Behn to avoid the 'Punk and Poetess' equation; to do so successfully required the strictest possible management of reputation and
of the conditions under which the writer sought to publish her
work. A germane example would be the queries and contributions
made to Dunton's *Athenian Mercury* in verse by 'the Pindarick
Lady', Elizabeth [Singer] Rowe, which Dunton anthologized and
published in 1696 as *Poems on several occasions. Written by*
PHILOMELA, and which in later life Mrs Rowe did not consider
polite enough to reprint.[14] In the case of the dramatist and poet
Susanna Centlivre, Pope and his fellow Scriblerians went out of
their way to drive home the 'Punk and Poetess' equation in the
collaborative play *Three Hours After Marriage*, which took the
stage in 1717. Although the play's most recent editor considers
that the character of Phoebe Clinket is a composite portrait of the
woman writer, it is assuredly a detailed and unmistakable likeness
of Centlivre.[15] References to Mrs Centlivre's œuvre, the prefaces
to her published plays, and the various controversies in which she
was embroiled are woven as thickly into the texture of the part as
are the portraits of dunces in *The Dunciad*. For the contemporary
audience, the pleasure of the portrayal lies precisely in this palpable disposition of detailed knowledge that is one source of *The
Dunciad*'s imaginative power, knowledge that spans almost two
decades of Centlivre's involvement in the English theatre.[16] In the

[13] Quoted from *The Twickenham Pope*, iv. 219–20. Recently, Murray G. H.
Pittock has suggested that this reference to Behn can provide a clue to his Jacobite
sympathies. See his *Poetry and Jacobite Politics in Eighteenth-Century Britain and
Ireland* (Cambridge University Press, 1994), 110.

[14] See Jeslyn Medoff, 'The Daughters of Behn and the Problems of Reputation', in
Isobel Grundy and Susan Wiseman (eds.), *Women, Writing, History, 1640–1740*
(London: Batsford, 1992), esp. 49–53. This is interesting on the later management of
Rowe's image to satisfy increasingly strict conceptions of politeness in the female
domain.

[15] See John Fuller's summary of the evidence and his conclusion in Gay's *Dramatic
Works*, i. 440–2. Quotations in the text are from this edition.

[16] To list just the most obvious identifying features, the scene in which Clinket's
play about Deucalion and Pyrrha in the flood is torn apart by the actors is a direct
reference to Centlivre's *The Man's bewitched; or, The Devil to Do About Her* (perf.
1709), the mutilation of which was extensively discussed in Bernard Mandeville's
periodical the *Female Tatler*, no. 69 (14 Dec. 1709) and by Centlivre herself in the
Preface to her play, where she denies that she was responsible for writing that number
of the *Female Tatler* and asserts that she was quite happy with Cibber's truncation of

previous chapter it was suggested that the critic John Dennis was
the victim of deliberate Popean acts of representation that put him
beyond the pale of politeness and ensured that, however significant his ideas, they would not be given due credit or attribution. In
Three Hours After Marriage, Dennis is brought face to face with
Mrs Centlivre in a Godzilla-versus-the-Hulk meeting of literary
monsters. Dennis (Sir Tremendous), presented as a knee-jerk
'ancient', rails at the emptiness and plagiarism of all modern
dramatists, doling out to them his brittle epithets, while Centlivre
(Phoebe Clinket) uses her sexuality to weasel her way into his
good opinion in a climax of *double entendres* made out of critical
terminology:

SIR TREMENDOUS. O what Felony from the Ancients! What Petty-
Larceny from the Moderns! There is the famous *Iphigenia* of *Racine*,
he stole his *Agamemnon* from *Seneca*, who stole it from *Homer*, who
stole it from all the Ancients before him. In short there is nothing so
execrable as our most taking Tragedys.
1ST PLAYER. O! but the immortal *Shakespear*, Sir.
SIR TREMENDOUS. He had no Judgment.
2ND PLAYER. The famous *Ben Johnson*!
CLINKET. Dry.

her ghost scene in the play but did not agree to the actor Estcourt's excising it almost
altogether. This gives point to Fossile's line in Act I of *Three Hours* that 'instead of
Puddings, she makes Pastorals; or when she should be raising Paste, is raising some
Ghost in a new Tragedy' (lines 65–7). This was not the first time Centlivre had had
trouble with her cast. The actor Wilks despised the script of her *The Busie Body*
(1709), as the *Tatlers* for 15 and 19 May 1709 had made known to all the town.
Although John Fuller fails to note it, the character name Plotwell used in *Three
Hours* had occurred in Centlivre's first comedy, *The Beau's Duel; or, A Soldier for
the Ladies* (1702), which has attached to it a Preface discussing the need for comedies
to maintain *vraisemblance*. That Preface, and the later one to *Love's Contrivance; or,
Le Médecin Malgré Lui* (1703) which discusses the relevance of Aristotelian precepts
to dramatic structure, are guyed in *Three Hours*. Apart from representing the
stereotype of the hack woman writer, Clinket is also a female virtuoso, a learned
philosophical lady: a type that Centlivre had presented in the character of Valeria in
The Basset-Table. All through *Three Hours*, sideswipes are being taken at Centlivre
through the character of Clinket; for example in II. 471 ff., when Clinket drinks
Fossile's virginity-testing preparation with the comment 'I can drink as freely of it, as
of the Waters of *Helicon*. My love was always Platonick,' which introduces extended
comic reference to her play *The Platonick Lady* (1706); or, when, in I. 558–9, Fossile
says to her 'you have got the poetical Itch, and are possess'd with Nine Devils, your
Nine Muses', referring to a collection of funeral poems dedicated to John Dryden
entitled *The Nine Muses; or, Poems Written by Nine Severall Ladies Upon the Death
of the late famous John Dryden, Esq.* (London, 1700), to which she is thought to have
contributed. It would be possible to demonstrate that the entire play could be read as
an extended parody of the typical structure of a Centlivre farcical comedy.

1ST PLAYER. The tender *Otway*!

SIR TREMENDOUS. Incorrect.

2ND PLAYER. Etheridge!

CLINKET. Meer Chit-chat.

1ST PLAYER. *Dryden*!

SIR TREMENDOUS. Nothing but a Knack of Versifying.

CLINKET. Ah! dear Sir *Tremendous*, there is that *Delicatesse* in your Sentiments!

SIR TREMENDOUS. Ah Madam! there is that Justness in your Notions!

CLINKET. I am so charm'd with your manly Penetration!

SIR TREMENDOUS. I with your profound Capacity!

CLINKET. That I am not able—

SIR TREMENDOUS. That it is impossible—

CLINKET . To conceive—

SIR TREMENDOUS. To express—

CLINKET. With what Delight I embrace—

SIR TREMENDOUS. With what Pleasure I enter into—

CLINKET. Your Ideas, most learned Sir *Tremendous*!

SIR TREMENDOUS. Your Sentiments, most divine Mrs. *Clinket*.

(I. 421–50)[17]

Phoebe Clinket is represented in the play as having all the demonic characteristics of the female aspirant to print: obsessive hunger for fame, vanity, sexual voracity which she is willing to market in her cause, and sluttish neglect for her physical appearance and domestic responsibilities. The stage direction that introduces her draws attention to her writing mania and to her inattention to personal hygiene. It reads: 'Enter *Clinket*, and her Maid bearing a Writing-Desk on her Back. *Clinket* Writing, her Head-dress stain'd with Ink, and Pens stuck in her Hair' (after I. i. 72; italics reversed). Even the necessary subterfuge to which Susanna Centlivre resorted to conceal her gender is mocked (she posed as a male in publishing *Love's Contrivance* and did not sign her plays, after the first one, until she was respectably married to Joseph Centlivre, one of the Queen's Yeomen of the Mouth, i.e. cooks), as Plotwell is reputed to be the author of Clinket's play, and, in this vicarious safety, cheerfully consents to its mutilation— much to the agony of Clinket.

There is, however, a very different way to see Centlivre, suggested in comments made by the later dramatist and literary

---

[17] Act I, lines 421–50 in Gay's *Dramatic Works*.

professional Elizabeth Inchbald in her influential twenty-five-volume anthology *The British Theatre*, published in 1808. In her introduction to Congreve's *Love for Love*, she writes: 'Idolized as this author [Congreve] was for his dramatic genius, he retired from the pursuit of fame to a country life, instigated by a jealousy of Mrs. Centlivre's superior influence with the town as a dramatist.'[18] Earlier, discussing Centlivre's *The Wonder! A Woman Keeps a Secret*, she had provided a more elaborate commentary on the respective merits of Congreve and Centlivre:

Merely as writers, the author of 'The Way of the World', and the authoress of 'The Wonder', hold distinct places among the literati; but as plays are productions that depend on action, and require talents of a nature, in which writing has perhaps the smallest share, Mrs. Centlivre has, from the time she commenced dramatic author to the present day, through all the vicissitudes of taste which have, in that period, intervened, still been more attractive on the stage than the great poet whom her success offended.[19]

Inchbald reprints only two of Congreve's plays in her monumental anthology, to Centlivre's three. And certainly when Inchbald wrote this, Centlivre was a very popular repertory dramatist.[20] When, for example, the denizens of the Austen rectory at Steventon wanted to stage amateur theatricals, it was to Centlivre's *The Wonder! A Woman Keeps a Secret* that they resorted for their text.[21] What emerges clearly, however, from the documentation of Congreve's critical reception compiled by Howard Erskine-Hill and Alexander Lindsay in *The Critical Heritage* is the extraordinary effort made on Congreve's behalf to create him as Mac Dryden. Congreve was intended to be a canonical writer, one of the great British worthies, before he had published a single word. As Howard Erskine-Hill's excellent introduction makes clear, Dryden was waiting for Congreve to happen so that he could designate him successor Laureate:

When in 1692 Thomas Southerne drew to the attention of Dryden the work of an unknown young playwright it was the chance Dryden had been

[18] Elizabeth Inchbald, *The British Theatre; or, A Collection of Plays, which are acted at the Theatres Royal, Drury Lane, Covent Garden, and Haymarket*, 25 vols. (London, 1808), xiii. 5–6.   [19] Ibid. xi. 3–4.
[20] On the performance history of *The Wonder! A Woman Keeps a Secret*, see Bowyer, *The Celebrated Mrs. Centlivre*, 179–86.
[21] Park Honan, *Jane Austen: Her Life* (London: Weidenfeld & Nicolson, 1987), 50–2.

looking for. Deposed from his laureateship by the revolution of the Prince of Orange, Dryden had little reason to admire his successor, and none to expect kindnesses from him. His pride as well as his sense of his own worth prompted him to name his own heir in the realm of letters. He needed someone of the younger generation whom he could himself recognize and assist; one whose talent, with assistance, could not fail to win applause; and one, not of Dryden's own religion and loyalty, who would be acceptable to the new Orange establishment. This heir might then protect his 'father' and mentor, and defend his reputation after death.[22]

Early poetic testaments to Congreve by Southerne, Swift, Yalden, Bevil Higgons, and in particular Dryden's own 'To my Dear Friend Mr. Congreve, On His Comedy, call'd, *The Double-Dealer*' (1694) convey the sense of a Congreve-shaped hole in the literary universe:

> Oh that your Brows my Lawrel had sustain'd,
> Well had I been Depos'd, if You had reign'd!
> The Father had descended for the Son;
> For only You are lineal to the Throne.
> Thus when the State one *Edward* did depose;
> A Greater *Edward* in his room arose.
> But now, not I, but Poetry is curs'd;
> For *Tom* the Second reigns like *Tom* the first.[23]

As the poet Thomas Yalden expressed it, the obstacle was likely to be a lack of financial independence that would result either in the poet's servility to a patron—private or public—or in his starvation:

> Trust not the ungrateful World too far;
> Trust not the Smiles of the inconstant Town:
> Trust not the Plaudits of a Theater,
> (Which *D——fy* shall, with *Thee*, and *Dryden* share)
> Nor to a Stages int'rest Sacrifice thy own . . .
> Small are the Trophies of his boasted *Bays*,
> The Great Man's promise, for his flattering Toyl,
> Fame in reversion, and the publick smile,
> All vainer than his Hopes, uncertain as his Praise.
> 'Twas thus in Mournful Numbers heretofore,
> Neglected *Spencer* did his Fate deplore:
> Long did his injur'd Muse complain,

[22] Howard H. Erskine-Hill and Alexander Lindsay (eds.), *William Congreve: The Critical Heritage* (London: Routledge, 1989), 2.
[23] Lines 41-8; quoted from *The Poems and Fables of John Dryden*, 490.

> Admir'd in midst of *Wants*, and *Charming* still in vain . . .
> Thus did the World thy great Fore-Fathers use,
> Thus all the inspir'd *Bards* before,
> Did their hereditary Ills deplore:
> From tuneful *Chaucer*'s, down to thy own *Dryden*'s Muse.[24]

Within five years of publication of his first play, however, the 'moral majority', spearheaded by Jeremy Collier, had put Congreve's form of licentious comedy under pressure, while unusually high-quality government patronage bestowed upon him robbed him of any incentive to endure the brickbats. Ironically, it was not imminent starvation, but rather material comfort stemming from his places first as a commissioner for licensing hackney carriages and stage-coaches and in 1705 as a commissioner for licensing wines (carrying a salary of £200 per annum) that ensured that Congreve would rely no further on the theatre after the cool reception of *The Way of the World*. Congreve's early celebrity and pre-publication packaging had taught him not to think of himself under the aspect of a professional writer. When Voltaire visited Congreve, he gained a strong impression of the latter's snobbery in this regard:

Mr. *Congreve* had one Defect, which was, his entertaining too mean an Idea of his first Profession, (that of a Writer) tho' 'twas to this he ow'd his Fame and Fortune. He spoke of his Works as of Trifles that were beneath him; and hinted to me in our first Conversation, that I should visit him upon no other Foot than that of a Gentleman, who led a Life of Plainness and Simplicity. I answer'd, that had he been so unfortunate as to be a mere Gentleman I should never have come to see him; and I was very much disgusted at so unseasonable a Piece of Vanity.[25]

Unlike the woman who became known as 'the celebrated Mrs Centlivre', Congreve could afford the luxury of desisting from writing plays when it ceased to suit him. This, doubtless, is part of what Alexander Pope meant when he said to Tonson at the end of November 1730, 'Aye, Mr. Tonson, he was Ultimus Romanorum! (with a sigh, speaking of poor Mr. Congreve, who died a year or

---

[24] Thomas Yalden, 'To Mr. Congreve: An Epistolary Ode Occasion'd by his late Play' (1693); quoted in Erskine-Hill and Lindsay (eds.), *Congreve*, 68–9.
[25] François-Marie Arouet de Voltaire, *Letters Concerning the English Nation*, trans. John Lockman (1733); quoted ibid. 213.

two before)'.[26] There is an instructive contrast with what he said about Centlivre and others, quoted earlier in this section.

II

We have only recently begun to recognize the full extent of the Pope perplex. However much he might have tried to mystify this in the *Epistle to Dr. Arbuthnot,* and in despite of *The Dunciad's* contempt for the entire commercial base of professional publishing, he was the most proficient literary entrepreneur of his era. *The Dunciad's* ridicule seems to be, to borrow Pope's charge against Addison, and use it against him, a case of hating for arts that caused himself to rise. But of course, as many commentators on *The Dunciad* have observed, it is not a simple case of *hating,* more of grim fascination. For the poem's ideology is rooted in the value systems that it ostensibly opposes, and much of its energy is borrowed from the lowbrow and demotic forms that it affects to despise. Pope subjected the culture of the populace and the market-place to the comic control of a dominating and prestigious cultural form—classical epic. And the heavy artillery of epic puts an ironic distance between itself and the meaningless triviality of such literary lives as are lived by the dunces. At this point, however, the argument that was conducted in Chapter 4 can be recalled: the authority of the controlling pre-text is itself destabilized by the valency of the new form. What Pope *actually* thought of Homeric epic, which comes through in the Preface to his *Iliad* translation and even more clearly in his textual footnotes, is at considerable odds with the official position that he was required to take as custodian of endangered classical culture. Embarrassment in the face of his material shows up at many points, in respect of the bloodthirstiness and savagery of the warriors and of the deities whose carnal antics he has to mediate to his readers. Pope's note to the *Iliad,* book xiv lines 359 ff., a passage in which Jupiter courts Juno by recounting his previous conquests, might serve as typical: 'This Courtship of *Jupiter* to *Juno* may possibly be thought pretty singular. He endeavours to prove the Ardour of his Passion

[26] Joseph Spence, *Observations, Anecdotes and Characters of Books and Men,* ed. James M. Osborn, 2 vols. (Oxford: Clarendon Press, 1966), vol. i, no. 488.

to her, by the Instances of its Warmth to other Women. A great many People will look upon this as no very likely Method to recommend himself to *Juno*'s Favour.'[27] Jupiter fails to behave like an eighteenth-century gentleman who has learned his gallantry from the advice pages of the periodicals.

Moving back a little in Pope's career to consider *The Rape of the Lock*, we can apply some of the above discussion to Pope's connection with Susanna Centlivre. I would contend that, amongst many other things that Pope was doing in his most celebrated poem, he was drizzling ironically reconstructed epic conventions over a social ambience already effectively imagined and embodied in Susanna Centlivre's plays. Current readings of the poem recognize a psychomachic dimension present in it. Belinda's identity as a woman is being fought over by two dimensions of femininity as constructed at that time, the coquette and the prude, partially externalized in the poem in the personae of Thalestris and Clarissa. In practice, there is a tendency for one character-type to fold into another because, as Ben Schneider observes in an article analysing the coquette-prude actress line in the contemporary theatre: 'The salient cultural fact is that in a society in which the female is the vehicle for transmitting economic stability from one generation to the next, she may not have the disposal of herself. This being so, she may not encourage any man whom she cannot marry without exposing herself to censure as a loose woman, and it follows that she certainly cannot encourage more than one man.'[28] This fundamental cultural datum entails that the poem sponsor an 'official' morality according to which proper female socialization consists in learning the lesson that you can't play the sex game without putting down a stake. Either the coquette's posture will cause men to become so inflamed that they will transgress the boundaries of decency—rape—or, if that is unthinkable, old age will come in the form of a nemesis. Clarissa's speech in Canto V carries most of the moral freight here. Speaking what appears to be a language of good sense, moderation, and compromise, Clarissa points out that 'She who scorns a man must die a maid', and she conjures up for Belinda the spectres of disfiguring disease and the loneliness of the long-distance virgin.

[27] Quoted from *The Twickenham Pope*, viii. 150. See also Weinbrot, *Britannia's Issue*, 296–307.

[28] Ben R. Schneider, 'The Coquette-Prude as an Actress Line in Restoration Comedy during the Time of Mrs. Oldfield', *Theatre Notebook*, 22/4 (Summer 1968), 143–59: 146–7.

Clarissa calls for the cultivation of the inner resources of personality—good sense, good humour, a sense of proportion—as an insurance policy against the inevitability of transience. Belinda must surrender her career of smiling on all alike and making the whole world gay, and also surrender her virginity in the time-honoured manner of all properly socialized women.

There are many possible ways of reacting to this version of necessary female conditioning, including a feminist reading that unmasks it as a patriarchal myth masquerading as natural good sense. Clarissa becomes a jealous, frustrated old spinster who is eager to deprive her younger rival of pleasure. My concern is not, at present, to offer a reading of *The Rape of the Lock*, but merely to emphasize that the coquette-prude character-type was entirely familiar to Pope's readership through its representation in a series of plays by Mrs Centlivre. In particular, in *The Gamester* and *The Basset-Table*, two plays written in 1705, Mrs Centlivre presented a world dominated by card-playing, in both of which the climactic scene would be a *vraisemblable* presentation of a card game (cf. *Rape of the Lock*, Canto III). Each would equate gambling and coquetry as the twin scourges of honourable behaviour. The milieux of these plays are, if not intentionally re-created in *The Rape of the Lock*, at least entirely familiar to its readers through dramatic representation. Indeed, one can read into the plot of *The Basset-Table* an acted-out version of the 'official morality' of Pope's poem. Lady Reveller is a coquette who is beloved of a man of sense, Lord Worthy. Her cousin Lady Lucy, 'a religious, sober lady', is the play's prude, its Clarissa.[29] Early in the play, Lady Lucy establishes what is to be the normative attitude both to gambling and to coquetry:

L. LUCY. Shou'd all the rest of the World follow your Ladyship's Example, the Order of Nature would be inverted, and every Good design'd by

---

[29] Later in Centlivre's career, the term 'prude' would come to be specifically attached to the Quaker sect: in *A Bold Stroke for a Wife* (1718), the following exchange occurs between Mrs Lovely and Mrs Prim the Quaker:

MRS. LOVELY. I know you have as much pride, vanity, self-conceit, and ambition among you, couched under that formal habit and sanctified countenance, as the proudest of us all; but the world begins to see your prudery.

MRS. PRIM. Prudery! What, do they invent new words as well as new fashions?   II. ii. (19–24)

Quoted from Susanna Centlivre, *A Bold Stroke for a Wife*, ed. Thalia Stathas (London: Edward Arnold, 1969), 28.

Heaven, become a Curse; Health and Plenty no longer would be known among us—You cross the Purpose of the Day and Night; you wake when you should sleep, and make all who have any Dependance on you wake, while you repose.

LADY [REVELLER.] Bless me! may not any Person sleep when they please?

L. LUCY. No; there are certain Hours that good Manners, Modesty, and Health, require your Care; for Example, disorderly Hours are neither healthful nor modest . . . Then you have such a Number of Lovers.

LADY. Oh, *Cupid*! is it a Crime to have a Number of Lovers? If it be, 'tis the pleasantest Crime in the World. A Crime that falls not every Day to every Woman's Lot . . . Oh, *mon cœur*! what Pleasure is there in one Lover? 'tis like being seen always in one Suit of Cloaths; a Woman, with one Admirer, will ne'er be a reigning Toast.

L. LUCY. I am sure those that encourage more, will never have the Character of a reigning Virtue.

LADY. I slight the malicious Censure of the Town, yet defy it to asperse my Virtue; Nature has given me a Face, a Shape, a Mein, an Air for Dress, and Wit and Humour to subdue: And shall I lose my Conquest for a Name?

ALP[IEW]. Nay, and among the unfashionable Sort of People too, Madam; for Persons of Breeding and Quality will allow, that Gallantry and Virtue are not inseparable.

L. LUCY. But Coquetry and Reputation are; and there is no Difference in the Eye of the World, between having really committed the Fault, and lying under the Scandal; for my own Part, I would take as much Care to preserve my Fame, as you would your Virtue.[30]

As the action unfolds, the connection between coquetry and gambling is spelled out. During the game of basset, Sir James Courtly, a reformable gamester in love with Lady Lucy, slips Lady Reveller a purse when her money is running low. Shortly afterwards, he comes to collect, and, having locked the door and laid violent hands on Lady Reveller, the scene proceeds thus:

L. REVEL. What shall I do? Instruct me Heaven.—Monster! Is this your Friendship to my Lord? And can you wrong the Woman he adores?

SIR JAM. Ay, but the Woman does not care a Souse for him; and therefore he has no Right above me; I love you as much, and will possess.

L. REVEL. Oh! Hold—Kill me rather than destroy my Honour;—what Devil has debauch'd your Temper? Or, how has my Carriage drawn

[30] *The Dramatic Works of the Celebrated Mrs. Centlivre*, 3 vols. (1761; repr. London: John Pearson, 1872), i. 208–9. Subsequent quotations are from this edition: the numerical reference is to page number, not line number.

this Curse upon me? What have I done to give you Cause to think you
ever should succeed this hated Way?   [*Weeps.*

SIR JAM. Why this Question, Madam? Can a Lady that loves Play so
passionately as you do,—that takes as much Pains to draw Men in to
lose their Money, as a Town Miss to their Destruction,—that caresses
all Sorts of People for your Interest, that divides your Time between
your Toilet and *Basset-Table*; can you, I say, boast of innate Virtue?—
Fye, fye, I am sure you must have guess'd for what I play'd so deep;—
we never part with our Money without Design,—or writing Fool upon
our Foreheads;—therefore no more of this Resistance, except you
would have more Money.

L. REVEL. Oh! horrid.

SIR JAM. There was fifty Guineas in that Purse, Madam,—here's fifty
more; Money shall be no Dispute.   [*Offers her money.*

L. REVEL. [*Strikes it down.*] Perish your Money with yourself—you
Villain—there, there; take your boasted Favours, which I resolv'd
before to have paid in *Specie*; basest of Men, I'll have your Life for this
Affront—what ho, within there.

SIR JAM. Hush!—Faith, you'll raise the House. [*Lays hold on her.*] And
'tis in vain—you're mine; nor will I quit this Room 'till I'm possess'd.
                                                    [*Struggles.*

L. REVEL. Raise the House! I'll raise the World in my Defence; help,
Murther! Murther—a Rape, a Rape—   (i. 249–50)

Lord Worthy enters to save her and, as it turns out, this was a
concerted plan between the two men, to make the point that card-
playing is a form of prostitution and that coquetry will eventually
meet its due reward. Lady Reveller is the victim of a simulated
rape as Pope's Belinda is the victim of a symbolic one.

In other less obvious respects, too, the texture of Centlivre's
dramatic universe is close to that of Pope's *Rape*. Commodification, the perversion of moral values resulting from a luxury culture
in which 'All Arabia breathes from yonder box' that is so essential
a backdrop to the game of Ombre in the *Rape*, is conveyed in *The
Basset-Table* through a trading couple called the Sagos. They are
one of several 'cit' couples in Centlivre's plays who identify themselves, in the best traditions of Jacobean city comedy and Otway,
by infantile pet names: in this case, 'Keecky' and 'Puddy'. Sago is
a druggist, whose wife is enamoured of gaming and Sir James
Courtly. She raises her gambling capital by wheedling money
out of her husband; and she engineers her welcome at Lady
Reveller's aristocratic table by means of expensive presents of

luxury commodities. One of the many social crimes of which Lady
Reveller stands accused is the promiscuous mixing of high- and
low-caste players at her basset table, a crime not mitigated by her
cynical exploitation of the cits and their social pretensions:

LADY. Have you heard from Mrs. *Sago* this Morning?
ALP. Certainly, Madam, she never fails; she has sent your Ladyship the
finest Cargo, made up of Chocolate, Tea, *Montifiasco* Wine, and fifty
Rarities beside, with something to remember me, good Creature, that
she never forgets. Well, indeed, Madam, she is the best-natur'd
Woman in the World; it grieves me to think what Sums she loses at
Play.
LADY. Oh, fye, she must; a Citizen's Wife is not to be endur'd amongst
Quality; had she not Money, 'twere impossible to receive her—
ALP. Nay, indeed, I must say that of you Women of Quality, if there is but
Money enough, you stand not upon Birth or Reputation, in either Sex;
if you did, so many Sharpers of *Covent-Garden*, and Mistresses of St.
James's, would not be daily admitted. (i. 217)

Speaking, in Chapter 3, of Garth's *Dispensary*, I made the point
that the poem brings the eternal verities of epic into collision with
a sharply defined world of quotidian reality. Pope's Rosicrucian
spirits are a far more creative solution to the credibility problem
created by epic machinery than are Garth's allegorical abstractions:
but the achievement of his poem is still to negotiate literature's
transition to contemporaneousness that the novel would be destined more fully to effect. And, as I have contended here, Susanna
Centlivre's *mise-en-scène* was of use to Pope in defining the
nature of the society that he represents satirically. Again, as with
the *Dunciad*, Pope borrows energy from forms that he also be-
littles. He anathematized Centlivre, but he also used her. It is a
pattern that careful readers of Pope have observed before. His
borrowings did not always have the immaculate classical pedigree
that he liked his readers to notice.[31] If this has been overlooked, it
is because our paradigms of reading have placed Pope in a great
tradition, rather than against the background of the local culture
in which he was fully immersed and which he did not transcend.
As for Susanna Centlivre, supposed victim of the male plot to
canonize Congreve, she turned out to be irrepressible in her own
era, partly because she had a knack of introducing the burning

---

[31] See e.g. Roger D. Lund, 'From Oblivion to Dulness: Pope and the Poetics of
Appropriation', *British Journal for Eighteenth-Century Studies*, 14 (1991), 171–90.

issues of the day into her plays, and with her rabidly anti-Jacobite, anti-Tory allegiance, she was taken up as something of an Hanoverian mascot after 1714; but more because she was actually an extremely competent dramatist. Readers who might want to celebrate her as a *woman* writer have a good deal of promising material. Some have discovered in the female virtuoso character of Valeria in *The Basset-Table* proto-feminist support for women's education, even if they do not agree that she is based on Mary Astell.[32] The precariousness of Centlivre's gender position, one might argue, pushed her into taking risks. Frequently, she goes further than a male writer might have done, as, for example, when in her first comedy, *The Beau's Duel; or, A Soldier for the Ladies* (1702), two cowards, Sir William Mode and Ogle, stage a duel with foiled rapiers and are not merely mocked but are soundly kicked and beaten by Clarinda and Emilia, the female gallants, dressed as men. In *The Gamester* (1705), again a woman in breeches beats a man at his own game, as Angelica defeats her lover Valere at dice and wins from him her own picture, which he has vowed never to lose. In the representation of sexuality, Centlivre is often outrageously explicit, perhaps providing a particular *frisson* for an audience that reflects on a woman playwright being thus daring.[33]

[32] See F. P. Lock's discussion of this in *Susanna Centlivre*, 53–4. Lock thinks that Valeria is not based on Astell, but does represent an enlightened attitude to women's education. In my own view, it is sufficiently clear from Sir Richard Plainman's speech in Act II that she is not a character to be altogether admired.

[33] My reader will want me to give an example. In Act 1 of *The Wonder! A Woman Keeps a Secret* (1714), a play set in Catholic Portugal, the 'Scotchman' Colonel Britton and the merchant Frederick have a man-to-man discussion that enables them to satirize sexual mores in Catholic and in Presbyterian countries:

FRED. Well, how do you like our Country, Colonel?

COL. Why Faith, *Frederick*, a Man might pass his Time agreeable enough with-inside of a Nunnery, but to behold such Troops of soft, plump, tender, melting, wishing, nay willing Girls too, thro' a damn'd Grate, gives us *Britons* strong Temptation to plunder. Ah *Frederick* your Priests are wicked Rogues. They immure Beauty for their own proper Use, and show it only to the Laity to create Desires, and inflame Accompts, that they may purchase Pardons at a dearer Rate.

FRED. I own Wenching is something more difficult here than in *England*, where Womens Liberties are subservient to their Inclinations, and Husbands seem of no Effect but to take care of the Children which their Wives provide.

COL. And does Restraint get the better of Inclination with your Women here? No, I'll be sworn not one even in fourscore. Don't I know the Constitution of the *Spanish* Ladies?

FRED. And of all the Ladies where you come, Colonel, you were ever a Man of Gallantry.

All of this was certainly enough to keep her in the repertory in her own time, but did not enable her to withstand Victorian prejudice against this licentious period of English drama, and women writers despite the hopes of the anonymous female author of the 'New Account' of Centlivre's life that prefaces the 1761 edition of her *Dramatic Works*:

Not only that barbarous Custom of denying Women to have Souls, begins to be rejected as foolish and absurd, but also that bold Assertion, that Female Minds are not capable of producing literary Works, equal even to those of *Pope*, now loses Ground, and probably the next Age may be taught by our Pens that our Geniuses have been hitherto cramped and smothered, but not extinguished, and that the Sovereignty which the male Part of the Creation have, until now, usurped over us, is unreasonably arbitrary: And further, that our natural Abilities entitle us to a larger Share, not only in Literary Decisions, but that, with the present Directors, we are equally intitled to Power both in Church and State.   (pp. x–xi)

She is ripe for a revival and surely the Swan Theatre in Stratford will perform one of her plays before very long.

III

At what many have recognized to be the imaginative epicentre of the 1729 *Dunciad Variorum*—amidst the heroic games in imitation of the *Aeneid*, book v—stands Eliza Haywood, represented in the lines I have already had occasion to quote:

> See in the circle next, Eliza plac'd;
> Two babes of love close clinging to her waste;
> Fair as before her works she stands confess'd,
> In flow'rs and pearls by bounteous Kirkall dress'd.
> The Goddess then: 'Who best can send on high
> The salient spout, far-streaming to the sky;

COL. Ah *Frederick*, the *Kirk* half starves us *Scotchmen*. We are kept so sharp at home, that we feed like Cannibals abroad.   (III. xi)

I think an argument can be made out for Centlivre similar to that made by Catherine Gallagher for Behn, that she uses the known fact of female authorship to titillate audiences with her unbridled sexuality. See her 'Who Was That Masked Woman? The Prostitute and the Playwright in the Works of Aphra Behn', in id., *Nobody's Story: The Vanishing Acts of Women Writers in the Marketplace, 1670–1820* (Oxford University Press, 1994), 1–48.

His be yon Juno of majestic size,
With cow-like-udders, and with ox-like eyes.
This China-Jordan, let the chief o'ercome
Replenish, not ingloriously, at home'.

(II. 149–58)

All the main allusions are typographical and they vividly re-create
the publishing circles in which Haywood moved. Elisha Kirkall is
the engraver who, Scriblerus' note claims, produced her likeness
for the 1724 four-volume edition of her *Works*.[34] The 'babes of
love' are the two secret histories she published in the 1720s: the
Memoirs of a Certain Island Adjacent to the Kingdom of Utopia
(1725) and the *Secret History of the Present Intrigues of the
Court of Caramania* (1727), works that Pope figures as bastardized
productions, the offspring of Haywood's lust for print. It was
not, as is sometimes said, the attack on Henrietta Howard in the
latter book that secured Haywood a place in *The Dunciad*, but
rather this vicious passage on 'Marthalia'—the inoffensive Martha
Blount—in the former that capitalizes on current rumours that
Pope and she were secretly married:

After a long Scene of continued Lewdness, she at last married an old
servant of the Necromancer's—he languishes under an incurable Disease,
and she has the Management of his Affairs . . . the Advantages of Dress
and Grandeur give her the Opportunities which before she wanted—she
is now caress'd by those, whose Servants once despised her, and the
Footman, who could not formerly be prevailed on to take her in his Arms,
sees her now in his Master's, and lights him to that Bed, he would not
once have ventured to go into himself . . . But there are some who of late
have severely repented trusting themselves to her Embraces, and cursed
the artificial Sweets and Perfumes, which hindred them from discovering
those Scents, that would have been infallible Warnings of what they
might expect in such polluted Sheets.[35]

[34] I have had no more success than Sarah Prescott in locating this portrait, which,
as Prescott says, is not to be found attached to the 1724 *Works*. See her article 'The
Palace of Fame and the Problem of Reputation: The Case of Eliza Haywood', *Bactyl*,
1/4 (Summer–Autumn 1994), 9–35: 20 and her expansion of the point in ch. 2 of her
Ph.D. thesis, 'British Women Writers of the 1720s: Feminist Literary History and the
Early Eighteenth-Century Novel' (Exeter University), currently in progress. I am
extremely grateful to her for permitting me to read this.
[35] Eliza Haywood, *Memoirs of a Certain Island* (1725), ed. Josephine Grieder
(New York: Garland, 1972), 12–13. Ros Ballaster repeats the claim that Pope's
venom was inspired by *Caramania* in *Seductive Forms: Women's Amatory Fiction
from 1684 to 1720* (Oxford: Clarendon Press, 1992), 161. See, however, Mack, *Pope*,
411.

Pope, in this version, is poxed by *Martha Blount*'s love: certainly, he was libelled by Eliza Haywood's hate. The two publishers who take up the challenge of the pissing contest, Chetwood and Curll, had both published Haywood. By some commentators, as we noted earlier, this passage is credited with having put paid to Haywood's novelistic endeavours after the 1720s. Until very recently, she has not been in the canon of studied eighteenth-century writing, and the reasons for that go beyond the bounds of Pope's admittedly considerable personal charisma and literary power.[36] They are wrapped up in the still-prevailing account of the 'rise of the novel', and in further aspects of the bourgeois public sphere, with which the rest of this chapter will be concerned.

Late-century and Victorian prejudice against lewd female writers might be a sufficient reason to explain the neglect of such as Haywood once Pope's formidable power of veto had expired. Clara Reeve's *The Progress of Romance* (1785), for example, presents Haywood's later novels as the acceptable products of a reformed muse, whereas her earlier amatory fiction deserves only neglect.[37] Our current sense, however, of what the novel is and when it began was defined for us by the phenomenal success of one particular version of literary history, Ian Watt's, in *The Rise of the Novel* (1957). Watt's title deliberately alludes to R. H. Tawney's epoch-making sociological study *Religion and the Rise of Capitalism*, because Watt considers that the conditions out of which the modern novel emerged were exactly the same conditions that produced the Protestant religion, early capitalism and the middle class, a set of developments that have in common a new emphasis on individual experience. For Watt, the novel proper is distinguished from earlier fictional forms by its narrative procedures designed to secure the objectives of formal realism. The modern novel, that is, encapsulates the experience of individual protagonists, particular people in particular circumstances, using original plots, as against the repetitive conventionalities of older romance. There is a new emphasis on the exploration of person-

[36] Sarah Prescott draws an interesting comparison between Penelope Aubin, a Catholic Jacobite sympathizer who was careful to keep on the right side of Pope, and Eliza Haywood, who so signally failed to do so: Haywood is in *The Dunciad*, Aubin is not. But neither has been in the canon until recently, which supports the point made in the text that Pope's personal animus is not the only relevant factor.

[37] I am indebted here to Prescott, 'Eliza Haywood: (Re)presenting the Disreputable', Ph.D. thesis, ch. 2.

ality in relation to the categories of time and space: characters are set in solidly imagined milieux, and there is a concern for the effect of the past upon present and future events, as well as a minutely discriminated time-scale, as the novel tries to get close to the texture of everyday occurrences. On this model, Daniel Defoe is the first unchallengeable exemplar.[38] 'Formal realism' is therefore, for Watt, the set of procedures through which the novel specifies the setting, time, and individual character of the events and personalities it creates. And the language most appropriate to securing these ends is a plain, neutral reportage such as is found in the unelaborated, non-figurative style of Defoe. Realism as delivered by Defoe was the preferred style of the new bourgeois reading public. The novel was supremely well fitted to supply the leisure-time needs of readers who required to be entertained, for growing amounts of time, with representations of the lives of individuals that they could recognize, identify with, and profit from. Individualism itself is the result of economic specialization produced by capitalism (division of labour and other productive forces breaking down traditional communities, and so forth) and by a Protestant emphasis on the primacy of individual conscience. Economic individualism flourishes in conditions of relative political liberty such as occurred in England after the Settlement of 1688 and in a society that is mobile and heterogeneous.

Thus it comes about that, consulting the standard reference books for the literature of the period, readers will find entries like the following in *The Oxford Illustrated History of English Literature* (1987): 'of several claimants to the title of our first true novel, the strongest is Daniel Defoe's *The Life and Strange Surprizing Adventures of Robinson Crusoe*'.[39] It is clearer now, some four decades after Watt, that a retrospective process of privileging, rather than empirical fact, dates the 'first novel' to 1719. The novel, we are now more fully aware, is not a category intrinsic to the material itself, but is a critical construct that can be argued over and contested. Once the race really got under way, in the 1970s and early 1980s, to replace Watt's account, very substantial modifications were made to it, of which I would single out

[38] Ian Watt, *The Rise of the Novel: Studies in Defoe, Richardson and Fielding* (1957; repr. London: Hogarth Press, 1987, 3rd imp. 1993).

[39] Pat Rogers (ed.), *The Oxford Illustrated History of English Literature* (London: Book Club Associates, 1987), 253.

three of the most important: the endurance of romance beyond its allotted span, the pointlessness of the search after origins, and the absence of women writers from the story. 'Formal realism' did not supersede romance in any simple way. The story of romance does not end in 1719. Romance conventions remain vitally important to the texture of Fielding's novels and even to those of Richardson. Thus Michael McKeon argues, in *The Origins of the English Novel* (1987), for the construction of a model capable of explaining the residual existence of romance within the developed novel. Such a model cannot be the linear one of 'rise' but requires to be dialectical. To account for the emergence of the novel, we must describe a series of dialectical engagements out of which it arose and comprehend the ideological work that it was developed to perform. His model is elaborated in terms of a dialectic of formal adaptation mediating the question of how to tell the truth in narrative; and a parallel dialectic of social change mediating the question of how to live the virtuous life.[40] On one point, J. Paul Hunter's account in *Before Novels* concurs with that of McKeon: looking for a point of origin of the novel is a wild-goose chase. Hunter's sense that there were *two* rises of the novel, or at least that there were two important phases in its rise—one occurring in the period from the 1690s to the 1720s, culminating in Defoe's novels and Swift's *Gulliver's Travels*; while the other was a much more self-conscious period in the 1740s and 1750s, when writers like Fielding and Richardson actually *knew* that it was novels they were writing and began to theorize consciously about the process—seems to me to be a very major modification of the traditional story.[41]

Yet in none of the male-authored accounts of the novel, however revisionist, do women writers receive significant attention, with the exception of McKeon's, who does discuss several at some length. Even on the terms in which the traditional accounts are expressed, Aphra Behn is as good a candidate to be the 'first' novelist as is Defoe. But if realism is to be the qualifying condition, it is not difficult to understand why the *later* women writers of the 1720s could not be accepted as having any defining role in

---

[40] Michael McKeon, *The Origins of the English Novel, 1600–1740* (1987; repr. London: Radius, 1988).

[41] J. Paul Hunter, *Before Novels: The Cultural Contexts of Eighteenth-Century Fiction* (London: W. W. Norton, 1990).

the process. Well before Watt, George Frisbie Whicher, early
twentieth-century biographer of Haywood, writes about her in
terms of a similar teleology: that realism is the condition to which
the novel aspires:

[Haywood's] purpose was not to paint a living portrait, but to create a
vehicle for the expression of vivid emotion, and in her design she was
undoubtedly successful until the reading public was educated to demand
better things . . . The romancer's purpose was not to reveal an accurate
picture of life and manners, but to thrill the susceptible bosom by scenes
of tender love, amorous rapture, or desperate revenge. The department of
sensationalism [was] especially exploited by women writers and [is]
generally allowed to be most suited to their genius.[42]

There is undoubtedly a problem, however, with defining the
English novel in such a way that a vast body of writing that
purports to be, and refers to itself as, the 'novel' is excluded from
it. It was to this problem that Jane Spencer's ground-breaking *The
Rise of the Woman Novelist* was addressed in 1986, but her
concern is mainly with the socio-economic conditions that constituted writing as 'the literate middle-class household's substitute
for the declining home industries which had once enabled the
housewife to contribute to the support of the family'.[43] Elegantly,
insouciantly, she side-steps the anguished male attempts to define
the novel by accepting anything at all that any female writer was
writing, assuming it was fictional and was not a play or a poem, as
a novel. Implicitly, she rejects the evaluative judgement built into
the progressivist assumption behind the 'rise' metaphor, as subsequent women writing on the subject have done explicitly.[44] To
some, however, issues of genre-definition and quality do not so
easily disappear. Ros Ballaster's absorbing and closely argued
introduction to *Seductive Forms: Women's Amatory Fiction from
1684 to 1720* (1992), for example, insists that 'women's writing
must be analysed within a history of genre if it is to find a
satisfactory place in accounts of the "rise" of the novel'.[45] Her own
way of imparting significance to the novels of Behn, Manley, and
Haywood is to use psychoanalytical approaches to the seduction

[42] George Frisbie Whicher, *The Life and Romances of Mrs. Eliza Haywood* (New
York: Columbia University Press, 1915), 43, 55–6.
[43] Spencer, *The Rise of the Woman Novelist*.
[44] See e.g. Janet Todd's Introduction to *The Sign of Angellica*, 1–10.
[45] Ballaster, *Seductive Forms*, 21.

plots embedded in them, educing the complexities in responding that female readers in particular would have experienced. Her readings I do not find entirely convincing, for reasons that will emerge later.

Of those who have examined the popular fiction of the early century, the most enduring and important contribution has been made by John Richetti. The significance that he accords to his account of early fiction in the introduction written specially for the 1992 reprint of *Popular Fiction before Richardson: Narrative Patterns, 1700–1739* (1969) is the one that I would also wish to emphasize. Early fiction 'helped to constitute, quite simply, a new kind of market-place for a newly aggressive fictional product':

Fiction of the kind I labelled 'popular' in the early eighteenth century offered certain pleasures to its readers, much like those which formula fiction has continued to provide ever since . . . A commodity produced by cheap labour hire by booksellers and publishers to satisfy a growing market, popular fiction is nothing less than the central and initiating line of the novel. To varying degrees, the art novel written by talented individuals is only an occasionally successful protest against this marketing strategy.[46]

Commencing in 1719 and spanning the 1720s, there appears to have been a competition between two professional writers, Eliza Haywood and Daniel Defoe, to capture what they perceived as a burgeoning market, with different kinds of prose fictional product. For 1719 did not *only* witness the publication of *Robinson Crusoe*, which by June had gone through three editions of 1,000 copies each.[47] Eliza Haywood's debut novel, *Love in Excess*, was also published and, although it was a somewhat slower burner than *Robinson Crusoe*, it was a major seller and had six editions by 1725.[48] Evidence exists to suggest that this template of market competition is not one arbitrarily cast over the writers by hindsight. Defoe and Haywood themselves saw it this way. Throughout the 1720s they competed with each other over versions of the story of the mute seer Duncan Campbell, Defoe concentrating more on the 'strange but true' elements of his biography and Haywood

[46] John J. Richetti, *Popular Fiction before Richardson: Narrative Patterns, 1700–1739* (Oxford: Clarendon Press, 1969; repr. 1992), pp. xxv, xxvi.

[47] Backscheider, *Defoe*, 412.

[48] See William H. McBurney (ed.), *Four before Richardson: Selected English Novels, 1720–1727* (Lincoln: Nebraska University Press, 1963), p. xxiii.

filling in romantic complications.[49] The real competition was
joined, however, when Haywood published *Idalia; or, The Unfortunate Mistress: A Novel* in 1723 and Defoe felt compelled to
respond with *The Fortunate Mistress* (the novel popularly known
as *Roxana*) in the following year. Obliquely, in the Preface, Defoe
refers to *Idalia* when he writes: 'He takes the liberty to say, That
this *Story* differs from most of the Modern Performances of this
Kind, tho' some of them have met with a very good Reception in
the World: *I say*, It differs from them in this Great and Essential
Article, *Namely*, That the Foundation of This is laid in Truth of
Fact; and so the Work is not a Story, but a History.'[50] In the body
of the text, Defoe takes opportunities to further distance himself
from those who were writing in the less valuable mode of the
romance. As Roxana says when she is being wooed by her French
Prince, 'it wou'd look a little too much like a Romance here, to
repeat all the kind things he said to me, on that Occasion' (p. 72),
thus making it clear that the standards of plausibility and verisimilitude operating in his fiction are entirely different from those that
prevail in such as Haywood. In terms of the market for which both
writers were competing, Defoe and Haywood are no different.
Beyond a shadow of doubt, however, they sought out different
ways of satisfying that market and of succeeding within it. That
difference need not be expressed in terms of the notoriously
slippery conception of realism. Lincoln Faller has recently argued
that the concrete particularity celebrated by Watt as a quintes-
sential feature of Defoe's fiction actually is more a feature of his
non-fictional writing. Faller thinks that Defoe's fictional writing is
marked out from contemporary criminal biography not by the bits
and quiddities of particular experience but by the greater degree of
complexity and the arresting uncertainties of narration that they
embody.[51] Complexity, however, is as relational a quality as is
realism, and it can be created by readers in places where Faller
would not expect it, as Ros Ballaster proves. She has some difficulty with Haywood as a writer in her book *Seductive Forms*.[52]

[49] See Whicher, *The Life and Romances of Mrs. Eliza Haywood*, ch. 4.

[50] Daniel Defoe, *Roxana: The Fortunate Mistress* (1724), ed. and intro. Jane Jack
(London: Oxford University Press, 1964; repr. 1976), 1 (italics reversed). Subsequent
references are to this edition.

[51] Lincoln B. Faller, *Crime and Defoe: A New Kind of Writing* (Cambridge
University Press, 1993), *passim*.

[52] The discussion is conducted in Ballaster, *Seductive Forms*, 167–75.

There is in Haywood only one way in which the genders are represented, she concedes. Women are everywhere the victims of predatory, unassuageable male desire. There is no ironic self-representation as in Behn and Manley, no means by which the writer herself is separable from the 'abused victims' who are her characters. This imparts to Haywood's writing a 'profound melancholia and pessimism' from which Ballaster is desperate to find her an escape. She finally locates 'a form of feminine resistance in the compulsive re-inscription and display of the hysterical female body'. Exploiting Freudian and Foucauldian accounts of a link between amatory and hysterical symptoms in the female body, where the latter are held to 'mimic' the former, Ballaster constructs an argument according to which, at the same time as Haywood's heroines manifest sexual desire through their bodies, they also show hysterical symptoms that constitute a form of resistance to the desire. If on a conscious level they invite male sexual attentions, on a deeper level they resist or remain opaque to them. To my mind, this is a forced and unconvincing attempt to psychologize such novels as *Idalia; or, The Unfortunate Mistress* (1723). As the plot summary that I offer below might confirm, the very hallmark of this story is the absence of any discourse that could plausibly be ascribed to 'character development' or 'psychology' or whatever else one wants to call the writing that, in novels, tells us more about characters than they can tell us about themselves. In my own view, the crucial distinction between Haywood (and, by and large, the other female writers of the 1720s) and Defoe should be made in terms of the entirely different conceptions of selfhood that underlie their writings, conceptions that dictate different narratological procedures. This distinction I should now like to investigate further.

IV

Here is a typical enough passage of Haywood's prose from *Love in Excess*. At this point, Amena is about to surrender to the blandishments of Count D'Elmont:

All Nature seem'd to favour his Design, the pleasantness of the Place, the silence of the Night, the sweetness of the Air, perfum'd with a thousand various Odours wafted by gentle Breezes from adjacent Gardens completed the most delightful Scene that ever was, to offer up a Sacrifice to Love; not a breath but flew wing'd with desire, and sent soft thrilling wishes to the Soul; CYNTHIA her self, cold as she is reported, assisted in the Inspiration, and sometimes shone with all her brightness, as it were to feast their ravish'd Eyes with gazing on each others Beauty; then veil'd her Beams in Clouds, to give the lover boldness, and hide the Virgins blushes. What now could poor AMENA do, surrounded with so many Powers, attack'd by such a charming force without, betray'd by tenderness within: Vertue and Pride, the Guardians of her Honour fled from her Breast, and left her to her Foe . . . she had only a thin silk Night Gown on, which flying open as he caught her in his Arms, he found her panting Heart beat measures of consent, her heaving Breast swell to be press'd by his, and every Pulse confess a wish to yield; her Spirits all dissolv'd sunk in a Lethargy of Love, her snowy Arms unknowing grasp'd his Neck, her hips met his half way, and trembled at the touch; in fine, there was but a moment between her and Ruine; when the tread of some body coming hastily down the Walk, oblig'd the half-bless'd Pair to put a stop to farther Endearments.[53]

The present-day reader's extreme familiarity with romantic writing might blunt the sensibilities to the novelty of a voice like this in the 1720s. Erotic but not pornographic, the passage creates a powerfully sensuous equivalence between the sumptuous exterior surroundings and the passions coursing through the veins of the lovers—long since a standard technique of romantic fiction. Narrative suspense, to a modern taste so cumbersomely managed, is a boldly experimental device, leaving the reader breathless with excitement at what might be the outcome of this dammed-up desire. In this strain of writing, plot-event is the prime mover of the narrative. Typically in a Haywood story, all possibility of psychological development is removed from the equation at an early stage. Thus in *Philidore and Placentia; or, L'Amour trop Delicat* (1727), for example, the title-page offers an epigram from Dryden that imposes on the narrative a psychological determinism: 'Each is himself disposer of his State. | 'Tis our own Faults, or Virtues, mold our Fate.' In *Idalia; or, The Unfortunate Mistress: A Novel* (1723), the heroine is described as perfect in beauty and grace but wilful, disdaining all control or advice; and 'the Consequence of such a Disposition could not be expected to be very fortunate'.[54] This

[53] Eliza Haywood, *Love in Excess; or, The Fatal Enquiry: A Novel*, 3 vols. (London, 1719–20), i. 28–9.

[54] Eliza Haywood, *Idalia; or, The Unfortunate Mistress: A Novel* (London, 1723), 3.

clears the way for the story-line to progress impeded only by the occasional narrative intrusion carrying a moral reflection. That story-line is as follows (I present it typographically as a pseudo-quotation to render it succinct and easier for the reader to grasp):

Idalia, the daughter of a Venetian nobleman, counts amongst her suitors one Florez, page to the Doge's nephew Don Ferdinand. Florez is relatively baseborn, foppish, altogether unworthy, but Idalia, through vanity, coquetry, and self-will, disobeys her father and encourages his advances in correspondence. Florez boasts of his conquest to his master, who lusts after Idalia, and, to ingratiate himself, the former agrees to set up an assignation between Idalia and Ferdinand in a house of ill repute. Only by threatening suicide can Idalia persuade Ferdinand not to ravish her and instead to alter his demeanour to that of a humble penitent. He claims that he will solicit her hand in marriage from her father, persuades Idalia to stay overnight, and 'in the midst of Shrieks and Tremblings, Cries, Curses, Swoonings, the impatient *Ferdinand* perpetrated his Intent, and finished her Undoing!' (p. 22). Since her father is on her trail, the conspirators remove Idalia to the house of Don Henriquez, who is charged with transporting her to Padua. Idalia's determination to end her life engages the sympathy, then the love, of Henriquez, whose affair with Donna Lawra has almost run its course, and 'what Tyes, what Obligations, what Engagements are sufficient to bind the roving Heart of faithless Man?' (p. 30) After a scene in which Henriquez is upbraided by Lawra and charged with having a new mistress, he removes Idalia to his villa in Vicenza, where she begins to conceive an esteem for him. Lawra meanwhile, vengeful and furious, has informed Idalia's father of her whereabouts, but they fail to find her in Padua. Henriquez concocts a story for Ferdinand's benefit that Idalia has escaped from his custody, but the latter does not believe it. A duel ensues: both are killed. The news of Henriquez's death is carried to Idalia by his brother Don Myrtano, who takes the opportunity to make love to her and she responds with love at first sight. Idalia is distracted by despair that Myrtano cannot return her feelings. He writes her a profession of love and a correspondence begins. They meet in Vicenza and the reader is treated to a verse 'Character of Myrtano' as it struck Idalia—a combination of heroic bearing and the almost effeminate deportment of a perfect lover. After suffering an attempted rape, Idalia demands that Myrtano marry her, but she is informed by an anonymous letter that he pays addresses to another. She endeavours to quit his Vicenza house and take to the cloister in Verona.

Of many candidates, perhaps the most implausible plot-element in this is the transfer of Idalia's allegiance from Henriquez to his brother Myrtano. Even the narrator herself suspects that this will be difficult to swallow and it prompts her to make the following statement:

I doubt not but the Reader will be pretty much surpriz'd to find she could so easily be brought from one Extreme to another, and that she who but a few days before was all Despair and Rage, was already grown so temperate and calm; but there was a happy Instability in this Lady's Nature, which prevented her from regretting anything for a long time together.   (p. 47)

This 'happy Instability' is what Haywood offers the reader in place of psychological investigation. In such a dense ratio of story to discourse as her novels maintain, where at least one event occurs on every page of the narrative, it is clear that there could scarcely *be* psychological development. When Defoe tells us in the Preface to *Roxana*, therefore, that his novel is based on 'truth of Fact', he is not merely referring to the possibility that there was a real-life model for Roxana in the bricklayer's daughter and whore Sally Salisbury.

   No one who has read *Roxana* could think that it at all resembles the story outlined in the plot summary that I have given above of *Idalia*, even if the issues surrounding seduction are central to both. If it is thought desirable on ideological grounds to deny that realism is a central distinguishing factor between these two novels (desirable because realism is equated with quality, which in turn has been a means of suppressing women's writing), there is never-theless an enormous difference in the reading experience of them that it is our critical duty to explain. The key difference is that the reader of *Roxana*'s interest is captured by elements other than the answer to the question 'what happens next?' and, at a simple level, what is the moral significance of what happens next. Defoe invites us to read, not only for the story, but for the involved reflections to which that story can give rise. Much has been written about the part played by Defoe's Protestantism, by habits of Bible-reading that would stress the comparison of one passage with another, by his inherited interest in Calvinist soteriology that provided him with 'casework' files extensible into novelistic situations, and in general by the accommodation of moral absolutes to the realities of life among the poorer classes, in shaping his fiction. Emphasizing as I have been doing the proliferations of the market-place, I would not be thought to neglect this influence, but neither do

I want to add, here, to the literature on this aspect of Defoe beyond saying that I do imagine that religious faith as well as gender must have played a part in distinguishing his fictional agenda from that of Haywood. *Roxana* is structured around *relationships* rather than around plot-events—five significant heterosexual bonds, to each of which substantial discourse is apportioned: with her first husband, her landlord the English jeweller, a French prince, a Dutch merchant, and an English lord. Three of them, the first husband, the French prince, and the merchant, exert an influence on the narrative beyond the termination of their relationships with Roxana; indeed the Dutch merchant later marries her. This marriage puts an end to the novel's interest in the socio-sexual economy of partnerships, and its last phase is dominated by Roxana's daughter Susan's obsessive search for identity, her single-minded quest to make Roxana own up to maternity. For the last third of the narrative, Roxana's Magwitchian desire to benefit her children, counterbalanced by what she experiences as an absolute requirement of anonymity, develops as a powerful nemesis—the price she has to pay for her material prosperity:

And let no-body conclude from the strange Success I met with in all my wicked Doings, and the vast Estate which I had rais'd by it, that therefore I either was happy or easie: No, no, there was a Dart struck into the Liver; there was a secret Hell within, even all the while, when our Joy was at the highest; but more especially *now*, after it was all over, and when according to all appearance, I was one of the happiest Women upon Earth; all this while, *I say*, I had such a constant Terror upon my Mind, as gave me every now and then very terrible Shocks, and which made me expect something very frightful upon every Accident of Life. (p. 260)

By the close, Roxana's fear of exposure by her own daughter has become so intense, forcing her as it does to live in a condition of bad faith with the husband she respects so much and imposing upon her a semi-nomadic existence, as to create an atmosphere of hunter and hunted that almost anticipates Godwin's *Caleb Williams.* Meanwhile the maid Amy, whose loyalty to her has been so powerful throughout her life, and with whom she has almost mystically bonded by the sharing of sexual partners, has become a loose cannon, pursuing her own monomaniacal mission to murder Susan. If the hunter–hunted theme anticipates later fiction, so also Roxana's tremulous uncertainty about what Amy might be doing at any point in the narrative brings Frankenstein and the monster to mind.

I stress the anticipatory, proto-Gothic elements in *Roxana* because I would wish to draw attention to their constitution in the split between the public and the private self that the novel so graphically imagines and that later fictions foreground. As the above quotation from the text illustrates, the retrospective first-person narrative articulates this self-division in a way that Haywood's omniscient tale-telling is neither able to do nor intends to do. The entire story is about the incongruence between Roxana's outward reality—her material circumstances—and her inner state of being. She is rich, but she is not happy. Where *Moll Flanders* is the dramatization of the coming together of the exterior and interior selves through the mechanism of penitence, *Roxana* is a radicalization of that earlier story. In *Roxana* the self splits into a series of social roles as the individual is forced to protect her past history and her innermost feelings from those closest to her. Even penitence is not a potent enough magic to cure this schizophrenia: hence the novel's insistence at various points on a distinction between genuine and fake penitence that is much more anguished than anything in *Moll Flanders*. Where Haywood drives on her fast-moving story, Defoe writes more static 'scenes' that permit the attribution of considerable discourse to discussion, debate, self-analysis. The retrospective narrative permits Roxana both to represent her ideology and to comment on it from the vantage-point of maturity and experience. One of the most celebrated and fascinating is the long altercation between the heroine and her Dutch merchant after he has bedded her and wishes now to solemnize their union in marriage, but is utterly dumbfounded by Roxana's refusal to accept his proposal and desire to remain a mistress. (People do not act like this in Haywood. No male who wishes to marry a woman in Haywood wishes to bed her first; and no male who beds a woman wishes to marry her afterwards.) As she freely admits, Roxana's grounds for refusal are strategic: she wishes to preserve her separate property. To disguise the mercenary nature of her motives, however, she adopts a feminist rhetoric of women's liberation, claiming that, even if as an individual her lover would take no advantage of her, on principle the laws of matrimony enabled him to do so. A married woman is her husband's slave: a 'whore' is her own mistress. As the debate develops, Roxana confesses that her partner's rhetoric of love, affection, mutual interest, and a virtuous liberty genuinely supported by religious principles amounts to a much stronger case than her own. The reader is left to conclude that only self-will and obstinacy in continuing to adhere to a stiff-necked pose prompts Roxana to refuse this advantageous match. Although this is Roxana's conclusion, the staging of such an inflammatory discussion at great length leaves the reader free to reach a different one. Whereas the opportunity to engage with advanced talk like this is one of the narrative satisfactions on offer in Defoe, Haywood is perhaps more concerned to satisfy the youthful appetites that she formulates thus in her novel *The Agreeable Caledonian* (a novel in which the hero rescues the heroine from a cloister by using the device of a 'diving machine' which is passed off to the Abbess as a sacred conveyance that has miraculously saved a ravished virgin from drowning): 'Young Virgins, long before they experience the Passion [of love] in reality, are animated by Desires that look somewhat like it; they are charm'd with being belov'd, and take as much Pains to attract a Number of Admirers, as she who doats on one, does to secure the Conquest she has gain'd.'[55]

To my mind, Lincoln Faller's insistence that Defoe intends to render Roxana unattractive to the reader is not quite correct.[56] Our privileged access to her inner thoughts and feelings, her frequently exercised kindness, and her attraction to Quakerism are a few of the elements that prevent alienation of the reader's sympathy. And we can perhaps go a little farther than Faller does in explaining why Defoe should have tried to capture the fiction market in such a distinctive way in the 1720s, capitalizing on what has already been said about the emergence of the bourgeois public sphere in the previous chapter. There occurs, in his *Complete English Tradesman* (1727), the following truly remarkable passage:

I heard once of a shop-keeper that behav'd himself [thus] to such an extreme, that when he was provok'd by the impertinence of the customers, beyond what his temper could bear, he would go upstairs and beat his wife, kick his children about like dogs, and be as furious for two or three minutes, as a man chain'd down in *Bedlam*; and again, when that heat

---

[55] Eliza Haywood, *The Agreeable Caledonian* (1728), ed. Josephine Grieder (New York: Garland, 1973), 61.

[56] Faller, *Crime and Defoe*, 231.

was over, he would sit down and cry faster than the children he had
abused; and after the fit he would go down into his shop again, and be as
humble, as courteous, and as calm as any man whatever; so absolute a
government of his passions had he in the shop, and so little out of it; in
the shop a soul-less animal that could resent nothing, and in the family a
madman; in the shop meek like a lamb, but in the family outrageous like
a Lybian lion.[57]

There could scarcely be a more graphic demonstration of the
split between the public and the private self that emerges in the
bourgeois sphere as a result of commercial ascendancy in the
early eighteenth century. Linda Colley, in her celebrated *Britons*,
makes a point about the growth and ubiquity of credit arrangements in this period. There were some 140,000 shopkeepers in
England and Wales, whose bills might be settled by customers
only once a year when rent income accrued to them.[58] No one was
more familiar than Defoe with the effects of the credit system on
the individual psyche, a point that he makes repeatedly in the
Review. The shopkeeper understands that his credit depends
entirely on his ability to please customers, to strike them as
gracious and reliable, to be perceived as unsparing of his time and
effort in suiting them with their purchases. On the presentation of
self, however, the effect is dramatic: destabilizing, fragmenting.
Personal identity dissolves into a series of nonce roles. The public
man and the private are discontinuous and unrecognizable to each
other. In his study of this era's visual art, David H. Solkin gives
the point a memorably pithy expression:

As far back as the sixteenth century, the English had begun to address
the problem of how to define motives and relations in a world where the
forms of exchange that had once been confined to the marketplace seemed
to be proliferating throughout society at large. The new circumstances of
agricultural and commercial capitalism raised profoundly unsettling questions about the 'authenticity, accountability, and intentionality' of human
subjects; and out of the various attempts to answer these questions there
emerged the modern consciousness of a private self, as a more or less
autonomous entity which existed in a tense relationship with the various
social roles it was called upon to play.[59]

[57] Daniel Defoe, *The Complete English Tradesman*, 2 vols., 2nd edn. (London,
1727), i. 94–5.
[58] Linda Colley, *Britons: Forging the Nation, 1707–1837* (London: Pimlico, 1991),
66.
[59] David H. Solkin, *Painting for Money: The Visual Arts and the Public Sphere in
Eighteenth-Century England* (New Haven: Yale University Press, 1993), 22.

It was Defoe's understanding of these new conditions of selfhood, and in particular his novelistic manipulation of the distinction between the public and the private self—which adds up to the invention of a psychological 'depth model' for novelistic character-ization—that distinguished his fictional writing most clearly from Haywood's.

V

What I have represented here as a market competition between the psychological fiction of Defoe and the amatory fiction of Haywood to capture the hearts and minds of readers is predicated on an assumption that the distance between potential readers of Defoe and Haywood is less than that between novel-readers and readers of other literary genres. As Paul Hunter expresses it:

Readers of poetry—pastorals, poetic epistles, social and political verses, philosophical poems, georgics—probably did often go on to read novels, but not as a replacement for poetry. Poetry, even when it was luxurious, lascivious, or occasional, was thought to be 'serious' and demanding in a way that new novels were not, and the movement from one to the other was not a natural one, for both the needs addressed and the pleasures afforded were thought to be quite different in the two modes.[60]

After 1750, in the wake of important novels by Fielding and Richardson, this situation changes. Powerful bids for the novel's importance as a genre begin to be launched. As we have already seen, Defoe takes the opportunity in *Roxana* (and in very many other places) to distinguish the fictions he writes from romance, by stressing their veracity. This is an early attempt to theorize fiction in a way that defends its seriousness and responsibility: if readers believe the story to be true, they will take it seriously enough to read and be morally improved by it. Later writers need to retain a defence of seriousness and responsibility, but without sacrificing fictionality itself. This is exactly the objective, however, of Char-lotte Lennox's *The Female Quixote; or, The Adventures of Ara-bella* (1752). Arabella has been brought up in seclusion on a diet of seventeenth-century French romance, which she has read as true history. Her value system and way of being in the world is

<hr />

[60] Hunter, *Before Novels*, 87.

entirely modelled on the conduct represented in these fantastic-
ated fictions. Consequently, she is unable to conduct a normal
relationship with her suitor Mr Glanville, or any of the people by
whom she is surrounded. Although in the time-honoured mode of
Quixotic satire, Arabella's idealism and unworldliness can put to
shame the mundane, petty, and calculating conduct of such as Mr
Glanville's vain, spoilt sister, the category mistakes that she makes
become increasingly dangerous. Her social blunders—mistaking a
thieving gardener for a banished nobleman and assuming even
respectable old gentlemen like Sir Charles Glanville to be potential ravishers—are embarrassing enough. Indeed, her misprision
of her prospective father-in-law is damaging to the social fabric, as
is her rescuing of a whore who is being beaten by her cully on the
mistaken assumption that she is a threatened noblewoman. As the
novel develops, one can perhaps discern three different 'worlds'
within it, governed by three different epistemologies: that of
French romance so implicitly credited by Arabella; the petty
sphere of sexual intrigues and 'adventures' inhabited by Charlotte
Glanville, Miss Groves, and various other unworthy women that I
would venture to suggest corresponds to the 'secret history' fiction
produced by Delarivier Manley and Eliza Haywood in England;
and the 'real world' of common sense, honour, decency, and moral
values inhabited by young Glanville, the Countess, and the Doctor
and beckoning to Arabella throughout. Naturally there is movement between these separate spheres, and some of the novel's
comic and narrative energy derives from the points at which
Arabella's behaviour threatens actually to turn Glanville's reality
into that of romance—as he finds himself fighting a duel with the
rakish Sir George, for example, who has designs upon Arabella
and exploits her obsession to attain his ends. While it is certainly
the case, as some critics maintain, that Arabella's romance addiction confers upon her certain forms of freedom and empowerment
with respect to men, it is to read the novel entirely against the
grain to wish that addiction longer life.

Romance's real danger is most apparent in Arabella's intellectual errors. These are perceived to be of profound concern.
In book VII, she is engaged in a dialogue with a know-all called
Selvin, who fancies himself as something of a historian. Arabella
confounds him with cod history derived from the romances;
and although the besting of the egregious Selvin is a source of

amusement to Glanville, he recognizes how seriously Arabella is deluded, and what a threat to all epistemological certainty her misinformation has become:

But Mr. *Glanville*, who knew all these Anecdotes were drawn from the Romances, which he found contradicted the known Facts in History, and assign'd the most ridiculous Causes for Things of the greatest Importance; could not help smiling at the Facility with which Mr. *Selvin* gave into those idle Absurdities. For notwithstanding his Affection of great Reading, his superficial Knowledge of History made it extremely easy to deceive him; and as it was his Custom to mark in his Pocket-Book all the Scraps of History he heard introduced into Conversation, and retail them again in other Company; he did not doubt but he would make a Figure with the curious Circumstances *Arabella* had furnish'd him with.[61]

At this point, there is some danger of false history seeping out and contaminating the entire knowledge-base of society. Arabella must be dehumoured, and she duly is so by a divine bearing a strong resemblance to Samuel Johnson at the novel's close. He takes it upon himself to prove to Arabella that there is no truth in the stories she has been reading. With the piercing naïvete of a Houyhnhnm questioning the efficacy of lying, Arabella asks what possible *use* writing can be that is not true. All fictions are 'empty Fictions, and from this Hour I deliver them to Moths and Mould' (p. 377). Shrewdly, the Doctor begins his response to this with a quotation from Shakespeare—the paradigm case of the poet-maker whose fictions are not empty:

Shakespear, said the Doctor, calls just Resentment the Child of Integrity, and therefore I do not wonder, that what Vehemence the Gentleness of your Ladyship's Temper allows, should be exerted upon this Occasion. Yet . . . Truth is not always injured by Fiction. An admirable Writer of our own Time, has found the Way to convey the most solid Instructions, the noblest Sentiments, and the most exalted Piety, in the pleasing Dress of a Novel, and, to use the Words of the greatest Genius in the present Age, 'Has taught the Passions to move at the Command of Virtue'.   (p. 377)

Thus, the Doctor vindicates the responsible novel as written by Richardson and endorsed by Samuel Johnson. And he goes on to lay down some of the epistemological conditions that such responsible fictions should meet, in distinction to those embodied

[61] Charlotte Lennox, *The Female Quixote; or, The Adventures of Arabella* (1752), ed. Margaret Dalziel with Duncan Isles, intro. Margaret Anne Doody (Oxford University Press, 1989), 273.

in romance: respect for known historical and geographical fact, truth to experience, plausibility that derives from our standards of what is commonplace and normal in living, and the recommendation of a system of moral values other than those of revenge and love—the dangerous passions that propel the bloodthirsty, unchristian actions of characters in romance. His manifesto for fiction is that it should embody a conception of the real similar to that recommended by philosophical empiricists: its invention based on past experience and the historical record, and its account of human behaviour based on inference. The social utility of responsible fictions, defined by the Doctor against the iniquity of romance, is one that the cult of sentiment would propagate widely: 'It is impossible to read these Tales [the romances] without lessening part of that Humility, which by preserving in us a Sense of our Alliance with all human nature, keeps us awake to Tenderness and Sympathy, or without impairing that Compassion which is implanted in us as an Incentive to Acts of Kindness' (p. 381).

By the mid-century, then, we can observe the realization that fiction could assume some of the traditional canons of poetic responsibility: it could be canonical, in short. Not all fiction would have to do this, however. It could address different sections of its potential readership differently. Writers might have a 'Design' similar to that expressed by Eliza Haywood in her Dedication of *Lasselia; or, The Self-Abandon'd: A Novel* (1724) to the Earl of Suffolk and Bindon, to 'remind the unthinking Part of the World, how dangerous it is to give way to Passion.'[62] Or they might develop aspirations to seriousness as profound as those expressed by Jane Austen in a famous passage in *Northanger Abbey*:

Although our productions have afforded more extensive and unaffected pleasure than those of any other literary corporation in the world, no species of composition has been so much decried . . . there seems almost a general wish of decrying the capacity and undervaluing the labour of the novelist, and of slighting the performances which have only genius, wit, and taste to recommend them. 'I am no novel reader—I seldom look into novels—Do not imagine that I often read novels—It is really very well for a novel.'—Such is the common cant.—'And what are you reading, Miss ——?' 'Oh! it is only a novel!' replies the young lady; while she lays down her book with affected indifference, or momentary shame.—'It is only

[62] Quoted from Vivien Jones (ed.), *Women in the Eighteenth Century: Constructions of Femininity* (London: Routledge, 1990), 153.

Cecilia, or Camilla, or Belinda'; or, in short, only some work in which the greatest powers of the mind are displayed, in which the most thorough knowledge of human nature, the happiest delineation of its varieties, the liveliest effusions of wit and humour are conveyed to the world in the best chosen language.[63]

Austen goes on to condemn the *Spectator*, in her time still considered in some quarters the epitome of approved reading for young women, as improbable, unnatural, dull, and—of all charges —coarse and impolite. Thus the publication that played so large a part, as we have seen, in the creation of polite literary discourse is condemned by that very form—the novel—that it helped to sponsor; and thus, as Shakespeare says, the whirligig of time brings in his revenges.

In October 1856 George Eliot's most famous review essay, 'Silly Novels by Lady Novelists', was published in the *Westminster Review*. At this historical juncture, she had enough confidence in the importance of the genre to speak of 'a sense of the responsibility involved in publication, and an appreciation of the sacredness of the writer's art'.[64] Although the novel had no particular rules or technique, which laid it open to 'mere left-handed imbecility' (p. 163), it was a form in which great achievement was possible, and that achievement was open to women. For Eliot, the reason why many female novelists brought the genre into disrepute was not the commonly given one that they wrote for bread:

Where there is one woman who writes from necessity, we believe that there are three women who write from vanity; and, besides, there is something so antiseptic in the mere healthy fact of working for one's bread, that the most trashy and rotten kind of feminine literature is not likely to have been produced under such circumstances. 'In all labour there is profit'; silly novels, we imagine, are less the result of labour than of busy idleness.　(p. 162)

Early in the essay, she has made a powerfully ironic point out of the observation that if such novels are written by 'lonely women struggling for a maintenance, or wives and daughters devoting themselves to the production of "copy" out of pure heroism' (p. 142), it is curious that none of this experience forms any part of

---

[63] Jane Austen, *Northanger Abbey* (1817), ed. Anne Ehrenpreis (Harmondsworth: Penguin, 1972; repr. 1975), 58.

[64] George Eliot, *Selected Essays, Poems and Other Writings*, ed. A. S. Byatt and Nicholas Warren (Harmondsworth: Penguin, 1990), 161.

the content of what they write, which is relentlessly patrician in its *mise-en-scène*. But, of course, the women producing this material are not patrician either. Absence of verisimilitude dogs everything they write: 'and their intellect seems to have the particular impartiality of reproducing both what they *have* seen and heard, and what they have *not* seen and heard, with equal unfaithfulness' (p. 143). Eliot has the confidence to pillory women writers and to distinguish several minor genres by comic nicknames (the '*mind and millinery* species', the '*oracular* species', the '*white neckcloth* species'), only because she has a strong belief in the centrality of the novel. Her criterion for great writing in this kind is also clear: verisimilitude, though not of the neoclassical Aristotelian stamp commended by such as John Dennis. 'Great writers . . . have modestly contented themselves with putting their experiences into fiction, and have thought it quite a sufficient task to exhibit men and things as they are' (p. 149). George Eliot formulates explicitly the criterion by which novels such as those of Haywood would be condemned as 'silly'.

7

'A Poet, and a Patron, and Ten Pound': Politics, Cultural Politics, and the Scriblerians

Swift's protégée Letitia Pilkington recalls in her *Memoirs* that Swift once showed her a letter from Pope which was 'filled with low and ungentlemanlike reflections both on Mr. Gay and the two noble persons who honoured him with their patronage after his disappointment at Court'. Pope receives only occasional mention in the *Memoirs*, but always dishonourable: he is shown to be an envious, two-faced, sneaking fellow. He is, for example, jealous of Gay's success with *The Beggar's Opera*—'The Dean very frankly owned he did not think Mr. Pope was so candid to the merits of other writers as he ought to be'.[1] Pope's compliment to Swift in *The Dunciad* is pronounced cold and forced by comparison with the warm, sincere fulsomeness of Swift's lines 'Hail happy Pope, whose generous mind' in his *A Libel on Dr. Delany*—lines which Pope subsequently came to regard as a considerable embarrassment. Later in the *Memoirs*, Mrs. Pilkington tells us that Swift had given her husband a letter of introduction to Pope, who invited him to stay at Twickenham for a fortnight on the strength of it. Whereas Pilkington writes back to his wife enthusing over the warmth of his welcome, Pope writes a letter to Swift in which he calls Pilkington a 'forward, shallow, conceited fellow' and tells Swift that he was sick of Pilkington's impertinence before the end of the third day. To Letitia Pilkington, there was a clear distinction to be drawn between Swift, whose behaviour was often eccentric but whose eccentricity derived from too much principle, and Pope, whose devious antics derived from too little. Her anecdotes remind us that contemporaries did not always regard Swift and Pope as entirely inseparable Siamese twins—the Castor

[1] *Memoirs of Mrs. Letitia Pilkington, 1712–1750* (1748–54), intro. Iris Barry (London, 1928), 62.

and Pollux of Tory satire—as has been a prominent tendency amongst more recent readers.[2] Characterizations of the friendship, like the very engaging one given in Pope's description of the *Miscellanies* project, are difficult to resist: 'Methinks we look like friends, side by side, serious and merry by turns, conversing interchangeably, and walking down hand in hand to posterity'; and on the basis of their many celebrations of it in the letters, one can see why Pope's most recent biographer, Felicity Rosslyn, invokes the friendship as 'the deepest and most sustaining' of Pope's lifetime.[3]

I will argue in this chapter that the tendency in recent liberal-humanist constructions of Pope, Swift, and Gay has been to bring the writers together into group solidarity despite the many temperamental and personal differences that are allowed to exist between them; but that the breakdown of the liberal-humanist consensus in scholarship and criticism apparent in eighteenth-century studies in the 1980s resulted in a fierce reaction to such brother-bonding, especially from feminists. Currently, scholars are more aware of the *distance* separating the writers than of their proximity. After this diagnostic exercise, I will make a case for reconceiving the writing of Pope, Swift, and Gay (as well as a writer upon whom I confer 'honorary' Scriblerian status, Henry Fielding) as informed by a *cultural* politics that is its most important distinguishing feature. While giving full weight to the very different ways in which it is embodied, I contend that a common cultural politics contours the writing of this group. It derives from a characteristic attitude towards professional writing and the shifting tectonics of patronage, and is elaborated in opposition to a set of literary developments that we can designate under the term 'novelization'. This cultural politics issues in the deployment of parodic literary forms—mock forms, hybrid forms—the common achievement of which is to borrow energy from the sincere forms they wish to explode, and recycle that energy in subversion. 'Cultural politics' implies an understanding of politics broader

[2] A. C. Elias, Jr., Pilkington's modern editor, offers an amusing and instructive account of her reliability as a witness in 'Laetitia Pilkington on Swift: How Reliable is She?', in Christopher Fox and Brenda Tooley (eds.), *Walking Naboth's Vineyard: New Studies of Swift* (Notre Dame, Ind.: University of Notre Dame Press, 1995), 127–42.

[3] Pope, *Correspondence*, ii. 426; Felicity Rosslyn, *Alexander Pope: A Literary Life* (Basingstoke: Macmillan, 1990), 83.

than the direct representation of issues on the party-political agenda. For the Scriblerians, the most important ideological struggle was that concerning the effect of the political and commercial organization of culture on the development of imaginative forms. Only a small part of this struggle was embodied in any explicit political programme. Very little of it generated parliamentary debate or legal reform, though, as my earlier discussion of the hard-fought campaign to define the products of literary endeavour as a form of property owned by its producer suggests, some of it did. The Scriblerians found their subject-matter and their most compelling forms, tropes, and techniques in the confusion generated by the growth of the literary market-place and in their resistance to the imperative of adjusting to it. Books, entertainment, theatre, and music—the semiotic domain of signs, images, and meanings—were the battlegrounds of most significance. Theirs was a cultural, more than a partisan, politics.

To conclude the chapter, I will give a brief account of Aaron Hill's career, a relatively neglected writer whose ubiquity and centrality is beyond doubt. His importance to this study is that he combines elements of the Whig-derived ideology of politeness and the aesthetic canons that derive from it with elements of the Scriblerian politics of decline referred to above. He is a particularly striking example of the confluence of 'progressive' and 'anti-progressive' strands in one complex and very human being.

I

Until the end of the 1960s Pope was, for scholars and critics, either the poet of couplet form or the poet of allusion. The weaponry of New Criticism was martialled to demonstrate the presence of 'devices'—antithesis, pun, irony, and ambiguity—that operated at a subtextual level to complicate the surface, attention to which would restore value to Pope's verse in the face of challenges to it that derive from Victorian attacks on his personal morality and Matthew Arnold's influential view that, on a particular definition of the term, Pope was not a poet at all. Alternatively, the poetry could be opened to a diachronic axis of contextualization. On this account, Pope was a poet saturated in a Christianized conception of classical writers—in particular the great writers of the Augustan age, Virgil, Horace, and Ovid, but naturally including Homer and reaching out to firmly embrace Lucretius and the other major Roman satirists Juvenal and Persius. In the modern period his poetic voice assimilates the laureate succession of the English poets: Chaucer, Milton, Dryden ... The ethical dimension to Pope's Christian humanism is emphasized in the volumes of the great Twickenham edition of Pope's poems that monumentalizes post-war scholarship.[4] It was the enormous achievement of Maynard Mack's *The Garden and the City* that, while he laid appropriate stress on the self-conscious Augustanism of Pope's retired life in his Twickenham villa and garden, he also restored Pope to contemporary English history by documenting that home and garden as a base for subversive political activity. Posing as Horace in retirement on his Sabine farm, cultivating in letters, poems, garden design, and iconography an environment that expressed this personality fully, Pope could camouflage his role as the orchestrator of the literary opposition to Sir Robert Walpole's Whig government. Mack's emphasis on contemporary history enabled him to combat both the formalist bias in literary criticism according to which literary texts never make reference to external reality but instead reveal to the expert eye an internal structure that subtly unites the disparate images and rhetorical figures; and the allusion-hunters who threaten to reduce Pope to a figure in some transcendental pageant of Great Writers Through the Centuries queuing up on the slopes of Parnassus. At the same time as Mack's influential book was published, Isaac Kramnick's *Bolingbroke and his Circle* provided what became a standard account of the anti-Whig Bolingbrokean ideology around which Pope, Swift, and Gay united in the period post-1726, after the commencement of *The Craftsman* and in the heady period of 'Scriblerian' effloration that witnessed the advent of *Gulliver's Travels*, *The Beggar's Opera*, and *The Dunciad*.[5] Kramnick

---

[4] The major works in this tradition are Reuben A. Brower, *Alexander Pope: The Poetry of Allusion* (Oxford: Clarendon Press, 1959); Earl Wasserman, *Pope's Epistle to Bathurst* (Baltimore: Johns Hopkins University Press, 1960); Maynard Mack, *The Garden and the City: Retirement and Politics in the Later Poetry of Pope, 1731–1743* (Toronto: University of Toronto Press, 1969); G. S. Rousseau and Pat Rogers (ed.), *The Enduring Legacy: Alexander Pope. Essays for the Tercentenary* (Cambridge University Press, 1988).

[5] Mack, *The Garden and the City*; Isaac Kramnick, *Bolingbroke and his Circle: The Politics of Nostalgia in the Age of Walpole* (Cambridge, Mass.: Harvard University Press, 1968).

242 THE SCRIBLERIANS AND THEIR ENEMIES

presented the Scriblerians as sharing a 'Country' ideology of nostalgic conservatism, a gloomy and reactionary lament for the passing of a society based on landed wealth and established social hierarchy, pitting themselves against writers like Defoe and Mandeville who sponsor the socially mobile, vigorous, and rising cadre of entrepreneurs and tradesmen. These progressive ideologues measure individual worth by enterprise, intelligence, survival instinct, and, increasingly, by the amassing of wealth. The great satirists of the early century formed their ideology as a conservative backlash to this mercantile upstartism. They were contemptuous of money circulation, deeply suspicious of credit, stockbroking— all forms of invisible assets and capital accumulation—despised financiers but tolerated honest tradesmen, and hated rapacious land stewards and other dishonest racketeers.

For many scholars working on Swift and Pope in the 1970s and early 1980s, the pressing imperative was to refine and sophisticate the literary judgements made in these seminal works, and to deepen their analysis of cultural politics. One landmark study was Bertrand A. Goldgar's *Walpole and the Wits*, a study that conceived the partisan affiliations of Walpole's literary opponents in the later 1720s and 1730s as the first era in which the entire question of cultural production becomes politicized.[6] Walpole was seen to be derelicting on his and his government's duty to patronize writers of merit. He was putting an exponentially increasing network of opportunity at the disposal of writers whose only qualification was that they would write on his side of any question. My own earlier book *Pope and Bolingbroke* contributed in some small measure to the enunciation of this complex of ideas, attitudes, and beliefs by emphasizing the importance of the Scriblerus Club as a matrix for satirical projects that implied absent norms, by dwelling on the period during which Pope and Swift were together in Twickenham as an *annus mirabilis* of creativity, and by foregrounding the part played by Bolingbroke and the *Craftsman* in the conversion of this ideology into a political persuasion in the 1730s (the 'Country' party). Assisted by J. G. A. Pocock's momentous history of republican civic humanism, I tried to show how the nexus of bad poetry and bad politics was cemented, through which Whig-sponsored hack writing became the manifestation on a

[6] Bertrand A. Goldgar, *Walpole and the Wits: The Relation of Politics to Literature, 1722–1742* (Lincoln: University of Nebraska Press, 1976).

cultural level of the 'corruption' that is seen to pervade the body politic.[7] Although this is a line of enquiry that has not been much pursued since then, two important recent books give renewed prominence to the politics of the Scriblerians, though they reach very different conclusions: Colin Nicholson's *Writing and the Rise of Finance* and Christine Gerrard's *The Patriot Opposition to Walpole*, which studies politics and patriotism in the early century.[8] Nicholson's argument, though securely in the line of Kramnick, Pocock, Erskine-Hill, and Mack, gains some torque from the observation that despite their public opposition to the manifestations of the 'financial revolution', the Scriblerians were all major players on the stock-market, who sought to benefit from it publicly. Nicholson's work is further valuable in suggesting that the new credit and banking system constituted a discourse that interpellated individuals differently and modified their subjectivities, forcing upon them new ways of conceiving human agency. This is his excellent formulation of issues that I addressed in Chapters 4 and 5:

> Writers steeped in the cognitive ideals of civic humanism found it increasingly difficult to grant self-interested individuals enmeshed in credit-driven commercial enterprise the autonomy and breadth of mind necessary for civic virtue. Simultaneously it became possible for the argument to be put (by Addison among others) that market forms of sociability, sympathy and honesty might be developed to redefine citizenship, and this was the project of *The Spectator*. The virtues of sociability in this view are substituted for civic virtues in an attempt to provide ideological coherence for a developing political economy.   (p. 3).

Christine Gerrard's work, on the other hand, refashions the existing landscape of cultural politics far more radically than does Nicholson. In place of a Newtonian universe in which every Tory has an equal and opposite Whig, she presents a much more complicated political scene in the 1730s. To Gerrard, the most significant cultural formation of Walpole's era is the group of writers that clustered round the so-called 'Boy Patriot' affiliation

---

[7] J. G. A. Pocock, *The Machiavellian Moment: Florentine Political Thought and the Atlantic Republican Tradition* (Princeton University Press, 1975); Hammond, *Pope and Bolingbroke*.

[8] Colin Nicholson, *Writing and the Rise of Finance: Capital Satires of the Early Eighteenth Century* (Cambridge University Press, 1994); Christine Gerrard, *The Patriot Opposition to Walpole: Politics, Poetry, and Natural Myth, 1725–1742* (Oxford: Clarendon Press, 1994).

of Opposition Whigs, young politicians like William Pitt, George Lyttelton, the Grenvilles, and Hugh Polwarth, third Earl March-mont, who took their lead from Lord Cobham and other dis-affected Whig grandees and who bestowed virtual cult status upon Frederick, Prince of Wales as the 'Patriot King' so much desired by Bolingbroke. To find the real literary opposition to Walpole, we need to examine not the work of the Scriblerians—especially not Pope, whom Gerrard represents as resolutely independent to the point of being a maverick—but the group of poets promoted by the patriot Whigs: James Thomson, Henry Brooke, Aaron Hill, Richard Glover, Gilbert West, George Lillo, and other more minor figures. This anti-Walpolean ideology certainly was not characterized by any conservative, land-based politics of nostalgia. It whole-heartedly embraced the spirit of mercantile enterprise and lost no opportunity to praise trade as the corner-stone of national prosperity.

If Christine Gerrard's work represents the high-water mark of scepticism about 'Bolingbroke and his circle' from one direction—she does not think Bolingbroke ever *had* a circle—recent feminist criticism raises its level from another. The 1980s was a major decade in Scriblerian literary biography, witnessing the publication of the long-awaited final volume of Ehrenpreis's *Swift: The Man, his Works, and the Age*, of Maynard Mack's *Alexander Pope: A Life*, and Martin and Ruthe Battestin's *Henry Fielding: A Life*.[9] The combined effect of these Herculean biographical labours was, by embracing the major Augustan authors in a liberal-humanist network of assumptions, to join them together. Critical reception of these biographies was not, however, as rapturous as a lifetime spent in research would have entitled their authors to expect. Irish reception of Ehrenpreis's biography was hostile in the main, leading Irish voices resenting the extent to which Ehrenpreis threatened to demythologize Swift, to pluck out the heart of his mystery and fail to give due weight to the savage residue of what Carole Fabricant calls the 'extreme, outrageous, and demonic side of Swift'.[10] When the Battestins' life of Fielding met with an even

---

[9] Irvin Ehrenpreis, *Swift: The Man, his Works, and the Age*, 3 vols. (London: Methuen, 1962–83); Mack, *Pope*; Battestin and Battestin, *Fielding*.

[10] Carole Fabricant, review, *Scriblerian*, 17/2 (1985), 167–9. For other similarly dissatisfied reactions, see Denis Donoghue's review, *Times Literary Supplement*, 4219 (1984), 143–4; and Andrew Carpenter's in *Irish University Review*, 14/2 (1984), 277–80.

more severe fate in 1989, one suspected that the kind of biography
called by Julian Barnes in *Flaubert's Parrot* a 'ten pound one',
the kind that 'stands, fat and worthy-burgherish on the shelf,
boastful and sedate', giving all the hypotheses as well as the facts,
was a form of 'master-narrative' discountenanced in our time.[11]
Recent literary theory has done so much to decentre intentionalist
accounts of authorship and unsettle organic accounts of the individual self that it is considered naïve in some quarters to express
whole-hearted approval of a mere biography. But Ian Campbell
Ross, in his review of Ehrenpreis published in *Hermathena*,
registers a very perceptive objection not merely fashionable. The
Swift that emerges from the biography is really an *accepted* Swift,
even a very familiar Swift, by the time Ehrenpreis publishes.
Ehrenpreis is really in dialogue with such as D. H. Lawrence and
Middleton Murry, who took him to be a dangerous lunatic. By
1983, however, the Swift we knew was a benevolist, convinced of
corrupt human nature and the need to adhere to rigid Christian
principles as a way of alleviating misery that corruption brings in
train.[12] And by 1983 many readers, feminists prominent among
them, did not believe in this Swift and wanted a different one.
This is presumably why David Nokes's *Jonathan Swift, a Hypocrite Revers'd* could win a prize only a year later. If any biography
ever lived up to its subtitle 'critical', this one does: Nokes's
biographical hypothesis is that Swift may have been a churchman,
but he was no Christian, finding central elements of Christ's
teaching unacceptable.[13]

The point about the big biographies representing the *end* of
something rather than the beginning—to wit, the end of the
liberal-humanist consensus—is more clearly made with respect to
Maynard Mack's biography of Pope published in 1985. Mack too
wanted to 'normalize' Pope, wanted to bring him within the
bounds of acceptable conduct, and by the time he came to publish
he too was combating a view of Pope (in this case, a Victorian
view) as a straw man. Reviewer after reviewer singles out the
central problem of Mack's biography as being his *advocacy* of Pope

[11] Battestin and Battestin, *Fielding*; Julian Barnes, *Flaubert's Parrot* (1984; repr.
London: Pan, 1985), 38.
[12] Ian Campbell Ross, '"If we Believe Report": New Biographies of Jonathan
Swift', *Hermathena*, 137 (1984), 34–49.
[13] David Nokes, *Jonathan Swift, a Hypocrite Revers'd; A Critical Biography*
(Oxford University Press, 1985).

and, allied to that, the densely allusive style, replete with scores of unacknowledged literary quotations, in which he conducts it. James McLaverty's review in *Notes & Queries* presented as its main strength just those aspects of Mack to which others took exception: 'This biography is . . . a powerful expression of Professor Mack's humanism; it is permeated by his sense of the importance of the past to the present, of the limitations always to be found in human nature, and of the value of moderation, tolerance, kindliness and friendship.'[14] Virtually the same point is made by Larry Lipking in a provocative review published in *American Scholar*, except that for Lipking this is the *problem*, not its solution. Pope is the poet of allusion. His work revels in its awareness of living amongst a 'club of wits' that perceives the continuity of human culture across widely separated times and places. The threnodic tone that connects Mack to his subject, giving Christopher Ricks his *aperçu* that '*Alexander Pope: A Life* is a worthy climax to Maynard Mack, a life', is also responsible for smudging the trail, for failing finally to distinguish Pope's life from the life of Pope's own creation in his art.[15] Mack is thrown back upon applying to Pope's life a moral calculus designed to assess whether he was more sinned against than sinning. Pope, in Mack's account, is a better writer than the dunces he attacked. He really *was*, as he said he was, trying to protect the cultural practice of writing from the depredations of the 'shifty, needy and incompetent', and his enemies deserved all they got. This is to fail to recognize an ideological dimension that *mediates* the poet and his age. The biographer permits Pope to set the agenda, when he should be setting up a model of the real social, political, and economic conditions that existed in the period, to which the poet relates imaginatively, partially, and in a way that cannot be disinterested. In the provinces of gender relations and of the economic conditions governing authorship, it was particularly evident that Swift and Pope could not speak anything like the entire truth about their cultures. In a recent article, Ellen Pollak puts the point thus: 'Critics would have to look beyond the surface of Swift's positive and negative images of women to ways in which gender is

---

[14] James McLaverty, review of Maynard Mack, *Alexander Pope: A Life*, *Notes & Queries*, 34/1 (1987), 89.
[15] Larry Lipking, review of Mack, *American Scholar*, 56/3 (1987), 435–9; Christopher Ricks, review of Mack, *Encounter*, 66/1 (1986), 38.

implicated in the production of meaning both in Swift's writing and in eighteenth-century British culture as a whole.[16] Swift's misogyny becomes a given, a fundamental condition of the production of intelligible meaning. The Marxist-feminist backlash of the mid- and late-1980s was fuelled by the inadequacy of the theoretical models adopted by Ehrenpreis and Mack. Pollak's work, and that of Laura Brown, Nussbaum and Brown, Margaret Anne Doody, and several others, was even more essential and overdue as a result of the big biographies.

There are, however, some peculiarities in the nature of recent feminist reaction to Swift and Pope. There is an amusing passage in Robert Graves's *Goodbye to All That* (1929), where he reports an Oxford college tutor as having said to him: 'I understand, Mr. Graves, that the essays which you write for your English tutor are, shall I say, a trifle temperamental. It appears, indeed, that you prefer some authors to others.'[17] Feminist critics of our period also prefer some authors to others. In *The Poetics of Sexual Myth*, Ellen Pollak reached conclusions that are deeply counter-intuitive to those who come at Pope and Swift from a biographical point of view—in the process driving Swift and Pope as far apart as they ever have been in any critical account.[18] Pope becomes the gender-villain and Swift the gender-hero, because while Pope accommodates himself comfortably to bourgeois sexual myths like that of 'passive womanhood', Swift exposes the contradiction inherent in the myths and refuses to naturalize them. *Ideologiekritik* arrives at conclusions that are difficult to sanction on the basis of what we know about the lives of the two writers. As contemporaries never failed to remind Pope, he was a scandal to masculinity, yet Pollak tells us that his poetry expresses canonical forms of sexism. Swift, whose entire life could be viewed as a flight from the responsibility of feeling for women, turns out to be a good guy who has written, in *Cadenus and Vanessa*, a great love poem. This can happen because, as Pollak puts it, Swift is better than Pope because worse, 'and "worse" is "better" when value is mediated by the poetic imperative of an alienating ideology'.[19] I concur entirely with John

[16] Ellen Pollak, 'Swift among the Feminists: An Approach to Teaching', *College Literature*, 19 (1992), 114–20: 116.

[17] Robert Graves, *Goodbye to All That* (1929; repr. Harmondsworth, 1977), ch. 27, p. 240.

[18] Ellen Pollak, *The Poetics of Sexual Myth: Gender and Ideology in the Verse of Swift and Pope* (Chicago: University of Chicago Press, 1985).   [19] Ibid. 183.

Sitter's review of Pollak in the *Scriblerian*, where he argues that what she has actually done is to reassign the qualities of savage indignation, unstable irony, and extremism that have always been recognized in Swift to a post-modernist conception of the authorial self: 'Pope's poetry looks for "balance" and "stability", Swift's for the point where "certainty dissolves". Pope's imposes "wholeness", Swift's "fractures" such impositions. Pope seeks to *re*center authorial presence, Swift to *de*center it. Pope's attempted fusion of new and classical modes is a "more accommodating response to modernism" than Swift's rejection of "the idea of the modern subject altogether".'[20] To Pollak, Swift is valuable because he is a deconstructor *avant la lettre*. Swift, the apostle of the 'post', the harbinger of cultural critiques that dispense with liberal-humanist emphasis on *evaluation*, is himself appropriated for a sweeping evaluative act that, like some eighteenth-century pantomimic special effect, transmutes Castor and Pollux into Punch and Judy. This is not the place to pursue the reasons why one might think that Swift's putative contribution to any 'post-modern' project would have been to stop it in its tracks rather than to welcome it with open arms. Suffice it to say here that although many readers of Swift have detected an excessive and inconsistent overdetermination of meaning in his writing, it is not the kind of ludic abstention from commitment that one detects either in theorists of the post-modern like Baudrillard and Lyotard or in practitioners of it.

Margaret Doody is a feminist of a very different methodological stamp to Pollak, but her conclusion that 'in any modern comparison of Swift and Pope in relation to their views on women, Swift is likely to come off much better: that is, if the person making the comparison be a woman' also gains critical éclat by means of a face-off between them.[21] In a fascinating article, she shows how Swift's iambic tetrameter and interest in 'that which is homely, unofficial, and truthful' (p. 79) enabled a succession of female poetic voices, including Letitia Pilkington's. Her claim that Swift, rather than Pope, was the true role model for eighteenth-century women poets might be hard pressed to stand up to statistical analysis; but it is yet more convincing than her claim that 'in

[20] John Sitter, review of Pollak, *Scriblerian*, 20/1 (1987), 61.
[21] Margaret Anne Doody, 'Swift among the Women', *Yearbook of English Studies*, 18 (1988), 68–92: 91.

his relations with women, Swift (inside and outside his own poems) never shuts them up' (p. 77).[22] This remark moves me to disclose the ending of the Letitia Pilkington story with which I began the chapter. Pilkington writes an abject letter to the Dean apologizing for her outburst and explaining her anxiety that Pope's poor opinion of her husband might prejudice Swift's. She quotes Swift's reply to her: 'You must shake off the leavings of your sex. If you cannot keep a secret and take a chiding, you will quickly be out of my sphere. Corrigible people are to be chid; those who are otherwise may be very safe from any lectures of mine: I should rather choose to indulge them in their follies than attempt to set them right. I desire you may not inform your husband of what has passed . . .'.[23] This appears to shut her up effectively enough, and also to come between husband and wife.

II

It is curious, then, that one of the greatest dangers to Pope's reputation in our time should be the rising stock of his closest friend, Swift.[24] In my view, this distortion is the result of an exaggeration of the stability of Pope's ideology and of the instability in Swift's. I should want to correct it by discerning the broad cultural territory upon which Pope and Swift, as well as Gay and Fielding, were in agreement. Readers who have been with me thus far will be aware that I see the decades following 1660 as a period of English cultural history in which a relatively rapid shift from patronage to marketing as the primary way of financing imaginative writing was accomplished; a period of growth in demand for what I have called, inelegantly, literary products. The emergence of writers capable of satisfying that demand occurred in symbiotic relationship with the development of the demand itself. Yet its

[22] For counter-balancing evidence of Pope's influence on subsequent generations of women readers and writers, see Claudia N. Thomas, *Alexander Pope and his Eighteenth-Century Women Readers* (Carbondale, Ill.: Southern Illinois University Press, 1994).

[23] Pilkington, *Memoirs*, 87.

[24] In an article entitled 'Beyond Consensus: *The Rape of the Lock* and the Fate of Reading Eighteenth-Century Literature', *New Orleans Review*, 15/4 (Winter 1988), 67–77, Robert Markley has defended Brown and Pollak against the 'old-line humanist criticism' of various antagonistic reviewers, but he has not taken on the full force of what the future is likely to be for Pope studies if feminist strictures are accepted.

very volume entailed that it could not be satisfied by the traditional means of patronage. New ways of satisfying it would have to be found. And the new writers who were summoned into existence by the Faustian powers of economic demand would be of a very different stamp from their amateur predecessors. The nature of writing would change, according to the altering social provenance of those who produced and those who consumed it. Bakhtin's conception of 'novelization' is one that I have appropriated earlier in the book to signify the aesthetic results of this historical process. By 'novelization' I understand first a tendency manifested in the imaginative writing of the later seventeenth and early eighteenth centuries towards a hybridization that breaks down traditionally observed generic boundaries. Secondly, my usage of the term denotes an 'aspiration' (if I may so put it) on the part of many disparate forms of writing towards the condition of narrative. Common both to the hybridization and the narrativization of writing is an altering requirement of plausibility and social relevance. In Chapter 3 I observed that whereas in the theatre of the early Restoration there is no difficulty in distinguishing comedy from tragedy—indeed, considerable ingenuity needs to be expended to perceive them as part of the same cultural formation, and for some readers their distinction points to a schizophrenic tendency within the culture—these boundaries become much more fluid as the various reform movements of the 1690s call for a softening of the edges of satirical comedy. I argued above that mock-epic is the product of 'novelization', mediating a profoundly experienced need for classical writing to compromise its cultural remoteness and become relevant to contemporary social concerns. In the area of prose fiction, too, contemporary relevance is a valuable commercial commodity, as is apparent from the success of Delarivier Manley's scandalous fictions *The New Atalantis* (1709) and *The Adventures of Rivella* (1713), which were imitated by Eliza Haywood a dozen or so years later. Social relevance is a central preoccupation of the early-century discourse of 'politeness', promoted both by the characteristic literary form it spawns —the periodical essay—and by the writing it recommends. Addison and Steele are at the centre of a network that includes writers like Thomas Tickell, Ambrose Philips, Susanna Centlivre, Nicholas Rowe, and Aaron Hill (at least in the latter's early days of working on the *British Apollo*). This coterie introduces some of the earliest exemplars of sentimental writing, based as it is on benevolist assumptions about human perfectibility and sociability; and sponsors drama like Rowe's 'she tragedies' which, as I have already remarked, embody a newly domesticated agenda later to be developed by George Lillo, and Addison's own *Cato*, which I have read as an embodiment of the Whig-sponsored cultural politics of *politesse* rather than as a direct enshrinement of Glorious Revolution libertarian principles.

Ambrose Philips might be a useful example. The *Spectator* pursued a campaign to promote his tragedy *The Distrest Mother* (1712), a play set in the aftermath of the Trojan war that tells the story of Pyrrhus, son of Achilles, who, after slaughtering Hector, has gone back to his kingdom with Hector's wife, Andromache, and young son Astyanax. Pyrrhus is betrothed to Hermione, daughter of Menelaus—a good, solid Greek damsel—but loves Andromache, an enemy Trojan. Orestes, son of Agamemnon, comes on a mission to persuade Pyrrhus to kill the Trojan boy lest he grows up and makes trouble, but Orestes is hopelessly in love with Hermione. If Orestes' mission succeeds, therefore, Pyrrhus will marry Hermione and he will lose his love. After numerous diagonal shifts of feeling between the four protagonists, Pyrrhus is murdered on Orestes' orders. Hermione is not grateful, however, and tells Orestes that he should have known better because she truly loved Pyrrhus. This drives Orestes spectacularly mad and he is dragged off-stage raving that the Furies are tearing his heart out, leaving Andromache, the 'distressed mother' of the title, undisputed victrix. Steele was enraptured by this dramatic action because it was a celebration of motherhood and family values. Political correctness à la bourgeois drips off his essay on it in the *Spectator*, no. 290 (1 February 1712):

Domestick Virtues concern all the World, and there is no one living who is not interested that *Andromache* should be an inimitable Character. The generous Affection to the Memory of her deceased Husband, that tender Care for her Son, which is ever heightned with the Consideration of his Father, and these Regards preserved in spite of being tempted with the Possession of the highest Greatness, are what cannot but be venerable even to such an Audience as at present frequents the *English* theatre.[25]

Mr Spectator reports that he was present at the read-through of the tragedy, and a hard-bitten troupe of actors could not avoid

[25] In Addison *et al.*, *The Spectator*, ed. Bond, iii. 32. Subsequent references are to this edition.

crying while they read their parts. This, he imputes to the 'Truth and humane life' of the action, which derives from the fact that, unusually, it is not merely the licentious passions unleashed by the sexual urge that motivates it. Characters in this play respect each other's 'Virtue and Merit; and the Character which gives Name to the Play, is one who has behaved her self with heroick Virtue in the most important Circumstances of a female Life, those of a Wife, a Widow, and a Mother' (p. 410). In many ways a manifesto for the polite tendency in early-century writing, this essay domesticates the world of classical epic beyond recognition, promotes a sentimental tear-shedding as an appropriate audience reaction, and hints broadly at the separate sphere to be occupied by women who stand to become wives, widows, and mothers.

Ambrose Philips continued to be the darling of the Whig-sponsored essayists. In the following year (1713), Thomas Tickell wrote five influential *Guardian* essays promoting Philips's version of pastoral, which was essentially that pastoral should give itself a local habitation and a name. It should take on the local colour of the country in which it is set: plausibility and verisimilitude, even in pastoral. The *Guardian*, no. 30 (15 April 1713) is the most forthright expression of this theory of 'naturalization': 'There are some things of an established Nature in Pastoral, which is essential to it, such as a Country Scene, Innocence, Simplicity. Others there are of a changeable kind, such as Habits, Customs and the like. The difference of the Climate is also to be considered, for what is proper in *Arcadia*, or even in *Italy*, might be very absurd in a colder Country.'[26] Pope's view of pastoral was that it represented an idealized community and landscape that could only render itself plausible and verisimilar at the expense of the kind of bathos that he exemplified (under the ironic pretence that he was praising it) from Philips's pastorals in the *Guardian*, no. 40 for 27 April 1713:

> Ah me the while! ah me! the luckless Day,
> Ah luckless Lad! the rather might I say;
> Ah silly I! more silly than my Sheep,
> Which on the flowery Plains I once did keep.[27]

[26] In Steele, *et al.*, *The Guardian*, 129. John Calhoun Stephens, recent editor of the *Guardian*, has an extremely helpful endnote to *Guardian* no. 22 on the dispute between the Pope faction and the Philips faction over the proper way to write modern pastoral. See pp. 625–6.

[27] Alexander Pope, *The Prose Works*, vol. i., ed. Norman Ault (Oxford: Basil Blackwell, 1936), 103.

Again, it is the question of domestication, of social relevance, that divides Pope from Philips and his Addisonian sponsors. It is interesting to note that when Pope chooses to involve himself in periodical writing on this occasion, he does so actually to subvert the strident sincerities of the form. In retrospect it is difficult to imagine how Steele could have admitted this serpent in his garden —this subversively ironic essay that undermines the entire ethos of the polite periodical. John Gay's early writing is also motivated by a desire to parody and burlesque the politeness manifesto, though it is clear from the outset of his career that works like *The Shepherd's Week* (1714) and *The What D'Ye Call It* (1715) had the capacity to outgrow their parodic roots. *The What D'Ye Call It* is directed at the condition of Addisonian drama in which long-established distinctions between genres were sunk into a sentimentalized and hybridized all-purpose tragicomedy. Gay represents this state of affairs in a play that alludes to Shakespeare's *A Midsummer Night's Dream*. Private theatricals are to be staged at the home of Sir Roger, a country justice, by his household servants. His son, Squire Thomas, is acting in the play within the play, in which two women, Kitty Carrot and Dorcas, claim him as father of their unborn children. (The 'stage' action is distinguished from the 'real' action by its employment of rhyming iambic pentameters.) Recruitment for the armed forces offers him a possible escape route. (In 'real life', Thomas has actually impregnated Kitty, who is the daughter of Sir Roger's steward. As manager of the play, the steward uses the dramatic action of a stage marriage to unite the wronged Kitty to Thomas.) Meanwhile, Dorcas's brother Timothy Peascod, played by the country booby Jonas Dock, has been arrested and faces a firing squad for desertion, but he is saved by a sudden reprieve (one of several anticipations of *The Beggar's Opera*). Readers of the *Complete Key to the last New Farce* The What D'Ye Call It (1715), probably the work of Gay himself, perhaps assisted by Pope, were alerted to a systematic series of parodies of lines and of situations, not only in the heroic tragedies of the last age by Otway and Dryden, but in the major contemporary monuments of Whig-sponsored drama: *Jane Shore, The Distrest Mother, Cato*. Perhaps the most celebrated example occurs at the opening of Act II, when the apprehended Peascod is brought in bound:

CORPORAL. Stand off there, Countrymen; and you, the Guard,
    Keep close your Pris'ner—see that all's prepar'd.
    Prime all your Firelocks—fasten well the Stake.
PEASCOD. 'Tis too much, too much Trouble for my sake.
    O Fellow-Soldiers, Countrymen and Friends,
    Be warn'd by me to shun untimely Ends:
    For Evil Courses am I brought to Shame,
    And from my Soul I do repent the same.
    Oft my kind *Grannam* told me—*Tim*, take warning,
    Be good—and say thy Pray'rs—and mind thy Learning.
    But I, sad Wretch, went on from Crime to Crime;
    I play'd at Nine-pins first in Sermon time:
    I rob'd the Parson's Orchard next; and then
    (For which I pray Forgiveness) stole—a Hen.
    When I was press'd, I told them the first Day
    I wanted Heart to fight, so ran away;
                         [*Attempts to run off, but is prevented.*
    For which behold I die. 'Tis a plain Case,
    'Twas all a Judgment for my Want of Grace.
                 [*The soldiers prime with their Muskets towards him.*
    —Hold, hold, my Friends; nay, hold, hold, hold, I pray;
    They may go off—and I have more to say.
1ST COUNTRYMAN. Come, 'tis no time to talk.
2ND COUNTRYMAN. Repent thine Ill.   [*Gives him a Book.*
PEASCOD. I will, I will.
    Lend me thy Handkercher—*The Pilgrim's Pro-*   [*Reads and weeps.*
    —*The Pilgrim's Progress—Eighth—Edi-ti-on*
    Lon-don—Prin-ted—for—Ni-cho-las Bod-ding-ton:
    With new Ad-di-tions never made before
    —Oh! 'tis so moving, I can read no more.   [*Drops the Book.*[28]

As the *Complete Key* made sure that readers knew, this action
parodies Cato's reading of Plato's treatise on the immortality of
the soul prior to taking his own life in the final act of Addison's
play. By this time, *Cato* was in its eighth published edition.
Peascod's looby dissenting piety, which moves him to see a providential pattern in his present predicament, his list of petty mis-
demeanours—offences that later 'idle apprentice' plays like Lillo's
London Merchant will take seriously—are in context hilariously
funny. His reading out of the printing information on the copy
of *The Pilgrim's Progress* is a fittingly bathetic ending to an

---

[28] II. i; quoted from Gay, *Dramatic Works*, i. 190–1. Subsequent references are to
this edition.

attempted funeral oration that begins by alluding to Mark Antony's famous lines in *Julius Caesar*. The stammer given to Peascod is thought to take off the well-known stammer of the popular writer Tom D'Urfey, doubtless brilliantly rendered by the actor Penkethman. Yet here, as throughout the play, there is a social satire that has very considerable force. These rustics are oppressed by a society in which punishments actually are as ill fitted to crimes as Peascod's case suggests. There are constant reminders of the harsh realities: corrupt justices, the ravages of press gangs, exploitation of child labour. Even the most ludicrously farcical moment in the action, the procession of ghosts (in parody of *Macbeth*) that includes the controversial ghost of an embryo, is socially concerned, since the ghosts are all victims of the Press Act (1703–4) as put into operation by the justiciary. And Peascod's walking in the shadow of death as the firing-squad shoulders arms is just one example of the play's black-comedy tonality, which *The Beggar's Opera* will later perfect. Although this play actually creates an entirely new form of black farce, in printed form Gay theorized it as a macaronic version of established genres. He prefaced it with a parodic critical treatise mocking the rule-governed, literal-minded approach to dramatic criticism manifested in the work of Dennis: the point of which is again the *mélange* of indistinguishable dramatic forms that Whig-sponsored domestic heroism had created:

> After all I have said, I would have these Criticks only consider, when they object against it as a Tragedy, that I design'd it something of a Comedy; when they cavil at it as a Comedy, that I had partly a View to Pastoral; when they attack it as a Pastoral, that my Endeavours were in some degree to write a Farce; and when they would destroy its Character as a Farce, that my Design was a Tragi-Comi-Pastoral.   (i. 177)

Gay's combination of social critique and generic subversion is one that was taken up later by Henry Fielding. There is, in my view, a distinctive cultural politics governing the form and content of such Scriblerian productions, which I now wish to investigate.

III

We are fortunate to have a new biography of John Gay by David Nokes that offers the most compelling and convincing account of the poet's personality to be found anywhere in the secondary literature. Gay lived his life in the shadow of his more charismatic and independent contemporaries Pope and Swift. In his satirical writings can be discerned, however, acts of minor rebellion against such self-effacement: what Nokes terms 'the suppliant's professional smile of ingratiation which curls, almost perceptibly, into a mocking grin'.[29] Nokes's key biographical hypothesis, and it is, as I have said, a powerfully explanatory one, is stated by him as follows:

His instinct for dependency was part of a psychological survival strategy which allowed Gay not only to preserve his wealth intact, but also to safeguard a private mental territory which found expression in his satires. Gay had internalized the beggar's technique of exploiting the society which he affected to flatter. Where Pope favoured a satiric pose of lofty independence, Gay adopted the more subversive role of a court favourite, biting the hand that fed him.   (p. 449)

As behoves the biographer, Nokes accounts for Gay's life and work with references to a model drawn from psychoanalysis. In my view, however, there is a dimension to the understanding of his career and his positioning in cultural history that is supra-psychological, not amenable to explanation from within an account of the poet's hidden personality because it is a very *constituting condition* of literary personality in the period. This is the dimension of cultural politics.

In Pope's extensively retouched poetic autobiography the *Epistle to Dr. Arbuthnot*, he took pains, through using the terms 'neglected' and 'the sole Return' and the metaphor of 'blooming', to create an impression of Gay as a great poet perishing in Mozartian poverty:

> Blest be the *Great*! for those they take away,
> And those they left me—For they left me GAY,
> Left me to see neglected Genius bloom,
> Neglected die! and tell it on his Tomb;
> Of all thy blameless Life the sole Return
> My Verse, and QUEENSB'RY weeping o'er thy Urn.
>
> (lines 255–60)

The stereotyped impression of Gay as a neglected poet starving to death in a garret, his genius all unrecognized, was disseminated from a variety of sources, expected and unexpected. Mary Barber, poetess and protégée of Swift, recounts in her poem 'A True Tale'

[29] Nokes, *Gay*, 8.

(published in her 1734 *Poems on Several Occasions*, which Swift introduced and to which Pope subscribed) the story of a mother who takes care to select appropriate reading for her son. She gives him Gay's *Fables*, and the boy is shocked by the autobiographical fable that chronicles the poet's neglect, 'The Hare with many Friends'. His mother, 'RESOLV'D to lull his Woes to rest', comforts him:

> This has been yet GAY'S Case, I own,
> But now his Merit's amply known:
> Content that tender Heart of thine,
> He'll be in the Care of CAROLINE.
> Who thus instructs the Royal Race,
> Must have a Pension, or a Place.
>   —MAMMA, if you were Queen, says he,
> And such a Book were wrote for me,
> I find, 'tis so much to your Taste,
> That GAY would keep his Coach at least.
> . . . WHAT I'd bestow, says she, my Dear?
> At least, *a thousand Pounds a Year.*[30]

This very palpable sense of Gay's neglect and the financial restitution for its remedy is one that Gay's own letters chronicle extensively. They are a litany of complaint about his failure to secure suitable court employment. His letters record that while he was ridiculing the efforts of Rowe and Philips in his early writings, they were busy advancing: Rowe as clerk of the council to the prince and Philips as a lottery paymaster on 29 January 1715. A process of gradual disenchantment with place-hunting climaxes in the letter he wrote to Pope in October 1727 after he had been insulted by the offer of a place as gentleman usher to the two-year-old Princess Louisa:

O that I had never known what a Court was! Dear *Pope*, what a barren Soil (to me so) have I been striving to produce something out of! Why did I not take your Advice before writing Fables for the Duke, not to write them? Or rather, to write them for some young Nobleman? It is my very hard Fate, I must get nothing, write for them or against them. I find myself in such a strange Confusion and Depression of Spirits, that I have not Strength even to make my Will; though I perceive by many Warnings, I have no continuing City here. I begin to look upon myself as one already dead.[31]

[30] Mary Barber, *Poems on Several Occasions* (London, 1734), 11–12.
[31] *The Letters of John Gay*, ed. C. F. Burgess (Oxford: Clarendon Press, 1966), 66.

The facts of Gay's case, however, hardly seem to justify the melancholic posturings of his letter. During his writing career, Gay had actually derived more benefit from patronage than most writers of his time. When he commenced his writing career in or around 1708, literary patronage had diversified into an unprecedented multiplicity of forms, and Gay benefited from all of them. As regards private patronage—the support of learning and the arts by the wealthy and the titled—Gay gained from the generosity of some of the handful of high-profile patrons who still recognized an obligation to put their hospitality at the disposal of the talented. Gay resided at Burlington House during the period when the earl was extending protection to Handel and making major alterations to the agriculture and landscape of Chiswick House with Pope's energetic collaboration.[32] The opening of Gay's *Epistle to Burlington* celebrates the grandeur of his patron's Palladian aspirations but in a domestic tone that takes in a private joke about Pope's diminutive stature and contrives to suggest the poet's intimacy with the great man:

> While you, my lord, bid stately Piles ascend,
> Or in your *Chiswick* Bow'rs enjoy your Friend;
> Where *Pope* unloads the Bough within his reach,
> Of purple Grape, blue Plumb, or blushing Peach;
> I journey far.—You knew fat Bards might tire,
> And, mounted, sent me forth your trusty Squire.[33]

This mawkish vision of himself as an overweight Sancho Panza is true to life. Gay lived a wandering life, frequently dependent on the bounty of the various wealthy and aristocratic hosts who provided for him: the Burlingtons, Pulteney, Mrs Howard, and the Queensberrys *inter alia*, had the pleasure of paying his bills in the 1720s. The somewhat desultory feeling that attaches to Gay's later life is the result of a certain rootlessness. Unlike Pope at Twickenham or Swift at the deanery, Gay is associated with no home of his own. Even his lodgings in Whitehall were obtained for him by the Earl of Lincoln and were again a form of patronage. Aristocratic patrons were prepared to go to considerable lengths for Gay; and if it is true that the Duchess of Monmouth slighted him by compelling him to wear livery early in his life, the Duchess

---

[32] See Jacques Carré, 'Burlington's Literary Patronage', *British Journal for Eighteenth-Century Studies*, 5 (1982), 21–33.
[33] Lines 1–6; all quotations from Gay's poetry are from Gay, *Poetry and Prose*.

of Queensberry was prepared to make a brazen show of support
for the banned play *Polly* later on in it, touting it around court
and soliciting subscriptions. With splendid *hauteur*, the Duchess
announced her break with George II's court over the incident:

the Dutchess of Queensberry is surprized, and well pleased, that the
King has given her so agreeable a Command as to stay from Court, where
she never came for Diversion, but to bestow a great Civility upon the King
and Queen. She hopes by such an unprecedented Order as this, the
King will see as few as he wishes at his Court, particularly such as dare
think or speak Truth; I dare not do otherwise, & ought not, nor could
have imagined, that it would not have been the very highest Compliment
I could possibly pay the King, to endeavour to support Truth and Innocence in his House.
    Particularly when the King & Queen both told me, that they had not
read Mr. Gay's play . . .[34]

Private patrons were also instrumental in securing government
patronage for Gay. Despite the sense of injured merit he constantly
projected, Gay did gain from the system of farming out sinecures
to talented writers, undemanding jobs that provided them with a
degree of financial security to support their writing. Gay became
Commissioner for State Lotteries in 1722, a post that paid £150
per annum for supervising the annual September draw. The only
other duty attaching to this post was to draw his salary. Pope's
remark in the 1728 *Dunciad* that 'Gay dies un-pension'd, with a
hundred Friends' (III. 326) was made, as we have seen, directly
after he had been offered £150 per annum from the civil list for
ushering the small Princess Louisa. It is difficult to see why he was
so insulted by this, since it appears to be exactly the kind of
lucrative soft number for which he appeared to be angling all his
life.
    There would appear, then, to be no factual basis whatsoever to
Gay's constant refrain that he was a neglected poet who never
achieved the quality of patronage that he deserved. That he felt it
is the result, in my view, of two related factors; the gradual
professionalization of writing, to which Gay, like Dryden before
him, found it enormously difficult to adjust; and the management
of his image by the other Scriblerians to whom Gay paid deference,
which made it virtually impossible for him to accept his success as

a paid professional writer who could make a prosperous and comfortable living by exploiting the talents demanded in the literary market-place. In *Britons*, Linda Colley comments on the diminishing role of royal patronage in the arts and on the British monarchy's progressive failure to achieve any degree of cultural magnificence equivalent to that of the French court. She associates the cramped spatial conditions of the Hanoverian monarchy especially with its restricted role as a social and cultural centre: 'The Royal Household under George I . . . included bands of musicians as well as a tame poet laureate, but it lacked the human or spatial resources to forge a discrete court culture or generate all of its own large-scale entertainments. Whenever George II or George III wanted to see an opera or a play, for example, they had to leave St. James's or Buckingham House and visit the London theatres, just like the rest of the public did.'[35] This is an analysis that is actually inherent in Gay's own poetry. To him, there was an uncomplicated relationship between the vigour of a court and the health of the nation's cultural life. Under the reigns of James I and Charles I, whatever the differences in moral tone, the literary and performance arts had received a good deal of direct encouragement. In *Trivia* (1716), Gay records an unqualified golden-age view of the Stuart era, as he exhorts his Barnstaple friend the lawyer Fortescue to:

> Behold that narrow Street, which steep descends,
> Whose Building to the slimy Shore extends;
> Here *Arundell*'s fam'd Structure rear'd its Frame,
> The Street alone retains an empty Name:
> Where *Titian*'s glowing Paint the Canvas warm'd,
> And *Raphael*'s fair Design, with Judgment charm'd,
> Now hangs the Bell-man's Song, and pasted here,
> The colour'd Prints of *Overton* appear.
> Where Statues Breath'd, the Work of *Phidias* Hands,
> A wooden Pump, or lonely Watch-house stands.
> There *Essex*' stately Pile adorn'd the Shore,
> There *Cecil*'s, *Bedford*'s, *Villier*'s, now no more.
> Yet *Burlington*'s fair Palace still remains;
> Beauty within, without Proportion reigns.
> Beneath his Eye declining Art revives,
> The Wall with animated Picture lives;

[35] Colley, *Britons*, 199.

> There *Hendel* strikes the Strings, the melting Strain
> Transports the Soul, and thrills through ev'ry Vein;
> There oft' I enter (but with cleaner shoes)
> For *Burlington*'s belov'd by ev'ry Muse.
>
> (481–500)

Mention of the Earl of Arundel here is especially significant. Arundel was perhaps the greatest of all Stuart collector-patrons, whose house (Arundel House) situated between the river and the Strand, incorporated a two-storeyed long gallery designed by Inigo Jones. This building housed the earl's unrivalled collection of paintings and statuary, both in architectural style and in function the result of the Arundels' earlier tour to Italy in Jones's company.[36] Celebrating 'Arundell's fam'd Structure', and lamenting its supersession by 'a wooden Pump, or lonely Watch-house', Gay is addressing himself to a particularly important instance of the *sic transit gloria mundi* theme. Since Arundel was the original patron of Palladianism, there is a natural transmission to Burlington, who can be usefully exploited both as the last of a noble line—'Yet *Burlington*'s fair Palace still remains'—and as the phoenix from whose ashes the new era of patronage will emerge: 'Beneath his Eye declining Art revives.' It is a remarkably flexible and economical passage, instinct with the poet's own personality—'(but with cleaner Shoes)'—but widening out to embrace the themes of architectural decline and artistic *risorgimento*. In the later *Epistle to the Right Honourable Paul Methuen, Esq.* (1720), Gay was one of the earliest writers to enunciate the view that Britain is no longer a soil in which genius can flourish because patronage now operates not to support writers of talent, but to harness mediocrities to the government-sponsored treadmill of the political press:

> Why flourish'd verse in great *Augustus*'s reign?
> He and *Mecaenas* lov'd the Muse's strain.
> But now that wight in poverty must mourn
> Who was (O cruel stars!) a Poet born.
> Yet there are ways for authors to be great;
> Write ranc'rous libels to reform the State . . .
> He, who his pen in party quarrels draws,
> Lists an hir'd bravo to support the cause;

---

[36] See Graham Parry, *The Golden Age Restor'd: The Culture of the Stuart Court, 1603–1642* (Manchester University Press, 1981), 114, 126–7.

> He must indulge his Patron's hate and spleen,
> And stab the fame of those he ne'er has seen.
>
> (lines 15–20, 27–30)

Gay goes on to advise that the commonly held view of particular arts being the accomplishment of particular nations is erroneous. The economic conditions of production are paramount, and a British-born painter like William Kent, the poem improbably contends, could be as great as Raphael if work were available for him in this country. But the general level of taste is now so low that artists of genius suffer detraction rather than encouragement. 'Sublime' art is readily distinguishable from the merely popular outpourings of hireling scribblers—and only the latter is funded:

> Had *Pope* with groveling numbers fill'd his page,
> *Dennis* had never kindled into rage.
> 'Tis the sublime that hurts the Critic's ease;
> Write nonsense and he reads and sleeps in peace:
> Were *Prior, Congreve, Swift* and *Pope* unknown,
> Poor slander-selling *Curll* would be undone.
> He who would free from malice pass his days,
> Must live obscure, and never merit praise.
>
> (lines 67–74)

In this view of cultural economics, according to which the need to rely on bookseller-publishers as brokers for public patronage was a guarantee of worthless, nonsensical art, John Gay was confirmed by Pope and Swift, who took upon themselves the management of his image. In the *Epistle to Dr. Arbuthnot*, Pope had represented himself as an independent, self-supporting man of genius who is not subject to the market forces that bring lesser writers into existence. Within this ideology, Gay functions as an example of genius less robust than his own, whose talents need to be nourished in the soil of patronage, 'the region where genius meets power', in Irvin Ehrenpreis's suggestive phrase.[37] The lines on Gay quoted earlier are an attempt to appropriate his image for Pope's own independence mythos, as we can see if we attend to the tombstone reference—'Neglected die, and tell it on his Tomb'. This is presumably to Gay's own mordant epitaph, 'Life is a Jest, and all Things show it; | I thought so once, but now I know it',

[37] Ehrenpreis, *Swift*, iii. 648. He discusses Mrs Howard's failure to obtain patronage for Gay at iii. 696–9.

considered so impious by Samuel Johnson. It also refers, however, to the inscription placed by the Queensberrys:

> Here lie the ashes of Mr. JOHN GAY,
> The warmest friend,
> The most benevolent man;
> Who maintained
> independence
> In low circumstances of fortune;
> Integrity
> In the middle of a corrupt age . . .

and so forth. After Gay had refused the usher's post, Pope's letter of condolence energetically recruited him for the independence posture, though political sloganizing *à la Craftsman* is easily detectable:

> I have many years ago magnify'd in my own mind, and repeated to you, a ninth Beatitude, added to the eight in the Scripture; *Blessed is he who expects nothing, for he shall never be disappointed.* I could find in my heart to congratulate you on this happy Dismission from all Court-Dependence . . . There is a thing, the only thing which Kings and Queens cannot give you (for they have it not to give) *Liberty*, which is worth all they have; and which, as yet, I hope *Englishmen* need not ask from their hands. You will enjoy that, and your own Integrity, and the satisfactory Consciousness of having *not* merited such Graces from them, as they bestow only on the mean, servile, flattering, interested, and undeserving.[38]

Swift also tried to manage Gay's image, but in a somewhat different direction. Just before *The Beggar's Opera* ended its Dublin run, he published an essay in the periodical he edited with Thomas Sheridan, the *Intelligencer*, no. 3 (?25 May 1728), in which he recognized that the strength of the play lay in the common touch of its 'humour':

> a Taste for *Humour* is in some manner fixed to the very Nature of Man, and generally Obvious to the Vulgar, except upon Subjects too refined, and Superior to their Understanding. And as this *Taste for Humour* is purely Natural, so is *Humour* it self, neither is it a *Talent* confined to Men of *Wit*, or *Learning*; for we observe it sometimes among common Servants, and the meanest of the People, while the very Owners are often Ignorant of the Gift they possess.[39]

[38] Pope, *Correspondence*, ii. 453.
[39] Jonathan Swift and Thomas Sheridan, *The Intelligencer*, ed. James Woolley (Oxford: Clarendon Press, 1992), 61–2.

Swift ought perhaps to have recognized the implication of his own judgement that the play was the product of an early Rice–Lloyd Webber who was on his audience's wavelength and had anticipated popular taste with a deft commercial instinct. As its modern editor rightly comments, however, Swift 'saw in Gay a principled and gifted writer victimized, like himself, by the false friendship and ingratitude of Queen Caroline and her dresser Mrs. Howard . . . Thus Gay's case seemed parallel to his own disappointment at not having been offered English preferment in the summer of 1727.'[40] So the essay devotes itself to the theme of Gay's shabby treatment at court and hints that the satirical attack on Walpole is the première's just desert for his neglect of such a meritorious writer. Swift's experience of patronage, at any rate after he left Temple's protection, was of repeated disappointment. When he might have seen his career progress as spectacularly as John Robinson's, who became Bishop of London and Lord Privy Seal, he was disappointed by the Earl of Berkeley. Later, he was eager to have his embittered view of patronage confirmed, as it was by Mrs Howard.[41] Swift repeatedly blames her, in his letters, for Gay's eventual disappointment at court, and in *A Libel on Dr. Delany* (1730), he sketches a Solomon Grundyish view of Gay's career as a trajectory of disappointment:

> Thus *Gay*, the *Hare* with many Friends,
> Twice sev'n long Years the *Court* attends,
> Who, under Tales conveying Truth,
> To Virtue form'd a *Princely* Youth,
> Who pay'd his Courtship with the Croud,
> As far as *Modest Pride* allow'd,
> Rejects a servile *Usher*'s Place,
> And leaves *St. James*'s in Disgrace.[42]

For Swift, finally, genius never really could meet political power because, as *A Libel* argues, political figures only ever entertain wits as an escape from business, and a poet asking for a place *is* business. In the poem Swift wrote *To Mr. Gay* in 1731, celebrating his supposed employment as steward to the Duke of Queensberry, he suggests that stewardship to a benevolent private individual is

---

[40] Swift and Sheridan, *The Intelligencer*, ed. Woolley, 57.
[41] Ehrenpreis, *Swift*, iii. 646–65.
[42] Lines 53–60; quoted from *Swift: Poetical Works*, ed. Herbert Davis (Oxford University Press, 1967), 418.

an ideal post for a poet, because poets feel about money as eunuchs do about concubines—it does not excite them.

Thus Gay's Scriblerian partners created for him a choice of roles—the neglected poet who is the living proof that existing forms of patronage are tainted, or the independent writer, poor but virtuous, who was born to blush unseen. For many years, Gay wrestled in his life and in his art with the Scylla and Charybdis of being a hack on the one hand and a client on the other. Right up until his very last works, such as the posthumously performed play *The Distress'd Wife* (in which a country landowner called Sir Thomas Willit has been ruined by attendance at court in hopes of receiving preferment from Lord Courtlove), Gay tried to exorcise his demons of disappointment and neglect. A lucrative and guaranteed position would have delivered him from financial insecurity and kept him above the market-place that works like Pope's *Dunciad* and Swift's *Progress of Poetry* encouraged him to despise. Yet in truth, throughout the years of servility and place-hunting, Gay was steadily advancing as a professional writer whose sure instinct for public taste saw a growing financial return on his labours. The success of *The Beggar's Opera* is entirely the result of its popular and commercial appeal, the 'something for everyone' likeability of its novel music-theatre form. Even early on in his career, Arbuthnot could joke about his poem *Trivia* that 'Gay has gott so much money by his art of walking the streets, that he is ready to sett up with equipage.'[43] Later in his career, the publication arrangements for the banned play *Polly* included marketing ploys as acute as any ever witnessed in the history of print. Gay retained the copyright and had the play printed at his own expense. Bowyer printed no fewer than 10,500 copies, vastly in excess of the usual print run. Subscription price was 1 guinea, calculated to appeal to the fashionable, whereas ordinary readers could purchase the play and its music for 6*s*. As Calhoun Winton reports, Gay's sales were damaged by pirated editions and he had to take action under the Copyright Act, but, despite that, he made a phenomenal profit out of printing *Polly* that Winton thinks might have been as much as £3,000, making it 'decidedly the highest remuneration for the publication of a single play, anywhere, to that time'.[44] When Gay died (for the record, not in

[43] Gay, *Letters*, 27.
[44] Calhoun Winton, *John Gay and the London Theatre* (Lexington: University of Kentucky Press, 1993), 135. On Gay's earnings, see also Nokes, *Gay*, 348–51, 421–3.

poverty, but in the Duke of Queensberry's fine Palladian town house, designed by Leoni and situated in the splendid new development of Burlington Gardens. There was an elaborately stage-managed funeral described vividly by Nokes in the biography pp. 534 ff.). He possessed a personal fortune in excess of £6,000. Had he deemed it an honourable calling to exchange his audience-pleasing skills for payment in the new market economy, he could have enjoyed that fortune. Sadly, however, Gay 'did but imperfectly know himself'.

IV

One of the few individuals who did not admire *The Beggar's Opera* was Daniel Defoe. In the pamphlets in which he used the soubriquet 'Andrew Moreton', Defoe took the government line on the play, which had been preached from the pulpit in March 1728 by Thomas Herring, preacher to the Honourable Society of Lincoln's Inn. This line was that the play presented thieves in 'so amiable a Light . . . that it has taught them to value themselves on their Profession, rather than be asham'd of it' and that it does not punish vice.[45] Swift, in the *Intelligencer*, no. 3, had argued the Opposition contention that this comedy 'contains likewise a *Satyr*, which, although it doth by no means affect the present Age, yet might have been useful in the former and may possibly be so in Ages to come. I mean where the Author takes occasion of comparing those *Common Robbers to Robbers of the Publick*; and their several Stratagems of betraying, undermining, and hanging each other, to the several Arts of *Politicians* in times of Corruption.'[46] Obviously there is a partisan issue at stake here, but the contention between Swift and Defoe is very much wider than that. The ironic *glissandi* of *The Beggar's Opera* are precisely directed at the conceptions of narrative and their ideological underpinnings that Defoe's fiction embodied. The ending of Gay's ballad opera, in which the Player asserts the polite taste of the town in the teeth of what the Beggar calls 'strict poetical Justice', a triumph of absurdity over plausibility as incompatible genres are spatchcocked together ('For you must allow, that in this kind of Drama, 'tis no matter how absurdly things are brought about'; III xvi. 12–13), is a

[45] Daniel Defoe, *Augusta Triumphans* (London, 1728), 48.
[46] In Swift and Sheridan, *The Intelligencer*, 64–5.

direct affront to narrative closure. This is the formal condition of an art in a world in which 'it is difficult to determine whether (in the fashionable Vices) the fine Gentlemen imitate the Gentlemen of the Road, or the Gentlemen of the Road the fine Gentlemen' (III xvi. 19–22).[47] In Gay's play, as recent commentators such as Nokes and Nicholson have suggested, money and trade generate ubiquitous metaphors, the cumulative effect of which is to subordinate all human relationships to their protean transformations.[48] Its ironic hopping up and down on the new commercial concepts of honour and credit amount to a virtual repudiation of Defoe's earnest sponsorship of such terms in *The Complete English Tradesman*. Even *Roxana*, despite the complexities of character and the relative openness of its narrative to which I have drawn attention, is evangelical in its enthusiasm for merchants and commerce (Sir Robert Clayton advises Roxana to settle her fortune on a merchant because 'an Estate is a Pond; but . . . a Trade was a Spring'[49]). Unsurprising, then, that the play most admired by Defoe was the *other* great theatrical triumph of 1728, Cibber's redaction of an earlier play by Vanbrugh, *The Provoked Husband*. By contrast to the volatile generic instability of *The Beggar's Opera*, *The Provoked Husband* is an over-policed text which subjects Lady Townly's fashionably delinquent behaviour to the heavy-handed correction of her husband. To Defoe, writing as Andrew Moreton in *Second Thoughts are Best*, this play preached a sound moral—as against the subversively unsound one that the Beggar tells us his Opera would have implied if he had been permitted to articulate it: "Twould have shown that the lower Sort of People have their Vices in a degree as well as the Rich: And that they are punish'd for them' (III xvi. 24–6). *The Provoked Husband* made an excellent job of disciplining women and upholding the sacrament of marriage.[50] In *The Beggar's*

---

[47] My argument here is being articulated in opposition, in certain crucial respects, to that of John Bender in *Imagining the Penitentiary: Fiction and the Architecture of Mind in Eighteenth-Century England* (University of Chicago Press, 1987), ch. 4. I have nevertheless learned a great deal from Bender, who employs the term 'novelization' and considers that *The Beggar's Opera* is a stage further advanced than are the novels of Defoe in that process because it assimilates the factual reality of Newgate Prison to generic permutation, thus bringing the literary work into a 'zone of contact' with the social practices of everyday life.

[48] Nokes, *Gay*, 436 ff.; Nicholson, *Writing and the Rise of Finance*, ch. 4.

[49] Defoe, *Roxana*, 170.

[50] Daniel Defoe, *Second Thoughts are Best; or, A Further Improvement of a Late Scheme to Prevent Street Robberies* (London, 1729).

Opera, of course, the Peachums view marriage as an unnatural perversion that is disastrous to the accumulation of money.

Defoe's critical judgements in the late 1720s, therefore, are those of a literary professional, deriving from the configuration of attitudes to trade, commerce, and politeness, and to the literary forms most capable of expressing them, that I denote under the term 'novelization'. Under such a taxonomy, Swift would have to be seen as an anti-novelist, and his greatest work, *Gulliver's Travels*, as an anti-novel. Certainly, one would not seek to deny that Swift was steeped in fictionality. Recently, Margaret Anne Doody has argued that on a structural level, as well as on a more precise level of direct influence, *Gulliver's Travels* belongs to a tradition deriving from ancient and Renaissance romance.[51] She draws attention to motifs present in *Gulliver's Travels* that recur in romance—the Curious Traveler, Metamorphozed Man, Man in Skins, Enslaved Person, Imprisoned Courtier—to mount the argument that it 'draws upon the deep traditions of prose fiction in the West and is itself a virtuoso performance within that tradition' (p. 123). Considered *sub specie aeternitatis*, *Gulliver's Travels* and *Robinson Crusoe* are stable-mates. This is unconvincing if we go into close-up on the cultural politics of the 1720s. Acquaintance with a range of Defoe's work, non-fictional and fictional, would suggest a writer who was, on most of the issues of his day, a progressive. He was all for some degree of democratization (as is clearly shown by the kinds of protagonists he chooses to write his novels about), criticized lazy élites, celebrated the virtues and productive energies of the middle sort: of tradesmen, economists, 'projectors'—those who had schemes to advance, ideas to air, business or social proposals. As book III of *Gulliver's Travels* makes apparent, Swift is not in favour of economically driven models of improvement. I suggested in the previous chapter that Defoe and Haywood were both looking for commercially successful deployments of narrative; and that Defoe found his solution in the creation and exploration of character, in the discussion of pressing social issues through the agency of a convincing literary approximation to a living human being. In Moll Flanders, Roxana, and Crusoe, Defoe has constructed convincing identities, forms of

[51] Margaret Anne Doody, 'Swift and Romance', in Christopher Fox and Brenda Tooley (eds.), *Walking Naboth's Vineyard: New Studies of Swift* (Notre Dame, Ind.: University of Notre Dame Press, 1995), 98–126.

consciousness to which events occur and who react to those events on an inner as well as an outer level. Admittedly the interior lives of Moll and Crusoe are not likely altogether to satisfy the sophisticated modern reader used to reading novels written in the post-Freudian psychologistic era. Maybe Crusoe is never as terrified as he should be of the extreme isolation in which he finds himself. Maybe Moll should have some *feelings*, rather than merely opinions, about what she does with her life. But they are consistent, enduring consciousnesses. That all the events in the novel happen to Moll or to Crusoe is an important aspect of the sense of aesthetic wholeness and satisfaction that the reader obtains. Swift and Gay, by contrast, deploy a parasitic system of characterization and narrative ordering that we might borrow Bertolt Brecht's later term 'epic' to designate. That Brecht found inspiration in *The Beggar's Opera* is not an arbitrary phenomenon. His knowledge of eighteenth-century English writing was surprisingly extensive. Certainly he knew Swift and Defoe, John Gay, and probably Fielding. In my view, he would have recognized that, to some extent, these writers had already arrived at an understanding of what he himself calls the 'epic' style. Scriblerian writing is characterized by an extraordinary degree of self-consciousness, by overt reflection on its own processes, and by what formalist theorists of our own century call 'alienation' and 'baring of the device'. Henry Fielding, in his ten-year career as a playwright before he came to write novels, had actually employed many of the 'alienation' effects that Brecht was to use two centuries later. In the Preface to his novel *Joseph Andrews*, Fielding claims to have written a 'comic epic in prose'; and all the major landmarks of early eighteenth-century writing employ an irony that distances the reader from the subject-matter, preserving a breadth of vision that we might read as 'epic' rather than as 'Aristotelian' in Brecht's taxonomy. Scriblerian writing is, as I have earlier sought to show, in conscious dialogue with epic, constantly reflecting on the world of the great epics as an age of militarism, of uncompromising honour, of heroism that contemporary life could only parody. In the writing of authors like Swift, Gay, and Fielding, there is a cynicism about human motives, about the purity of politics, about mercantile expansionism and national 'greatness' that is often expressed through a comic juxtaposition of epic and domestic. This leads to the kind of 'unmasking' that Brecht's drama also undertakes, for different ideological reasons. Scriblerian 'unmasking' works through parasitic devices designed to steal the clothes of the 'host' forms and relay them back in parodic form. Whereas Defoe is trying, in Robinson Crusoe, to create a character who is a credible approximation of a human being and whose *experience* gets moral issues across to us, in Gulliver Swift is trying to create a device that can be exploited for satiric purposes. Gulliver can be the vehicle of the satire, as he is in Lilliput, or the target of it, as he is when he tries to purvey to the King of Brobdingnag the secret of gunpowder. When he comes under suspicion of conducting an affair with a six-inch-high court lady in Lilliput, there is surely a satire intended on the metaphorical 'littleness' of the sexual intrigue that is the stuff of 1720s romance; in particular of the 'secret history' variety favoured by Haywood. Even if it is true that the reader does become involved in the Gulliver-device and treats it as if it is a Defovian character, there is an ideological distinction that we must continue to draw. Ultimately, Swift is not trying to co-operate in the developing process of novelization. If anything, he is trying to retard it. If it is true therefore, as on some level it is, that Swift is steeped in romance, his set towards it is an alienating and defamiliarizing one. Earlier in the book, I suggested that the hack-persona in *A Tale of a Tub* is, *inter alia*, a parody of irresponsible fictional forms such as are represented in Dunton's *New Voyage Round the World*. Paul Hunter is, in my view, correct to argue that *A Tale* is an attack on the energies that would culminate in the first wave of true novel-writing in the 1720s:

To isolate the attitudes and features of contemporary writing that Swift attacks as reprehensible involves making a comprehensive list of features that found their labyrinthine way into the novel as it emerged in the half century after the *Tale*—subjectivity, novelty, contemporaneity, interest in individual lives, digressiveness, circumstantiality, the eccentric, and the bizarre. *A Tale of a Tub* is not exactly a parody of the novel—it is hard to parody something that has as yet no concrete form, tradition, or definitive example—but it is an exposure of the cast of mind and set of values that ultimately produced novels, and its attack upon the tastes and desires of contemporary audiences suggests that Swift understood modern readers early and well.[52]

[52] Hunter, *Before Novels*, 108. I therefore tend to disagree with Robert Phiddian in *Swift's Parody* (Cambridge University Press, 1995), when he argues in respect of *A Tale of a Tub* that 'the lines between the parody and the texts parodied are never stable. This instability leaks everywhere and grounds for certainty recede as this

What is true of *A Tale* is even more apparent in *Gulliver's Travels*. It is ideologically opposed to the set of attitudes and beliefs that was fuelling the development of the novel as a genre.

Readers of *Gulliver's Travels*, book IV, in particular, who are also familiar with *Robinson Crusoe*, find themselves haunted by a sense of *déjà lu*, an insistent subtext of the familiar that never quite articulates itself as clear parody. Gulliver arrives in Houyhn-hnmland through the same mechanism of mutiny that brings the English captain and his crew to Crusoe's island. Defoe's providential disposition of significant dates is imitated by Swift. Gulliver's infuriatingly easy acceptance of the term 'Master' used in reference to the Houyhnhnm who discovers him and rescues him from the Yahoos is surely an ironic comment upon Crusoe's usage for Friday, whom he likewise saves from mortal danger: 'I likewise taught him to say Master, and then let him know, that was to be my name.'[53] More generally, the educative process that Crusoe undertakes with respect to Friday, the principles of natural religion that he instils in him are ironically inverted in the comparative education that Gulliver gains at the hands of his 'Master'. Gulliver, playing Man Friday to the Houyhnhnm, learns that European culture and civilization is to Houyhnhnm as Friday's belief in Benamuckee is to ours in Christian revelation. In both narratives, kindly and humane Portuguese sea-captains play a crucial role in ensuring the safety and prosperity of the protagonists, though again, Swift's deployment of that narrative token is not as straight-forward as Defoe's and might be read as an ironic comment on the misanthropy that Gulliver is developing. Whereas Crusoe's most fervent wish is to gain his deliverance from the solitary island, Gulliver appears to be cocking a snook at him and his readers when he tells us in book IV, chapter vii that 'I had not been a Year in this Country, before I contracted such a Love and Veneration for the Inhabitants, that I entered on a firm Resolution never to return to human Kind.'[54] At times, this *sotto voce* conjuring with

parody of Modern bookishness becomes an archetype of Modern bookishness' (p. 194). In the final analysis I think we must distinguish between the parodic text and its implied target.

[53] Daniel Defoe, *The Life and Strange Surprizing Adventures of Robinson Crusoe, of York, Mariner* (1719), ed. Angus Ross (Harmondsworth: Penguin, 1965), 209. Subsequent quotations are from this edition.

[54] Jonathan Swift, *Gulliver's Travels* (1726), ed. Christopher Fox (Boston and New York: St Martin's Press, 1995), 235. Subsequent quotations are from this edition.

Robinson Crusoe is more clearly enunciated, for example at the end of book IV, chapter ii, when Gulliver spends some time explaining to us how he makes a rudimentary form of oatcake. Crusoe's struggle to make an acceptable bread is expounded at a length that meets with Swiftian reproach: 'This is enough to say upon the Subject of my Dyet, wherewith other Travellers fill their Books, as if the Readers were personally concerned, whether we fare well or ill. However, it was necessary to mention this Matter, lest the World should think it impossible that I could find Sustenance for three Years in such a Country, and among such Inhabitants' (p. 215). With insouciant economy, Swift allows this one instance to stand as a metonymy for the wealth of description of Crusoe's attempt to reconstruct industrial and agricultural processes from first principles—description that partly comprises the 'realism' of *Robinson Crusoe* and that is a major source of the book's fascination, nostalgically invoking an integrated way of living before the onset of divided labour and luxury. Gulliver's bread-making implies the triviality of such writing, and a respect in which its claim to realism insults the sophisticated reader's intelligence.

Even in respects in which there might seem to be a superficial congruence between *Crusoe* and the *Travels*, one comes to suspect that Swift may be parodying the striking of Defovian attitudes. Since it is a critical commonplace to cite *Crusoe* as an example of the congeries of attitudes towards trade and colonizing that define mercantile expansionism in the early modern period, readers are often surprised to find passages coming out strongly against—if not all forms of colonialism—certainly the genocidal dimensions of the Spanish conquest of America. After Crusoe has discovered the cannibals practising their abominations on his island, he debates whether his loathing for their customs justifies his murdering them. In an early anticipation of the anthropological relativism that would follow Captain Cook's expeditions in the later century, Crusoe concludes that they are acting according to their lights and that, whatever he thinks of it, cannibalism is a practice that might make sense within a greater cultural entity: and this leads him to excoriate Spanish practices in America. True, Crusoe does not continue to live up to the liberalism of these insights. As many have pointed out, the building of his 'castle' and 'bower' on the island apes an aristocratic English way of life, though actually this is treated in the novel with an uncommon element of self-mockery. When Providence delivers him up some subjects, he is only too willing to *subject* them, setting himself up as a governor supported by imperial authority. Again, though, Crusoe is really sporting with ideas of absolute feudal monarchy and religious toleration:

My island was now peopled, and I thought myself very rich in subjects; and it was a merry reflection which I frequently made, how like a king I looked. First of all, the whole country was my own meer property; so that I had an undoubted right of dominion. 2dly, my people were perfectly subjected: I was absolute lord and lawgiver, they all owed their lives to me, and were ready to lay down their lives, if there had been occasion of it, for me. It was remarkable too, we had but three subjects, and they were of different religions. My man Friday was a pagan and a cannibal, and the Spaniard was a Papist: however, I allowed liberty of conscience throughout my dominions.   (pp. 240–1)

At the end of *Gulliver's Travels* there is a famous passage in which Gulliver explains why he has not claimed the lands he has discovered for the British flag. There are similarities between this passage and the one referred to earlier in *Crusoe*. Here are the two passages, set out in parallel:

Robinson Crusoe

This would justify the conduct of the Spaniards in all their barbarities practised in America, where they destroyed millions of these people, who, however they were idolaters and barbarians, and had several bloody and barbarious rites in their customs, such as sacrificing human bodies to their idols, were yet, as to the Spaniards, very innocent people; and that the rooting them out of the country is spoken of with the utmost abhorrence and detestation by even the Spaniards themselves at this time, and by all other Christian nations of Europe, as a meer butchery, a bloody and unnatural piece of cruelty, unjustifiable either to god or man; and such, as for which the

Gulliver's Travels

I had conceived a few Scruples with relation to the distributive Justice of Princes upon those Occasions. For Instance, A Crew of Pyrates are driven by a Storm they know not whither; at length a Boy discovers Land from the Top-mast; they go on Shore to rob and plunder; they see an harmless People, are entertained with Kindness, they give the Country a new Name, they take formal Possession of it for the King, they set up a rotten Plank or a Stone for a Memorial, they murder two or three Dozen of the Natives, bring away a Couple more by Force for a Sample, return home, and get their Pardon. Here commences a new Dominion acquired with a Title by *Divine Right*. Ships

very name of a Spaniard is reckoned to be frightful and terrible to all people of humanity, or of Christian compassion; as if the kingdom of Spain were particularly eminent for the product of a race of men who were without principles of tenderness, or the common bowels of pity to the miserable, which is reckoned to be a mark of generous temper in the mind. (p. 178)

are sent with the first Opportunity; the Natives are driven out or destroyed, their Princes tortured to discover Gold; a free Licence given to all Acts of Inhumanity and Lust; the Earth reeking with the Blood of its Inhabitants: And this execrable Crew of Butchers employed in so pious an Expedition, is a *modern Colony* sent to convert and civilize an idolatrous and barbarous People. (p. 264)

On one level, of course, Swift's passage continues the narratological joke of insisting upon the book's veracity, parodying such claims made by Defoe in his various prefaces. On another, Swift's experience of Irish life imparted a testamentary authenticity to his attack on colonialism practised in the name of trade, which he may have considered to be absent in Defoe's case. What is clear from Swift's *next* paragraph is that he has in his sights Defoe's convenient assumption that such atrocities were only perpetrated by the *Spaniards*, and there is perhaps a side-swipe at Crusoe's evangelizing with respect to Friday: 'But this Description, I confess, doth by no means affect the *British* Nation, who may be an Example to the whole World for their Wisdom, Care and Justice in planting Colonies; their liberal Endowments for the Advancement of Religion and Learning; their Choice of devout and able Pastors to propagate *Christianity*' (p. 265).

If we seek a *sigillum* for *Robinson Crusoe*, a sign to represent the claims made for narrative in that novel, we could not find a better one than the single footprint that Crusoe finds in the sand: 'it happened one day about noon going towards my boat, I was exceedingly surprized with the print of a man's naked foot on the shore, but which was very plain to be seen on the sand. I stood like one thunder-struck, or as if I had seen an apparition' (p. 162). Unexplained, indeed inexplicable, this ultimate sign of noncoincidence (there aren't even *a pair* of prints) might stand for the difference between Haywoodian romance, the life-blood of which is coincidence, and the new form of the novel with its commitment to narrative, to stories of singularity, of individuals who interest us for their own sakes. A comparable emblem in *Gulliver's Travels* would be the female Yahoo's impassioned embrace of Gulliver in book IV, chapter viii. The ethical significance of this incident is paramount to Swift: in view of it, Gulliver cannot wholly repudiate his affinity with the Yahoos because he is recognized by one of them as a desirable mate. The context of suppressed but continuous parody has already led Paul Hunter to suspect that *Gulliver's Travels* is

an accreting generic or class parody not only of travel narratives per se but also of a larger developing class of first-person fictional narratives that make extraordinary claims for the importance of the contemporary, the knowableness through personal experience of large cosmic patterns, the significance of the individual, and the imperialistic possibilities of the human mind—a class parody, in short, of what we now see as the novel and the assumptions that enable it.[55]

Given the opportunity, Swift would have stopped the developing novel in its tracks.

V

Henry Fielding's early career as a dramatist is also more easily explicable on a broad conception of cultural politics than on a set of determinations based on party affiliations. Until relatively recently, the standard view was that of his early-century biographer Wilbur L. Cross who read the plays as a sclerotic hardening into anti-Walpolean opposition, commencing with the rewriting of *Tom Thumb* as *The Tragedy of Tragedies* in 1731.[56] The reasoning was essentially syllogistic: at this time, all writers of genius and moral fibre were united in opposition to Walpole; Fielding was a writer of genius and morale fibre; therefore, Fielding was part of the Tory opposition to Walpole. To this, there is a simple, Fieldingesque objection, namely, that it is not true. Fielding developed an early antipathy to the Scriblerians, especially to Pope. The *Grub-Street Journal*, with which Pope was connected, kept up a continual campaign of harassment against Fielding; and, for his part, Fielding in his unpublished 'Epistle to Mr. Lyttleton' (*sic*)

---

[55] J. Paul Hunter, '*Gulliver's Travels* and the Novel', in Frederik N. Smith (ed.), *The Genres of* Gulliver's Travels (Newark, NJ: University of Delaware Press, 1990), 69.
[56] Cross, *The History of Henry Fielding.*

satirized Pope in terms as scabrous and personal as any employed by the hacks.[57] More recent accounts of his politics emphasize his family connections to powerful Whigs, though few accept Brian McCrea's view that he was a lock, stock, and barrel convert to the financial revolution: 'for [Fielding] the stock exchange and the national debt are as much a part of British life as the Anglican church and English common law'.[58] Fielding nowhere represents the world of city finance sympathetically in his writing. He held trade and commerce in high regard, certainly. As recent commentators like Christine Gerrard have stressed, however, so did Bolingbroke and the Country opponents to Walpole. Fielding's attitude to paper credit and invisible earnings, like his attitude to trade, was entirely compatible with Bolingbroke's. Behind the most recent analysis of Fielding's partisan affiliations is a view of politics refreshingly less reificatory and rigid than those based on binary oppositions like Whig and Tory, court and Country, ministry and Opposition. Thomas R. Cleary and Robert D. Hume represent Fielding as non-partisan and apolitical at least until 1735, when his standpoint can be identified with the 'Broad-bottom' Whig opposition to Walpole.[59] Politics in this conception is a fluid matter of shifting alliances between family and interest groups. To them, Fielding's primary concern was to attract quality patronage, and he wrote even-handed pro- and anti-ministerial satire in an endeavour to see which side buttered his bread. As Hume trenchantly expresses it: 'the plain, dull truth is that Fielding was a freelance writer who peddled his plays where he could

---

[57] One of Fielding's earliest works is a poem, 'To the Right Honourable Sir Robert Walpole', an amusing attempt to solicit patronage; while the 'Epistle to Mr. Lyttleton' includes the following lines:

> Say, Wretch, why should her charms [Lady Mary's] thy Anger move?
> Too ugly thou! too impotent for Love!
> 'Twere capital to suffer thy Embrace,
> For thou art Surely not of human Race.
> An evil Sprite, like Satan; sent to tell
> Those Lies on Earth, thy Brother spreads in Hell.

(lines 38–43)

See Isobel M. Grundy, 'New Verse by Henry Fielding', *PMLA*, 87 (Mar. 1982), 213–45, esp. 241.

[58] Brian McCrea, *Henry Fielding and the Politics of Mid-Eighteenth-Century England* (Athens: University of Georgia Press, 1981), 33.

[59] Thomas R. Cleary, *Henry Fielding: Political Writer* (Waterloo, Ont.: Wilfred Laurier University Press, 1984); Hume, *Henry Fielding and the London Theatre.*

get them accepted' (p. 52). Martin and Ruthe Battestin's biography further shows how precarious Fielding's living was in the 1730s, and how far his life was dominated by financial exigency.[60] Fielding's professionalism is stressed in these accounts, which are important in effecting at least a partial recuperation of earning a living as a motive in the production of valuable art. Because they cannot identify any clear partisan commitment running through his work, however, these critics tend to regard professionalism as a readiness to prostitute the muse—to say anything for money— which is incompatible with any consistent ideology. Fielding had, to be sure, a desire to be rewarded for writing in the same way as one is rewarded for other productive enterprises. More explicitly than Pope, Gay, or Swift, he considered writing for money a legitimate enterprise: as he says in defence of his one-time collaborator James Ralph in the *Jacobite's Journal*, he does not think 'a Writer, whose only Livelihood is his Pen, to deserve a very flagitious Character if, when one Set of Men deny him Encouragement, he seeks it from another, at their Expence'.[61] Yet there is a real ideological consistency running through all of his early work which inheres not in a partisan commitment but an aesthetic programme, which is collateral to that of the Scriblerians in its opposition to the novelization of culture.

Fielding is the natural successor to John Gay in his analysis of the state of contemporary culture. Like Gay, he saw the theatrical art of the post-Restoration period as receding towards an indeterminate tragicomic form that was incapable of expressing any clear dramatic imperative. As Albert J. Rivero puts the point, 'a careful study of Fielding's dramatic career reveals that playwrights in the 1720s and 1730s were keenly aware that traditional plots and techniques of regular comedy and heroic tragedy had run their course'.[62] Richard Steele's Prologue to *The Conscious Lovers*, which had spoken of 'a Joy too exquisite for Laughter' as the true objective of the comedy, is an early high-water mark of the polite-sentimental benevolism that was inaugurated in the earlier periodicals.[63] It was against this tendency that Fielding published his first

---

[60] Battestin and Battestin, *Fielding, passim.*

[61] No. 17 (26 Mar. 1748), in *'The Jacobite's Journal' and Related Writings*, ed. W. B. Coley (Middletown, Conn.: Wesleyan University Press, 1975), 215.

[62] Albert J. Rivero, *The Plays of Henry Fielding: A Critical Study of his Dramatic Career* (Charlottesville: University of Virginia Press, 1989), 2–3.

[63] Richard Steele, *The Conscious Lovers: A comedy* (1722); quoted from *The*

prose essay, a piece on the 'Benefit of Laughing', arguing the therapeutic power of burlesque in *Mist's Weekly Journal* for 3 August 1728. That the threat to sensible, rational cultural forms was widely felt is apparent from a remarkable ironic tract written by the man who was later to become Fielding's collaborator on the *Champion*, James Ralph. Ralph's *The Touch-Stone* (1728) makes the connections between generic miscegenation and the decline of taste that would become the major strands of Fielding's subsequent cultural critique. The seven chapters of this treatise enact the hierarchization of contemporary forms, ranging as they do from opera at the top of the social scale, through mimes and pantomimes, masquerades, ridottos, and assemblies, down as far as bear-baitings, prize-fighting, cock-fighting, puppet shows, fairs, and public auctions. To demonstrate the suggestibility of Ralph's writing to Fielding, we can excerpt what he has to say on the present state of dramatic genres:

THE second Mismanagement I charge upon our *Poets*, is their Ignorance in, or Neglect of the true Design and Nature of a *Stage-Play*; by presenting us with merry *Tragedies*, or sad *Comedies*. This Disease is in a Manner *Epidemick* amongst that Tribe; yet by the strictest Enquiry into the original Seeds of POETRY, I cannot fix upon a natural Reason, whence so general a Malignity can spring; of consequence, I must be pretty much at a Loss in proposing a remedy.

I believe it often happens, that an old, or a young *Poet*, takes Pen, Ink and Paper,—sits down to his Scrutore—or perhaps a Table—he finds it necessary to write a PLAY—he turns over God knows how many Volumes for a Story—or he makes one, and then—he writes a PLAY: The Dispute is, Must it be a *Tragedy* or *Comedy*? The Arguments of both Sides are weighty—it cannot be decided, the Reasons are so equal—At last he wisely counts his Buttons—or trusts to Cross and Pile—As Fortune would have it, *Tragedy* wins the Day; you see in the Play-Bill and Title-Page, *TRAGEDY*, in large Red Letters, like a Saint in a *Calendar*: Of Consequence, we must be Spectators and Readers of that Performance, in a Deluge of Tears. Another writes a *Comedy* by the same Rules, and wonders, that an Excess of Mirth does not crack our Voices, and split our Sides: When, alas! the World does not laugh at the Absurdities of the first, and is griev'd at the Stupidity of the other.[64]

This argument about the arbitrariness and hybridization of genre

Plays of Richard Steele, ed. Shirley Strum Kenny (Oxford: Clarendon Press, 1971), 299.

[64] Ralph, *The Touch-Stone*, ed. Freeman, 56–7.

fed into a wider cultural critique being articulated in the late 1720s by the Scriblerians, which calls attention to the transgressiveness created by the promiscuous mingling of high and low literary and dramatic forms in popular stage entertainment and in opera. After 1730, in the wake of Pope's *Dunciad* and *Peri Bathous*, aesthetic arguments about genre become fully absorbed into a politicized debate over cultural degeneration, and a two-way traffic between Pope and Fielding develops. Very soon after reading *The Dunciad*, Fielding was drawn to the Scriblerian vision of commodified culture, of classical learning polluted by a money-grubbing group of impresarios and marketeers. In his burlesque plays he developed an ideally fissile and layered dramatic form to express these anxieties. The demotic genres of pantomime and farce, and the nice-but-dim genre of opera, could be telescoped and exploited for the undoubted energies they possessed while simultaneously being placed within a frame that exposed them as degenerate. This might be the 'rehearsal' device exploited in his later plays like *Historical Register for the Year 1736* and *Pasquin*; or a device such as the Preface by H. Scriblerus Secundus and *Dunciad*-style footnotes to *The Tragedy of Tragedies; or, The Life and Death of Tom Thumb the Great* (1731), with its parody of the critical methods of John Dennis, 'proving' that the play corresponds to Aristotle's rules and following Horace to 'demonstrate' that only bombast or doggerel are usable in tragedy. I have already drawn attention, in Chapter 1, to *The Author's Farce*, from which my book derives its title, and in which an entire range of commercial practices governing literary production are also on display, as every aspect of making a living by means of the pen is explored. Witmore, in that play, makes a normative statement of Fielding's educated, anti-popular position on the present state of wit:

'Sdeath! In an age of learning and true politeness, where a man might succeed by his merit, it would be an encouragement. But now, when party and prejudice carry all before them, when learning is decried, wit not understood, when the theatres are puppet shows and the comedians ballad singers, when fools lead the town, would a man think to thrive by his wit? If you must write, write nonsense, write operas, write entertainments, write Hurlothrumbos, set up an Oratory and preach nonsense, and you may meet with encouragement enough.[65]

---

[65] Act I scene v, quoted from Fielding, *The Author's Farce*, ed. Woods.

From 1730 onwards Fielding consistently attacks a range of targets
that define his cultural project as similar to that of the Scriblerians:
dunces and pedants like Theobald, Bentley, and Burmann (who
may have taught him at Leiden); unintelligent entertainment like
opera, puppetry, and pantomime; theatre managers; the Royal
Society; and in particular Colley Cibber. Cibber was Fielding's
invention more than he was Pope's. Fielding it was who first
discovered in Colley Cibber an epitome of the prostituting of
talent to popularity and made him the mast-head for an age of
proliferating print and pop art.[66] From his first appearance on
Fielding's stage as Marplay in *The Author's Farce* to his last as
Ground-Ivy in *The Historical Register*, Cibber is represented as
an 'improver' of Shakespeare who can scarcely string together a
grammatical sentence: 'Shakespeare was a pretty fellow and said
some things which only want a little of my licking to do well
enough,' says Ground-Ivy, to which the author Medley later
responds: 'I have too great an honour for Shakespeare to think of
burlesquing him, and to be sure of not burlesquing him, I will
never attempt to alter him, for fear of burlesquing him by accident,
as perhaps some others have done.'[67] After his playwriting career
was terminated, Fielding continued to find in Cibberian grammar
and Cibberian solecism an emblem of cultural pollution. In the
Champion for 25 December 1739, for instance, Hercules Vinegar
poses as a philistine enemy to learning:

I would by no means be here understood to be an Enemy to all good
Learning, a Competency of which (I mean to write and read, an Height to
which I myself have arrived) may possibly be necessary to all such as are
bred to Divinity, Law, or Physic. The utmost I contend for, being to
banish from among us those dead Tongues which are not only useless,
but, as I am informed, have much contributed to introduce the Religion
of the Ancients as well as their Language.

In this context of a rupture with learning, a breach of the laureate

[66] On this connection, see Houghton W. Taylor, 'Fielding upon Cibber', *Modern
Philology*, 29 (1931–32), 73–90; George Sherburn, '*The Dunciad*, Book Four', *Texas
Studies in English*, 24 (1944), 174–90; J'nan Sellery, 'Language and Moral Intelligence in the Enlightenment: Fielding's Plays and Pope's *Dunciad*', *Enlightenment
Essays*, 1 (1970), 17–26, 108–19; Nancy A. Mace, 'Fielding, Theobald, and *The
Tragedy of Tragedies*', *Philological Quarterly*, 66 (1987), 457–72.
[67] Act III, ll. 92–5, 142–5; Henry Fielding, *The Historical Register for the Year
1736* (1737), ed. William W. Appleton (Lincoln: University of Nebraska Press,
1967), 42, 44.

tradition that connects great writers with scholarship and study, Cibber is introduced:

Poetry . . . stands so little in need of [learning], that the Poet of our Age, most cherished at Court, never pretended to more than to read. I know it may be objected, that the *English Apollo*, the Prince of Poets, the great *Laureat* abounds with such a redundancy of *Greek* and *Latin*, that not contented with the vulgar Affectation of a Motto to a Play, he hath prefixed a *Latin* Motto to every Act of his *Caesar in Egypt*; some of which, as appears by the said Motto's, he had no Temptation, but his aforesaid Redundancy, to place there; and in one other of his Plays, he hath introduced a Footman talking *Greek*. So that one may say of him with *Hudibras*,

> —*He could speak* Greek
> *As naturally as Pigs squeak;*
> *For* Latin *'twas no more difficil*
> *Than for a Blackbird to whistle.*

Nay, his Learning is thought to extend to the oriental Tongues, and I myself heard a Gentleman reading one of his Odes, cry out, *Why, this is all Hebrew.*[68]

In the attacks upon Cibber, Fielding's cultural politics are most nakedly displayed. He spoke for a status group to whom the preservation of classical learning as an index of social stratification was important. Pantomime, combining as it did low action derived from the Italian *commedia* and a serious classical main plot staged with all the scenic elaboration of the early Stuart masque, resulted in a toy-shop farrago of special effects, brainless spectacle, and supernatural quackery.[69] Lewis Theobald, John Rich, and Colley Cibber were ready to exploit a nickel-and-dime version of classical learning, but, as a professional playwright, Fielding could not gainsay the box-office success of such hybrids or fail to take advantage of it. This he did by attacking the perpetrators while employing their forms in mannerist exaggerations that showed how close they were to disappearing down the whirlpool of meaninglessness. In *The Covent-Garden Tragedy*, Fielding revisited Philips's *The Distrest Mother*, rendering Andromache and Hermione through the two whores Kissinda and Stormandra, while the noble Pyrrhus and Orestes become two rakes, Bilkum and

---

[68] Henry Fielding and James Ralph, *The Champion: Containing a Series of Papers Humorous, Moral, Political, and Critical*, 2 vols. (London, 1741), i. 129.

[69] See Peter Lewis's helpful account of pantomime in *Fielding's Burlesque Drama*, 159–80.

Lovegirlo. The noble mother herself is transformed into Mother Punchbowl, an alcoholic brothel madam. Plots for burlesque after-pieces like *Eurydice, a Farce* (1737) and *Tumbledown Dick; or, Phaeton in the Suds* (1736) are macaronic versions of classical myth, building in ridicule of the audience's ignorance. The former begins by satirizing its audience's loose grasp on classical myth-ology and literature, rivalled by the author's, who took the story from 'Littleton's dictionary'. Hell becomes the world of fashion-able London society and Orpheus becomes Signor Orfeo, an opera singer. Comedy lies in the incongruous juxtaposition of classical myth, infernal deities, and identifiably modern attitudes towards marriage and cuckoldom: so that this particular Eurydice is having too good a time in the underworld to wish to return with her husband.

We can follow a curious web of relationship between Fielding, Cibber, and Haywood that might furnish a final perspective on Fielding and 'novelization'. In *The Author's Farce*, the publisher Bookweight buys a play from the writer Luckless called *The Pleasures of the Town*. This is a puppet show performed by humans in which the goddess Nonsense is wooed by Signior Opera, Don Tragedio, Sir Farcical Comic, Dr Orator, Monsieur Pantomime, and Mrs Novel. Here is represented the entire pan-oply of popular and debased cultural forms. Indebted to *The Dunciad*, the texture of this play-within-a-play resembles Lantern Leatherhead's classical burlesque in Jonson's *Bartholomew Fair*. There is a similarly carnivalesque atmosphere, as each of the characters sings, rants, intones, whines, in the idiolect of his own art form. Its linguistic Babel exemplifies what Bakhtin would term 'heteroglossia', the impulsion of language towards eccentric sub-cultural specificities. The inset play ends with a character called Murdertext entering to stop the show—clearly a clone of Jonson's Zeal-of-the-Land Busy—subsiding suddenly into the arms of Mrs Novel in a typically Jonsonian ending: the silencing or imploding of the killjoy. At the same time, however, the unmotivated pairing is a parody on the arbitrary affections that consummate love-intrigues in the romantic novellas of Eliza Haywood, of whom Mrs Novel is a representation. For her 1727 novel *Philidore and Placentia*, Haywood had written one of the most infelicitous dedications ever composed. Lady Abergavenny is therein addressed as 'the ornament and example of the age and the happiness of your illustrious consort'.[70] Within two years, that illustrious consort was prosecuting her through the lawcourts, having caught her in the act of adultery with one Richard Lydell. Suspicion soon arose, however, that this was a set-up: that Abergavenny had actually connived at the affair in order to exploit the prevailing laws of 'criminal conversation', laws that emphasized the non-status of women as chattels by allowing a husband to sue his wife's lover for damages if he could prove 'criminal conversation' with her body, his property. This litigation was behind Fielding's play *The Modern Husband* (1732), excoriated in its own time by the *Grub-Street Journal*, whose 'Dramaticus' spoke of 'the affectation and inordinate desire of saying something new, [which] has made our Author draw some of the vilest characters that ever yet entered into Comedy'.[71] Using a pre-Chekhovian conversational form that proceeds through discussion and encounter, a form owing something to Southerne's *The Wives' Excuse* and *The Maid's Last Prayer*, Fielding conveys a dark vision that gains its power from authenticity. The Moderns contrive to trap Lord Richly into an actionably compromising situation with Mrs Modern, while Richly tries to suborn Bellamant into prostituting his virtuous wife. Bellamant, to complete the symmetry, is hopelessly infatuated with Mrs Modern. Throughout the play, there is a powerful attack on lowbrow high-society entertainment, impressively integrated with a critique of sexual commodification. Vacuous entertainment is seen to be a contributory cause of a pervasive moral nullity:

GAYWIT. I think, my Lord, we have improv'd on the Italians. They wanted only Sense—We have neither Sense nor Musick.
RICHLY. I hate all Musick but a Jigg.
GAYWIT. I don't think it would be an ill Project, my Lord, to turn the best of our Tragedies and Comedies into Operas.
RICHLY. And, instead of a Company of Players, I wou'd have a Company of Tumblers and Ballad-singers.
BELLAMANT. Why, Faith, I believe it will come to that soon, unless some sturdy Critick should oppose it.[72]

---

[70] Eliza Haywood, *Philidore and Placentia; or, L'Amour trop Delicat* (1727); repr. in *Four before Richardson: Selected English Novels, 1720–1727*, ed. William H. McBurney (Lincoln: University of Nebraska Press, 1963), 155.

[71] No. 117 (30 Mar. 1732). The case for this play's basis in the Abergavenny litigation was first put by C. B. Woods, 'Notes on Three of Fielding's Plays', *PMLA* 52 (1937), 359–73: 362–8.

[72] Henry Fielding, *The Modern Husband: A comedy* (Dublin, 1732), II. v.

This play is Fielding's answer to the relentlessly bourgeois norms of Cibber's *The Provoked Husband*, in which Lord Townly, his sensible friend Manly, and exemplary sister Grace act as a moral mafia to intimidate Lady Townly. Fielding exorcizes Cibber's sentimental facilities in his much darker vision of how modern marriages can be cynically exploited. Despite the obeisance he makes to Cibber's play in the Preface of his own début play *Love in Several Masques*, its enduring legacy for Fielding was a preface in which Cibber's solecisms (using 'paraphonalia' instead of 'paraphernalia') suggest that he could scarcely control the English language.[73]

Cibber's vanity and unctuous self-satisfaction continued to be a target for Fielding until very late in his career. The publication of his autobiography in 1740 was one of the many targets aimed at in *Joseph Andrews*.[74] And it is tempting to suggest that another of Fielding's targets in *Joseph Andrews* was the romantic novella as exemplified by such as Eliza Haywood's *Philidore and Placentia*. In Haywood's novel, Philidore is hopelessly in love with Placentia, but because his fortune is unequal to hers, he thinks himself unworthy of her. Disguised as a servant, he enters her household just to be near her, and does the most menial tasks. He gives much evidence of his superior quality, however, and before long he is noticed by his mistress: singing a beautiful and cultured love-song, replying to her commands in courtly phrases, saving her from attack by two ruffians—the usual exploits of heroes in the romantic novella. Matters come to a head when he is offered, but refuses, promotion, certain that this will blow his cover. Placentia threatens him with dismissal, and the following scene occurs:

[73] Cibber's Preface to *The Provoked Husband* is burlesqued by Fielding in the Preface to the 1730 version of *Tom Thumb*: 'Mr Lock complains of confused Ideas in Words, which is entirely amended by suffering them to give none at all: This may be done by adding, diminishing, or changing a Letter, as instead of Paraphernalia, writing Paraphonalia: For a Man may turn Greek into Nonsense, who cannot turn Sense into either Greek or Latin' (Henry Fielding, *The Tragedy of Tragedies* (1730), ed. James T. Hillhouse (New Haven: Yale University Press, 1918), 49.

[74] 'But I pass by these and many others, to mention two Books lately published, which represent an admirable Pattern of the Amiable in either Sex. The former of these which deals in Male-Virtue, was written by the great Person himself, who lived the life he had recorded, and is by many thought to have lived such a Life only in order to write it . . . The Reader, I believe, already conjectures, I mean, the Lives of Mr. *Colley Cibber*, and of Mrs. *Pamela Andrews*' (Henry Fielding, *The History of the Adventures of Joseph Andrews and of his Friend Mr. Abraham Adams* (1742), ed. Douglas Brooks (London: Oxford University Press, 1970), 16).

Philidore who, on being told she wanted to speak with him, imagined now the fatal hour was arrived in which he was to be discharged, approached with so trembling an air that scarce had he the power of obeying her. Having, however, executed the first part of his commission, that of locking the door, she again repeated the other, on which, 'No more of this unnecessary homage', resumed she, perceiving he stood aloof and bowing. 'If I had not told you so, 'tis alas too easy for you to observe the pain it gives me. I charge you, therefore, to sit down, and near me, too, because I know not but there may be eavesdroppers of our private conference.'

'I shall obey you, madam,' replied he, 'in all things in which I can do without forfeiting that respect which it is not even in your power to banish from my soul. Thus will I attend your commands.'

With these words he drew near the couch and stooped down his head in the posture of a bow that he might the more easily hear what she had to say without obliging her to speak aloud.

'Must I then make use of force to draw you to me?' said she, catching suddenly one of his hands and pulling him to a chair close to the couch. 'I once more tell you,' pursued she, 'that I am assured you were not born for offices such as I have received from you. Reveal to me the secret which has engaged you to undertake them, and I swear to you by everything that we esteem great and sacred there is nothing you can ask I will refuse you' . . .

'All that I am is yours,' cried he hastily. 'I wish to live but to do you all the services that are in my poor power. My whole soul is devoted to you, nor does one wish rise in my breast but for your happiness and peace of mind.'

'Yet you alone have robbed me of it,' sighed she out; and at that instant the violence she did her modesty in acting in this manner deprived her of the power of proceeding, and she sunk motionless and fainting.[75]

Perhaps this particular Haywood novel stuck in Fielding's mind because of its dedication to Lady Abergavenny, given his own appropriation of that notorious case in *The Modern Husband*. Haywood's contacts with Fielding were quite extensive in the 1730s. With William Hatchett, she had reworked his *Tragedy of Tragedies* into a very successful *Opera of Operas* performed in 1733. And in 1737 she actually appeared as an actress in Fielding's troupe at the Little Haymarket, performing in his *The Historical Register* and *Eurydice Hiss'd*. By this time, she had herself been recruited, perhaps by Fielding, for the anti-Walpole literary opposition, as her exceptionally original *roman-à-clef The*

---

[75] Haywood, *Philidore and Placentia*, 175–6.

Adventures of Eovaai, Princess of Ijaveo (1736) would attest.[76] There is every reason, then, to think that Fielding kept her and her work in mind throughout the decade. At all events, as a scene of gender reversal in which a woman makes the first move, offering herself to a man and to a seeming servant, it might call to mind the exquisite scene (*Joseph Andrews*, book I, chapter 8) in which Lady Booby offers herself to Joseph and is turned to stone by his refusal of her on the grounds of his 'virtue'. The structural similarities are suggestive. Like Philidore, Joseph is summoned to Lady Booby's presence. Like Placentia, Lady Booby has to bridge the physical gap between them and like Philidore, Joseph has a supernal virtue that makes him somewhat slow in taking the point: '"What would you think, *Joseph*, if I admitted you to kiss me?" *Joseph* reply'd, "he would sooner die than have any such Thought".' Like Placentia, Lady Booby exposes herself to the refusal of her footman and, while the strain placed on Placentia's modesty actually causes her to lose consciousness, Lady Booby has a metaphorical black-out: 'You have heard, Reader, Poets talk of the *Statue of Surprize*.' The virtuous manservant is employed by Fielding as a device to expose the sexual politics of virtue in Richardson's *Pamela*, where it has become a reified commodity that the maidservant is finally able to exchange for marriage and social elevation. Like *Gulliver's Travels*, however, the novel is also a high-cultural repudiation of the narrative energies going into romantic novellas. The 'forward female', Fielding suggests, is a creature of romantic fiction who, when she is encountered in 'real life', is a grotesque and monstrous embodiment of carnal riot.

VI

When John Dennis died in 1729 there were relatively few to mourn him, but one enthusiastic mourner was Aaron Hill. Hill's 'Verses on the Death of Mr. Dennis' are much more accurate and sincere in representing Dennis as a neglected figure dying in

[76] On contacts between Fielding and Haywood, see John R. Elwood, 'The Stage Career of Eliza Haywood', *Theatre Survey* 5/2 (Nov. 1964), 107–16, and 'Henry Fielding and Eliza Haywood: A Twenty Year War', *Albion*, 5 (Fall 1973), 184–92; and Marcia Heinemann, 'Eliza Haywood's Career in the Theatre', *Notes & Queries* (Jan. 1973), 9–13.

poverty than are Pope's verses on Gay. At unflinching length, Hill specifies Dennis's faults of character, but asserts that posterity will discover a proper sense of his true worth:

> ADIEU! unsocial excellence! at last
> Thy foes are vanquish'd, and thy fears are past:
> Want, the grim recompence of truth like thine,
> Shall now no longer dim thy destin'd shine.
> Th' impatient envy, the disdainful air!
> The front malignant, and the captious stare!
> The furious petulance, the jealous start,
> The mist of frailties that obscured thy heart,
> Veil'd in thy grave shall unremember'd lie.
> For these were parts of Dennis born to die . . .
> The rising ages shall redeem his name,
> And nations read him into lasting fame.[77]

Aaron Hill was the cultural glue, one comes to think, that held this literary period together. For Hill was personally acquainted with every single author discussed in this section. Eliza Haywood was part of the so-called 'Hillarian circle' in the 1720s, and her rivalry with the poetess Martha Fowke Sansom (perhaps for Hill's affections) was public knowledge.[78] Sansom was the other Martha (other than Pope's Martha Blount) to be lampooned in Haywood's *Memoirs of a Certain Island*. As Robert Inglesfield correctly discerns, Hill was the missing link between John Dennis and the later writers like David Mallet and James Thomson who were destined to become the Whig 'patriots' of the 1730s.[79] In the periodical he edited with William Popple in the 1720s, the *Plain Dealer*, Hill sponsored David Mallet's somewhat ersatz ballad 'William and Margaret' and printed early poems by Savage and Thomson. For some years previously, he had been tirelessly disseminating Dennis's enthusiasms for biblical poetry and the sublime. In the Preface to his 1720 poem 'The Creation', addressed to Pope, for example, Hill spoke of the 'divine Spirit, glowing forcibly in the Hebrew Poetry, a kind of terrible Simplicity! a magnificent Plainness! which is commonly lost, in Paraphrase, by our mistaken Endeavours after heightening the Sentiments, by a

---

[77] Aaron Hill, *Poetical Works*, in Robert Anderson (ed.), *Complete Edition of the Poets of Great Britain*, 11 vols. (London, 1793), 8. 708.

[78] See Dorothy Brewster, *Aaron Hill: Poet, Dramatist, Projector* (New York: Columbia University Press, 1913), ch. 5.

[79] Inglesfield, 'James Thomson, Aaron Hill and the Poetic "Sublime"', 215–22.

figurative Expression'.[80] Arguing that the 'Hebrew poetry' of the Authorized Version is destroyed by metaphorical elaboration, 'Dropsical Wordiness' as he phrases it, Hill culled examples of the false sublime from Trapp, Blackmore, Philips, and Addison. 'Naturalness' in poetry was Hill's watchword, and it could be found in primitive forms as represented by biblical poetry and by the ballad.

Yet despite this predominantly Whig, even Addisonian, provenance, Hill thought of himself as an honorary Scriblerian. In the *Plain Dealer*, Hill set himself up in judgement upon contemporary culture, attacking a range of debased art forms such as pantomime and opera that would become the focus of *The Dunciad*. The *Plain Dealer*, no. 59 for 12 October 1724, for example, is a more than usually ironic paper that takes off from a playbill for a puppet show *Hero and Leander* to be performed, 'at the White Hart in St Margaret's Lane, by a Company of ARTIFICIAL ACTORS, whose Diversions are very *Changeable*, and *Consistivarious*'. The *Plain Dealer* affects to think that this may be advertising Cibber's new tragedy *Caesar in Egypt*, which, as we have seen, would become a target for Fielding later: 'I assure all Christian People, that though *Caesar*, may stand, in Capitals, on the *Title Page*, yet that shou'd only be consider'd as an *Error of the Press*; which the Buyer may *correct* with Ease, by reading CIBBER *in Egypt*.'[81] Satirizing Cibber, the *Plain Dealer* also lavished much praise on Pope ('the Praise of Mr. *Pope* will be a theme for Wit, and Learning, when all the *Dukes*, his *Patrons*, shall be *lost* in the Dust that covers them!'), though it made the excellent point that the glittering subscription list for Pope's Homer was an index not necessarily of critical sophistication but more of fashionability: 'But, let me see these shining Names to Mr. *Dennis's Miscellaneous Tracts*, which he is now publishing by a Subscription, scarce the Sixth Part so chargeable, and I will afterwards suppose, that They can *read*, as well as *purchase*.'[82] Small recompense for Hill's efforts, then, that

[80] Aaron Hill, 'The Creation: A Pindaric Illustration of a Poem, originally written by Moses, on that Subject. With a Preface to Mr. Pope, concerning the Sublimity of the Ancient Hebrew Poetry' (London, 1720), 4.

[81] Aaron Hill and William Popple, *The Plain Dealer: Being Select Essays on Several Curious Subjects Relating to Friendship, Love, and Gallantry, Marriage, Morality, Mercantile Affairs, Painting, History, Poetry, and Other Branches of Polite Literature*, 2 vols. (London, 1730), ii. 15.

[82] Ibid. i. 119, 452.

he found himself transfixed by the lepidopterist's needle as a 'flying fish', example of the foolish sublime, in Pope's *Peri Bathous* (1728). This must have been the more galling as the satiric technique employed by Pope of analysis and example had already been used by Hill: not for the first time, Pope steals the clothes of a writer that he would impersonate to attack.

More than for anything else, Hill has earned the honorific title of 'the most colossal bore in the eighteenth century' for his badgering Pope over dismissing him as a dunce in Scriblerian texts like *Peri Bathos* and *The Dunciad*. Yet Hill's earnestness cannot be doubted. He was incensed that Pope could make the error of casting *him*, Aaron Hill, into the outer darkness of duncehood. Was he not an energetic campaigner on behalf of improving cultural standards? Throughout the 1730s Hill sought to ameliorate the economic conditions of authorship by challenging the stranglehold that booksellers held over authors. He was a founder in 1736 of the Society for the Encouragement of Learning, discussed earlier; and he lost no opportunity to remind anyone listening that, as Caesar puts it in Hill's play *The Roman Revenge*, 'Where wit wants patronage—a *state* wants wisdom.'[83] In 1731 he wrote directly to Walpole to advise him that the encouragement of able writers is the best way to seek popularity. Hill's letters are studded with references to his plan to establish an 'academical Theatre, for improving the taste of the stage, and training up young actors and actresses for the supply of the Patent Theatres'. If the plan succeeded, then perhaps a theatrical cosmos could be transformed in which:

meaning is silently *pardoned*, while *folly* is mis-called *entertainment*, and received with *uproar* and *transport*: They are awake to nothing but *hurry*; and that too, to the most dark and dirty kinds of it. They approve of nothing, that they are able to see through. Their taste, as they wrongfully call it, is a kind of muddy vivacity; which, like the working of a *beer-barrel*, fills the body of the vessel with confusion, and throws the noise, and the dross, to the surface.[84]

Hill thought himself to be what he later in actuality became, a cultural ally of Pope's. Always eschewing financial gain as a reason

---

[83] Aaron Hill, *The Roman Revenge: A tragedy* (1753), from *Dramatic Works*, 2 vols. (London, 1760), ii. 279.

[84] Aaron Hill, *Works*, 4 vols. (London, 1754), 31 Aug. 1733; 16 Oct. 1734.

for writing (he always left the profits gained from his benefit nights to the theatre, though assuredly these did not amount to much), Hill was early into the field with 'Advice to the Poets' (1731), an exalted manifesto for poetry that conceived the true poet as the creation of much time and study, as the immortalizer of statesmen and the exhorter to virtue:

> But when the deathless poet is to shine,
> Long-lab'ring ages swell the slow design.
> At length he comes: the birth of time appears!
> And heav'n smiles satisfy'd a thousand years.[85]

Combining elements both of the Whig manifesto of the polite, the sublime, and the primitive and of the Scriblerian manifesto of cultural decline, while working in a practical and pragmatic way for the actual improvement of conditions both of production and consumption of culture, Hill was in many ways the perfect encapsulation of the prevailing tendencies of his era. Assuredly, he could never *be* a Scriblerian. The absence of humour in his later plays makes that evident, as does the deadly seriousness with which he took himself. It is to his credit that despite the tedious indirection of the epistolary style he assumed for Pope's benefit, he actually got far closer to understanding him, and perhaps to 'rumbling' him, than any other contemporary. Hill noticed that Pope's life did not altogether live up to the billing that he gave it. In a letter of June 1738, he ventured to suggest that:

we are, All of us, in some Lights, or other, the *Dupes* of our natural Frailties: and when Mr. *Pope*, with the Warmth that becomes a great Mind, tells me how far he is from despising Defects in men's *Genius*— never feeling any contempt but for the Dirt of their *Actions*; I am sure he says nothing but what he firmly believes to be true. And yet there are Pieces, well known to be *his*, many Passages whereof no Man, less appris'd than himself of his Heart's secret Views and Intentions, can read, without being strongly convinc'd of a Scorn, that regards *Genius* only.[86]

That scorn was, of course, absolutely central to Scriblerian irony and, unsympathetic to it, Hill was finally outside the club. Yet he understood that Pope's heart had 'secret views and intentions'; and it is to these that I turn in the next chapter of this book.

[85] In Anderson, *Complete Edition of the Poems of Great Britain*, viii. 682.
[86] Pope, *Correspondence*, iv. 104.

8

Piddling on Broccoli:
Pope's Menu and his Ideology

Alexander Pope has cast a long shadow over this book, despite his well-known short stature. He is the 'onlie begetter' of it, in two major respects. His *Dunciad* is readable as an intervention against various forms of cultural seepage and transgressive mingling of social strata. It dramatizes conflict between prestigious forms—the classical epic—and the forms produced for the populace and the market-place. Commercial culture, and popular culture, are presented in the poem as aspects of the same ideological formation. *The Dunciad* is a good example of what Stephen Greenblatt terms 'symbolic acquisition', where a set of social practices, or 'modes of social energy', is transferred to the domain of literature by means of metaphorical and metonymical representation.[1] Secondly, *The Dunciad* pickled a large number of contemporary writers in aspic as 'dunces', writers without a true vocation whose 'works' were entirely reducible to the material forms of their dissemination—to the paper and print out of which they were manufactured. Writers like James Ralph are rendered by Pope's dismissive couplet an early comic prototype of Wordsworth's Winander Boy:

> Silence, ye Wolves! while Ralph to Cynthia howls,
> And makes Night hideous—Answer him, ye Owls!
>
> (bk. iii, lines 165–6)

Pope's verdicts on such as John Dennis, Ned Ward, Eliza Haywood, Colley Cibber—even the manifestly indefensible pillorying of Lewis Theobald—have been accepted as just and true, rather than as ammunition in an ongoing struggle between a dominant culture and the emergent forms that it seeks to disorganize,

---

[1] Stephen Greenblatt, *Shakespearean Negotiations: The Circulation of Social Energy in Renaissance England* (Oxford University Press, 1988), 10–11.

reorganize, and finally contain.[2] These aspects of the poem's achievement have demanded the reinvestigation that has resulted in this study.

And yet it has become increasingly apparent, as Pope's typographical preferences and publishing habits have come under scrutiny, that there is a massive paradox here. Pope has a fair claim to be the first great professional writer in English letters: the first writer to make a fortune by applying extraordinary commercial acumen to the exploiting of his literary talents. At a tentative stage in his career, before he had finished the Homer translation, Pope made a bid for the status of genius in the Preface to the 1717 edition of his *Works*. Here he was careful to stress the complexity involved in arriving at value judgements and gave the reading public a significant role to play in the process:

I think a good deal may be said to extenuate the fault of bad Poets. What we call a Genius, is hard to be distinguish'd by a man himself, from a strong inclination: and if it be never so great, he can not at first discover it any other way, than by that prevalent propensity which renders him the more liable to be mistaken. The only method he has, is to make the experiment by writing, and appealing to the judgment of others . . . We have no cause to quarrel with [the worst of authors] but for their obstinacy in persisting, and this too may admit of alleviating circumstances. Their particular friends may be either ignorant, or insincere; and the rest of the world too well bred to shock them with a truth, which generally their Booksellers are the first that inform them of. This happens not till they have spent too much of their time, to apply to any profession which might better fit their talents; and till such talents as they have are so far discredited, as to be but of small service to them.[3]

A would-be genius (such as John Dennis, say), Pope argues, has the same sense of needing to write, as has the genuine article. What separates them is not anything in nature, but the thumbs-down of the reading public. Thereafter, the crime lies in continuing to write. Writing becomes a displacement profession, substituting for more seemly and serious callings. As for Pope himself, he puts much distance between himself and professional writers: 'I writ because it amused me; I corrected because it was as pleasant to me to correct as to write; and I publish'd because I was

---

[2] On this eternal contest, see Stuart Hall, 'Notes on Deconstructing "the Popular"', in Raphael Samuel (ed.), *People's History and Socialist Theory* (London: Routledge & Kegan Paul, 1981), 227–40.

[3] Pope, *Prose Works*, ed Ault, i. 290. Subsequent references are to this edition.

told I might please such as it was a credit to please' (i. 292). But
however Pope sought to distance himself from the taint of professionalism, it is clear that, in respect of the Homer translation,
business considerations interacted with aesthetic desiderata to
produce beautiful books and considerable profits. What emerges
so clearly from David Foxon's study of Pope's relations with the
early eighteenth-century book trade is not so much that Pope
made vast profits out of his translation of Homer—of the order of
£5,000 for each of the *Iliad* and the *Odyssey*—but rather that,
despite the extraordinary tightness of the publisher Lintot's agreement with him, Pope outsmarted him. The poet ended up making
an enormous profit out of the venture by securing numerous
subscriptions for fine-paper, quarto copies, while Lintot was
left with considerable difficulty trying to sell large numbers of
ordinary-paper copies.[4] In comparison to Dryden, who left it up to
Jacob Tonson to secure subscribers for the Virgil translation, Pope
was indefatigable in persuading his influential friends to interest
their influential friends in subscribing. In Pope's case it is clear
that the marketing elements of subscription publishing are less
important than the paternalistic ones. As Foxon further demonstrates, one result of Pope's financial independence gained
through Homer translation was 'to extract the maximum profits
from his publication and to keep the copyright of his works under
his own control' (p. 102). Hiring his own printer (John Wright)
and distributing his publications through two publishers whom he
had helped to establish in business (Lawton Gilliver and Robert
Dodsley), Pope's control over every aspect of the production of his
own books—from the business arrangements to the aesthetic
considerations that favoured the smaller octavo formats over their
more majestic relations the quartos and folios and resulted in a
printed page that was much closer to what we now take for granted
than to the standard eighteenth-century page of verse, with its
capitalized substantives, italics, erratic punctuation, catchwords,
and the like—is quite astonishing.

This ideological contradiction speaks to Pope's position as a
writer whose career is shaped by the changing economics of authorship. Those who are familiar with Pope's writing will be aware of
the extent to which his bid for cultural centrality was based on a
representation of his art and his life as a triumph for moderation

4 Foxon, *Pope and the Eighteenth-Century Book Trade*, ch. 2, *passim.*

and the middle way, a steering between extremes. In politics he supported a government of national unity, subscribing to a 'patriot' programme capable of uniting all those elements not already recruited to the banners of Whig plutocracy or Tory legitimism. In matters religious he played down his Catholicism in order to foreground those aspects of a reasonable Christianity calculated to appeal to all but extremists and fanatics. To the extent that Pope's bid for cultural centrality has succeeded, it has done because in *The Dunciad* he presented a powerfully mythologized system of distinctions between valuable and valueless cultural forms; and, in the Horatian poems written in the 1730s, he made his own exemplary life stand as guarantor for the ethical norms that under-propped *The Dunciad*'s evaluative system. To the extent that it has failed, it has done because not everyone has been prepared to take Pope at his own word. Many have noticed that his life did not altogether square with the sterilized account of it given in the autobiographical poems. From his Victorian editors Elwin and Courthope down to his recent biographer Maynard Mack, a major concern has been to determine to what extent Pope's way of living actually justified the version of it he purveyed in, for example, the *Epistle to Dr. Arbuthnot*. In very recent years, however, the terrain on which this debate has been conducted has shifted from the personal to the ideological. The point is not to establish whether Pope was a man more sinned against than sinning, but to question, as Laura Brown puts it, 'remorselessly', 'the political, social and even aesthetic positions of his poetry'.[5] In materialist-feminist analysis there is a strong tendency to represent Pope as the embodiment of a stable ideology that was powerful and dominant in its era. Ellen Pollak contends, for example, that 'Pope fetishizes the female as a way of eliminating visible traces of anxiety and violence from the interior of his texts ... Pope accommodates women comfortably within his texts by objectifying them in such a way that they give back the image of himself he wants to see.'[6] But the ideological impasse examined above, that Pope was a consum-mate professional writer whose major poems stand as an attack on professional and commercial writing, is one of the reasons why I claimed in the previous chapter that Pope cannot altogether be so represented. Laura Brown believes that 'Pope's major works stand

[5] Brown, *Pope*, 3.
[6] Pollak, *The Poetics of Sexual Myth*, 160.

as documents of the ideological structures of the period' (p. 3). I should like to examine that view, with respect to the country and the city polarity, undoubtedly one of the ideological structures of the period, and with reference to some of the major works in which Pope employs that structure.

Pope's career can be understood partly in terms of the developing phenomenon of suburbanization. The rapid growth of London after 1660 generated the need to get away from the place, if not as far as a wilderness like Hampshire, certainly to suburban areas like Richmond and Twickenham that could mediate between city congestion and intolerable rusticity. Prevented by anti-Catholic legislation from living within twelve miles of central London, Pope turned his involuntary rustication to Twickenham into a power-base, a vantage-point from which he could observe and comment on political affairs while claiming the neutrality of retirement. The title of my chapter alludes to Pope's version of Horace's *Second Satire of the Second Book*, in which the poet gives us one of the most memorable portraits of suburban living in all his work:

> In South Sea days not happier, when surmised
> The lords of thousands, than if now *excised*;
> In forests planted by a father's hand,
> Than in five acres now of rented land.
> Content with little, I can piddle here
> On broccoli and mutton, round the year;
> But ancient friends (though poor, or out of play)
> That touch my bell, I cannot turn away.
> 'Tis true, no turbots dignify my boards,
> But gudgeons, flounders, what my Thames affords:
> To Hounslow Heath I point and Banstead Down,
> Thence comes your mutton, and these chicks my own:
> From yon old walnut-tree a shower shall fall;
> And grapes, long lingering on my only wall,
> And figs, from standard and espalier join;
> The devil is in you if you cannot dine:
> Then cheerful healths (your mistress shall have place)
> And, what's more rare, a poet shall say grace.
>
> (lines 133–50)

These lines were affixed to the only print of Pope's house published in his lifetime, an engraving by Nathaniel Parr after an original drawing by Peter Rysbrack: word and image seem to come together in a representation of perfect balance.[7] The verbal message compliments the visual message conveyed by the villa-style architecture. Alluding to the building styles of the Roman architect Vitruvius and the sixteenth-century Italian architect Andrea Palladio, the villa is a severely classical response to the extravagantly exaggerated architecture of large and impressive country seats, with a new emphasis on comfort and human scale. Implicitly in this passage Pope defines his way of living against two alternatives: the conspicuous consumption characteristic of the English baroque style of architecture in houses like Castle Howard and Blenheim built to proclaim aristocratic and courtly power; and on the other hand the cramped conditions endured by the growing urban proletariat. Elsewhere in his poetry, Pope also gives us the most memorable representations anywhere to be found, both of garret life and of life in the baroque show-house. In his *Epistle to Burlington*, Pope consciously identifies himself with Richard Boyle, third Earl of Burlington and his Palladian manifesto. Houses like Marble Hill and Burlington's own villa at Chiswick were designed as temples of the arts, to set off the owner's exquisite taste as a collector but built on a scale that would not sabotage the possibility of convivial hospitality and friendship. Contrast to this, on the one hand the well-known satiric vignette of Timon's Villa in the *Epistle to Burlington*, and on the other the magnificent garret set-piece in the first book of the revised *Dunciad*, the portrait of the theatre-impresario, actor, and playwright Colley Cibber.

Pope's vision of himself in the cited passage from the *Imitations of Horace, Satires*, II. ii, can legitimately be read as an attempt to steer between the extremes of Cibber and Timon. It is suburban man's view of the excesses both of urban congestion and of country-estate opulence and show. This is more or less the standard reading of the passage, as found in discussions like those of Virginia Kenny and Jacob Fuchs:

Pope's frugality is symbolized in the rejection of luxury as he trifles with simple foods:

> Content with little, I can piddle here
> On Broccoli and mutton, round the year.

[7] Morris Brownell, *Alexander Pope's Villa: Views of Pope's Villa, Grotto and Garden. A Microcosm of English Landscape* (London: GLC, 1980), 23, 30.

The meal is plain but his appreciation of frugality makes Pope relish the knowledge of its provenance. Not for him the townsman's diet of foods bought from among the promiscuous jumble of the market-place; his mutton comes from well-known pastures, the poultry from his land and the palatable fish are caught beneath his windows. The absence of an extensive estate does not therefore deny him the pleasure of feeling that over much that he sees, even where it is not in his care, he extends the sovereignty of grateful use.[8]

Behind Kenny's ringing phrase 'the sovereignty of grateful use', one detects the entire tradition of country-house poetry, within which she wishes to accord Pope a secure position. Some years ago, George Hibbard published an extremely influential article entitled 'The Country House Poem of the Seventeenth Century', the argument of which was that there is a short-lived, but distinct, genre of poems that begins with Ben Jonson's *To Penshurst*, is visible in other poems by Jonson, Carew, and Herrick, and is already beginning to mutate in Andrew Marvell's poem *Upon Appleton House*.[9] For Hibbard, the poems comprising the tradition have at their heart a country house like the Sidneys' Penshurst Place, which functions in its community as 'the centre of a complex web of relationships which make up the fabric of civilised living'. Houses like Penshurst express fully the owners' personality, and the reciprocal relationship between house and master is mirrored in the harmonious relationship between the estate and its tenants. Hibbard writes as if the Jonsonian literary representation is a direct reflection of social truth. The Sidney estate at Penshurst *was* like that: the tenants of the Sidneys really weren't exploited but entered into a reciprocal relationship of duties and responsibilities freely and gladly. Jonson only had to come along and write it up. It was left to Raymond Williams, in his important book *The Country and the City*, to point out that literature just does not work like that. It is never a straightforward reflection of social realities, but a more or less complex mediation of them. In arguing for an unbroken genre of country-house poems, Hibbard was occluding the ways in which those poems were positioned in

[8] Virginia Kenny, *The Country-House Ethos in English Literature, 1688–1750: Themes of National Expansion and Personal Retreat* (Brighton: Harvester Press, 1984), 146; Jacob Fuchs, *Reading Pope's Imitations of Horace* (Lewisburg, Pa.: Bucknell University Press, 1989), 80 ff.

[9] George Hibbard, 'The Country House Poem of the Seventeenth Century', *Journal of the Warburg and Courtauld Institute*, 19 (1956), 159–74.

their own shifting, mobile history. For Williams, the ancient town-versus-country opposition on which Hibbard bases his account of such poems as Jonson's *Penshurst* was always a falsification because, by the time *Penshurst* came to be written, there was no possibility of hiving off 'innocent' enclaves of land use, where the land was securely owned by some Edenic title and worked for the good of its tenants without involvement in any city-based mercantile transactions. As Williams insists, 'we need not, at any stage, accept this town-and-country contrast at its face value':

> For in the transaction that mattered, who was it, after all, who came from the country? It was not the labourer or the cottager; the hunger of their families kept them in the fields. It was the landowner and his endowed son, the landowner's wife and her prospecting daughter, who came on their necessary business . . . What they brought with them, and what they came to promote, rested on the brief and aching lives of the permanently cheated: the field labourers whom we never by any chance see; the dispossessed and the evicted; all the men and women whose land and work paid their fares and provided their spending money.[10]

Virginia Kenny is certainly more conscious than was Hibbard of the respects in which Pope's account of his life on the Twickenham Sabine farm is a mediated one: but her fundamental commitment is still to what we might term, borrowing an expression from Catherine Belsey, 'expressive realist'.[11] Pope expresses what his form of living is really like. Laura Brown, on the other hand, though she does not treat this particular passage, discovers a poem like the *Epistle to Burlington* to be ideological in the classic Marxist sense of expressing 'false consciousness'; to her, it is a poem that promotes and legitimizes the sectional interests of aristocratic capitalist-imperialists: 'Its aim is . . . the definition of a cultural ideal for the ruling class, an ideal constructed from the superimposition of an abstract and neo-classical system of aesthetic valuation upon a concrete programme for mercantile capitalist economic expansion.'[12]

But Pope's poetry is very often not quite what it appears. Let us look at the 'piddling on Broccoli' passage again. The middle-way ideal, the rhetoric of moderation, the shadowy figure of Horace on

---

[10] Raymond Williams, *The Country and the City* (1973; repr. London: Hogarth Press, 1993), 54.

[11] Catherine Belsey, *Critical Practice* (London: Methuen, 1980), 7–14.

[12] Brown, *Pope*, 124.

the Sabine farm enjoying domesticated retirement that is behind this passage, and yet the wholesome Englishness created by the brilliant paraphrase, is not quite the whole effect of it. Both in its details and in its broad implications, the passage is subversive of the poetic posture that it ostensibly promotes. Some details that might impede an easy reading would include the word 'piddle': yes it means toying with one's food, but 'piddling' on broccoli also suggests to the reader a method of food-preparation that would be *far* from satisfactory. And on *broccoli*. Pope is claiming to eschew the fashionable tastes of expensive gourmets, but in fact broccoli, although it was a vegetable known to John Evelyn, was only beginning to be exploited in England after 1720 and at the time of writing of Pope's poem, would still be exotic. The pioneering gardener Stephen Switzer's *A Compendious Method for the raising of Italian brocoli, Spanish Cardoon, Celeriac, Finochi, and other Foreign Kitchen-Vegetables* (5th edn 1731) still found it necessary to be evangelical about broccoli, which he describes as a 'Sallad that has been some Time among us; but our not knowing how to manage it, has brought a kind of Disreputation upon it.'[13] So has the fact that Italian seed-gatherers have been in the habit of shipping turnip-seed over, posing as broccoli! Switzer tells us that Edward Wortley Montagu's gardener at Twickenham is a great expert in its cultivation. Pope was clearly part of the Twickenham broccoli Mafia, and knew perfectly well that broccoli was an unusual choice of vegetable in this homely menu. A manuscript draft of the *Epistle to Fortescue* had a line about Lord Peterborow (another member of the broccoli mafia) dressing 'Brocoli' which Pope excised presumably because it did sound too exotic.[14] In February we find Pope recruiting Swift for the broccoli mafia by sending him some seeds; and in a note the editor George Sherburn contends that it was Peterborow who introduced Pope to the vegetable. Pope's friend William Cleland is also an initiate.[15] And what about the reference to 'turbots'? E. Smith's very popular manual *The Complete Housewife* (17th edn 1766) tells us that

[13] Stephen Switzer, *A Compendious Method for the raising of Italian brocoli, Spanish Cardoon, Celeriac, Finochi, and other Foreign Kitchen-Vegetables* (5th edn. London, 1731), p. vi.

[14] Maynard Mack, *The Last and Greatest Art: Some Unpublished Poetical Manuscripts of Alexander Pope* (Newark, NJ: University of Delaware Press; London: Associated University Presses, 1984), 181 (line 80).

[15] Pope to Swift, 17 Feb. 1727 (Pope, *Correspondence*, ii. 425).

it should be served with butter and lobster sauce, and garnished with horse-radish and lemon, but does not suggest that it was uncommon. But those readers in Pope's time who knew their Horace well (and there were plenty around) might think of a different context for the word. In Horace's *Satires*, I. ii, he is discussing the virtues of adultery with married Roman matrons as against fornication with freedwomen. And he puts the following question:

> num, tibi cum fauces urit sitis, aurea quaeris
> pocula? num esuriens fastidis omnia praeter
> pavonem rhombumque? tument tibi cum inguina, num, si
> ancilla aut verna est praeto puer, impetus in quem
> continuo fiat, malis tentigine rumpi?

(lines 114–18)

[When your throat is parched with thirst do you insist on having a golden | tankard? When famished do you turn up your finicky nose at all | except peacocks and turbots? When your organ is stiff, and a servant girl | or a young boy from the household is near at hand and you know | you can make an immediate assault, would you sooner burst with tension?][16]

For those who knew this intertext, the entire passage of Pope's imitation of Horace's *Satire*, II. ii, quoted above, in which he describes his domestic life, has a lewd and libidinous undercurrent. Hounslow Heath and Banstead Down may be excellent sheep pastures, but they are also notorious haunts of highwaymen. 'Mutton' was an Elizabethan slang term for a prostitute.[17] The tolerant inclusiveness of permitting mistresses to 'have place' is put into question by the placing of an apostrophe—'mistress' or 'mistress's'? Is one's mistress to have a place, or only her health? What exactly are the implications of a poet saying grace? More generally, the passage begins by proclaiming the poet's happiness and security despite his position as a Roman Catholic and a political outcast—a position that forces him to be only a tenant, not an owner-occupier of the villa that was imagined to be so deeply expressive of his personality. And, as it goes on, the satire widens out to a subversion of the entire land-tenure system that underpins country-house culture:

[16] Quintus Horatius Flaccus (Horace), *Satires, Epistles, Ars Poetica*, Loeb translation (London: William Heinemann; New York: G. P. Putnam's Sons, 1929), 28. The translation is that of Niall Rudd (Harmondsworth: Penguin, 1973; repr. 1976), 35–6.   [17] *OED*, 'mutton' (3).

'Pray heaven it last!' cries SWIFT, 'as you go on;
I wish to God this house had been your own:
Pity! to build, without a son or wife:
Why, you'll enjoy it only all your life.'
Well, if the use be mine, can it concern one,
Whether the name belong to Pope or Vernon?
What's *property*? dear Swift? you see it alter
From you to me, from me to Peter Walter;
Or, in a mortgage, prove a lawyer's share;
Or, in a jointure, vanish from the heir . . .
Let lands and houses have what lords they will,
Let us be fixed, and our own masters still.

(lines 161–70, 79–80)

Why use *Swift* of all people, one of the most notorious bachelors in all literary history, to act as apologist for marriage, procreation, and heredity? 'What's *Property*?' There are so many ways of losing it, the market is currently so mobile . . . and the passage ends with a firm distinction drawn between mastery of *self* and mastery of one's estate. It is a trifle ironic, after all, that Pope's villa at Twickenham, one of the best-known literary landscapes in existence, an iconographic legend in its own and later times, was actually Vernon's villa and was rented by Pope on insecure terms. Interestingly, a few years before the publication of this poem in July 1734, Pope and Swift were both exhorting John Gay to settle down and, as David Nokes says, 'the property he set his sights on was the widow Vernon's house by the Thames near Pope at Twickenham'.[18] Swift's letter to Gay of March 1730 might have provided Pope with a few suggestions for his poem: 'I hope when you are rich enough you will have some little oeconomy of your own, either in town or country, and be able to give your friend a pint of port and a bit of mutton; for the domestic season of life will come on.'[19] But whereas for Gay home-ownership was a castle in the air, for Pope it was a domestic ideal that his position as an outsider forced him to subvert. Although we now know a great deal more about country-house or 'estate' poetry, as Alasdair Fowler teaches us to call it, than we did when Hibbard published his ground-breaking article, it still appears, even when considering Pope's passage against Fowler's vastly extended account, that

[18] Nokes, *Gay*, 479.
[19] Swift, *Correspondence*, iii. 381.

Pope's poem is intentionally written against the grain of the central generic assumptions made in such poems.[20] A remark of Sir Henry Wotton's cited by Fowler might suggest the distance between the seventeenth-century estate poet's sense of 'home' and Pope's transitory tenancy: 'Every man's proper mansion house and home, being the theatre of his hospitality, the seat of self-fruition, the comfortablest part of his own life, the noblest of his son's inheritance, and kind of private princedom; nay, to the possessors thereof, an epitomy of the whole world . . .'. '*To the possessors thereof* . . .' In his poem, Pope is subverting the very idea of country-house poetry itself, which, as has been said, traditionally depended on a close identification between the values of the property owner and the characteristics of his house and grounds—precisely the fusion that Pope is here driving apart. If this passage is any 'document of the ideological structures of the period', it is a samizdat document.

The reading of a passage of Pope offered above is what I might term a 'symptomatic' one. I suggest that a reading like this, in which one finds that Pope does not quite mean what he is ostensibly saying, could be made of many passages in Pope's *œuvre*; and it might go some way towards explaining why, although Pope ought to be in some respects the 'villain' of this book's story— the oppressor of other writers, the Canute trying to send back the waves of professional progress, the satirist who attempted to preserve the property of literary appreciation in the hands of his own and his adopted class-fraction—he is not quite. His poetry keeps us there, reading.

---

[20] Alasdair Fowler, *The Country House Poem* (Edinburgh University Press, 1994). Fowler's collection of poems includes over seventy items. His introduction makes clear that this poetry is much more concerned with grounds than with houses—hence 'estate'; that it comprises several sub-genres; that it has a rich classical and medieval ancestry; and that its provenance is georgic, not pastoral.

[21] Ibid.

Conclusion

The conclusion to this book has to be of the Johnsonian kind, following *Rasselas*, in which nothing is concluded. Johnson's name is in many respects an appropriate one to invoke at this stage, because my book's allotted timespan just reaches the point of departure of his career and because recent work on Johnson has constructed him as the first hero of the age of print.[1] Johnson's letter to Chesterfield on the occasion of the latter's post-publication interest in the *Dictionary*, reminding him that he was never interested in it *pre*-publication, is very frequently cited as sounding the death-knell to the patronage system: 'Is not a Patron, My Lord, one who looks with unconcern on a Man struggling for Life in the water, and, when he has reached ground encumbers him with help?'[2] In this book's argument, Johnson would be part of the process that I have used the term 'novelization' to designate rather than the revolutionary herald of a new age. Novelization is the set of material, cultural, and institutional changes responsible for the promotion of prose narrative to its undisputed pre-eminence as the most widely consumed form of imaginative writing, a process that extinguished the long poem, marginalized all other poetic forms, and rendered the theatre a minority interest. Novelization brings about, if the reader will pardon the bathos, the novel. Its energies continued well into our own century and, arguably, can only be spoken of in the past tense when print comes to be replaced by visual image media as the primary forms in which products of the imagination are received. We are familiar with its effects on school and university students of literature, many of whom evince a reluctance to engage with forms of imaginative writing not expressed in prose.

Such a process cannot be given chronological boundaries. The time-frame into which this book is set is not invested with the

---

[1] Alvin Kernan, *Samuel Johnson and the Impact of Print* (Princeton University Press, 1987; repr. 1989).

[2] *The Letters of Samuel Johnson*, ed. Bruce Redford, 5 vols. (Oxford: Clarendon Press, 1992), i. 96.

significance that some authors wish to confer on their chrono-
logies. This period corresponds roughly to the lifetimes of Swift
and Pope and closely to the decades that engage most fully my own
particular interests in literary history. The book is the most
sustained attempt I have made so far to define those interests. I
have tried to convey a sense of the instability of literary culture
and literary genre, connected to changes in the means of literary
production and consumption. My early emphasis on the emergent
problems of proprietorship, originality, plagiarism, and the conflict between regulatory and proprietary models of ownership and
between amateur-aristocratic and professional-bourgeois postures
intends to suggest some of the hazards of the literary terrain that
authors had to negotiate. Of novelization as such, I do not suggest
that the authors caught up in it were aware. This might be given as
an example of the functioning of ideology in a Machereian or
Jamesonian sense: the historical 'unconscious', the play of history
on the margins of literary works that determines the limits of what
such works can say. Novelization is a term that tries to relate the
history of social formations to that of literary forms. It speaks to
the emergence of a market for imaginative writing and of professional writers who saw an opportunity to gain a living by developing and satisfying it, coeval with the attenuation of literary genres
that could not satisfy such a market and the development of new
ones. For me one fascination of reading a writer like John Dryden,
caught in the web of such changes, is to observe the extent to which
aspects of this wider process are to some degree apparent to
consciousness, but in dim and contradictory fashion, lending a
pathos to his writing career. Rochester's aristocratic hauteur conflicts with Dryden's enforced professionalism. This is clear. Less
clear, however, is Dryden's opposition to Shadwell, with whom he
felt himself to be in sharp dispute over such topics as wit versus
humour and speech versus action, but with whom the logic of
novelization would suggest that he had, finally, much more in
common. Dryden was deeply sensitive to the emergent protocols
of professionalism and could not affect Shadwell's insouciance
about them precisely because for Dryden the residual claims of an
older, allusive literary tradition were much stronger. The immortal
longings of epic ambition pressed urgently upon him, I have
argued, and yet he was at some level aware of the accommodations
that needed to be made with the domesticating tendencies of

novelization—accommodations that necessarily entailed mixing. Mock-heroic in Dryden, Garth, and early Pope is such an accommodation, perilously close to the acceptance that it just will not work. What distinguishes Dryden from the ineptitude of such as Blackmore is this awareness. Blackmore naïvely believes that the difference can be overcome. His attitudes, expectations, and motives for writing are myopic and insensitive therefore.

'Politeness' or 'refinement' is a pan-cultural discourse that gathers momentum in the post-Revolutionary period. It is to a large extent the executive arm of the novelization project, but is not entirely coextensive with it. The various practices sanctioned by politeness, aimed as they were at the regulation of speech and behaviour, had a liberating, class-surpassing agenda that brought into being the 'public sphere', within which access to political and cultural involvement was granted to greater numbers. Reading over what I have written, I have perhaps failed to emphasize this as much as I should have done. I have dwelt too much on the regulatory, disciplinary aspects of politeness protocols. My main concern has been to show that there are many distinct strands in the warp and weft of politeness and that contributions were made to its formation by figures who, in so far as they intuited its intentions, were not fully comprehended by them—were not brought on board. Polite aesthetics, through its figure of aesthetic possession, empowers those who have no substantial holdings in *real* property to possess landscape, nature, affordable literature, and art, while it also retains a class-stratifying sense of privilege (in leisure time and education) necessary for even this less exalted form of ownership. John Dennis was, I have suggested, a key figure in bringing about this aesthetic empowerment of the bourgeoisie by laying the groundwork for an appreciation of the sublime, the Miltonic, and the vernacular (within which one might include the sponsorship of Hebraic verse forms in the Psalms and Authorized Version). In his own person, however, and in his typical paradigms of argument, Dennis was entirely outside the pale of politeness— one of the most impolite men who ever lived.

The impulse to create polite and refined forms of writing is a relatively *visible* aspect of novelization, even in its own time. Alexander Pope, for instance, could see for himself what the Addison and Steele camp was up to and could use their strategies for his own advancement in the *Essay on Criticism* and, more subversively, in *The Rape of the Lock*. Under the pressure of subsequent vilification, however, and shaped by a developing political agenda of opposition to Walpole's manipulation of writing to shore up corrupt power, Pope self-consciously abandoned polite sociability, employing 'filthy rhymes' and 'beastly similes' to show his contempt for its limitations and increasingly adopting the rhetoric of *ego contra mundum* in the *Imitations of Horace*. In *The Dunciad*, Pope set his face against the professionalization and proliferation of writing that increasing the participation rate in print culture and in imaginative writing (an aim of the polite movement) would necessarily bring in train. In this reactionary stance, I have suggested, the other Scriblerians also participated; indeed, it is what defines them as a coherent grouping within literary history. None more so, in my view, than Jonathan Swift, whose scepticism is so much more consistent and corrosive than Pope's and whom I have defined in opposition to Centlivre, Defoe, Haywood, and the early development of the novel. Swift's obsessive enunciation of the cloacal signals clearly his refusal of polite limitations on discourse.

In what I have said about Pope, Swift, and the Scriblerians, however, I have tried to stress, but perhaps have still insufficiently stressed, the extent to which they were a part of the novelization process even while they stood in conscious opposition to some of its more visible aspects. I have shown them borrowing energy quanta, the provenance of which they affect to despise. The forms they adopted are parodic of the generic mixing and domestic realism that characterizes the novel. Yet, in the larger analysis, not only were they unable to resist the imperatives of novelization, but they actively assisted its forward march through the professional practices they adopted: witness Pope's tactics for marketing his poetry and Swift's for marketing *Gulliver's Travels*. There is no absolute distinction to be drawn between writers like Addison and Pope or Tickell and Pope or Defoe and Swift, because they all inhabit the same city of professional writing even if they live in different suburbs. Addison domesticates the world of the classical epic and forecasts the ideology of separate spheres for men and women; but how different is this from *The Rape of the Lock* and Clarissa's moral? Pope, Philips, and Tickell are all involved in the domestication of pastoral and, from one point of view, Gay's parody of Philips in *The Shepherd's Week* employs polite

condescension against the homely rusticity of the latter's Spen-
serianisms. Attacks by Gay and Fielding on the heroic drama and
high tragedy are launched in the interests of a more bourgeois
conception of the tragic.

I have aimed, therefore, at a dialectical view of literary professionalization, which needs to be understood as both integral and
coherent, and yet as composed of divergent elements that entail a
distinct cultural politics. It is the respects in which Pope and
Addison resemble one another, the extent to which both were
affected by the developing capitalization of the publishing industry, that permits us to distinguish the qualities of difference on
which their literary identities are based. Both are interpellated by
the same set of ideological questions posed by history, but the
artistic statements they made in response to this historical
situation are experienced by us as startlingly distinctive. My most
profound hope for the book I have written is that it has something
to say about that distinctiveness in individual writers as well as
about the historical conditions that produced it.

Bibliography

The place of publication is London wherever it is omitted.

MANUSCRIPT SOURCES

British Library (BL) Add. MSS 47131, fo. 96.
—— Upcott Collection, Original assignments of MSS between authors and publishers principally for dramatic works, from the year 1703–1810. BL Add. MS 38, 728.
Bodleian Library, MS Rawlinson 72, fo. 65.
Wiltshire Record Office, Salisbury Museum Collection, MS 164/13/5.

PRINTED SOURCES

A Biographical Dictionary of Actors etc., 1660–1800, ed. Philip H. Highfill, Jr., Kalman A. Burnim, and Edward A. Langhans, 16 vols. (Carbondale, Ill., 1973–93).
A Dictionary of British and American Women Writers, 1660–1800, ed. Janet Todd (1987).
ADDISON, JOSEPH, *Cato* (1713).
—— *Dialogues upon the Usefulness of Ancient Medals especially in Relation to the Latin and Greek Poets* (1721).
—— *The Miscellaneous Works*, ed. A. C. Guthkelch, 2 vols. (1914).
—— *et al., The Spectator*, ed. Donald F. Bond, 5 vols. (Oxford, 1965).
—— RICHARD STEELE, *et al., The Spectator* (1711–14).
AMIS, MARTIN, *The Information* (1995).
ASTBURY, RAYMOND, 'The Renewal of the Licensing Act in 1693 and its Lapse in 1695', *Library*, 33 (1978), 296–322.
A Transcript of the Registers of the Worshipful Company of Stationers from 1640 to 1708 A.D., ed. G. E. Briscoe Eyre and C. R. Rivington, 3 vols. (1913; repr. New York, 1950).
ATTERBURY, FRANCIS (John Clarke), *The Virgin Seducer* in *Miscellanea. In Two Volumes. Atterburyana. Being Miscellanies, by the Late Bishop of Rochester* (1727).
AUSTEN, JANE, *Northanger Abbey* (1817), ed. Anne Ehrenpreis (Harmondsworth, 1972; repr. 1975).

BACKSCHEIDER, PAULA R., *Daniel Defoe: His Life* (Baltimore, 1989).

BAKHTIN, MIKHAIL, 'Epic and Novel: Towards a Methodology for the Study of the Novel', in Michael Holquist (ed.), *The Dialogic Imagination: Four Essays*, trans. Caryl Emerson and Michael Holquist (Austin, Tex., 1981).

BALLASTER, ROS, *Seductive Forms: Women's Amatory Fiction from 1684 to 1720* (Oxford, 1992).

BARBER, MARY, *Poems on Several Occasions* (1734).

BARKER-BENFIELD, G. J., *The Culture of Sensibility: Sex and Society in Eighteenth-Century Britain* (Chicago, 1992).

BARNES, JULIAN, *Flaubert's Parrot* (1984; repr. 1985).

BARRELL, JOHN, and HARRIET GUEST, 'On the Use of Contradiction: Economics and Morality in the Eighteenth-Century Long Poem', in Felicity Nussbaum and Laura Brown (eds.), *The New Eighteenth Century: Theory, Politics, English Literature* (New York, 1987; repr. 1991).

BATTESTIN, MARTIN and RUTHE, *Henry Fielding: A Life* (1989).

BEHN, APHRA, *The Fair Jilt* (1688).

—— *Oroonoko* (1688).

—— *Oroonoko, The Rover and Other Works*, ed. Janet Todd (Harmondsworth, 1992).

—— *The Rover* (1677), ed. Frederick M. Link (1967).

—— *The Rover* (1677), ed. Janet Todd (Harmondsworth, 1992).

BELSEY, CATHERINE, *Critical Practice* (1980).

BENDER, JOHN, *Imagining the Penitentiary: Fiction and the Architecture of Mind in Eighteenth-Century England* (Chicago, 1987).

BERTLESEN, LANCE, *The Nonsense Club: Literature and Popular Culture, 1749–1764* (Oxford, 1986).

BICKERSTAFFE, ISAAC, *The Maid of the Mill: A comic opera* (Dublin, 1765).

BLACKMORE, SIR RICHARD, *King Arthur: An Heroick Poem* (1697).

—— *Prince Arthur: An Heroick Poem* (1695; repr. Menston: Scolar Press, 1971).

BLOOM, EDWARD, A. and LILLIAN D. BLOOM, *Joseph Addison's Sociable Animal* (Providence, RI, 1971).

BLOUCH, CHRISTINE, 'Eliza Haywood and the Romance of Obscurity', *Studies in English Literature*, 31 (1991), 535–53.

BOILEAU-DESPRÉAUX, N., *Satires*, ed. Albert Cahen (Paris, 1932).

BOND, RICHMOND P., 'The Pirate and the *Tatler*', *Library*, 5th ser., 28/4 (1963), 257–74.

BOWYER, JOHN WILSON, *The Celebrated Mrs. Centlivre* (Durham, NC, 1952).

BREWSTER, DOROTHY, *Aaron Hill: Poet, Dramatist, Projector* (New York, 1913).

BROICH, ULRICH, *The Eighteenth-Century Mock-Heroic Poem*, trans. David Henry Wilson (Cambridge, 1990; original German version 1968).

BROME, RICHARD, *The Novella: A comedie* (1632; repr. 1653).

BROOKE, HENRY, *Gustavus Vasa, the Deliverer of His Country* (1739).

BROWER, REUBEN A., *Alexander Pope: The Poetry of Allusion* (Oxford, 1959).

BROWN, LAURA, *Alexander Pope* (Oxford, 1985).

BROWNELL, MORRIS, *Alexander Pope's Villa: Views of Pope's Villa, Grotto and Garden. A Microcosm of English Landscape* (1980).

BUCKINGHAM, GEORGE VILLIERS, DUKE OF, et al., *The Rehearsal* (1672), ed. D. E. L. Crane (Durham, 1976).

BURNEY, FRANCES, *Camilla; or, A Picture of Youth*, 5 vols. (1796).

BURNIM, KALMAN A., *David Garrick: Director* (Pittsburgh, 1961).

BYWATERS, DAVID, *Dryden in Revolutionary England* (Berkeley and Los Angeles, 1991).

CALDWELL, TANYA, 'Towards a Carmen Perpetuum: Dryden's *Georgics* and *Aeneis*', Ph.D. thesis (Toronto, 1996).

CARPENTER, ANDREW, Review of Irvin Ehrenpreis, *Swift: The Man, his Works, and the Age*, *Irish University Review*, 14/2 (1984), 277–80.

CARRÉ, JACQUES, 'Burlington's Literary Patronage', *British Journal for Eighteenth-Century Studies*, 5 (1982), 21–33.

The Cases of the Appellants and Respondents in the Cause of Literary Property Before the House of Lords (1774).

CENTLIVRE, SUSANNA, *A Bold Stroke for a Wife* (1718), ed. Thalia Stathas (1969).

—— *The Artifice: A comedy* (1723).

—— *The Basset-Table: A comedy*, 2nd edn. (1706).

—— *The Beau's Duel; or, A Soldier for the Ladies* (1702).

—— *The Busie Body* (1709), 5th edn. (1723).

—— *The Cruel Gift: A Tragedy* (1717).

—— *The Dramatic Works of the Celebrated Mrs. Centlivre*, 3 vols. (1761; repr. 1872).

—— *The Gamester: A comedy* (1705).

—— *Love's Contrivance; or, Le Médecin Malgré Lui* (1703).

—— *The Man's Bewitch'd; or, The Devil to Do About Her* ([1710?]).

—— *The Platonick Lady: A comedy* (1707).

—— *The Wonder! A Woman Keeps a Secret: A comedy* (1714).

CHAMBERS, E. K., *The Elizabethan Stage*, 4 vols. (Oxford, 1923).

CIBBER, COLLEY, *Caesar in Egypt: A tragedy* (1725).

—— *Love's Last Shift; or, The Fool in Fashion* (1696).

—— *The Non-Juror: A comedy* (1718).

—— *The Provoked Husband; or, A Journey to London* (1728).

CLAPP, SARAH L. C., 'The Beginnings of Subscription Publication in the Seventeenth Century', *Modern Philology*, 29 (1931–2), 199–224.

—— 'Subscription Publishers Prior to Jacob Tonson', *Transactions of the Bibliographical Society: Library*, 4th ser., 13 (1932–3), 158–83.

CLARK, J. C. D., *English Society, 1660–1832: Ideology, Social Structure and Political Practice during the Ancien Regime* (Cambridge, 1985).

CLEARY, THOMAS R., *Henry Fielding: Political Writer* (Waterloo, Ont., 1984).

COLLEY, LINDA, *Britons: Forging the Nation, 1707–1837* (1992).

COLOMB, GREGORY C., *Designs on Truth: The Poetics of the Mock-Epic* (University Park, Pa., 1992).

CONGREVE, WILLIAM, *The Double Dealer: A comedy* (1694).

—— *Incognita; or, Love and duty reconcil'd* (1692).

—— *Letters and Documents*, ed. John C. Hodges (1964).

—— *The Mourning Bride: A tragedy* (1697).

—— *The Way of the World: A comedy* (1700).

COOK, HAROLD J., 'Living in Revolutionary Times: Medical Change under William and Mary', in Bruce T. Moran (ed.), *Patronage and Institutions: Science, Technology and Medicine at the European Court, 1500–1750* (Rochester, NY, 1991).

COPLEY, STEPHEN, 'Commerce, Conversation and Politeness in the Early Eighteenth-Century Periodical', *British Journal for Eighteenth-Century Studies*, 18/1 (Spring 1995), 63–77.

CORMAN, BRIAN, *Genre and Generic Change in English Comedy, 1660–1710* (Toronto, 1993).

COTTON, CHARLES, *Scarronides; or, Virgile Travestie: A Mock-Poem on the First and Fourth Books of Virgil's* Aenaeis *in English Burlesque* (1670; 10th edn. 1715).

CROSS, WILBUR L., *The History of Henry Fielding*, 3 vols. (New Haven, 1918).

CROWNE, JOHN, *Daeneids; or, The Noble Labours of the Great Dean of Notre-Dame in Paris, for the Erecting in his Quire a Throne for his Glory, and the Eclipsing of Pride of an Imperious, Usurping Chanter. An Heroique POEM in Four Canto's, Containing a True History, and shews the Folly, Foppery, Luxury, Laziness, Pride, Ambition and Contention of the Romish Clergy* (1692).

—— *The History of the Famous and Passionate Love, between a Fair Noble Parisian Lady and a Beautiful Young Singing-Man; a Chanter in the Quire of Notre Dame in Paris and a Singer in Opera's Being in Imitation of Virgil's Dido and Aeneas* (1692).

CUNNINGHAM, ROBERT NEWTON, *Peter Anthony Motteux, 1663–1718: A Biographical and Critical Study* (Oxford, 1933).

DANCHIN, PIERRE (ed.), *The Prologues and Epilogues of the Eighteenth Century*, 2 parts, 4 vols. (Nancy, 1990–3).

DEFOE, DANIEL, *An Essay on the Regulation of the Press* (1704), ed. J. R. Moore (Oxford, 1948).

—— *Augusta Triumphans* (1728).

—— *The Complete English Tradesman*, 2 vols., 2nd edn. (1727).

—— *The Fears of the Pretender Turn'd into the Fears of Debauchery with a Hint to Richard Steele, Esq.* (1715).

—— *The Life and Strange Surprizing Adventures of Robinson Crusoe, of York, Mariner* (1719), ed. Angus Ross (Harmondsworth, 1965).

—— *The Review* (1712).

—— *Roxana: The Fortunate Mistress* (1724), ed. and intro. Jane Jack (1964; repr. 1976).

—— *Second Thoughts are Best; or, A Further Improvement of a Late Scheme to Prevent Street Robberies* (1729).

DEKKER, THOMAS, *Satiromastix* (1602), ed. Fredson Bowers (Cambridge, 1953).

DENNIS, JOHN, *The Advancement and Reformation of Modern Poetry* (1701).

—— *Appius and Virginia* (1705).

—— *The Characters and Conduct of Sir John Edgar, Call'd by Himself Sole Monarch of the Stage in Drury-Lane; and his Three Deputy-Governors. In Two Letters to Sir John Edgar* (1720).

—— *Critical Works*, ed. E. N. Hooker, 2 vols. (Baltimore, 1939).

—— *The Grounds of Criticism in Poetry* (1704).

—— *The Impartial Critick; or, Some observations upon a late book, entituled, A Short View of Tragedy* (1693).

—— *The Invader of his Country; or, The Fatal Resentment: A tragedy* (1720).

—— *Reflections on An Essay Upon Criticism* (1711).

—— *Remarks on* Prince Arthur *(1696).*

—— *Remarks upon* Cato, *A Tragedy* (1713).

—— *The Stage Defended, from Scripture, Reason, Experience, and the Common Sense of Mankind for Two Thousand Years. Occasion'd by Mr. Law's Late Pamphlet Against Stage-Entertainment* (1726).

—— *The Usefulness of the Stage, etc.* (1698).

DIAPER, WILLIAM, *Dryades; or, The Nymphs prophecy: A poem* (1713).

—— *Nereides; or, Sea-Eclogues* (1712).

DONALDSON, ALEXANDER, *Some Thoughts on the State of Literary Property humbly submitted to the Consideration of the Public* (1764).

DONNE, JOHN, *Letters to Severall Persons of Honour: Written by John Donne, Sometime Deane of St. Paul's London*, 2 vols. (1654).

DONOGHUE, DENIS, Review of Irvin Ehrenpreis, *Swift: The Man, his Works, and the Age*, *Times Literary Supplement*, 4219 (1984), 143–4.

DOODY, MARGARET ANNE, 'Swift among the Women', *Yearbook of English Studies*, 18 (1988), 68–92.

—— 'Swift and Romance', in Christopher Fox and Brenda Tooley (eds.), *Walking Naboth's Vineyard: New Studies of Swift* (Notre Dame, Ind., 1995).

DOWNES, JOHN, *Roscius Anglicanus; or, An Historical Review of the Stage* (1708), ed. Judith Milhous and Robert D. Hume (1987).

DOWNES, KERRY, *Sir John Vanbrugh: A Biography* (1987).

DRYDEN, JOHN, *A Defence of an Essay of Dramatique Poesie* (1668).

—— *All for Love; or, The World well lost* (1678).

—— *Amboyna: A tragedy* (1673).

—— *Amphitryon; or, The Two Sosia's* (1690).

—— *An Evening's Love* (1671).

—— *A Parallel Betwixt Painting and Poetry* (1695).

—— *The Assignation; or, Love in a Nunnery* (1673).

—— *Cleomenes, the Spartan Heroe* (1692).

—— *Discourse concerning Satire* (1692).

—— *Don Sebastian, King of Portugal: A tragedy* (1690).

—— *Dramatic Works*, ed. George Saintsbury, 8 vols. (Edinburgh, 1882).

—— *Eleonora: A panegyrical poem. Dedicated to the memory of the late Countess of Abingdon* (1692).

—— *Of Dramatic Poesy and Other Critical Essays*, ed. George Watson, 2 vols. (1962; repr. 1968).

—— *Marriage à la Mode: A comedy* (1673).

—— *The Poems and Fables*, ed. James Kinsley (Oxford, 1958; repr. 1962).

—— *Preface of the Translator* [of Du Fresnoy's *De Arte Graphica*], containing a Parallel of Poetry and Painting (1695).

—— *Sir Martin Mar-all; or, The Feign'd Innocence: A comedy* (1668).

—— *Works*, ed. H. T. Swedenberg, Jr., *et al.*, 20 vols. (Berkeley and Los Angeles, 1956–). (The California Dryden.)

—— (trans.) *The Works of Virgil* (1697).

—— and SIR WILLIAM DAVENANT, *The Tempest; or, The enchanted island* (1670).

DUFFET, THOMAS, *Psyche Debauch'd* (1678).

DUFFY, MAUREEN, *The Passionate Shepherdess: Aphra Behn, 1640–1689* (1977).

DUNTON, JOHN, *The Athenian Oracle: Being an Entire Collection of all the Valuable Questions and Answers in the Old Athenian Mercuries*, 3 vols. (1703–4).

—— *A New Voyage Round the World; or, A Pocket Library* (1691).

—— *The Life and Errors of John Dunton, Citizen of London*, 2 vols. (1818).

——*The Life and Errors of John Dunton, late Citizen of London; written by Himself in Solitude* (1705).

D'URFEY, THOMAS, *The English Stage Italianiz'd in a New Dramatic Entertainment, called Dido and Aeneas; or, Harlequin, a Butler, a Pimp, a Minister of State, Generalissimo, and Lord High Admiral; dead and alive again, and at last crown'd King of* Carthage *by* Dido (1727)

EAGLETON, TERRY, *The Function of Criticism: From the* Spectator *to Post-Structuralism* (1984).

EARLE, PETER, *The Making of the English Middle Class: Business, Society and Family Life in London, 1660–1730* (1989).

EHRENPREIS, IRVIN, *Swift: The Man, His Works, and the Age*, 3 vols. (1962–83).

EISENSTEIN, ELIZABETH L., *The Printing Revolution in Early Modern Europe* (Cambridge, 1983; repr. 1990).

ELIAS, A. C., Jr., 'Laetitia Pilkington on Swift: How Reliable is She?', in Christopher Fox and Brenda Tooley (eds.), *Walking Naboth's Vineyard: New Studies of Swift* (Notre Dame, Ind., 1995).

ELIOT, GEORGE, *Selected Essays, Poems and Other Writings*, ed. A. S. Byatt and Nicholas Warren (Harmondsworth, 1990).

ELWOOD, JOHN R., 'Henry Fielding and Eliza Haywood: A Twenty Year War', *Albion*, 5 (Fall 1973), 184–92.

—— 'The Stage Career of Eliza Haywood', *Theatre Survey*, 5/2 (Nov. 1964), 107–16.

Enquiry into the Nature and Origin of Literary Property (1762).

ERSKINE-HILL, HOWARD H. and ALEXANDER LINDSAY (eds.), *William Congreve: The Critical Heritage* (1989).

ETHEREGE, SIR GEORGE, *The Man of Mode; or, Sir Fopling Flutter: A comedy* (1676).

FABRICANT, CAROLE, Review of Irvin Ehrenpreis, *Swift: The Man, his Works, and the Age*, *Scriblerian*, 17/2 (1985), 167–9.

FALLER, LINCOLN B., *Crime and Defoe: A New Kind of Writing* (Cambridge, 1993).

FARLEY-HILLS, DAVID, *Rochester's Poetry* (Totowa, NJ, 1978).

FARQUHAR, GEORGE, *The Constant Couple; or, A trip to the Jubilee* (1700).

—— *The Recruiting Officer: A comedy* (1706).

FEATHER, JOHN, 'The Book Trade in Politics: The Making of the Copyright Act of 1710', *Publishing History*, 8 (1980), 19–44.

—— 'The Commerce of Letters: The Study of the Eighteenth-Century Book Trade', *Eighteenth-Century Studies*, 17 (1983–4), 405–24.

FIELDING, HENRY, *The Author's Farce* (1730), ed. C. B. Woods (repr. Lincoln, Nebr., 1966).

—— *The Covent-Garden Tragedy* (1732).

—— *Eurydice Hiss'd; or, A word to the wise* (1737).

—— *The Grub-street Opera* (1731), ed. Edgar V. Roberts (1969).

—— *The Historical Register for the Year 1736* (1737), ed. William W. Appleton (Lincoln, Nebr., 1967).

—— *The History of the Adventures of Joseph Andrews and of his Friend Mr. Abraham Adams* (1742), ed. Douglas Brooks (1970).

—— *'The Jacobite's Journal' and Related Writings*, ed. W. B. Coley (Middletown, Conn., 1975).

—— *The Letter Writers; or, A new way to keep a wife at home* (1731).

—— *The Lottery: A farce* (1732).

—— *Miscellanies*, I, ed. Henry Knight Miller (Oxford, 1972).

—— *The Miser* (1733).

—— *The Modern Husband: A comedy* (Dublin, 1732).

—— *Pasquin: A dramatick satire on the times* (1736).

—— *Tom Thumb: A tragedy* (1730).

—— *The Tragedy of Tragedies* (1730), ed. James T. Hillhouse (New Haven, 1918).

—— *Tumbledown Dick; or, Phaeton in the Suds* (1736).

—— *The Wedding Day: A tragedy* (1730).

—— and James Ralph, *The Champion: Containing a Series of Papers Humorous, Moral, Political, and Critical*, 2 vols. (1741).

FLYNN, SHANE, 'The Scriblerus Club and the Interaction of Politics and Literature, 1710–1714', Ph.D. thesis (Aberystwyth, 1994).

FOUCAULT, MICHEL, 'What is an Author?' (1969), in *Language, Counter-Memory, Practice (ed. and introd. Donald F. Bouchard)*, trans. Donald F. Bouchard and Sherry Simon (Oxford, 1977).

FOWLER, ALASDAIR, *The Country House Poem* (Edinburgh, 1994).

FOXON, DAVID, *Pope and the Eighteenth-Century Book Trade*, rev. and ed. James McLaverty (Oxford, 1991).

FUCHS, JACOB, *Reading Pope's Imitations of Horace* (Lewisburg, Pa., 1989).

FURBANK, P. N., and W. R. OWENS, *The Canonisation of Daniel Defoe* (New Haven, 1988).

GALLAGHER, CATHERINE, 'Who was that Masked Woman? The Prostitute and the Playwright in the Works of Aphra Behn', in id., *Nobody's Story: The Vanishing Acts of Women Writers in the Marketplace, 1670–1820* (Oxford, 1994).

GARTH, SIR SAMUEL, *A Short Account of the Proceedings of the College of*

Physicians, London, in Relation to the Sick Poor of the said City and Suburbs thereof (1697).

—— *The Dispensary* (1699; 9th edn. 1725), ed. Jo Allen Bradham (Delmar, NY, 1975).

GAY, JOHN, *The Beggar's Opera* (1728).

—— (?)*Complete Key to the last New Farce* The What D'Ye Call It (1715).

—— *The Distress'd Wife: A comedy* (1743).

—— *Dramatic Works*, ed. John Fuller, 2 vols. (Oxford, 1983).

—— *Fables: In two parts* (1750).

—— *Letters*, ed. C. F. Burgess (Oxford, 1966).

—— *Poetry and Prose*, ed. Vinton A. Dearing with Charles E. Beckwith, 2 vols. (Oxford, 1974).

—— *Polly: An opera. Being the second part of the Beggar's Opera* (1729).

—— *The Present State of Wit, in a Letter to a Friend in the Country* (1711).

—— *The Shepherd's Week: In six pastorals* (1714).

—— *The What D'Ye Call It: A tragi-comi-pastoral farce* (1715).

—— *The Wife of Bath: A comedy*, 2nd edn. (1730).

—— and GEORG FRIEDRICH HANDEL, *Acis and Galatea: An English pastoral opera* (1718).

—— ALEXANDER POPE, and JOHN ARBUTHNOT, *Three Hours after Marriage: A comedy* (1717).

GERRARD, CHRISTINE, *The Patriot Opposition to Walpole: Politics, Poetry, and Natural Myth, 1725–1742* (Oxford, 1994).

GOLDGAR, BERTRAND A., *Walpole and the Wits: The Relation of Politics to Literature, 1722–1742* (Lincoln, Neb., 1976).

GOREAU, ANGELINE, *Reconstructing Aphra: A Social Biography of Aphra Behn* (Oxford, 1980).

GRAHAM, WALTER, *English Literary Periodicals* (New York, 1930).

GRAVES, ROBERT, *Goodbye to All That* (1929; repr. Harmondsworth, 1977).

GREENBLATT, STEPHEN, *Shakespearean Negotiations: The Circulation of Social Energy in Renaissance England* (Oxford, 1988).

GREG, W. W., *Some Aspects and Problems of London Publishing between 1550 and 1650* (Oxford, 1956).

GRUNDY, ISOBEL M., 'New Verse by Henry Fielding', *PMLA*, 87 (Mar. 1972), 213–45.

GUBAR, SUSAN, 'The Female Monster in Augustan Satire', *Signs*, 3 (1977), 380–94.

HABERMAS, JÜRGEN, *The Structural Transformation of the Public Sphere: An Inquiry into a Category of Bourgeois Society* (Darmstadt, 1962), trans. Thomas Burger with Frederick Lawrence (Cambridge, Mass., 1989; repr. 1993).

HALL, STUART, 'Notes on Deconstructing "the Popular"', in Raphael Samuel (ed.), *People's History and Socialist Theory* (1981).

HAMMOND, BREAN S., ' "Guard the sure barrier": Pope and the Partitioning of Culture', in David Fairer (ed.), *Pope: New Contexts* (New York, 1990).

—— *Pope* (1986).

—— *Pope and Bolingbroke: A Study of Friendship and Influence* (Columbia, Mo., 1984).

HARRIS, JOHN, *The Palladian Revival: Lord Burlington, his Villa and Garden at Chiswick* (New Haven, 1995).

HAWKINS, HARRIET, *Classics and Trash: Traditions and Taboos in High Literature and Modern Popular Genres* (1990).

HAYWOOD, ELIZA, *The Adventures of Eovaai, Princess of Ijaveo* (1736).

—— *The Agreeable Caledonian* (1728), ed. Josephine Grieder (New York, 1973).

—— *Idalia; or, The Unfortunate Mistress: A Novel* (1723).

—— *Lasselia; or, The Self-Abandon'd: A Novel* (1724).

—— *Love in Excess; or, The Fatal Enquiry: A Novel*, 3 vols. (1719–20).

—— *Memoirs of a Certain Island Adjacent to the Kingdom of Utopia* (1725), ed. Josephine Grieder (New York, 1972).

—— *Philidore and Placentia; or, L'Amour trop Delicat* (1727); repr. in William H. McBurney (ed.), *Four before Richardson: Selected English Novels, 1720–1727* (Lincoln, Nebr., 1963).

—— *Secret History of the Present Intrigues of the Court of Caramania* (1727).

—— *Works*, 4 vols. (1724).

—— and WILLIAM HATCHETT, *Opera of Operas; or, Tom Thumb the Great* (1733).

HEINEMANN, MARCIA, 'Eliza Haywood's Career in the Theatre', *Notes & Queries* (Jan. 1973), 9–13.

HELGERSON, RICHARD, *Self-Crowned Laureates: Spenser, Jonson, Milton, and the Literary System* (Berkeley, 1983).

HEPBURN, JAMES, *The Author's Empty Purse and the Rise of the Literary Agent* (1968).

HEWISON, P. E., 'Rochester, the Imitation and *An Allusion to Horace*', *Seventeenth-Century*, 2/1 (1987), 73–94.

HIBBARD, GEORGE, 'The Country House Poem of the Seventeenth Century', *Journal of the Warburg and Courtauld Institute*, 19 (1956), 159–74.

HILL, AARON, 'The Creation: A Pindaric Illustration of a Poem, originally written by Moses, on that Subject. With a Preface to Mr. Pope, concerning the Sublimity of the Ancient Hebrew Poetry' (1720).

—— *Dramatic Works*, 2 vols. (1760).

—— *Poetical Works*, in Robert Anderson (ed.), *Complete Edition of the Poets of Great Britain*, 11 vols., viii (1793).

—— *The Roman Revenge: A Tragedy* (1753).

—— *Works*, 4 vols. (1754).

—— and WILLIAM POPPLE, *The Plain Dealer: Being Selected Essays on Several Curious Subjects Relating to Friendship, Love, and Gallantry, Marriage, Morality, Mercantile Affairs, Painting, History, Poetry, and Other Branches of Polite Literature*, 2 vols. (1730).

HONAN, PARK, *Jane Austen: Her Life* (1987).

HORACE (Quintus Horatius Flaccus), *The Satires of Horace and Persius*, trans. Niall Rudd (Harmondsworth, 1973; repr. 1976).

—— *Satires, Epistles, Ars Poetica* (1929).

HOWARD, EDWARD, *The Women's Conquest: A tragedy* (1671).

HUME, ROBERT D., *Henry Fielding and the London Theatre, 1728–1737* (Oxford, 1988).

—— 'Henry Fielding and the Politics at the Little Haymarket, 1728–1737', in John M. Wallace (ed.), *The Golden and the Brazen World* (Berkeley, 1985).

—— 'The London Theatre from *The Beggar's Opera* to the Licensing Act', in id., *The Rakish Stage: Studies in English Drama, 1660–1800* (Carbondale, Ill., 1983).

HUNTER, J. Paul, *Before Novels: The Cultural Contexts of Eighteenth-Century Fiction* (1990).

—— '*Gulliver's Travels* and the Novel', in Frederik N. Smith (ed.), *The Genres of* Gulliver's Travels (Newark, NJ, 1990).

HUTCHESON, FRANCIS, *Inquiry into the Original of our Ideas of Beauty and Virtue* (1725).

INCHBALD, ELIZABETH, *The British Theatre; or, A Collection of Plays, which are acted at the Theatres Royal, Drury Lane, Covent Garden, and Haymarket*, 25 vols. (1808).

—— *The Mogul Tale; or, The Descent of the Balloon: A farce* (1788).

INGLESFIELD, ROBERT, 'James Thomson, Aaron Hill and the Poetic "Sublime"', *British Journal for Eighteenth-Century Studies*, 13/2 (Autumn 1990), 215–22.

JOHNSON, SAMUEL, *The History of Rasselas, Prince of Abissinia* (1759), ed. D. J. Enright (Harmondsworth, 1976).

—— *Letters*, ed. Bruce Redford, 5 vols. (Oxford, 1992).

—— *Life of Addison*, in *The Lives of the English Poets*, 3 vols. (1779–81).

—— *London: A poem, in imitation of the third Satire of Juvenal* (1738).

—— *The Oxford Authors: Samuel Johnson*, ed. Donald Greene (Oxford, 1984).

JONES, VIVIEN (ed.), *Women in the Eighteenth Century: Constructions of Femininity* (1990).

JONSON, BEN, *Bartholomew Fayre: A comedie* (1614).

—— *Epicoene; or, The Silent Woman* (1620).

—— *The New Inn* (1631), ed. Michael Hattaway (Manchester, 1984).

—— *Poems*, ed. Ian Donaldson (Oxford, 1975).

—— *Poetaster; or, The Arraignment* (1602).

—— *Volpone; or, The Foxe* (1607).

—— *Works*, ed. C. H. Herford and Percy and Evelyn Simpson, 11 vols. (Oxford, 1935–52).

Journals of the House of Commons, 16 (1803), 16 Nov. 1708–9 Oct. 1711.

KANT, IMMANUEL, *Critique of Judgement* (1790), trans. J. C. Meredith (Oxford, 1952).

KENNY, VIRGINIA, *The Country House Ethos in English Literature, 1688–1750: Themes of National Expansion and Personal Retreat* (Brighton, 1984).

KENT, ROBIN, *Agony: Problem Pages throughout the Ages* (1979; repr. 1987).

KERNAN, ALVIN, *Samuel Johnson and the Impact of Print* (Princeton, 1987; repr. 1989).

KETCHAM, MICHAEL G., *Transparent Designs: Reading, Performance and Form in the* Spectator *Papers* (Athens, Ga., 1985).

KILLIGREW, THOMAS, *Comedies and Tragedies* (1664).

KLEIN, LAWRENCE E., 'Liberty, Manners, and Politeness in Early Eighteenth-Century England', *Historical Journal*, 32/3 (1989), 583–605.

—— 'The Third Earl of Shaftesbury and the Progress of Politeness', *Eighteenth-Century Studies*, 18 (1984/5), 186–214.

KOON, HELENE, *Colley Cibber: A Biography* (Lexington, Ky., 1986).

KRAMNICK, ISAAC, *Bolingbroke and his Circle: The Politics of Nostalgia in the Age of Walpole* (Cambridge, Mass., 1968).

KUPERSMITH, WILLIAM, *Roman Satirists in Seventeenth-Century England* (Lincoln, Nebr., 1985).

LADDIE, HUGH, PETER PRESCOTT, and MARY VITORIA, *The Modern Law of Copyright* (1980).

LANGBAINE, GERARD, *Momus Triumphans; or, The Plagiaries of the English Stage* (1687), ed. David Stuart Rodes (Los Angeles, 1971).

LANGFORD, PAUL, *A Polite and Commercial People: England, 1727–1783* (Oxford, 1992).

LAW, WILLIAM, *The Absolute Unlawfulness of the Stage-Entertainment Fully Demonstrated* (1726).

—— *A Serious Call to a Devout and Holy Life* (1729).

LEE, NATHANIEL, *Lucius Junius Brutus, Father of his country: A tragedy* (1681).

LENNOX, CHARLOTTE, *The Female Quixote; or, The Adventures of Arabella* (1752), ed. Margaret Dalziel with Duncan Isles, intro. Margaret Anne Doody (Oxford, 1989).

LEVINE, JOSEPH M., *The Battle of the Books: History and Literature in the Augustan Age* (Ithaca, NY, 1991; repr. 1994).

LEWIS, PETER, *Fielding's Burlesque Drama: Its Place in the Tradition* (Edinburgh, 1987).

LILLO, GEORGE, *The London Merchant; or, The History of George Barnwell* (1731).

LINDEY, ALEXANDER, *Plagiarism and Originality* (New York, 1952).

LIPKING, LARRY, Review of Maynard Mack, *Alexander Pope: A Life*, *American Scholar*, 56/3 (1987), 435–9.

LOCK, F. P., *Susanna Centlivre*, Twayne English Authors, 254 (Boston, 1979).

LOCKE, JOHN, *Two Treatises of Government* (1690).

LODGE, DAVID, 'After Bakhtin', in id., *After Bakhtin: Essays on Fiction and Criticism* (London, 1990).

LOEWENSTEIN, JOSEPH, 'For a History of Literary Property', *English Literary Renaissance*, 18/3 (Autumn 1988), 389–412.

—— 'The Script in the Marketplace', *Representations*, 12 (Fall 1985), 101–14.

The London Stage, 1660–1800: A Calendar of Plays, Entertainments and Afterpieces etc., ed. William Van Lennep (part 1), Emmett L. Avery (part 2) (Carbondale, Ill., 1960–).

LUND, ROGER D., 'From Oblivion to Dulness: Pope and the Poetics of Appropriation', *British Journal for Eighteenth-Century Studies*, 14 (1991), 171–90.

LYNCH, KATHLEEN M., *Jacob Tonson: Kit-Cat Publisher* (Knoxville, Tenn., 1971).

McBURNEY, WILLIAM H. (ed.), *Four Before Richardson: Selected English Novels, 1720–1727* (Lincoln, Nebr., 1963).

McCREA, BRIAN, 'The Canon and the Eighteenth Century: *A Modest Proposal* and *A Tale of Two Tubs*', *Modern Language Studies*, 18/1 (Winter 1988), 58–73.

—— *Henry Fielding and the Politics of Mid-Eighteenth-Century England* (Athens, Ga., 1981).

MACE, NANCY A., 'Fielding, Theobald, and *The Tragedy of Tragedies*', *Philological Quarterly*, 66 (1987), 457–72.

MACK, MAYNARD, *Alexander Pope: A Life* (New Haven, 1985).

—— *The Garden and the City: Retirement and Politics in the Later Poetry of Pope, 1731–1743* (Toronto, 1969).

—— *The Last and Greatest Art: Some Unpublished Poetical Manuscripts of Alexander Pope* (Newark, NJ, and London, 1984).

MCKEON, MICHAEL, *The Origins of the English Novel, 1600–1740* (1987; repr. 1988).

MCLAVERTY, JAMES, Review of Maynard Mack, *Alexander Pope: A Life*, *Notes & Queries*, 34/1 (1987), 89.

MANDEVILLE, BERNARD, and MARY DELARIVIER MANLEY (eds.), *The Female Spectator*, 4 vols. (1745).

MANLEY, MARY DELARIVIER, *The Adventures of Rivella; or, The History of the Author of the Atalantis* (1714).

—— *Secret Memoirs . . . of several persons of quality . . . from the New Atalantis* (1709).

MARKLEY, ROBERT, 'Beyond Consensus: *The Rape of the Lock* and the Fate of Reading Eighteenth-Century Literature', *New Orleans Review*, 15/4 (Winter 1988), 68–77.

MARLOWE, CHRISTOPHER, *The Tragedy of Dido, Queen of Carthage*, in *The Complete Plays*, ed. J. B. Steane (Harmondsworth, 1969).

MARVELL, ANDREW, *The Rehearsal Transpros'd and The Rehearsal Transpros'd, the Second Part (1672)*, ed. D. I. B. Smith (Oxford, 1971).

—— *Works*, ed. Frank Kermode and Keith Walker (Oxford, 1990).

MEDOFF, JESLYN, 'The Daughters of Behn and the Problems of Reputation', in Isobel Grundy and Susan Wiseman (eds.), *Women, Writing, History, 1640–1740* (1992).

MILHOUS, JUDITH, and ROBERT D. HUME, 'Receipts at Drury Lane: Richard Cross's Diary for 1746–1747', *Theatre Notebook*, 49/1 (1995), 12–26; 49/2 (1995), 69–90.

MILTON, JOHN, *Areopagitica; a speech of Mr. John Milton for the liberty of unlicens'd printing* (1643).

—— *Complete Poems*, intro. Gordon Campbell (1980).

—— *The Complete Prose Works*, 8 vols. (New Haven and London, 1953–82).

MOTTEUX, PETER, *The Gentleman's Journal; or, The Monthly Miscellany. By Way of Letter to a Gentleman in the Country*, 2 vols. (1692).

—— and JOHN ECCLES, *Rape of Europa by Jupiter* [1694] and *Acis and Galatea* [1701], ed. Lucyle Hook, Augustan Reprint Society, 208 (Los Angeles, 1981).

MUMBY, F. A., and IAN NORRIE, *Publishing and Bookselling*, part 1: *From the Earliest Times to 1870* (1930; rev. edn. 1974).

MURPHY, ARTHUR, *Alzuma: A tragedy* (1773).

—— *The Apprentice: A farce* (1756).

MURPHY, ARTHUR, *The Grecian Daughter: A tragedy* (1772).

—— *Zenobia: A tragedy* (1768).

MYERSON, GEORGE, *The Argumentative Imagination: Wordsworth, Dryden, Religious Dialogues* (Manchester, 1992).

NICHOL, DON, 'Warburton (not!) on Copyright: Clearing up the Misattribution of *An Enquiry into the Nature and Origin of Literary Property* (1762)', *British Journal for Eighteenth-Century Studies* (forthcoming).

—— *Pope's Literary Legacy: The Book-Trade Correspondence of William Warburton and John Knapton with Other Letters and Related Documents (1744–1780)* (Oxford, 1990).

NICHOLS, JOHN, *Literary Anecdotes of the Eighteenth Century*, 9 vols. (1812–15).

NICHOLSON, COLIN, *Writing and the Rise of Finance: Capital Satires of the Early Eighteenth Century* (Cambridge, 1994).

The Nine Muses; or, Poems written by Nine Severall Ladies Upon the Death of The Late Famous John Dryden, Esq. (1700).

NOKES, DAVID, *John Gay: A Profession of Friendship* (Oxford, 1995).

—— *Jonathan Swift, A Hypocrite Revers'd: A Critical Biography* (Oxford, 1985).

ODEN, RICHARD L. (ed.), *Dryden and Shadwell. The Literary Controversy* (Delmar, NY, 1977).

OLDMIXON, JOHN (ed.), *The Muses Mercury; or, The Monthly Miscellany* (1707).

OTWAY, THOMAS, *Don Carlos, Prince of Spain: A Tragedy* (1676).

—— *The Orphan; or, The Unhappy Marriage: A tragedy* (1680).

—— *Works*, ed. J. C. Ghosh, 2 vols. (Oxford, 1932).

PARKS, STEPHEN, *John Dunton and the English Book Trade: A Study of his Career with a Checklist of his Publications* (New York, 1976).

PARRY, GRAHAM, *The Golden Age Restor'd: The Culture of the Stuart Court, 1603–1642* (Manchester, 1981).

PATEY, DOUGLAS LANE, 'The Eighteenth Century Invents the Canon', *Modern Language Studies*, 18/1 (Winter 1988), 17–37.

PATTERSON, ANNABEL, *Censorship and Interpretation: The Conditions of Writing and Reading in Early Modern England* (Madison, Wis., 1984).

PEBWORTH, TED-LARRY, 'John Donne, Coterie Poetry, and the Text as Performance', *Studies in English Literature*, 29 (1989), 61–75.

PEDICORD, H. W., *The Theatrical Public in the Time of Garrick* (New York, 1954).

PERRAULT, CHARLES, *Parallèle des anciens et des modernes* (Paris, 1688–92).

PHIDDIAN, ROBERT, *Swift's Parody* (Cambridge, 1995).

PHILIPS, AMBROSE, *The Distrest Mother: A tragedy* (1712).
—— *Pastorals, Epistles, Odes, and other original poems* (1748).
PILKINGTON, LETITIA, *Memoirs of Mrs. Letitia Pilkington, 1712–1750* (1748–54), intro. Iris Barry (1928).
PITTOCK, MURRAY G. H., *Poetry and Jacobite Politics in Eighteenth-Century Britain and Ireland* (Cambridge, 1994).
PIX, MARY, *The Deceiver Deceived: A comedy* (1698).
—— and CATHERINE TROTTER, *The Plays of Mary Pix and Catharine Trotter*, ed. Edna L. Steeves, 2 vols. (New York, 1982).
PLANT, ARNOLD, 'The Economic Aspects of Copyright in Books', *Economica*, NS 1–4 (May 1934), 167–95.
PLANT, MARJORIE, *The English Book Trade: An Economic History of the Making and Sale of Books* (1939; repr. 1974).
POCOCK, J. G. A., *The Machiavellian Moment: Florentine Political Thought and the Atlantic Republican Tradition* (Princeton, 1975).
POLLAK, ELLEN, *The Poetics of Sexual Myth: Gender and Ideology in the Verse of Swift and Pope* (Chicago, 1985).
—— 'Swift among the Feminists: An Approach to Teaching', *College Literature*, 19 (1992), 114–20.
POPE, ALEXANDER, *Correspondence*, ed. George Sherburn, 5 vols. (Oxford, 1956).
—— *The Narrative of Dr. Robert Norris concerning the strange and deplorable frenzy of Mr. John Dennis, an Officer of the Custom-house* (1713), in *The Prose Works of Alexander Pope: The Earlier Works, 1711–1720*, ed. Norman Ault (Oxford 1936; repr. 1968).
—— *Prose Works*, ii, ed. Rosemary Cowler (Oxford, 1986).
—— *The Twickenham Edition of the Poems of Alexander Pope*, ed. John Butt *et al.*, 11 vols. (1939–69). (The Twickenham Pope.)
—— and JONATHAN SWIFT, *Miscellanies in Prose and Verse*, 4 vols. (1727–32).
PRESCOTT, SARAH, 'British Women Writers of the 1720s: Feminist Literary History and the Early Eighteenth-Century Novel', Ph.D. thesis (Exeter, in progress).
—— 'The Palace of Fame and the Problem of Reputation: The Case of Eliza Haywood', *Baetyl*, 1/4 (Summer–Autumn 1994), 9–35.
PRICE, CURTIS, *Henry Purcell and the London Stage* (Cambridge, 1984).
PRIOR, MATTHEW, *Literary Works*, ed. H. Bunker Wright and Monroe K. Spears, 2nd edn. (Oxford, 1971).
—— *Poems on Several Occasions* (1718).
PROBYN, CLIVE T., *English Fiction of the Eighteenth Century, 1700–1789* (1987).
RADCLIFFE, ANN, *The Italian* (1797).

324 BIBLIOGRAPHY

RADCLIFFE, ANN, *The Mysteries of Udolpho* (1794).

RALPH, JAMES, *The Case of Authors by Profession or Trade, Stated with Regard to Booksellers, the Stage and the Public* (1758).

—— *The Touch-Stone* (1728), ed. Arthur Freeman (New York, 1973).

RANSOM, HARRY, 'The Rewards of Authorship in the Eighteenth Century', *University of Texas Studies in English*, 18 (1938), 47–66.

RAWSON, CLAUDE, 'Pope's *Waste Land*: Reflections on Mock-Heroic', in id., *Order from Confusion Sprung: Studies in Eighteenth-Century Literature from Swift to Cowper* (1985).

REEVE, CLARA, *The Progress of Romance . . . With remarks on the good and bad effects of it*, 2 vols. (1785).

RICHETTI, JOHN J., *Popular Fiction before Richardson: Narrative Patterns, 1700–1739* (Oxford, 1969; repr. 1992).

RICKS, CHRISTOPHER, Review of Maynard Mack, *Alexander Pope: A Life*, in *Encounter*, 66/1 (1986), 38.

RIGGS, DAVID, *Ben Jonson: A Life* (Cambridge, Mass., 1989).

RIVERO, ALBERT J., *The Plays of Henry Fielding: A Critical Study of his Dramatic Career* (Charlottesville, Va., 1989).

ROBINSON, A. J. K., 'The Evolution of Copyright, 1476–1776', *Cambrian Law Review*, 21–2 (1990–1), 55–77.

ROGERS, PAT, 'An Allusion to Horace', in *Spirit of Wit: Reconsiderations of Rochester*, ed. Jeremy Treglown (Oxford, 1982).

—— *Grub Street: Studies in a Subculture* (1972).

—— *Henry Fielding: A Biography* (1979).

—— (ed.), *The Oxford Illustrated History of English Literature* (1987).

ROSE, MARK, 'The Author as Proprietor: *Donaldson v. Becket* and the Genealogy of Modern Authorship', *Representations*, 23 (Summer 1988), 51–85.

—— *Authors and Owners: The Invention of Copyright* (Cambridge, Mass., 1993).

ROSS, IAN CAMPBELL, '"If we Believe Report": New Biographies of Jonathan Swift', *Hermathena*, 137 (1984), 34–49.

ROSSLYN, FELICITY, *Alexander Pope: A Literary Life* (Basingstoke, 1990).

ROUSSEAU, G. S. and PAT ROGERS (eds.), *The Enduring Legacy: Alexander Pope. Essays for the Tercentenary* (Cambridge, 1988).

ROWE, ELIZABETH (Singer), *Poems on several occasions. Written by PHILOMELA* (1696).

ROWE, NICHOLAS, *The Fair Penitent* (1703), ed. Malcolm Goldstein (1969).

—— *The Tragedy of Jane Shore. Written in imitation of Shakespeare's style* (1714).

RUMBOLD, VALERIE, *Woman's Place in Pope's World* (Cambridge, 1991).

S[ettle], E[lkanah], *The New Athenian Comedy, containing the Politicks,*

Oeconomicks, Tacticks, Crypticks, Apolcalypticks, Stypticks, Scepticks, Pneumaticks, Theologicks, Poeticks, Mathematicks, Sophisticks, Prognosticks, Dogmaticks, etc. Of that most Learned Society (1693).

SAMBROOK, JAMES, *The Eighteenth-Century: The Intellectual and Cultural Context of English Literature, 1700–1789* (1986).

—— *James Thomson, 1700–1748: A Life* (Oxford, 1991).

SAUNDERS, J. W., *The Profession of English Letters* (London and Toronto, 1964).

SCHNEIDER, BEN R., 'The Coquette-Prude as an Actress Line in Restoration Comedy during the Time of Mrs. Oldfield', *Theatre Notebook*, 22/4 (Summer 1968), 143–59.

SCOUTEN, ARTHUR M., 'The Increase in Popularity in Shakespeare's Plays in the Eighteenth Century', *Shakespeare Quarterly*, 7 (Spring 1956), 189–202.

SELLERY, J'NAN, 'Language and Moral Intelligence in the Enlightenment: Fielding's Plays and Pope's *Dunciad*', *Enlightenment Essays*, 1 (1970), 17–26, 108–19.

SHADWELL, THOMAS, *Bury-Fair: A comedy* (1689).

—— *The Complete Works of Thomas Shadwell*, ed. Montague Summers, 5 vols. (1927; repr. New York, 1968).

—— *The Humorists: A comedy* (1671).

—— *The Lancashire Witches, and Tegue o Divelly the Irish Priest* (1682).

—— *The Medal of John Bayes: A satyr against folly and knavery* (1682).

—— *Psyche* (1675).

—— *The Squire of Alsatia* (1688): *A Critical Edition*, ed. J. C. Ross (New York, 1987).

—— *The Sullen Lovers; or, The Impertinents: A comedy* (1668).

—— *The Virtuoso: A comedy* (1676).

SHAFTESBURY, ANTHONY ASHLEY COOPER, 3RD EARL OF, *An Inquiry concerning Virtue and Merit in Two Discourses* (1699).

—— *Characteristics of Men, Manners, Opinions, Times, etc.* (1711), ed. John M. Robertson, 2 vols. (1900).

—— *The Moralists: A Philosophical Rhapsody. Being a recital of certain conversations upon natural and moral subjects* (1709).

—— *Soliloquy; or, Advice to an Author* (1710).

SHAKESPEARE, WILLIAM, *The Tempest*, ed. Frank Kermode (1954; repr. 1980).

—— *The Tempest*, ed. Stephen Orgel (Oxford, 1987; repr. 1994).

SHERBURN, GEORGE, '*The Dunciad*, Book Four', *Texas Studies in English*, 24 (1944), 174–90.

SHEVELOW, KATHRYN, *Women and Print Culture: The Construction of Femininity in the Early Periodical* (1989).

SINFIELD, ALAN, *Faultlines: Cultural Materialism and the Politics of Dissident Reading* (Oxford, 1992).

SITTER, JOHN, Review of Ellen Pollak, *The Poetics of Sexual Myth: Gender and Ideology in the Verse of Swift and Pope*, in *Scriblerian*, 20/1 (1987), 61.

SMITH, E., *The Complete Housewife*, 17th edn. (1776).

SMOLLETT, TOBIAS, *Travels through France and Italy* (1766), ed. Frank Felsenstein (Oxford, 1979; repr. 1992).

SOLKIN, DAVID H., *Painting for Money: The Visual Arts and the Public Sphere in Eighteenth-Century England* (New Haven, 1993).

SOUTHERNE, THOMAS, *The Fatal Marriage; or, The Innocent Adultery* (1694).

—— *The Maid's Last Prayer; or, Any, rather than Fail* (1693).

—— *Oroonoko; A tragedy* (1696).

—— *Sir Anthony Love; or, The Rambling Lady: A comedy* (1691).

—— *The Wives' Excuse; or, Cuckolds make themselves* (1692).

—— *Works*, ed. Robert Jordan and Harold Love, 2 vols. (Oxford, 1988).

SPENCE, JOSEPH, *Observations, Anecdotes and Characters of Books and Men*, ed. James M. Osborn, 2 vols. (Oxford, 1966).

SPENCER, JANE, *The Rise of the Woman Novelist: From Aphra Behn to Jane Austen* (Oxford, 1986).

STACK, FRANK, *Pope and Horace* (Cambridge, 1985).

STALLYBRASS, PETER, and ALLON WHITE, *The Politics and Poetics of Transgression* (1985).

STEDMOND, J. M., 'Another Possible Analogue for Swift's *Tale of a Tub*', *Modern Language Notes*, 72 (1957), 13–18.

STEELE, RICHARD, *The Christian Hero; or, An Argument Proving that no Principles but those of Religion are Sufficient to make a Great Man* (1701).

—— *The Conscious Lovers: A comedy* (1723).

—— *The Lying Lover; or, The Ladies Friendship* (1704).

—— *The Plays of Richard Steele*, ed. Shirley Strum Kenny (Oxford, 1971).

—— *The Tender Husband; or, The Accomplished Fool* (1705).

—— *Tracts and Pamphlets*, ed. Rae Blanchard (Baltimore, 1944).

—— et al., *The Guardian*, ed. John Calhoun Stephens (Lexington, Ky., 1982).

—— and Joseph Addison, *Selections from the* Tatler *and the* Spectator, ed. Angus Ross (Harmondsworth, 1982; repr. 1988).

—— —— *The Tatler and the Guardian* (Edinburgh, 1880).

STONE, GEORGE WINCHESTER, JR. and GEORGE M. KAHRL, *David Garrick: A Critical Biography* (Carbondale, 1979).

SWIFT, JONATHAN, *A Compleat Collection of Genteel and Ingenious Conversation, according to the most polite Mode and Method, now used at Court, and in the best Companies of* England. *In several Dialogues. By* Simon Wagstaff, *Esq.* (1738).

—— *A Tale of a Tub . . . To which is added, An Account of a Battel etc.* (1710).

—— *Correspondence*, ed. Harold Williams, 5 vols. (Oxford, 1965).

—— *Gulliver's Travels* (1726), ed. Christopher Fox (Boston, 1995).

—— *The Importance of the Guardian Considered, in a Second Letter to the Bailiff of Stockbridge* (1713).

—— *Journal to Stella*, ed. Harold Williams, 2 vols. (Oxford, 1948; 2nd edn. 1974).

—— *Poetical Works*, ed. Herbert Davis (Oxford, 1967).

—— *The Prose Works*, ed. Herbert Davis *et al.*, 16 vols. (Oxford, 1939–74).

—— and THOMAS SHERIDAN, *The Intelligencer*, ed. James Woolley (Oxford, 1992).

SWITZER, STEPHEN, *A Compendious Method for the raising of Italian brocoli, Spanish Cardoon, Celeriac, Finochi, and other Foreign Kitchen-Vegetables*, 5th edn. (1731).

TATE, NAHUM, *Brutus of Alba; or, The Enchanted Lovers: A tragedy* (1678).

—— *The History of King Richard the Second; acted under the name of The Sicilian Usurper* (1681).

TAWNEY, R. H., *Religion and the Rise of Capitalism* (1926; repr. Harmondsworth, 1987).

TAYLOR, HOUGHTON W., 'Fielding upon Cibber', *Modern Philology*, 29 (1931–2), 73–90.

THEOBALD, LEWIS, *A dramatick Entertainment, call'd Harlequin, A Sorceror* (1725).

—— *The Rape of Proserpine*, 4th edn. (1727).

THOMAS, CLAUDIA N., *Alexander Pope and his Eighteenth-Century Women Readers* (Carbondale, Ill., 1994).

THOMAS, DAVID, and ARNOLD HARE (eds.), *Theatre in Europe: A Documentary History. Restoration and Georgian England, 1660–1788* (Cambridge, 1989).

THOMAS, KEITH, *Religion and the Decline of Magic* (1971).

THOMSON, JAMES, *The Seasons* (1730).

—— *The Tragedy of Sophonisba* (1730).

THURMOND, JAMES, *Harlequin Dr. Faustus: with the masque of the deities* (1724).

TICKELL, THOMAS, *The First Book of Homer's Iliad* (1715).

TODD, JANET, *The Sign of Angellica: Women, Writing and Fiction, 1660–1800* (1989).

TUKE, SIR SAMUEL, *The Adventures of Five Hours: A tragi-comedy* (1663).

TURNER, CHERYL, *Living by the Pen: Women Writers in the Eighteenth Century* (1992; repr. in paperback 1994).

VARNEY, ANDREW, 'Advertising and Vindicating Eighteenth-Century Novels', *Connotations*, 3/2 (1993–4), 133–46.

VOLTAIRE, FRANÇOIS-MARIE AROUET DE, *Letters Concerning the English Nation*, trans. John Lockman (1733).

WARBURTON, WILLIAM, *A Letter from an Author . . . Concerning Literary Property* (1747).

WASSERMAN, EARL, *Pope's Epistle to Bathurst* (Baltimore, 1960).

WATT, IAN, *The Rise of the Novel: Studies in Defoe, Richardson and Fielding* (1957; repr. 1987; 3rd imp. 1993).

WEAVER, JOHN, *The Loves of Mars and Venus; a Dramatick Entertainment of dancing, etc.* (1718).

WEINBROT, HOWARD D., 'The "Allusion to Horace": Rochester's Imitative Mode', *Studies in Philology*, 69 (1972), 348–68.

——— *Britannia's Issue: The Rise of British Literature from Dryden to Ossian* (Cambridge, 1993).

WHICHER, GEORGE FRISBIE, *The Life and Romances of Mrs. Eliza Haywood* (New York, 1915).

WILLIAMS, RAYMOND, 'Base and Superstructure in Marxist Cultural Theory', *New Left Review* (1973); repr. in id., *Problems in Materialism and Culture: Selected Essays* (1980).

——— *The Country and the City* (1973; repr. 1993).

WILMOT, JOHN, EARL OF ROCHESTER, *The Poems*, ed. Keith Walker (Oxford, 1984).

WINN, JAMES A., *John Dryden and his World* (New Haven, 1987).

WINTON, CALHOUN, *John Gay and the London Theatre* (Lexington, Ky., 1993).

WITHER, GEORGE, *Fidelia* [1615] *Newly corrected and augmented* (1619).

——— *The Hymnes and Songs of the Church etc.* (1623).

——— *Miscellaneous Works of George Wither: First Collection* (1872).

——— *The Schollers Purgatory, Discovered in the Stationers Commonwealth* ([c.1624]).

WOLLSTONECRAFT, MARY, *A Vindication of the Rights of Men in a Letter to the Right Honourable Edmund Burke* (1790), ed. Janet Todd (1993).

WOODMAN, THOMAS, *Poetry and Politeness in the Age of Pope* (1989).

WOODMANSEE, MARTHA, 'The Genius and the Copyright: Economic and Legal Conditions of the Emergence of the "Author"', *Eighteenth-Century Studies*, 17 (1983–4), 425–48.

WOODS, C. B., 'Notes on Three of Fielding's Plays', *PMLA* 52 (1937), 359–73.

YOUNG, EDWARD, *The Complete Works, Poetry and Prose, of the Rev. Edward Young, LL.D.*, 2 vols. (1854).

—— *Conjectures on Original Composition in a Letter to the Author of Sir Charles Grandison* (1759).

Index

Compiled by Shaun Regan

patronage (*cont.*):
  by government 190–1, 242, 259, 261
  by theatre audience 49–51, 53
Patterson, Annabel 33 n.
Pebworth, Ted-Larry 23
Pedicord, H. W. 53
Penkethman, William (actor) 255
Pepys, Samuel 67–8
Perceval, Sir John 58–9
periodical literature 5, 32, 73–4, 145–6, 156–7
  and aesthetics 9–10, 154–5, 185–90, 199
  and gender 145–6, 151, 172
  and politeness 8, 145–6, 147, 150, 152–3, 154, 156–8, 172, 175, 181–2, 183, 185, 199, 200–1, 210, 236, 250, 252–3, 277
  and professional writing 8, 73–4, 147, 154, 156–8, 181–2, 190–1
  and reading public 9–10, 157, 172, 182–4
Perrault, Charles:
  Parallèle des anciens et des modernes 126–7
Perseus and Andromeda (pantomime) 63
Persius 241
Peterborow, Charles Mordaunt, third Earl of 202, 299
Phiddian, Robert 270–1 n.
Philips, Ambrose 250, 251–3, 257, 288, 306–7
  Distrest Mother, The 114, 251–2, 253, 280–1
Philips, Katherine 200
Phoenix Theatre 55
Physicians, Royal College of 139–43
Pilkington, Letitia 248
  Memoirs 238–9, 249
piracy, literary 20, 34–5, 66–7, 182, 265
Pitt, William, earl of Chatham 244
Pittock, Murray G. H. 203 n.
Pix, Mary 75
  Deceiver Deceived, The 60
plagiarism 7, 20, 21, 37–8, 43, 87, 304
  and dramatic writing 21, 44, 84, 86, 97–8, 99–103, 198
  and professional writing 97–103, 198
  see also originality
Plain Dealer, The 287, 288
Plant, Arnold 36

Plant, Marjorie 27
Plato 126, 159
plausibility, narrative 106, 110–11, 112–21, 123–4, 126–33, 135–6, 142–4, 147, 172, 175–7, 223, 232–5, 250, 252, 266–7
play-writing, *see* theatre
Pocock, J. G. A. 242–3
poetomachia 98–9
poetry, pastoral 9, 252–3
poetry, religious 128–32, 177–8, 287–8
politeness 8–10, 32, 106, 126–7, 147, 148, 150–4, 158–60, 162–8, 169–71, 173–5, 176–8, 178–80, 204, 251, 252, 253, 290, 304–6
  and aesthetics 9–10, 154–5, 165–8, 170, 177–8, 185–90, 199, 240, 305
  and commerce 147, 153, 162
  and conversation 9, 151–3, 180–1, 187
  and criticism, literary 152–3, 168–71, 175–8, 187
  and gender 145–6, 172–4, 203 n.
  and gentility 151, 153–4, 164, 165, 179, 181, 185, 187, 188, 195
  and periodical literature 8, 145–6, 147, 150, 152–3, 154, 156–8, 172, 175, 181–2, 183, 185, 199, 200–1, 210, 236, 250, 252–3, 277
  and professional writing 8–9, 73–4, 147, 154, 156–8, 159–60, 161–2, 162–5, 181–2, 190–1, 268
  and reading public 9–10, 147, 157, 162, 178, 182–4, 186–7, 252
  and sentimentalism 179, 235, 250–1, 252, 253
  and social behaviour 9, 145, 148, 150–1, 152, 156, 173–5, 177, 178–9, 243, 251
politics, cultural 239–40, 242, 243–4, 256, 268, 275, 307
Pollak, Ellen 246–8, 249 n., 294
Polwarth, Hugh Hume, third Earl of Marchmont 244
Pope, Alexander 2, 3, 4, 12, 13, 40, 72, 85, 154, 171, 188, 196, 202–3, 217–18, 252–3, 291, 292, 296, 304, 306
  and Addison 171, 195, 209, 306, 307
  and the canon 2, 12, 195–7, 200, 240–1
  and Catholicism 3, 294, 295, 300